Governing Guns, Preventing Plunder

# GOVERNING GUNS, PREVENTING PLUNDER

*International Cooperation against Illicit Trade*

Asif Efrat
*Interdisciplinary Center (IDC) Herzliya*

OXFORD
UNIVERSITY PRESS

# OXFORD
## UNIVERSITY PRESS

Oxford University Press, Inc., publishes works that further
Oxford University's objective of excellence
in research, scholarship, and education.

Oxford   New York
Auckland   Cape Town   Dar es Salaam   Hong Kong   Karachi
Kuala Lumpur   Madrid   Melbourne   Mexico City   Nairobi
New Delhi   Shanghai   Taipei   Toronto

With offices in
Argentina   Austria   Brazil   Chile   Czech Republic   France   Greece
Guatemala   Hungary   Italy   Japan   Poland   Portugal   Singapore
South Korea   Switzerland   Thailand   Turkey   Ukraine   Vietnam

Efrat, Asif.
Governing guns, preventing plunder : international cooperation against illicit trade / Asif Efrat
    p.   cm.
Includes bibliographical references and index.
ISBN 978-0-19-976030-5 (hbk. : alk. paper) 1. Smuggling—Prevention—International
cooperation. 2. Illegal arms transfers—Prevention. 3. Human trafficking—Prevention.
4. Classical antiquities thefts—Prevention. I. Title.
HJ6619.E47   2012
364.1'336—dc23      2011047119

9 8 7 6 5 4 3 2 1

Printed in the United States of America
on acid-free paper

*To my mother Pnina, my sister Hila, and my brother Maor;*
*and in memory of my father Moshe*

# CONTENTS

# ACKNOWLEDGMENTS

This book was made possible thanks to the help of many individuals and institutions. It is, in the first place, the product of my graduate studies in the Department of Government at Harvard University. Beth Simmons, chair of my dissertation committee, gave invaluable advice, encouragement, and support at every step of the way. I am deeply grateful not only for her great contribution to my research, but for her kindness and warmth. I was fortunate to have Beth as a mentor and role model. Many thanks are also owed to my other advisors. Jack Goldsmith offered his advice, guidance, and friendship when they were most needed. Michael Hiscox provided many useful comments and suggestions. Andy Kydd contributed helpful feedback and insights. Lisa Martin's incisive criticism allowed me to clarify my ideas and hone my arguments.

My academic home at Harvard was the Weatherhead Center for International Affairs. The Center's financial and logistical support made much of the research for this project possible. Most importantly, however, the Center provided an extraordinary intellectual and social environment that facilitated the research and writing and made them such an enjoyable experience. I am especially grateful to Steve Bloomfield, Steve Levitsky, Alex Noonan, and Clare Putnam. My fellow GSAs, Warigia Bowman, Manjari Miller, and Sonal Pandya, have been a welcome source of support and encouragement.

I received helpful comments and suggestions at Harvard's research workshops on international security and political economy, as well as at the International Law–International Relations Seminar. Jee Young Kim shared with me her knowledge of conducting surveys. Yev Kirpichevsky helped to conduct the survey on which Chapter 3 is based. Jeff Blossom and Giovanni Zambotti assisted with the geographic analysis in that chapter. The Graduate School of Arts and Sciences, the Center for European Studies, and the Center for American Political Studies provided generous funding.

Cornell Law School was a wonderful setting in which to work on the book phase of this project. For their advice and support, I thank Greg Alexander, Eduardo Peñalver, Jeff Rachlinski, Steve Shiffrin, and Josh Teitelbaum. Thanks also go to Peter Katzenstein and Alex Tsesis for providing helpful guidance on the book publishing process.

The Interdisciplinary Center (IDC) Herzliya has been an ideal environment in which to complete the writing of this book. At the Lauder School of Government, Diplomacy and Strategy, under the deanship of Alex Mintz, I found an intellectually vibrant, supportive, and congenial atmosphere, as well as wonderful colleagues. I owe thanks to Dima Adamsky, Assaf Moghadam, Lesley Terris, and Udi Eiran for their comments and suggestions. I also thank Zeev Maoz for his advice and continued friendship.

This book could not have been written without the cooperation of many individuals—government officials, activists, and others. Through my interviews with them, I gained valuable information and insights that contributed immensely to my understanding of decisions, events, and processes. Whether their names appear in the book or remain confidential, I am indebted to each and every one of them. I especially thank Clemency Coggins and Michael Horowitz for giving me access to their personal files.

At Oxford University Press, it was a pleasure to work with Dave McBride. I thank Dave for his enthusiasm about the project and for efficiently managing the review process. I am very grateful to the two anonymous reviewers, whose extensive and insightful comments improved the book considerably. Elina Sluzhman Carmona copyedited the manuscript, and Ryan Sarver and Anitha Chellamuthu ensured the smooth and professional production of the book. In Herzliya, Ruvik Danieli provided another pair of very helpful eyes. Yotam Kreiman and Elan Nyer helped with the preparation of the index.

Parts of Chapter 3 have appeared in *International Organization* 64(1). I thank Cambridge University Press for the permission to use the material.

Last but not least, to my family I owe the largest debt of gratitude. My father Moshe z"l, my mother Pnina, my sister Hila, and my brother Maor have shown me endless love and devotion. Without their support and encouragement, this book would never have been written. It is gratefully dedicated to them.

Asif Efrat
Herzliya, Israel
January 2012

Governing Guns, Preventing Plunder

# 1

## INTRODUCTION

---

The illicit trade in small arms is a grave international concern: it sustains civil wars, fuels crime, and facilitates terrorism. Human trafficking is another major problem. Every year, hundreds of thousands of men, women, and children are trafficked across borders, falling victim to brutal sexual or labor exploitation. Yet, despite the severity of these problems, international cooperation against them has been difficult to establish. Governments have sharply disagreed about the extent of—and even the need for—international action to curb these illicit trades. Similar controversies have hindered the international efforts against other types of illicit commerce, such as the trade in looted antiquities and the drug trade.

This book explores the global cooperative efforts against illicit trade, focusing on the domestic and international political conflicts underlying these efforts. Specifically, the book seeks to answer two central questions. First, why are cooperative endeavors against illicit trade so controversial? Why do some governments support these endeavors, while others vehemently resist them? Second, when and how do governments overcome the international disagreements and establish cooperation against illicit trade?

These questions are not answered by the literature on international cooperation—the body of work that identifies obstacles to joint action among governments and examines how international institutions may overcome these obstacles.[1] From preventing war to removing trade barriers to reducing environmental harm, studies of cooperation have examined how governments collectively tackle a variety of challenges. Yet among the challenges studied, the suppression of illicit trade has received little attention. In an article published in 1990, Ethan Nadelmann examined "global prohibition regimes" aimed against transnational criminal activities.[2] Since that pioneering article, the field of international cooperation has seen few studies on this subject. As a result, we lack a thorough, systematic understanding of the international efforts to curb illicit trade. This book develops such an understanding, by identifying the problems that impede cooperation against illicit trade and examining how they may be resolved. Given the far-ranging implications of illicit trade for human welfare and world politics, filling the gap in the cooperation literature is long overdue.

While overlooked in the literature on international cooperation, illicit trade has been the subject of investigation by scholars of transnational crime and crime control.[3] This book differs from the transnational-crime literature both in focus and substantive argument. In terms of focus, much of the transnational-crime literature is concerned with the relationship between states and illegal markets: it examines the state's role in and power over these markets. This book, as a study of *cooperation*, explores interactions among governments and domestic political influences that shape those interactions. My goal is to explain the origins, evolution, and dynamics of intergovernmental cooperative endeavors aimed at curbing illicit trade. Substantively, this book offers a new account of the difficulties of suppressing illicit trade. As an explanation for the persistence of illicit trade, the transnational-crime literature points, first and foremost, to the capacity of criminals: flexible, highly adaptive, and empowered by technological innovations, criminal groups are able to escape law enforcement. Moreover, criminals' enormous profits allow them to corrupt the state apparatus, create a climate conducive to criminal activities, and in some cases capture local or national policymaking. By contrast, the capacity of governments to fight crime is constrained by their bureaucratic and hierarchic nature and by limited resources.[4]

Government constraints, corruption, or capture by criminals can certainly hinder the suppression of illicit trade. This book, however, advances a different explanation that centers on the conflicting interests of governments, as shaped by their respective domestic arenas. Some governments identify benefits from cooperating against illicit trade, while other governments conclude that a cooperative endeavor would bring much loss and little gain to domestic actors. The main obstacle to cooperation is thus the absence of shared interest among governments, rather than the corrupting influence of criminals. Furthermore, this book highlights the role of legal, legitimate actors as agents of resistance to the efforts against illicit trade. From arms and drug manufacturers to museums that acquire looted antiquities to banks that launder money, it is *legal* actors who have often sought to hinder, delay, or obstruct attempts to curb illicit trade.

In a nutshell, international regulation against illicit trade encounters a large variation in government preferences and fuels an international political conflict. Certain governments are concerned about the negative externalities that the trade imposes on their own countries or on foreign countries; they favor strong international regulation as a means of suppressing illicit trade and its externalities. Other governments, however, vehemently oppose international regulation, as they are protecting the interests of exporters or consumers who benefit from unregulated trade. In the absence of common ground, the cooperative outcome typically reflects the preferences of the powerful governments. Through coercion, powerful governments can establish more robust international regulation than can weaker governments, yet international regulatory campaigns led by the latter may still have important effects. I support this argument through an in-depth empirical investigation of the cooperative efforts against the illicit trade in small arms, the trade in looted antiquities, and human trafficking. Using original materials and primary documents, the empirical chapters explore the political obstacles to the suppression of illicit trade and the implications for international cooperation. Three shorter cases—drugs, money laundering, and counterfeits—further demonstrate the challenges of cooperation and how they are being met.

## Cooperation against Illicit Trade: An Overview

Illicit trade is a cross-border commercial activity for the provision of goods or services that violates the laws of the exporting and/or importing country.[5] As such, illicit trade is not a new phenomenon and neither are international agreements for its suppression. Abolition of the slave trade was the subject of several bilateral and multilateral treaties in the 19th century.[6] Treaties signed at the very beginning of the 20th century tackled drugs and trafficking of women.[7] Over time, and especially since the 1980s, the number of agreements has increased and so has the range of practices that they target, from the sale of small arms to criminals, rebels, and terrorists, to the plunder of antiquities, to the funding of civil wars through conflict diamonds. In part, the expanding cooperation reflects the growth of American power throughout the 20th century. Its increasing influence has allowed the United States to lead international campaigns against drugs, money laundering, counterfeiting, and human trafficking. The expansion of cooperation has also resulted from the rising influence of new actors—developing countries and transnational civil society—that demanded international action against the illicit trade in small arms, antiquities, hazardous wastes, and conflict diamonds. International institutions, especially the United Nations (UN) system, have facilitated the conclusion and implementation of agreements to suppress illicit trade. Yet the proliferation of agreements has also stemmed from a growing *need* to tackle illicit trade—the result of new challenges (such as money laundering and conflict diamonds) and an escalation in the magnitude and negative effects of longstanding problems (such as the illicit drug trade, human trafficking, and the looting of antiquities). To a large extent, the explosion of illicit trade in recent decades has been an unintended consequence of globalization and the lowering of barriers to economic exchange. Improvements in technology and transportation have made illegal export and import cheaper and easier; the liberalization of world trade has substantially increased its volume, inadvertently providing cover for illicit cargo and making its detection and seizure more difficult.[8] The collapse of the Soviet Union played an important role in the process of globalization. That dramatic event also fueled illicit trade by creating economic and social turmoil and leaving governance gaps in which illegal activities flourished.[9]

For more than a century, governments have sought to jointly counter illicit trade through international agreements: treaties or nontreaty arrangements. Yet the long list of agreements may be deceiving. The establishment of cooperation against illicit trade has been anything but simple. In fact, it has been fraught with controversies not only over the form and substance of agreements, but over their utility and desirability. In some cases, governments have gone so far as to suggest that tight cooperation may be unnecessary, unfeasible, or even detrimental. In many instances, following the negotiation and adoption of an agreement, certain governments have declined to join it or have joined but not fully complied. Why has illicit trade been the subject of heated international disputes, rather than determined international action? How have these disputes been resolved? These are the main questions that this book addresses. Before I lay out my answers, however, let us consider where this book stands in relation to the main body of literature in which it is situated: studies of international cooperation.

## Illicit Trade and the Study of International Cooperation

Since the early 1980s scholars have been examining how self-interested governments may establish cooperation in an anarchical environment and how international institutions can facilitate this task. Traditionally, studies of international cooperation have been divided into four issue areas: security, economics, human rights, and the environment.[10] Within these four broad areas, more specific areas have been distinguished. Cooperation in matters of security includes arms control, alliances, and the laws of war, while economic cooperation encompasses trade liberalization, finance, investment, and monetary affairs. Scholars have identified the problems that impede governments' cooperative efforts in each area; they have also examined the institutional arrangements designed to mitigate these problems and promote cooperation.[11] Efforts against illicit trade, however, have received relatively little attention in the literature on international cooperation and institutions. To the extent that cooperative endeavors against illicit trade have been studied, they have mostly been classified into one of the familiar issue areas. For example, the efforts against the illicit trade in small arms have been studied as a matter of security;[12] the international action against money laundering has been examined as a case of financial regulation;[13] the agreement against counterfeit and pirated goods—TRIPS[14]—has been seen as a part of the multilateral trade regime;[15] and the efforts to curb the illicit movement of hazardous wastes have been considered an environmental initiative.[16] Yet blending these cooperative enterprises into the familiar issue areas misses their distinctiveness. The efforts against illicit trade constitute a separate area of cooperation with its own logic. Only few studies have, in fact, examined illicit trade as a distinct domain of international cooperation. While offering important insights, these studies have left central issues unexplored—issues that an account of cooperation should address.

Ethan Nadelmann brought illicit trade into the study of international cooperation in an article on global prohibition regimes: regimes aimed at criminalizing and suppressing certain cross-border activities, such as maritime piracy, drug trafficking, human trafficking, and the killing of endangered species.[17] In an updated version of that article, Nadelmann and coauthor Peter Andreas outline five stages in the evolution of a prohibition regime: (1) Most societies consider the activity to be proscribed as legitimate; (2) The activity is redefined as a problem and an evil—often by transnational moral entrepreneurs such as religious groups; (3) Regime proponents—powerful governments as well as moral entrepreneurs—push for the suppression and criminalization of the activity by all states and the establishment of international conventions. To this end, they employ various measures, from diplomatic pressure to military intervention to propaganda campaigns; (4) If the regime's proponents are successful, the activity becomes prohibited through criminal laws in much of the world; and (5) Some prohibition regimes indeed manage to accomplish their goal of significantly reducing the incidence of the prohibited activity.[18] Andreas and Nadelmann argue that the success of a prohibition regime ultimately depends "on the nature of the criminal activity and its susceptibility to criminal justice measures"—for example, whether the activity is easily concealed.[19] Political disincentives to cooperate receive less attention in their account. While acknowledging that prohibition regimes face "dissident or deviant states that refuse to conform to the regime's mandate,"[20] it does not explain why these states are reluctant to cooperate.

Another notable study is that of Christine Jojarth, who explores the variation in the design of international institutions aimed at suppressing illicit trade. Adopting a functionalist approach, Jojarth assumes that "the optimal design of an international institution is largely determined by the particular constellation underlying the problem on which international actors seek to cooperate"—for example, the difficulty of detecting noncompliance.[21] Jojarth examines whether institutions' actual design conforms to their optimal design, while recognizing that institutional design may be suboptimal. For domestic political reasons, powerful states may not be interested in effective international institutions.[22] Yet the power-related and domestic politics-based influences that may explain the mismatch between optimal and actual design are left to future research.[23]

Overall, existing studies fail to offer a systematic account of governments' goals and interests and of the international political conflict that stems from the divergence of interests. While these studies acknowledge that governments may vary in their willingness to suppress illicit trade, they do not adequately explain the existence or absence of that willingness. In particular, little consideration is given to domestic political concerns that diminish governments' motivation to suppress illicit trade. Domestic political pressures are at the center of this book; so is the international political conflict among governments with different domestically shaped preferences. The following section outlines my central argument.

## Analytical Approach and Argument

International agreements against illicit trade are regulatory in nature. They seek to curb illicit transactions in goods or services by establishing uniform standards to be adopted and applied worldwide. The stringency of regulation, however, varies between the different agreements. At the extreme, international regulation amounts to a total prohibition of the trade. This is the case with human trafficking, for example. In most cases, however, international regulation does not involve a complete ban. Rather, it seeks to curb *illicit* trade by setting rules, guidelines, and requirements for the proper conduct of *legitimate* trade. The 1961 Single Convention on Narcotic Drugs requires the parties to allow the manufacture, trade, and distribution of drugs only under license and to permit the export of drugs to any country only in accordance with the laws of that country. This convention also empowers the International Narcotics Control Board to oversee the international drug trade in order to "limit the cultivation, production, manufacture and use of drugs to an adequate amount required for medical and scientific purposes . . . and to prevent illicit cultivation, production . . . and use of, drugs."[24] The Forty Recommendations, originally issued by the Financial Action Task Force in 1990, require governments to criminalize money laundering. The Recommendations also ask banks and other financial institutions to take measures to prevent money laundering in the course of their business, such as through verifying the identity of customers. To stem the trade in conflict diamonds, the Kimberley Process Certification Scheme requires that standardized certificates accompany international shipments of rough diamonds, certifying the diamonds as conflict-free. Whether they mandate import and export controls, administrative measures for controlling production, or criminal offenses, the regulatory agreements establish internationally coordinated rules and practices for the conduct of trade. By ensuring responsible conduct of legitimate trade, international regulation seeks to suppress the other side of the coin: illicit trade.

This book explains why governments disagree on the means, the extent, and even the desirability of international regulation aimed at curbing illicit trade. My goal, in other words, is to account for the large variation and conflict in government *preferences* on international regulation. This, I argue, is the most fundamental obstacle to the cooperative efforts against illicit trade. Governments vary in their preferences to such a degree that they do not identify a shared interest in combating illicit trade.

The focus on government preferences and their variation is the hallmark of the liberal theory of international relations (IR), as stated by Andrew Moravcsik.[25] In the liberal conception, world politics is shaped by government preferences—that is, the fundamental goals and purposes that underlie and motivate foreign policy. Government preferences, liberals argue, have societal origins: various domestic groups pressure governments to pursue international policies consistent with their respective goals. The nature of political institutions determines which societal actors have voice and the extent to which their demands influence policymakers. Government preferences are thus the product of social pressures channeled through domestic political institutions. The preferences that arise from the domestic political arena, in turn, shape governments' behavior in the international arena. Each government seeks to realize its distinct preference under the constraints imposed by the preferences of other governments. For liberals, government preferences and their variation is therefore the key to understanding international interactions and outcomes. Conflicting preferences could lead to political disputes, whereas a convergence of preferences facilitates cooperation.

Inspired by liberalism, my analysis of cooperation against illicit trade takes a two-stage approach. The first stage disaggregates the state and examines the domestic actors, considerations, and processes that shape government preferences on international regulation. The second stage moves the analysis from the domestic sphere to the international arena, taking government preferences as given and explaining the cooperative outcome as a function of the variation in preferences and the distribution of power.[26] In other words, the dependent variable that I explain first is government preferences on international regulation. This dependent variable then becomes an explanatory variable. The variation in government preferences, combined with the distribution of power, accounts for a second dependent variable: the robustness of international regulation. For liberals, however, government preferences and their variation are of utmost causal importance. When synthesizing preferences and power, it is preferences that enjoy analytical priority.[27] Therefore, the main dependent variable to be explained is government preferences on international regulation. Specifically, my goal is to account for three kinds of preference variation: across countries, across trades, and across time.

The first type of variation—across countries—refers to the divergent views of governments on the proper regulatory measures required to curb a given illicit trade. Indeed, governments often sharply disagree about the method and degree of international regulation. For example, certain governments may prefer targeting supply, whereas others may wish to reduce demand; some governments seek stringent regulation, whereas others favor looser control or oppose regulation altogether. These disagreements are easily observable. They have various manifestations, such as acrimonious international negotiations, failure to reach an agreement, or refusal of certain governments to join an agreement. One example is the controversy that has surrounded the international efforts against the illicit trade in small arms since the inception of these efforts in the mid-1990s. African governments have advocated tight international regulation of small arms in order to curb the illicit trade. However, other governments—including those of the United States and China—have opposed such regulation. In 2006 this controversy led to the failure of the UN conference that met to review the efforts against the illicit trade in small arms (hereafter the Review Conference),[28] but ended with no outcome document.

The second type of preference variation—across trades—refers to the differing preferences that a given government may hold with respect to different kinds of illicit trade. A government may support international regulation to combat a certain trade while resisting the efforts against another. Consider the American preferences on human trafficking, small arms, and antiquities. The United States has been at the forefront of the efforts to eliminate human trafficking since 2000 and has coerced foreign governments to tackle this problem. By contrast, the United States has favored weak international regulation of small arms. On the efforts against the illicit trade in antiquities, American policy has been ambivalent. The United States has sought to contribute to the suppression of that trade, while safeguarding the interests of the U.S. art market.

The evolution of Britain's view on looted antiquities demonstrates the third type of preference variation: over time. For decades, Britain had resisted the international efforts to control antiquities and prevent their plunder. Yet, in 2002 the British government reversed its opposition to international regulation and joined the relevant agreement: the Convention on the Means of Prohibiting and Preventing the Illicit Import, Export and Transfer of Ownership of Cultural Property, 1970 (hereafter the UNESCO Convention). The United States went through a similar preference change some three decades earlier.

An account of cooperation against illicit trade should systematically explain the three preference variations. It should also explain a fourth variation: differences in the robustness of international regulation across trades. Some regulatory agreements establish far-reaching commitments through legally binding rules with mechanisms to ensure compliance. Other agreements are weaker in their substantive obligations or form. For example, international drug control is based on three legally binding treaties and involves a delegation of monitoring authority to international organs. By contrast, the primary agreement against the illicit trade in small arms is merely a political declaration that lacks monitoring mechanisms.

This book sheds light on the four types of variation in an analysis that highlights the political conflicts over illicit trade: why these conflicts occur and how they are overcome. The analysis has two underlying premises. First, the principal motivation for cooperation is the negative externalities that illicit trade imposes on society. These include, for example, gun violence, drug abuse, and archaeological destruction caused by the looting of antiquities. Governments unable or unwilling to bear the burden of curbing these externalities seek international regulation in order to shift the burden elsewhere. Second, outlawed actors such as criminals and terrorists are important actors in illicit transactions. The key to the analysis of cooperation, however, are the legitimate market-actors—exporters or consumers—who are involved in these transactions. The goal of international regulation is to make these actors behave responsibly and to prevent them from abetting illicit trade. Examples of such legitimate actors include arms manufacturers, banks, the diamond industry, and consumers of antiquities: antiquities dealers, museums, and private collectors.

Building on these foundations, I argue that two groups of governments support the international regulatory efforts against illicit trade. Certain governments favor international regulation in order to curb the *primary externalities* of illicit trade—its negative effects on their own countries. Other governments support international regulation out of concerns about *secondary externalities*— the trade's negative effects on foreign countries. Concern about secondary externalities may result from the advocacy of moral entrepreneurs who are committed to worldwide suppression of illicit trade. Yet international regulation and its restrictions on trade could harm the exporters and consumers of the goods. Governments that protect the interests of these actors thus tend to oppose international regulation. From their point of view, it unjustifiably shifts onto them the burden of addressing problems that plague other countries.

The large variation in government preferences creates a significant cooperation problem: lack of shared interest. Certain governments stand to benefit from international regulation; for other governments, however, it is undesirable. In the absence of common interest, the distribution of power plays an important role in shaping the cooperative outcome. When the governments favoring regulation are weak, they struggle to bring on board powerful noncooperative governments, and the resulting international regulation is typically diluted, both in substance and in form. Yet when powerful governments support regulation, they can employ coercion to overcome the resistance of weaker governments and establish robust regulation. In addition to coercion, the international political conflict over illicit trade may also be resolved through a transformation of government preferences over time. Change in the underlying determinants of preferences can make noncooperative governments—even powerful ones—more inclined to cooperate.

In short, different governments face different constellations of the four influences: exporters, consumers, primary externalities, and secondary externalities. They therefore hold divergent preferences on international regulation against illicit trade. The result is an intense international political conflict. This conflict may be overcome in two ways: either coercion exercised by powerful governments or a temporal change in preferences can bring initially reluctant governments to cooperate. The four aforementioned influences account for the variation in preferences across countries, across trades, and across time. Governments' preferences, together with the distribution of their power, explain the varying robustness of international regulation.

## *Scope of the Analysis*

The establishment of cooperation against illicit trade is a long and arduous process. This process has five main stages: (1) placing an issue—a certain kind of illicit trade—on the international agenda; (2) negotiations and the adoption of a regulatory agreement to suppress that trade; (3) commitment to the agreement; (4) compliance with the agreement; and (5) effectiveness—actual suppression of the trade. By combining preferences and the distribution of power, this book explains much, though not everything, about the process of cooperation.

Preferences account for agenda setting. Governments that wish to eliminate the trade are those who put the issue on the international agenda and initiate a regulatory campaign. The variation in government preferences accounts for the controversies that arise in the process of negotiations; preferences combined with power distribution explain the form and substance of the resulting agreement. A similar combination accounts for governments' commitment to the agreement—that is, their expression of willingness to participate in the agreement and to behave in a manner that is consistent with its terms. Governments supportive of regulation will embrace the regulatory agreement and commit to it. If the agreement takes the form of a treaty, commitment is manifested through ratification. By contrast, governments opposed to regulation will decline to join the agreement, unless coerced to do so by more powerful governments.

The same logic applies to compliance. Governments that favor regulation will introduce the measures and policies required by the agreement and enforce them; governments that consider regulation antithetical to their interests will implement and enforce the agreement only under external pressure. Yet compliance has an additional dimension. Even governments that are willing to comply and have established the necessary laws and regulations may still fail to enforce them. Enforcement may be hampered by scarce government resources, bureaucratic inefficiency, or lack of technical know-how. Another reason for enforcement failure is that agreements against illicit trade seek not only to regulate the behavior of governments themselves: they ask governments to enforce standards of conduct upon private, nongovernmental actors, from banks and arms manufacturers to drug cartels. Monitoring and sanctioning nongovernmental entities, some of which operate outside the boundaries of the law, can prove extremely difficult. But even full compliance with international regulation does not guarantee effectiveness—that is, trade eradication or reduction. The trade may persist since the regulatory agreement did not go far enough or simply chose the wrong means. Furthermore, international regulation may yield perverse, unintended consequences, such as the creation of a criminal black market.

The existing literature on illicit trade highlights the latter elements of the story—especially the difficulties of enforcing criminal prohibitions—to the neglect of the previous stages that are more strongly shaped by government preferences and their variation. Yet preferences have causal priority over the challenges of enforcement on the ground. Before inquiring why governments have failed to enforce prohibitions and suppress illicit trade, one has to establish that trade suppression was, in fact, their goal. Indeed, governments may not actually be interested in abolishing the trade. A prior account of government preferences is therefore necessary if we are to understand cooperation. Preferences allow us to explain why international regulation takes the form and includes the content that it does, and why governments vary in their willingness to commit to regulation and comply with it. This is the main concern of this book. An intention to fight illicit trade, however, may not suffice. Successful regulatory enforcement and elimination of the trade depend on additional factors that lie outside the purview of my analysis.

The scope of inquiry is also limited primarily to the *global* efforts against illicit trade. Illicit trade is the subject of various bilateral and regional arrangements, and the theoretical argument generally applies to those as well. Homogeneity of domestically shaped government preferences facilitates bilateral and regional initiatives. When preferences diverge, bilateral and regional cooperation is more difficult to establish and may require coercion. To make the analysis feasible, however, I focus on the global endeavors.

As defined above, illicit trade can be in goods or in services. This book focuses mainly on trade in goods, but also examines human trafficking, whose purpose is to provide sexual or labor services, and money laundering, a service of another type.

## Case Selection

Of the various illicit trades, I have chosen the following three as the main subjects of empirical investigation: small arms, antiquities, and human trafficking. Several considerations motivated this case selection. Most important were the multiple variations in the main phenomenon of interest: government preferences on international regulation. As discussed earlier, this book seeks to shed light on the variation in preferences across countries, trades, and time. The selected cases provide fertile ground for exploring and explaining these variations through a theory of preference formation. Indeed, all three trades display cross-country preference variation. Certain governments have demanded vigorous action against the illicit trade in small arms, while others have offered no more than lip service; similar disputes have plagued the efforts against looting of antiquities and human trafficking. Variation across trades is manifested in the different American views on small arms, antiquities, and human trafficking. Preference variation over time is clearly seen in the case of antiquities: the United States and Britain shifted from rejection of regulation to cautious acceptance. The three selected cases also vary on the explanatory variable of power distribution that, combined with government preferences, shapes the cooperative outcome. It was the United States that launched an international campaign against human trafficking in 2000, while developing countries have been at the forefront of the international campaigns against the illicit trade in small arms and in antiquities. The three cases thus demonstrate how cooperation evolves when its proponents enjoy a power advantage—and what happens when they are inferior in power.

Two additional considerations for case selection were policy relevance and significance, as well as the novelty of the research. Small arms and human trafficking are among the most important types of illicit trade in terms of their far-reaching humanitarian, social, and economic implications. These two cases, as well as that of antiquities, have also received scant attention in the literature on international cooperation. Small arms kill many more people than any other weapon and are the weapons of choice in the vast majority of contemporary conflicts, yet they have been almost entirely absent from the scholarship on arms control; looted antiquities have been a subject of research for archaeologists and legal scholars, but not for political scientists; and studies of international human rights have largely overlooked human trafficking. Furthermore, small arms and antiquities have received little coverage in the transnational-crime literature that has been preoccupied with drugs, money laundering, and human trafficking. In order to push the study of international cooperation and transnational crime into new areas, I focus on small arms, antiquities, and human trafficking. Of the three, the small-arms case is the latest in time. Yet it is this case that opens the empirical investigation, as it offers a broad, cross-national analysis of government preferences and their determinants. The antiquities and human trafficking cases follow, where I zoom in on specific episodes and offer a close look at the domestic politics of international cooperation.

## Plan of the Book

Chapter 2 lays out a theoretical framework for analyzing the cooperative efforts against illicit trade. This framework specifies the principal influences on government preferences, identifies the cooperation problem that results from the variation in preferences, and examines how this problem may be resolved. The empirical chapters that follow provide evidence in support of the theory and demonstrate its explanatory power. By employing the theory, these chapters account for observed variations in government preferences and cooperative outcomes. At the same time, the empirical analysis puts flesh on the theory and deepens our understanding of actors' preferences and interactions. The theory gives us the essence of the political dynamic; actual cases show this dynamic unfolding through an in-depth analysis of the domestic and international controversies over cooperation.

On the basis of an original survey, Chapter 3 examines the international efforts against the illicit trade in small arms. The survey included interviews with officials from 118 countries, conducted at the 2006 UN Review Conference. The survey data shed light on the variation in government preferences on the international control of small arms. Consistent with the theoretical expectations, governments facing high homicide rates—the negative externalities of the illicit arms trade—are found to favor strict international regulation; so are governments whose humanitarian foreign policy inspires concern about the deleterious effects of small arms abroad. By contrast, governments protecting the interests of state-owned arms exporters tend to oppose regulation; so do nondemocratic governments that are anxious to secure their own arms supply. Proponents of small-arms regulation, first and foremost the African governments, were unable to overcome this heterogeneity of preferences, especially the resistance of powerful actors such as the United States and China. Consequently, small arms are regulated internationally in a weak manner through a vaguely phrased, non-legally binding agreement: the Program of Action to Prevent, Combat and Eradicate the Illicit Trade in Small Arms and Light Weapons in All Its Aspects, 2001. Overall, this chapter demonstrates that the establishment of cooperation against illicit trade is an uphill battle—one that weaker governments might be ill-equipped to win.

And yet, weaker governments' efforts are not destined to fail. The agreements they initiate may, over time, be accepted by powerful governments that had initially resisted them. Moreover, by raising public awareness of the negative effects of illicit trade, these agreements may influence the market actors complicit in the trade. These are some of the findings of Chapter 4, which investigates the efforts against the illicit trade in antiquities and against the archaeological plunder that feeds the trade. I first examine the international political conflict over the main agreement addressing this problem: the 1970 UNESCO Convention. Primary UNESCO documents reveal considerable variation in government preferences on this regulatory agreement. Support for the UNESCO Convention came from poor countries unable to curb the plunder of their archaeological sites. By contrast, the antiquities-importing countries of Western Europe vigorously opposed the convention, fearing it would harm their art markets and impose a heavy burden on their bureaucracies.

Chapter 4 next examines the domestic political debate over international regulation and the process of national-preference formation and change. My goal here is to explain the puzzling transformation of U.S. policy over time: the American decision in the early 1970s to reverse the laissez-faire approach to antiquities and join the UNESCO Convention, in stark contrast to other market countries that had rejected it. I find that U.S. policymakers became concerned about plunder abroad following a series of scandals that exposed the involvement of American museums and collectors with looted material. In addition, advocacy efforts of American archaeologists educated policymakers about the loss of historical knowledge caused by looting and the necessity of regulation. Also examined are the lobbying of antiquities dealers and certain museums against regulation and the ultimate compromise: limited implementation of the UNESCO Convention. The analysis relies on records of the congressional debate over the UNESCO Convention in the 1970s and early 1980s; interviews with key actors in that debate, including the State Department official who negotiated the convention and spearheaded its implementation; documents from the personal files of the archaeologist who led the advocacy efforts in support of the convention; and interviews with participants in the contemporary U.S. debate on antiquities regulation, from both the art and archaeological communities.

The final part of Chapter 4 maintains the focus on the domestic politics of international cooperation while turning the attention to Britain. The goal here is to understand the change in government preferences over time by examining Britain's surprising accession to the UNESCO

Convention in 2002—which reversed more than three decades of British opposition to the convention. I find that Britain's loss of its own cultural objects, scandals involving the London art market, and the change of government in 1997 all contributed to the transformation of the British preference. The analysis draws primarily on interviews with members of the archaeological, museum, and art-market communities.

Chapter 5 examines the use of coercion to establish cooperation against illicit trade, first explaining why the United States launched an international campaign against human trafficking in 2000. It was an unusual coalition of evangelical Christians and women's groups that convinced the U.S. government to engage in unilateral coercive efforts: monitoring the conduct of governments worldwide and threatening to impose sanctions for failure to act against human trafficking. Interviews with members of this coalition and documents from the personal files of the coalition's founder reveal these actors' motivations, advocacy methods, and strategies for overcoming obstacles, such as the Clinton administration's opposition to sanctions. Next, the chapter explores Israel's policy on sex trafficking and labor trafficking, based on interviews with Israeli policymakers and activists. I find that the reputational effects of the American criticism motivated the Israeli authorities to combat sex trafficking, a problem to which they had been indifferent throughout the 1990s. The analysis further shows that concern for the interests of employers diminished the Israeli government's determination to suppress labor trafficking.

As the reader will discover, the small arms, antiquities, and human trafficking chapters vary in their emphasis and methodology. Before pointing out the differences, however, let us consider the two fundamental commonalities that connect these chapters.

The first commonality is the determinants of government preferences. Government preferences on international regulation are shaped by four main influences: exporters, consumers, primary externalities, and secondary externalities. Two of these influences—consumers and secondary externalities—are highlighted in all three chapters. Nondemocratic governments—as consumers of arms—have been an obstacle to small-arms cooperation; antiquities dealers and museums—consumers of antiquities—have sought to weaken the efforts against the illicit antiquities trade; and Israeli farmers and contractors—"consumers" of trafficked migrant workers—have had little interest in vigorous government action against human trafficking. By contrast, secondary externalities—the trade's negative effects on foreign countries—have motivated cooperation. Humanitarian concerns about gun violence in Africa have fueled European support for the efforts against the illicit trade in small arms; concerns about archaeological plunder and human trafficking in foreign countries have been central to the cooperative endeavors against these problems.

The second commonality that ties the three chapters together is the cooperation problem. The principal challenge to international action against the illicit trade in small arms, the trade in looted antiquities, and human trafficking has been an absence of shared interest in cooperation. Different combinations of the four aforementioned influences have resulted in a large variation in government preferences; certain governments—indifferent to the trade's negative effects, concerned for the interests of legitimate market-actors, and anxious to avoid a law-enforcement burden—have had little desire to cooperate. Concerns for the profitability of state-owned arms industries or art markets have made governments reluctant to accept stringent international controls on small arms or antiquities; the Israeli government had more urgent law-enforcement priorities than the sexual enslavement of foreign women and the severe exploitation of migrant workers. In all these cases, the main obstacle to cooperation has not been an inability to enforce the law and suppress illegal activities, but rather a lack of political motivation to do so. Governments have faced domestic pressures and concerns that militated against cooperation, while failing to identify countervailing benefits.

Beyond these key similarities, the small arms, antiquities, and human trafficking cases (Chapters 3, 4, and 5, respectively) highlight different aspects of cooperation against illicit trade.

First, the small-arms chapter paints a static picture: conflicting government preferences on the international regulation of small arms, as of 2006. The antiquities case demonstrates one mechanism that may resolve the international political conflict: temporal change in preferences. The United States and Britain, initially opposed to international control of antiquities, moderated their resistance over time and became more cooperative. The human trafficking case demonstrates a second mechanism for overcoming preference variation: coercion. The Israeli government, at first indifferent to human trafficking, ultimately tackled this problem under American pressure. Both these mechanisms are absent in the case of small arms. The United States has not exercised coercion to promote small-arms cooperation, and coercion is obviously not in the menu of options for the African countries, the primary beneficiaries of international action on small arms. As for change over time, the international regulation of small arms was established in 2001. By 2006 there had not yet been a significant change in preferences along the lines of international antiquities regulation, which dates back to 1970. As a result, small-arms cooperation does not demonstrate the same progress apparent in the cases of antiquities and human trafficking.

Second, the small-arms chapter tests the theoretical model of government preferences and their determinants. The appropriate tool for this purpose is a large-N study that combines statistical, geographic, and qualitative methods. The purpose of the analysis is to identify a correlation between the theoretically expected influences on government preferences and the empirical pattern of preference variation, as captured by the cross-national survey data. The antiquities and human trafficking chapters, by contrast, explore the domestic politics of international cooperation and offer in-depth accounts of preference formation. Through qualitative analysis, my intention is to examine the goals of societal actors, how these goals are conveyed to the government, and how the government establishes its preference. The analysis traces the cost-benefit calculation that guides governments' thinking about illicit trade and the changes to this calculation over time or under external pressure, through five case studies: (1) the United States and the efforts against the looting of antiquities; (2) Britain and the efforts against the looting of antiquities; (3) the origins of the American efforts against human trafficking worldwide; (4) Israel's policy on sex trafficking; and (5) Israel's policy on labor trafficking. Each of these case studies includes a cross-time comparison (for example, Britain's hostility to the efforts against looting of antiquities between 1970 and 2000, compared to its willingness to support these efforts after 2000; Israel's inaction against sex trafficking during the 1990s, compared to the rush to action following the rebuke of Israel in the 2001 State Department report on human trafficking). The analysis also includes comparisons across case studies. For example, American museums' opposition to international antiquities regulation is contrasted with British museums' support for regulation.

A third difference among the chapters is that the analysis of small arms primarily addresses material influences on government preferences; by contrast, the antiquities and human trafficking chapters highlight moral concerns over the deleterious effects of illicit trade abroad. The reason for this distinction is that the small-arms chapter tests the entire model of government preferences. This model includes three material influences: exporters' interests, consumers' interests, and primary externalities. The chapter does address humanitarian concerns over gun violence in Africa, but only as one among several influences on governments. Yet moral concerns are a truly puzzling aspect of the efforts against illicit trade: why would governments worry about the negative impact of trade on foreign countries? For this reason, I highlight moral concerns about secondary externalities in the antiquities and human trafficking chapters. The use of qualitative methods in these chapters facilitates the analysis of moral concerns and of the civil society campaigns that stimulate them.

Chapter 6 complements the three primary empirical chapters with three shorter cases that demonstrate the broader applicability of the book's theoretical framework. Each of these cases identifies the negative externalities that motivated cooperation alongside commercial concerns that had the opposite effect, followed by an outline of the international political conflict. Particular emphasis is given to the role of coercion in inducing reluctant governments to cooperate and tackle illicit trade. The chapter first analyzes a century of international drug control that began in 1909. The analysis examines the political conflict between drug-exporting and drug-consuming countries and the American efforts to compel drug cooperation through political and economic pressure. Next, I examine the Financial Action Task Force's use of countermeasures against countries that fail to suppress money laundering. The chapter concludes with the U.S.-led campaign against counterfeit and pirated goods, in which the threat of trade sanctions has played a major role.

Chapter 7 examines the broader contribution of this book to the analysis of illicit trade and international relations. I explore, among other things, the implications for understanding the persistence of illicit trade, the effects of international institutions, and the evolution of norms. This chapter also offers insights and lessons for policy. Indeed, illicit trade presents one of the greatest policy challenges and threats of our time. Countering this threat requires international cooperation, the establishment of which is fraught with political difficulties. Yet while these obstacles are indeed significant, they are not insurmountable. To overcome them, we need to learn from existing experience through theoretical and empirical analysis. This is what the following chapters set out to do.

## 2

# THEORIZING COOPERATION AGAINST
# ILLICIT TRADE

This chapter develops a theoretical framework for analyzing the international cooperative efforts against illicit trade. At the heart of these efforts are regulatory agreements whose purpose is to suppress illicit trade and its negative effects. These agreements are the subject of much international contention: they fuel intense political conflicts among governments. The theoretical framework sheds light on the origins of these conflicts—and what they mean for cooperation.

The analysis begins by laying the foundations: identifying the purpose of cooperation, specifying the relevant actors, and choosing the appropriate theoretical lens to combine these elements. I posit that international regulation seeks to shift the burden of fighting illicit trade, from the countries that bear the trade's negative externalities onto the countries that generate those externalities. The targets of regulation are criminals and, no less importantly, *legitimate* actors who are complicit in the trade. Given its social purpose and the societal actors it seeks to influence, international regulation is best analyzed through the liberal theory of international politics: an analytical approach that highlights state-society relations.

In accordance with liberalism, the crux of the theoretical framework is the variation in government preferences on international regulation. It is this variation that holds the key to understanding cooperation. The theory turns to the domestic political arena and derives government preferences from four main influences: the primary negative externalities of illicit trade; the trade's secondary externalities—that is, its deleterious impact on foreign countries; the concerns of exporters; and the concerns of consumers. Next, the theory identifies the cooperation problem that emerges from the conflicting preferences: an absence of shared interest between governments. This problem may be overcome in two ways. First, preferences may shift over time. When the underlying determinants of preferences change, noncooperative governments may become more favorable to international regulation and more willing to suppress illicit trade. Second, coercion can compel cooperation. Under external pressure, reluctant governments may be forced to combat illicit trade that they once tolerated. The central role of coercion in resolving the cooperation problem has an important implication: the distribution of power significantly affects the cooperative outcome, that is, the robustness of international regulation. Since only powerful governments are able to employ coercive means, they can establish more robust regulation than can weaker governments.

Overall, the theory captures the essence of the international contestation over the efforts to eliminate illicit trade. By combining the trade's negative effects and the market actors involved, it accounts for the large variation in government preferences on international regulation. This variation sparks a political struggle among governments. Preferences—combined with the distribution of power—shape the dynamic and outcome of that struggle.

## Theoretical Foundations

### The Purpose of Cooperation

A preliminary question that an account of cooperation need address concerns the goal of the cooperative endeavor. What do governments seek to achieve through mutual coordination of their policies that cannot be obtained through unilateral action? I argue that the primary goal of cooperation against illicit trade is to curb the negative externalities of that trade, that is, its detrimental effects on society. In some cases, societies in *importing* countries bear the negative externalities. For example, the illicit trade in small arms allows criminals, rebels, and terrorists to acquire guns, and thereby raises the risk of gun violence in gun-importing countries. Gun violence causes injuries and killings, destruction of physical infrastructure, refugee flows, and disruption of social services and economic activity.[1] The illicit drug trade creates a variety of externalities in drug-importing countries, including crime and violence, healthcare costs, and lower workforce productivity.[2] Indeed, certain actors within society, such as gun-wielding criminals and drug users, may welcome illicit trade; but the cost of the trade to society at large is enormous.

In other cases, *exporting* countries bear the negative externalities of illicit trade. The trade in conflict diamonds funds civil wars in diamond-exporting countries;[3] the illicit trade in antiquities fuels looting and destruction of archaeological sites in archaeologically rich countries.[4] As with guns and drugs, certain societal actors benefit from the illegal movement of antiquities and diamonds. Rebel groups use conflict diamonds to finance their military activities. Looters receive financial compensation for the antiquities they plunder, and the middlemen who move those antiquities out of the country and sell them abroad make much larger financial gains. For society, however, the illicit trades in diamonds and antiquities have dire consequences.

Third countries, neither the exporting nor importing countries, may also face the negative externalities of illicit trade. For example, the illicit trade in small arms threatens not only those countries that are awash in guns: neighboring countries might also feel the effects of gun violence through refugee inflows and obstruction of commerce. Counterfeit goods are another case in point. When country A exports counterfeits to country B, the result is lost revenue to the legitimate producer in country C.

Illicit trade imposes damaging externalities on society. The purpose of international cooperation is to curb illicit transactions and their externalities by introducing common regulatory standards for the proper conduct of legitimate trade. Through international regulation of small arms, governments attempt to deny guns to criminals, rebels, and terrorists, while allowing gun use by security forces and law-abiding citizens. International regulation of the drug trade aims at restricting the use of drugs to medical and scientific purposes. Control of the diamond trade enables consumers to purchase and enjoy the precious stones without inadvertently financing conflicts in Africa. The efforts against money laundering seek to ensure the legitimacy of banking services and to prevent their misuse to disguise criminal proceeds or fund terrorism. In short, the purpose of international regulatory standards is to keep trade within the boundaries that governments deem permissible and to curtail the illicit trade and its negative effects.

### Why Is National Regulation Insufficient?

Given that the purpose of international cooperation is to mitigate the negative externalities of illicit trade, an immediate question presents itself: Why can't governments reduce these externalities through national regulation and why is there a need for *international* regulation? In some cases—when the bearers of the externalities are third countries not directly involved in the trade—national trade regulation is not a viable option. More commonly, governments do establish national controls in an attempt to suppress illicit trade and its externalities. Indeed, illicit trade is first established as such in national regulation. National laws define legal and illegal transactions in guns, antiquities, and drugs: who may—and may not—buy, sell, or possess these goods and for what purposes. National regulation, however, often proves insufficient and ineffective, and at times is merely words on paper. Trade contrary to national laws endures, and so do its negative effects. African and Latin

American countries have imposed restrictions on the import, circulation, and possession of small arms,[5] yet they suffer from high rates of gun violence. Many antiquities-rich countries have laws that make all antiquities—including those still unexcavated—the property of the state. Such laws often prohibit any export of antiquities.[6] Nevertheless, the looting and export of antiquities continue uninterrupted, notwithstanding the prohibiting legislation. Needless to say, national laws banning nonmedical drug use are routinely violated.

Several reasons explain the insufficiency of national controls. One reason is that trade controls do not stifle consumers' demand. Demand for guns persists despite restrictions on their import and possession; limitations on the export of antiquities do not lessen the interest of museums and private collectors in acquiring them. Suppliers and consumers thus seek to carry on the trade, regardless of restrictions. Suppliers have powerful incentives to flout national regulation, since many of the relevant commercial activities—such as the looting of antiquities, drug export, and human trafficking—promise a high yield with a relatively low-cost investment. Second, and most importantly, law enforcement and administrative agencies have limited capacities. They often lack the human, financial, and technical resources required for suppressing illicit trade. National regulation is meaningful only if the police apprehend violators and courts' sentences are enforced; in many countries, these conditions do not obtain. Customs and border control are never fully effective even in developed countries, let alone in developing countries where trained and equipped law-enforcement personnel are scarce. The increasing volume of trade in recent decades has further diminished the intensity and effectiveness of customs inspections, compounding the challenge of enforcing trade controls.[7] Geography also affects the magnitude of that challenge: the larger the territory and the longer the borders, the more difficult it is to restrict the production, outflow, inflow, or use of controlled goods. Corruption among law-enforcement authorities is yet another obstacle.

An alternative approach to curbing illicit trade through national means would treat the roots of the problem. Demand for small arms stems from, among other things, personal-security concerns, poverty and lack of educational and professional opportunities, especially among youth, and sociocultural attitudes, such as the association of guns with masculinity or freedom. Governments could attempt to lower small-arms demand through police and court reform to improve security, the provision of education and employment, and campaigns to stigmatize guns and gun violence.[8] The same applies to drugs and antiquities. Social, health, and educational measures to lower the demand for drugs would go a long way toward diminishing the drug trade and its negative externalities. The plunder of antiquities by poor communities may be prevented by providing those communities with alternative sources of income or educating them about the value of preserving the archaeological heritage. The problem, of course, is that such means are costly, burdensome, and extremely complex. They may yield the anticipated results only in the long run, if at all. Governments therefore seek an easier, faster solution to the challenge of illicit trade—one that does not require them to address socioeconomic problems such as poverty, or to transform ingrained cultural attitudes. International regulation is such a solution.

### The Asymmetry of Illicit Trade's Externalities

As a means of overcoming governments' failure to mitigate negative externalities, international regulation against illicit trade is hardly unique: governments typically resort to international cooperation to tackle problems that they cannot resolve on their own. It is therefore not the goal of reducing externalities that distinguishes cooperation against illicit trade. Rather, it is the highly asymmetric nature of those externalities.

Much of the literature on international cooperation examines situations of symmetric externalities, as captured, for example, by prisoners' dilemmas or tragedies of the commons. As Ronald Mitchell and Patricia Keilbach explain, in those situations the actors are simultaneously perpetrators *and* victims. They generate externalities that harm others; at the same time, they are harmed by the externalities of others. These situations are symmetric in two respects: all the relevant actors engage in the externalities-generating behavior, and all are concerned about the externalities and would benefit from their mitigation. In symmetric situations, the actors have mixed motives: they want to maintain their own harmful behavior, but want others to change their behavior and alleviate the harm it causes. By contrast, situations of asymmetric externalities involve a clearer distinction between victims and perpetrators: the actors concerned about the problem have not caused it, while those perpetrating the problem do not consider themselves harmed by it. In asymmetric situations, actors thus have one of two motives. Victims seek to alter the status quo and reduce the externalities that they bear; perpetrators wish to maintain the status quo and persist in their damaging behavior, whose costs are borne by others.[9]

Asymmetry of externalities is sometimes known as an "upstream/downstream" problem. It is manifested most visibly in certain environmental contexts, such as the pollution of rivers by upstream countries to the detriment of downstream countries. Asymmetry of externalities is also the key to the analysis of cooperation against illicit trade. Illicit trade involves victims—countries that bear an overwhelming share of the trade's externalities—and perpetrators, that is, countries that generate those externalities and are content with the status quo. Gun violence exists in virtually any country, but has reached enormous proportions in sub-Saharan Africa—a region flooded with small arms; by contrast, China and Egypt, two major exporters of small arms, have very low levels of gun violence. Fueled by the demand of art markets in the West, the illicit antiquities trade has caused major losses in archaeologically rich countries, such as Peru, Cambodia, and Mali; market countries, however, have benefited financially and culturally from the flow of looted antiquities. Some countries—first and foremost, the United States—suffer an enormous drug-abuse problem; other countries consider drugs an important export. The trade in counterfeit goods provides employment and income in developing countries while harming industries in developed countries.

The distinction between externalities-bearing countries and externalities-generating countries is useful for analytical purposes. In reality, certain countries may both generate and bear the externalities of illicit trade. These countries sometimes overlook the externalities that they bear and act *as if* they were pure perpetrators, reluctant to change the status quo. In other cases they may behave *as if* they were victims, seeking a solution to the problem of externalities. A reconciliation of their mixed motives could also lead these countries to adopt an intermediate position. But the fundamental dynamic of cooperation against illicit trade is not shaped by mixed motives. Cooperation is so contentious precisely because certain countries would like to suppress trade that they consider detrimental, whereas others consider that trade beneficial. While some countries act as both victims and perpetrators, other countries behave as victims *or* as perpetrators; and it is the tension between these two opposing camps that drives the political dynamic.

What, then, is the purpose of international regulation and how does it augment and supplement national efforts? The asymmetry of the externalities leads to variation in national regulation between perpetrators and victims. Countries that generate the negative externalities and benefit from the trade take a permissive approach and establish loose national controls; by contrast, externalities-bearing countries impose strict controls in an attempt to curb the trade. But given the insufficiency of national control, the externalities-bearing countries turn to international regulation in order to tackle the externalities at their source. Through international regulation, they attempt to shift the burden of control and induce the establishment of adequate restraints by the externalities-generating countries. Countries that fail to reduce gun violence by preventing the illegal import and possession of guns seek to shift the burden to arms-exporting countries; the aim of international regulation of small arms is to set standards for arms exports and thereby thwart gun acquisition by criminals or rebels. Countries that fail to prevent the illegal import and use of drugs compensate by passing the burden onto drug-exporting countries; international drug control seeks to limit drug production and export in order to reduce consumption and abuse. Poor countries that cannot stop the illegal removal and export of antiquities seek to shift the regulatory burden to rich market-countries; the purpose of regulating antiquities internationally is to lower market countries' demand for antiquities and suppress the archaeological plunder that is fueled by that demand. In short, the goal of international regulation is to overcome the limitations and difficulties of national efforts to stem illicit trade: to narrow the gaps in national control and to effectuate a convergence of regulatory practices on the stringent side of the spectrum. By requiring that all countries, especially those that are the source of the externalities, establish appropriate controls, international regulation aligns national practices in order to curb illicit trade and its negative effects.

### The Role of Commercial Interests

What role do private economic interests play in motivating efforts to suppress illicit trade? Cooperation against illicit trade is not a "Baptists and bootleggers" story—a metaphor that originated from tales of American states' efforts to ban the sale of alcohol on Sundays. Baptists endorsed the ban on moral and religious grounds; for bootleggers, the ban was a commercial boon that limited competition and increased their illegal alcohol sales. By analogy, the metaphor captures unlikely coalitions whose members pursue similar goals for different reasons. Some members are morally motivated or act on behalf of the public interest; others, typically industries, seek private economic gain. The joint pursuit of coinciding goals facilitates their realization: the morally driven actors provide legitimacy, whereas the industries bring political clout.[10] One example is Elizabeth DeSombre's account of the internationalization of American environmental regulations since the 1970s. DeSombre documents how coalitions of environmentalists and industries convinced the U.S. government to ensure that foreign countries abided by environmental standards similar to those of the United States. The key to the success of these regulatory campaigns was the convergence of public and private interests: environmental concerns intersected with industries' concerns about their diminished competitiveness due to domestic environmental regulations.[11]

By contrast, the international regulatory efforts against illicit trade do not require an overlap between public interest—mitigating the trade's externalities—and private commercial interests. Such an overlap exists in the case of counterfeits, in which the bearers of the externalities are themselves private industries. In other cases, however, the trade's negative externalities are the main driver of international regulation, even in the absence of coinciding commercial motivations. Indeed, governments typically seek to limit the adverse commercial effects of regulation on legitimate businesses. Furthermore, international regulation may sometimes *benefit* business by leveling the playing field in the global market or by enhancing the reputation of regulation-compliant firms. Such benefits reinforce the impetus for regulation provided by the trade's externalities. Yet the promotion of commercial interests in itself is not a necessary or principal motivation. The international efforts against illicit trade are aimed, first and foremost, at curbing the trade's negative externalities. The question is which *actors* are best positioned to achieve this goal.

## The Actors

International cooperative agreements seek to influence the behavior of certain actors. In many cases, these actors are governments. The purpose of human rights treaties is to shape governments' treatment of their own citizens in a manner consistent with human dignity. Agreements on trade liberalization require governments to lower barriers to trade. Security agreements govern the conduct of governments by establishing alliances and arms control and by setting the laws of war. International environmental agreements, by contrast, target not only governments. They are also aimed at influencing the behavior of a variety of private actors, especially firms and industries.[12] I have noted above the similarity between illicit trade and environmental problems that involve asymmetric externalities. This analogy extends to the actors as well. International regulation against illicit trade makes demands on governments, but it also seeks to alter the behavior of the nongovernmental, private actors involved in the trade.

Illicit trade is an international commercial activity. As in legal trade, the participants in this activity are market actors: exporters and consumers. A key distinction between legal and illicit trade, however, is that many of the exporters and consumers involved in illicit trade are criminals. Indeed, illicit markets encompass a broad and diverse range of criminal actors, from individual offenders and small gangs to loose criminal networks to major syndicates, such as the Italian mafia and the Japanese Yakuza. Accordingly, studies and policy debates typically associate illicit trade with organized crime and conceive of illicit markets as the domain of criminal groups. In his seminal book *Illicit*, Moisés Naím explains that the "story [of illicit trade] is about smuggling and, more generally, about crime."[13] Naím thus focuses on global criminal networks: "stateless traders in illicit goods" that, he argues, "are changing the world."[14] Yet criminals are not the only actors in illicit trade. Contrary to popular image, illicit trade is not entirely underground, hidden from view. It is, in fact, closely tied with legal trade and involves a host of legitimate actors. The international regulatory efforts against illicit trade may directly target the criminal actors involved; but often they take advantage of the legal-illicit nexus and attack the illicit market indirectly. Their goal is to curb illicit transactions by regulating the legal dimensions of the trade—the more exposed links in the chain. By targeting the *legitimate* actors who are complicit in illicit trade, governments seek to suppress the activities of illegitimate actors.

The legitimate actors taking part in illicit trade are diverse. These may be banks that launder the proceeds of crime; diamond companies that trade in conflict diamonds; museums that acquire and display looted antiquities; or arms manufacturers that sell guns indiscriminately, including to purchasers that might misuse the weapons. These and other legitimate actors feed, fuel, or assist illicit trade—knowingly at times, but often out of willful neglect to ensure the integrity of their business. They turn a blind eye to the dubious origin or destination of goods, to the questionable nature of transactions, and to the involvement of criminals and other outlaws. These otherwise legitimate actors benefit from illicit trade while remaining indifferent to its negative consequences, and it is this indifference and recklessness that international regulation seeks to end. Its goal is to make the actors behave more responsibly and to increase their accountability by establishing proper standards and closing regulatory gaps.

Why suppress the illicit economy by regulating legal economic activities? Put simply, legitimate actors are more convenient targets. Their behavior is easier to influence and alter than that of criminals who operate outside the realm of the law. While the legitimate actors may act in an unscrupulous, irresponsible manner that abets illicit trade, their activity overall is in the open and not underground. They operate inside the territory of the law, within the reach of regulators. Therefore, it is possible to monitor their conduct, shape their incentives so as to encourage compliance with regulatory standards, and punish them for noncompliance. It is much more difficult to target clandestine activity and deter or punish criminals.

I illustrate this logic—curbing illicit trade by regulating the conduct of legal, legitimate actors—through two examples.

Consider the trade in small arms and its two spheres: the legal and the illicit trade. Within the legal sphere there are a variety of legitimate actors involved in the manufacture, trade, possession, or use of small arms. These include the arms industry, governments and their police and military forces, and law-abiding civilian gun owners. The illicit sphere is occupied by actors unauthorized to acquire guns, such as criminal groups, rebels, terrorists, and embargoed governments. The primary method by which these unauthorized actors obtain arms is *diversion*: the movement of arms from the legal sphere to the illicit realm. Diversion can take various forms, among them theft from military or civilian stocks, "straw purchasing" from a gun dealer through an eligible intermediary, diversion of an international arms shipment en route to an ostensible end-user, and diversion of the arms after their delivery to the end-user.[15]

The international efforts against the illicit trade in small arms are aimed at preventing unauthorized actors from acquiring arms and misusing them.

The principal means of achieving this goal, however, is not by targeting the unauthorized actors directly, but rather by tightening the control over the *legal* dimensions of the small-arms market to close loopholes and reduce the risk of diversion. Responsible behavior on the part of actors transacting in small arms and careful government scrutiny of arms sales and transfers can go a long way toward thwarting diversion. Indeed, enhanced control over the legal small-arms trade is the aim of the international regulatory framework established in 2001: the Program of Action to Prevent, Combat and Eradicate the Illicit Trade in Small Arms and Light Weapons in All Its Aspects. For example, the Program of Action calls upon states "[t]o assess applications for export authorizations according to strict national regulations and procedures that cover all small arms and light weapons and are consistent with the existing responsibilities of States under relevant international law, taking into account in particular the risk of diversion of these weapons into the illegal trade. Likewise, to establish or maintain an effective national system of export and import licensing or authorization."[16] These measures have two addressees: arms exporters who are required to go through more rigorous checks and meet more stringent licensing requirements; and governments' regulatory authorities whose task it is to monitor the export process and ensure the legitimacy of transactions. Licensing officers can disrupt diversion schemes and prevent arms from falling into the wrong hands by collecting all relevant documentation, verifying its authenticity, and confirming the legitimacy of the end-user and of the requested arms-transfer.[17]

A similar logic is at work in the case of money laundering. Money laundering is a paradigmatic example of the entanglement of legal and illegal activities: the proceeds of crime receive a veneer of legitimacy as they pass through financial institutions. The international efforts against money laundering are aimed at preventing criminals from converting their illegal gains into seemingly legal assets; yet these efforts do not focus on the criminals themselves. Rather, they target the actors whose conduct is more easily monitored and controlled. The primary targets of anti-money laundering regulations are *legitimate* financial institutions—banks and others—that provide the legal cover for proceeds of crime. The Forty Recommendations— the international standards of anti-money laundering measures—require financial institutions to verify the identity of customers, prohibit anonymous accounts, maintain records of transactions for at least five years, and examine the background and purpose of unusual transactions.[18] Governments are responsible for ensuring that financial institutions are under adequate regulation and supervision and are implementing the Forty Recommendations effectively.[19]

Other regulatory campaigns similarly target legitimate actors or both legitimate and criminal actors. The Kimberley Process Certification Scheme seeks to eliminate rebels' trade in diamonds through regulation of the legal diamond industry. International antiquities regulation aims at the legitimate, visible actors who buy the loot and fuel the thievery: antiquities dealers and auction houses, museums, and private collectors. International drug control is directed at drug traffickers, drug-cultivating peasants, and pharmaceutical companies, among others. The efforts against human trafficking target criminal organizations as well as legitimate actors, from bars and clubs that exploit trafficked women to farmers and contractors who employ trafficked migrant workers. Initiatives against counterfeit goods seek to stop the production of and trade in these goods by legitimate firms as well as criminal groups. The efforts against the illicit movement of hazardous wastes are aimed at preventing rich-country industries from exporting those wastes to poor countries.

As primary targets of these international efforts, legitimate societal actors are central to the analysis of cooperation against illicit trade. Furthermore, these actors can legitimately and openly sound their voice in the political arena. They may participate in the domestic political process relating to international regulation: present their views in parliamentary debates and other public forums, lobby policymakers, and take part in policymaking sessions. Governments can legitimately translate the views and preferences of these actors into official policy that they will espouse in the international arena. The legitimate societal actors may also have direct access to the international political process as part of states' delegations to negotiations or even on an independent basis.[20]

An analysis of cooperation against illicit trade must, of course, take into account the criminal actors as well. Yet the criminals' access to and impact on international political processes is more limited than that of the legitimate actors who can influence policymaking directly and openly. It is difficult for a government to justify its position in the international arena based on the preferences of criminals. Criminal actors are thus less likely to shape the form and substance of international regulation. Their influence is typically manifested on the ground. Through bribery, corruption, and intimidation, they may seek to thwart the enforcement of and compliance with international regulation.

## Theoretical Lens

Since the principal purpose of cooperation is to curb illicit trade's negative externalities on society, and given that the cooperative endeavors seek to shape the conduct of societal actors, our theoretical perspective should highlight state-society relations and their impact on international interactions and outcomes. Such an emphasis makes *liberal* international relations theory a fruitful lens through which to theorize cooperation against illicit trade. The premise of liberal IR theory—as stated by Andrew Moravcsik—is that domestic and transnational society shapes the goals and social purposes that governments pursue in world politics.[21] In other words, for liberals, international behavior has societal roots: the preferences that governments seek to realize internationally originate from the preferences, views, and demands of individuals and groups in society. My analysis builds on this general assumption and on two specific variants of liberalism derived from it: ideational liberalism and commercial liberalism.

Ideational liberalism sees the origin of government preferences in domestic social identities and values. These include, among others, societal preferences on socioeconomic regulation and on the provision of public goods such as personal safety, healthcare, and environmental protection.[22] To provide public goods in an interdependent world, governments often resort to international cooperative efforts. Applied to illicit trade, this variant of liberalism captures the motivation for cooperation: curbing the *primary negative externalities* of the trade—that is, the negative effects of the trade within the national territory. Society wishes to combat public bads like gun violence, drug abuse, and the plunder of antiquities; governments thus attempt to diminish these problems and enhance social welfare through international regulation. Yet societal concerns can extend beyond the national boundaries. Individuals and groups in society may worry—on moral or humanitarian grounds—about the negative effects of illicit trade abroad. These actors demand international action to curb *secondary externalities*—the trade's negative effects on foreign countries—and press their governments to initiate or participate in such an endeavor. Whether the concerns are over the trade's externalities at home or abroad, ideational liberalism traces government preferences to domestic society. Societal actors pressure governments to seek the suppression of illicit trade; governments then pursue this goal through international cooperative efforts.

Whereas ideational liberalism captures the motivation for cooperation—society's desire to mitigate the externalities of illicit trade—commercial liberalism highlights the market actors involved in the trade. Commercial liberalism posits that private actors who benefit from cross-border transactions typically pressure governments to facilitate such transactions. These actors oppose measures that could obstruct commerce or otherwise lessen the rewards that it yields. Commercial liberal theory thus expects that actors involved in illicit trade—exporters and consumers—will seek to maintain the private benefits that they enjoy. Accordingly, they would resist international efforts directed against the trade.[23]

Liberal factors account for government preferences. Integrating ideational liberalism and commercial liberalism allows the construction of government preferences shaped by opposing societal influences: on the one hand, concerns over the trade's externalities and demands for their mitigation and, on the other hand, the concerns of actors involved in the trade and their desire to prevent its suppression. Yet preferences alone do not determine international outcomes. Preferences are the goals that governments pursue. Their pursuit takes place within a strategic environment and is subject to the constraints imposed by that environment, first and foremost those relating to national capabilities. Powerful governments are more capable of promoting and achieving their goals than are weaker governments. An analysis of cooperation must therefore integrate the variation in preferences with the distribution of power. In other words, theory synthesis is necessary. While liberal IR theory is the main premise of the theoretical framework, only its combination with a realist element—power distribution—will produce a full theory.[24] This synthesis takes the form of a two-stage process. In the first stage, governments define their preferences. They determine whether to support international regulation against illicit trade and, if so, what kind of regulation they favor. In the second stage, governments interact. The variation in government preferences fuels an international political conflict, and the distribution of power determines who prevails and what the regulatory outcome is. The stage of preference formation is analytically prior to the international interaction: Governments first determine what their respective goals are; their aggregated decisions then determine the magnitude and contours of the ensuing political conflict.[25]

## Government Preferences on International Regulation

Why do governments sharply disagree about the extent and means of—and even the need for—international regulation against illicit trade? To solve the puzzle, this section combines several building blocks: the purpose of cooperation—curbing primary or secondary negative externalities—and the market actors: exporters and consumers. Taken together, these influences give rise to highly divergent preferences, from strong support for international regulation to outright opposition. I begin, however, with several underlying assumptions.

The first assumption is that governments care about aggregate social welfare as well as the wishes of specific societal groups.[26] Policymakers may seek to increase social welfare since they are genuinely concerned for the wellbeing of domestic or foreign publics and may derive pleasure from pursuing policies that they view as socially beneficial. At the same time, policymakers may believe that such policies will garner public support and enhance their prospects of political survival. Governments are also attentive to the concerns of specific societal groups—both legitimate groups and groups that operate outside the boundaries of the law. These groups may benefit policymakers directly—for example, through political contributions, bribes, or votes. But policymakers may also believe—or be persuaded—that policies consistent with these groups' wishes increase social welfare; for example, by providing jobs or tax revenue.

The analysis employs a weak rationality assumption, maintaining that domestic political systems produce identifiable preferences that governments pursue within the limitations of the available political means.[27] This implies that government preferences need not be uniform across trades. A government may favor tight international regulation of one trade while vigorously resisting the regulation of another. Nor need preferences be consistent over long periods of time. When their underlying determinants change, so will government preferences themselves. Most importantly, the rationality assumption does *not* mean that preferences must be grounded exclusively in material incentives. Moral concerns about the effects of illicit trade may indeed influence governments' calculations.

The theoretical framework takes the preexisting national regulation as its point of departure. As explained above, national regulation varies between the generators and bearers of illicit trade's externalities, and the purpose of international regulation is to reduce that variation. Government preferences on international regulation typically mirror their respective preferences on national regulation. Governments that bear the trade's externalities enact stringent national regulation; the insufficiency of such regulation leads them to advocate strict international regulation. By contrast, governments whose countries generate the externalities establish loose national controls; when the trade becomes an international issue, these governments typically favor minimal international constraints. For the sake of parsimony, and since my focus is international cooperation, I theorize only preferences on international regulation.

The theoretical framework assumes that governments act as unitary actors *in the international arena*. The framework's first stage disaggregates the state and examines how national preferences are shaped by domestic society. The unitary-actor assumption only means that once specific preferences arise from the domestic arena, governments pursue them as unitary actors vis-à-vis other governments.[28] One critique of this approach is that government agencies and ministries may differ in their views and policies, thus precluding us from ascribing a single preference to the government.[29] Yet even when such differences exist domestically, governments typically seek to speak with a single voice in the international arena. Prior to international negotiations, competing government bodies attempt to reconcile their differences and establish a coherent joint position. During negotiations, delegations composed of representatives of various ministries usually bargain as a team with a coordinated position. The clearest manifestation of the government's unified preference is the decision whether or not to commit to the resulting agreement. This decision may be the product of conflicting views, but these views eventually produce a single act of either joining the agreement or rejecting it. A unitary-actor assumption is therefore appropriate when analyzing governments' negotiating positions and their willingness or reluctance to commit. At the stages of implementation and enforcement, differences between ministries and agencies may surface. When this is the case, the unitary-actor assumption is relaxed.

## Determinants of Government Preferences

### Primary Negative Externalities

Primary externalities of illicit trade are the negative effects on one's own country resulting from the production, sale, or use of the goods or the provision of the service. Examples include gun homicide and drug-user crime (externalities from use); financing of rebel military campaigns through proceeds from diamonds (externalities from sale); and archaeological destruction caused by the looting of antiquities (externalities from production). These negative effects are felt mainly by the importing or exporting countries, but third countries could face them as well.

Governments may have several motivations for suppressing illicit trade and its negative effects. First, the externalities of illicit trade threaten and undermine social welfare. Policymakers concerned for political survival may thus perceive a connection between the trade's externalities and public support. The public might disapprove of governments that fail to solve pressing problems like rampant gun violence or widespread drug abuse. Second, policymakers may be genuinely concerned about public welfare. Their sense of duty and responsibility could lead them to tackle the trade's externalities. A third possibility is that specific actors may demand the suppression of illicit trade, as they bear its externalities. One example is corporations whose products are the subject of counterfeiting; another is governments themselves that are directly threatened by large-scale gun violence or the financing of rebel movements through conflict diamonds.

How do the trade's primary externalities affect government preferences on international regulation? Following are several expectations.

1. *Governments will prefer stronger international regulation when the negative externalities are larger in magnitude.* As the rate of gun violence or drug abuse rises, governments will seek stronger international restraints on the trade in small arms or drugs. The greater the scale of archaeological plunder, the stronger should be governments' support for international control of the antiquities trade.

2. *Governments will prefer stronger international regulation when the negative externalities are perceived as more severe.* The perceived severity of the externalities may reflect a construction more than an objective harm. For example, some countries see the plunder of antiquities not merely as theft, but as the loss of objects that are part of their national identity. Such a perception may be of benefit to governments seeking to fuel nationalist sentiments. Another example is the moral panic over drug use by minority groups in the United States in the late 19th and early 20th centuries. Minorities' use of drugs was thought to disrupt the social restrictions that kept these groups under control, inciting violence and sexual assault.[30]

3. *Governments will prefer stronger international regulation when the national capacity to curb the negative externalities is lower.* The need for international regulation arises from the insufficiency of national trade control. Governments whose control measures fail to suppress illicit trade seek to overcome this failure through international regulation. By shifting the burden of control, international regulation allows these governments to make up for their regulatory inadequacy. The lower the capacity of the importing (exporting) countries to curb the trade's externalities, the more dependent they are on the efforts of the exporting (importing) countries, and the greater their support for international regulation.

4. *Governments will prefer stronger international regulation when the domestic costs of curbing the negative externalities are higher.* Even when governments have the capacity to suppress illicit trade and its externalities, doing so could still be costly—both financially and politically. Governments would therefore seek international regulation to spread the burden. For example, policymakers may prefer to fight drug abuse by limiting drug production abroad rather than expend resources, curtail civil liberties, and raise political controversies at home.[31]

## Secondary Negative Externalities

The negative externalities of illicit trade are of concern not merely to governments whose countries bear those externalities. Certain governments may worry about the trade's negative impact on foreign countries. I term this impact *secondary externalities*, that is, the externalities borne by countries other than one's own. The question is what fuels these other-regarding concerns, and why governments would wish to suppress trade whose deleterious effects are felt abroad. Why would the United States seek to eliminate human trafficking worldwide? Why would European governments wish to reduce gun violence in Africa?

Concern about secondary externalities may be instrumental and self-interested. Exhibiting concern about the problems plaguing foreign countries may improve relations with those countries. A government seeking to enhance its international image or influence will similarly demonstrate concern about the negative effects of illicit trade abroad. Governments may also believe that their own countries' economy or security is influenced by the wellbeing of foreign countries; hence, the problems and disruptions that illicit trade causes abroad might indirectly threaten one's homeland and interests. Secondary externalities, in other words, could potentially turn into primary externalities. For example, gun violence in country X may have spillover effects in neighboring countries and could adversely affect X's political and economic ties with countries outside its immediate neighborhood.

Concern about secondary externalities may also be morally inspired. Some policymakers genuinely care about the welfare of foreign countries: illicit trade's externalities abroad resonate with their values. For example, they may truly abhor the worldwide death toll of the illicit trade in small arms. Policymakers may also believe that action against the trade will earn them the support of elites and mass publics who care about welfare abroad.[32] Another source of concern about secondary externalities is moral entrepreneurs: civil society groups that place the trade and its negative effects on the agenda and lobby governments to initiate or participate in an international regulatory campaign. These groups are committed to worldwide suppression of illicit trade that they deem harmful and repugnant. In some cases, the moral entrepreneurs are domestic actors. Chapter 4, for example, examines the advocacy of American archaeologists for regulation to eliminate the illicit trade in antiquities. Other entrepreneurs take the form of transnational networks of nongovernmental organizations (NGOs). An example is the coalitions of European and American NGOs that formed in the late 1990s and early 2000s to advocate against conflict diamonds.[33]

Why would moral entrepreneurs push for action against illicit trade? While these actors sometimes have self-interested reasons to stem the trade, their principal motivation comes from values and normative principles.[34] The source of these values may be religion; for other entrepreneurs, motivation comes from a diverse set of values and goals, such as human rights and humanitarianism, peace, development, environmental protection, and women's rights. The efforts of the archaeological community against the illicit trade in antiquities are in the interest of historical knowledge. In fact, regulatory campaigns may bring together quite different moral entrepreneurs. In the late 1990s evangelical Christians teamed up with women's groups, normally their bitter rivals, to demand U.S. action against sex trafficking.

Moral entrepreneurs advocate the elimination of illicit trade and its negative effects abroad. Why would governments pay attention to their demands? Some entrepreneurs are politically powerful and represent important constituencies. This allows them to wield significant influence over governments.[35] More typically, entrepreneurs seek to educate policymakers and raise their awareness of illicit trade and its detrimental consequences. To educate and raise awareness, these actors take advantage of their expertise and knowledge about the trade and even their first-hand experience with the trade's damaging effects. The provision and dissemination of *information* is the entrepreneurs' key strategy for gaining influence and shaping preferences.[36] Their provision of information may involve various techniques, such as meeting with policymakers, sending letters, giving oral and written testimonies, and publishing reports. While entrepreneurs' advocacy highlights moral and normative reasons for suppressing illicit trade, it may also identify instrumental motivations—for example, warning policymakers that failure to take action against the trade would tarnish the country's international reputation.

Moral entrepreneurs seek to promote regulation directly by lobbying policymakers and educating them, but they also exert influence indirectly by shaping the public atmosphere and fostering public opinion that is conducive to regulation. Through such means as publications and lectures, entrepreneurs may raise public awareness and galvanize popular concern about the externalities of illicit trade abroad. Such a public climate can motivate policymakers to pursue regulation, while making it harder for proponents of the status quo to resist and obstruct the regulatory efforts. A notable example is the campaign to control the diamond trade. To encourage action against conflict diamonds, the campaigning NGOs distributed posters, leaflets, and videos and published reports. They called upon the public to ask governments and diamond companies for effective controls.[37]

Although the theoretical framework distinguishes between primary and secondary externalities, it should be noted that governments could be concerned about both at the same time. They may worry about the trade's negative effects upon their own countries as well as its impact abroad. The empirical chapters of the book will provide several examples of such dual concerns.

## Exporters

The international regulatory efforts against illicit trade involve both criminal exporters and legitimate exporters. The two groups have somewhat different concerns and an unequal exposure to the risk of enforcement. International regulation, however, may carry adverse consequences for both types of exporters.

### Criminal Exporters

Drug cartels are one example of criminal exporters; another is sex traffickers who recruit women and transfer them abroad. These actors may generally benefit from regulation that serves as an entry barrier. Such regulation drives out competition and allows the outlawed exporters who shield themselves from enforcement to increase their profits.[38] Yet tight, effective *international* regulation may not work to the exporters' advantage.

First, international regulation strengthens the government's incentives to suppress illicit trade, making it more difficult for the criminal exporters to keep escaping the law. International regulatory agreements may bring the conduct of the government under the scrutiny of foreign governments or that of an international organ. Compliance may be tied to benefits that the government covets, such as foreign aid. International regulation can thus generate pressures for stronger law enforcement and motivate governments to step up the efforts against the trade. Governments that have previously turned a blind eye to illicit commercial activity will find inaction more difficult to sustain. The upshot for the criminals is an increased risk of apprehension and punishment and the additional costs of avoiding that risk.

Second, international regulation might adversely affect criminal exporters by narrowing the gaps in national control and inducing all countries to establish adequate regulatory measures. In the countries of origin, especially where the bureaucracy and law-enforcement agencies are weak or corrupt, criminals may be able to persist in their commercial activities despite international regulation. Yet once loopholes are closed in transit countries and countries of destination, these actors will face a more formidable challenge. Not only is it more difficult for them to exercise their tools of influence— bribery, corruption, and intimidation—across borders, but law enforcement abroad may be more robust and not easily compromised. Antiquities looters may be able to smuggle the plundered objects out of the source countries, where the bureaucratic apparatus is weak; but there is little they can do if U.S. Customs seizes the antiquities at the point of entry. Drug traffickers may be able to get the drugs out of the producing countries, but heightened enforcement in transit and destination countries could force them to seek alternative routes and markets.[39] By strengthening the control throughout the chain of trade, international regulation complicates or altogether obstructs illegal commercial transactions, even if the exporters can still evade the law in their own countries.

Governments will welcome international regulation when they are concerned about the negative externalities that criminal activities create within the national territory. Plunder of antiquities is an example. But other governments are less concerned about crime's negative effects, especially those borne abroad. Sometimes, especially in failing states, illicit trade is part of a political strategy: the government uses its control of the illicit market to channel resources and provide economic opportunities to its supporters.[40] Or, a symbiotic criminal-political relationship may exist, in which the authorities tolerate or even protect criminal activities in exchange for economic benefits and political subordination.[41] Cracking down on illicit exports is thus not only a costly and risky law-enforcement endeavor; it jeopardizes the interests of officials under whose auspices the trade flourishes. Governments that tolerate or collude with criminal exporters would therefore favor weak international regulation, which does not pressure them to suppress the trade.

### Legitimate Exporters

How does international regulation affect exporters and service providers in *legitimate* industries, such as arms manufacturers, diamond companies, or banks? Unlike criminal exporters, legitimate exporters operate in the open and are more exposed to the risk of enforcement. Their conduct may be monitored by the authorities and they cannot easily escape criminal or regulatory sanctions. Therefore, these exporters' base assumption is that they will have to comply with international regulation and bear its adverse commercial consequences, such as a ban on certain transactions, administrative requirements that could slow down or block the export process, and higher production costs. Consider a possible prohibition on the export of arms when these might be used for human-rights violations. Such a prohibition is intended to diminish small-arms misuse and curb gun violence; yet for exporters, the screening of buyers means diminished sales and lost income. Anti-money laundering regulations could have similar implications for banks: reduced financial activity and lower profits. These regulations also entail significant administrative costs, such as the filing of reports on suspicious transactions.[42] Noncompliance with these and other regulatory requirements carries a dual risk: not only a state-imposed penalty, but also a tarnished reputation and the loss of public trust.[43] Maintaining reputation and public trust is obviously not a concern for criminal groups, but it may be important to legitimate businesses.

While international regulation entails costs for exporters, it may also offer them some benefits.[44] One benefit is a level playing field in the global market. Exporters subject to stringent national regulation suffer a competitive disadvantage compared to their loosely controlled foreign competitors. This disadvantage translates to loss of business.[45] Arms exporters required to comply with strict export standards and ascertain the legitimacy of buyers lose sales to exporters who sell freely to any buyer. Banks that take measures to prevent money laundering could see financial flows—both legitimate and illegitimate—redirected to foreign banks that are less heavily regulated. For the tightly controlled exporters, international regulation promises to spread the burden to their competitors as well. By requiring all exporters to comply with uniform regulatory standards, international regulation could eliminate the competitive disadvantage that stems from variation in national regulation. Furthermore, international regulation may serve as a barrier that eliminates the competition from small, unscrupulous exporters and leaves the market to the larger, regulation-compliant firms. A second benefit of international regulation is the standardization of exporters' operating environment, obviating the need to accommodate multiple national regulatory regimes. Clear, predictable international rules also lessen exporters' uncertainty. They facilitate accurate expectations and understanding of regulatory requirements and how those requirements might evolve.[46] The third benefit of international regulation is reputational. Compliance with international rules aimed at curbing illicit trade can demonstrate exporters' social responsibility and burnish their public image. Positive reputation, in turn, can attract consumers and business partners, boost shareholder confidence, and raise employee morale.[47] In this sense, international regulation is consistent with the trend of industry self-regulation. Since the early 1990s, a growing number of multinational corporations have adopted voluntary codes of conduct to protect and enhance their reputation.[48] Nonvoluntary, public welfare-oriented international regulation may achieve a similar reputational effect.

The benefits of international regulation do not accrue equally to all exporters: they vary across industries and countries. Maintaining public trust and a reputation for integrity is essential for banks, less so for arms manufacturers. Businesses in industrialized countries are more likely to face media and public criticism for unethical conduct; they would be more concerned for their reputation than their counterparts in developing countries. Leveling the playing field is a concern for those exporters who find their competitiveness diminished by stringent national regulation. Those exporters would seek to impose similar constraints on their competitors through international control.

While international regulation brings exporters both costs and benefits, I expect them to prefer weak regulation to strict regulation. Exporters likely seek the least restrictive international regulation—diluted to the minimum necessary to reap the benefits of international regulatory standards. The reason is that the costs of international regulation are certain, immediate, and fairly easily quantifiable. Whether it is loss of sales or licensing and reporting requirements, the regulatory burden weighs heavily on exporters. By contrast, the benefits of international regulation are less clearly evident. Their realization is uncertain or may take a long time. The benefits may also be difficult to measure and will not necessarily outweigh the costs that regulation entails. Exporters may desire the reputational boost that international regulation could yield, but the magnitude of this boost and its salutary effect on business are difficult to assess. Exporters thus tend to focus on regulation's immediate costs and tangible constraints. Their utmost priority is to avoid an onerous burden.

The expectation of exporters' resistance to international regulation finds support in the area of environmental cooperation. International environmental agreements impose costs on businesses, but may also benefit them by spreading the regulatory burden. Nevertheless, firms and industries over-whelmingly oppose national and international regulation to address envi-ronmental problems. Their primary concern is the immediate onus of compliance, and the regulatory benefits are typically discounted. Businesses resist environmental regulation as long as they believe that it can be obstructed and that a nonregulation status quo can be maintained. Only when the government or market developments eliminate that option, does business support stricter environmental policy.[49] A similar pattern should hold in the realm of illicit trade. We would expect exporters to prefer minimal regulatory interference with their commercial activity. If international regu-lation cannot be thwarted altogether, exporters will seek to dilute the regula-tory agreement and lighten the burden it imposes on them. They may also try to prevent the ratification of the agreement or weaken the implementing legislation. The question is whether the exporters can indeed bring the gov-ernment to espouse their preference for minimal constraints.

Unlike criminal exporters who do not operate openly in the political arena, legitimate exporters may resist regulation through conventional channels of political activity. Typical impediments to the political involve-ment of exporters have a smaller effect in the present context. Exporters, gen-erally speaking, may not always be willing to act politically due to the uncertainty of economic gain that trade liberalization would bring. Exporters may judge that there are limited profits in new markets or that the costs of collective political action overwhelm the benefits of trade liberalization. The need to counter pressures from import-competing industries may also lessen exporters' enthusiasm to organize politically.[50] Such considerations, how-ever, are less likely to diminish the political activity of the exporters addressed here. International regulation against illicit trade involves a high certainty of significant loss for exporters that serves as a strong motivation for political action. The countervailing forces that exporters may have to overcome—pro-regulation civil society groups—are typically less formidable than import-competing industries and their significant political clout. Further-more, the collective action problem that exporters face is not severe. Like in-ternational environmental agreements, regulation against illicit trade adversely affects a limited number of commercial entities. The highly con-centrated burden gives exporters a strong incentive to organize politically in opposition to regulation. They may employ various lobbying means, such as financial contributions, provision of information, and development of per-sonal and social ties with politicians and bureaucracies.[51] The ability to wield these tools of influence varies across exporters as a function of their organi-zational capacity, resources, and access to the policymaking process.

Exporters may influence government preferences through political ac-tivity. Yet governments may still heed exporters' concerns and protect their interests even if they avoid direct political involvement. The exporters' commercial activity may be an important source of employment, income, and tax revenue; exporters such as arms manufacturers and drug companies may be vital to national security and healthcare. International regulation, however, constrains businesses and could diminish their benefits to society. The adverse effects of regulation—such as lowering employment and income—might also endanger governments' political survival.[52] By resisting international regulation of trade, governments seek to maintain the flow of benefits that the trade provides.

### Consumers

The consumers involved in illicit trade constitute a diverse group. In certain trades, consumers are numerous, while in others they are relatively few. The number of illegal drug users, for example, dwarfs that of antiquities collectors and museums. Consumers also vary in their legal status. Some are legitimate actors who overall engage in legal activity; examples include museums, employers of trafficked migrant workers, and otherwise law-abiding citizens who buy counterfeit goods. Other consumers, however, are unlawful actors, such as rebels, terrorists, and criminals who use small arms or money-laundering services.

Consumers may be interested in the trade for various reasons. Collectors purchase antiquities because of their aesthetic or historical value or as a financial investment; rebels obtain arms to overthrow the government; counterfeits are simply cheaper than the original. Whatever the source of interest, I assume that consumers typically care about their own welfare and are indifferent to the negative externalities of illicit trade. Accordingly, I expect them to resist international regulation and the costs it entails: administrative requirements, restrictions on the access to and availability of the goods and services, and price increase. International regulation could significantly limit or altogether suppress consumption—a consequence that consumers would strongly wish to avoid. Therefore, they will prefer loose controls and reluctantly accept those that are inevitable. Consumers who are themselves commercial actors, such as antiquities dealers, may reap competitive and reputational gains from international regulation. Yet like exporters, these consumers typically perceive the costs of regulation as outweighing its benefits. They would therefore prefer the weakest regulation possible.

But can consumers press the government to pursue minimally controlled trade? Their political activity might face obstacles. One obstacle is a collective action problem, the constraint on consumer influence emphasized by the literature on conventional trade.[53] Another possible impediment—unique to illicit trade—is the illegal status of certain consumers. Criminals, for example, cannot openly lobby governments to allow money laundering or easy gun acquisition. Where drug use is prohibited, illegal users may find it difficult to lobby for liberalized trade in drugs. Nevertheless, their interests may still find indirect public expression. Most notably, since the 1980s the U.S. prohibitionist drug policy has come under criticism from a range of actors calling for alternative approaches.[54] These advocates include, among others, civil libertarians, public health practitioners, and civil society groups committed to human rights and social justice.[55] They are all concerned about the negative effects of a strict prohibition: erosion of civil rights, exacerbation of public health problems such as HIV/AIDS, and overwhelming of the criminal justice system, to name a few.

Other consumers, however, enjoy legitimate political influence that they would use to press for weak international regulation. This is obviously the case when the government itself is among the consumers. Small arms are a notable example. Another category of politically active consumers includes actors such as employers of trafficked migrant workers, antiquities dealers, and museums. In those cases, the number of consumers is sufficiently small and the benefits of the trade are concentrated enough to lessen the collective action problem and motivate political activity. But as with exporters, governments may also respond to consumers' concerns in the absence of explicit lobbying. Aware of the economic and cultural benefits of a thriving art market, for instance, governments might hesitate to curb the inflow of antiquities, even though many of them are likely looted.

## Variation in Government Preferences on International Regulation

I have identified four possible influences on government preferences: the pro-regulation pull of primary and secondary negative externalities and the anti-regulation push from exporters and consumers. The weight of these influences will vary as a function of different underlying variables, such as exporters' and consumers' level of political activity; the magnitude of the trade's negative externalities as well as the national capacity to curb them; and the influence of moral entrepreneurs. Combining the four influences along two dimensions, as shown in Figure 2.1, leads one to expect a large heterogeneity of government preferences on international regulation.

At one extreme are pro-regulation governments (Quadrant II). These include two subgroups: "victim" governments whose countries bear the primary externalities of illicit trade; and governments concerned about secondary externalities, that is, sympathizers with the victims. Worried about the trade and its negative effects, these governments do not face considerable anti-regulation pressure from exporters or consumers. We would therefore

## Influence of Primary/Secondary Negative Externalities

|  |  | Low | High |
|---|---|---|---|
| **Exporter/Consumer Influence** | **Low** | I.<br>Bystander governments<br>*Moderate regulation* | II.<br>Pro-regulation governments |
|  | **High** | III.<br>Anti-regulation governments | IV.<br>Cross-pressured governments<br>*Preference varies* |

**Figure 2.1** Expected Government Preferences on International Regulation

expect them to prefer strong international regulation, which potentially offers these governments important benefits—reducing the trade's negative externalities—at little cost.

At the other extreme are anti-regulation governments: "perpetrator" governments whose countries generate illicit trade's externalities, and other governments that might be anxious about the costs of international regulation (Quadrant III). These governments hold little concern over the trade's negative effects at home or abroad; yet they are strongly influenced by exporters or consumers who oppose regulation. Furthermore, an international regulatory agreement may require these governments to invest in bureaucracy and law enforcement—for example, by strengthening export or import controls—to the benefit of foreign countries. Such an agreement would also entail sovereignty costs. From these governments' point of view, international regulation unjustifiably and unnecessarily shifts onto them the burden of tackling the problems of other countries: it imposes costs on exporters, consumers, or the bureaucracy while bringing little benefit in return. If the status quo of no regulation cannot be maintained, we would expect these governments to prefer the weakest international regulation possible.

A third group of bystander governments has little concern over primary or secondary externalities and faces little anti-regulation pressure from exporters or consumers (Quadrant I). These governments have neither strong incentives to support international regulation nor motivation to resist it. We would expect them to adopt an intermediate position and favor moderate international regulation.

Finally, a fourth group includes cross-pressured governments (Quadrant IV). Primary or secondary negative externalities pull these governments toward strong international regulation. At the same time, exporters or consumers push them to minimize regulatory constraints. Cross-pressured governments likely vary in their preferences: they may adopt a victim preference for strong regulation, a perpetrator preference for weak regulation, or an intermediate preference for moderate regulation. These governments' support for international regulation increases as the negative externalities increase; their support for regulation declines as the influence of exporters or consumers rises.

Figure 2.1 combines the four influences to capture the cross-country variation in preferences: the divergent views of different governments on the proper regulatory measures for a given trade. The same influences account for the variation in government preferences across trades. A specific constellation of exporters' and consumers' influence, as well as primary and secondary externalities, may lead a government to strongly support the international regulation of a certain trade. A different constellation could bring the same government to oppose the international regulation of another trade. As the empirical chapters of this book will document, the United States has led the international efforts to control drugs and to curb human trafficking and money laundering. Yet the United States has failed to endorse the international regulation of small arms and has been ambivalent with respect to the international control of antiquities. Variation in the four underlying influences accounts for the differing American views across trades.

Government preferences may also vary over time. Such temporal preference change may come about in two ways. First, a change of government may lead to a preference change. A government preference is the result of balancing the negative externalities of illicit trade against the interests of exporters or consumers. A new government in power may weigh the competing influences differently than the previous government and strike a different balance. It may be attentive to domestic actors different than those that its predecessor had privileged. In accordance with its ideology and agenda, the new government may also differ from its predecessor in its concern about illicit trade's externalities at home or abroad. For example, a government pursuing a humanitarian foreign policy will have a greater interest in tackling the trade's effects abroad than a previous, non-humanitarian motivated government. Second, government preferences may shift as a result of exogenous changes in the domestic or transnational environment. Governments that previously faced only pressure from exporters or consumers may have to face the trade's negative externalities and become cross-pressured. Externalities that were initially small may increase in magnitude or perceived severity. Moral entrepreneurs that were previously inactive could wage an advocacy campaign and spur government concern about illicit trade. New information that comes to light can increase awareness by exposing the scale of the trade, its consequences, and the actors involved. These various developments may strengthen governments' pro-regulation incentives and bring them to prefer stronger regulation than they previously favored. The reverse may also occur. For example, intensified lobbying by actors demanding weak regulation may bring governments to pursue the liberalization of controls. Government preferences are therefore dynamic: they may change following shifts in their underlying determinants.

Turning back to Figure 2.1, the large variation in preferences is a major obstacle to the international regulatory efforts against illicit trade. While certain governments stand to benefit from international regulation, others find it costly and undesirable. The following section examines whether and how this international political conflict is overcome and cooperation established.

## The Establishment of Cooperation

### The Cooperation Problem

Identifying the cooperation problem is a critical step in an analysis of international cooperative efforts. By understanding the nature of the strategic interaction among governments, one can understand the factors that facilitate or impede joint international action.[56] I argue that the problem underlying the efforts against illicit trade is an absence of joint gains and a lack of shared interest among governments. Certain governments seek mutual cooperation through a regulatory agreement; yet other governments prefer the status quo of no agreement to mutual cooperation.

Why is there no shared interest? The benefits of international regulation flow to victim governments concerned about the negative externalities of the trade. International regulation helps these governments address serious social problems and shifts the burden of addressing these problems abroad. Victim governments thus have a strong interest in eliciting the cooperation of perpetrator governments—the governments from whose territories the trade's externalities emanate. Yet for perpetrator governments, international regulation is not welfare-enhancing but welfare-reducing. Indeed, international regulation would leave them and some of their domestic constituents worse off. As the trade does not adversely affect their countries or other countries they care about, these governments have no need for international control. From their point of view, regulatory measures would only limit the ability of exporters to make profits or the ability of consumers to obtain the goods. Moreover, regulation would entail costly law-enforcement efforts. Since cooperation imposes significant costs and offers little gain for them, these governments favor the noncooperative status quo.

The following two examples illustrate the cooperation problem. Consider the preferences of Somalia and China on the international regulation of the small-arms trade. The Somali government, seeking to prevent militias from obtaining arms, favors strong international regulation. International regulation would make up for Somalia's inability to curb the illicit import and circulation of guns. It would shift the responsibility for tackling Somalia's gun violence to arms-exporting countries, such as China. China, however, has a low rate of gun violence and no need for international regulation of small arms. From the Chinese point of view, international regulation is an unnecessary and damaging constraint on arms exports. China and Somalia therefore hold diametrically opposed preferences: whereas Somalia prefers tight international regulation, China favors no regulation or the weakest possible. The two countries do not share an interest in cooperation; only Somalia has such an interest. A similar problem characterizes the antiquities market. Consider the preferences of Mexico and Switzerland on the regulation of the antiquities trade. As a country suffering significant looting and loss of antiquities, Mexico—together with Peru—initiated the international control of antiquities in 1960. Such regulation would have made up for the Mexican government's failure to curb the plunder and illegal export of antiquities. It would have shifted the regulatory burden to market countries, such as Switzerland, by requiring those countries to control imports and block the inflow of looted material. Switzerland, however, preferred free trade in antiquities.[57] Strict regulation to allow Mexico to retain its antiquities would have disrupted the supply of antiquities to the Swiss art market, causing financial damage and job loss. Whereas Mexico had a strong interest in cooperation, Switzerland considered cooperation detrimental. As in the case of China's position on small arms, Switzerland was reluctant to shoulder the burden of solving the problem of plunder—a problem for which it bore some responsibility.

The root of the cooperation problem is that the international efforts against illicit trade do not promise mutual gains, and perpetrator governments lack any motivation to participate in these efforts. These governments consider the noncooperative status quo—absence of international control—their preferred outcome, whereas tight control is their worst outcome. They have little to gain by cooperating, regardless of what other governments do. China has no incentive to strictly regulate arms exports, even as arms-importing countries struggle to curb gun inflows. Switzerland saw no reason to control the import of antiquities, even as archaeologically rich countries failed to stop the plunder and illegal export of those antiquities.

The absence of shared interest poses a dual challenge, hindering both commitment and compliance. First, perpetrator governments will be reluctant to sign on to international regulation. Comfortable with the status quo, they see no reason to upset it by endorsing the regulatory efforts and committing to suppress illicit trade. Second, perpetrator governments that *do* join regulatory agreements have little motivation to comply with them.[58] This exacerbates the already complex challenge of compliance in the area of illicit trade. International agreements in other realms—such as human rights treaties and trade liberalization pacts—require governments to follow certain rules. By contrast, agreements against illicit trade ask governments not only to bring their own behavior into conformity with regulatory requirements, but also to ensure that the behavior of private actors conforms to regulation. This requires governments to monitor and take enforcement measures against various actors, from legitimate commercial entities—such as the arms industry and banks—to criminal groups. Bringing a government to comply with an agreement and ensure the compliance of private actors is all the more difficult when the government does not identify gains from cooperation. Governments have little appetite for costly compliance efforts that would ultimately leave them and their constituents worse off.

Absence of shared interest also means that self-enforcement is off the table. As Beth Simmons observes, international agreements are often self-enforcing—that is, they do not rely on third parties for enforcement. The agreement itself and the nature of the interaction give the parties incentives to comply, even without external enforcement. Underlying self-enforcement is each actor's expectation that the agreement will yield her long-term benefits, and that those benefits will be greater than the present value of violation. The parties themselves can "enforce" the agreement by curtailing the future flow of benefits.[59] The self-enforcement logic, however, does not apply to agreements that are not mutually beneficial, such as agreements that tackle illicit trade. Perpetrator governments do not benefit from an agreement that they did not want in the first place, and nonexpectation of future benefits gives them little reason to comply. Under such conditions, victims cannot elicit perpetrators' cooperation by responding to compliance or violation in kind. In other words, reciprocity—a key mechanism of self-enforcement—is not a viable option.

Lack of mutual gains and weakness of self-enforcement are not unique to illicit trade. The absence of mutual gains and an inability to employ reciprocity can hinder environmental cooperation in situations of asymmetric externalities. Human rights agreements exhibit a similar problem. They do not yield mutual gains and cannot be self-enforced through reciprocity. A government is unlikely to change its rights practices in response to human rights violations elsewhere.[60] Environmental and human-rights agreements are thus sometimes enforced through domestic accountability mechanisms. These agreements mobilize societal groups and provide them the leverage to demand government compliance.[61] In the realm of illicit trade, however, domestically motivated compliance is less likely. Domestic enforcement of international agreements requires a domestic pro-compliance constituency—be it voters, activists, or businesses—that has the motivation and means to hold the government accountable. For illicit trade, however, the actors with the largest stake in compliance are abroad: the foreign victim-countries. At home, perpetrator governments could face a pro-compliance constituency that is too small, if it exists at all, or does not possess enough political leverage. Rather, those governments are attentive to *anti*-compliance constituencies: exporters or consumers. As long as those constituencies and their concerns dominate policymaking, governments will have little motivation to comply.

## Overcoming the Cooperation Problem

International regulation against illicit trade does not meet the Pareto principle. While benefiting victim governments, it makes perpetrator governments worse off. Two mechanisms can facilitate cooperation under these inauspicious conditions. I have hinted at one of them earlier: the transformation of preferences over time. When the underlying determinants of preferences change, noncooperative governments may moderate their aversion to regulation and turn more cooperative. For example, moral entrepreneurs may appear on the political stage and pressure a previously noncooperative government to suppress the trade; or primary externalities could emerge, turning what used to be other governments' problem into a government's own problem. In addition, preferences may shift as a new government comes to power and adopts a more favorable attitude toward regulation than its predecessor's. A temporal preference change, however, does not necessarily solve the cooperation problem altogether. Governments that previously resisted regulation will not immediately become staunch supporters. More typically, they will come to hold mixed motives and favor moderate international control, which somewhat diminishes illicit trade without imposing an onerous burden on exporters or consumers. Cross-pressured, these governments may thus be reluctant to entirely commit to international regulation or to fully comply with it. Nevertheless, a preference change may partly alleviate the cooperation problem and move governments from a state of irreconcilable preferences to one of partial preference convergence. Replacing "no shared interest" with "some shared interest" enhances the prospects of cooperation, as Chapter 4 will demonstrate.

Change in government preferences is domestically (or transnationally) induced. By contrast, the second mechanism for resolving the cooperation problem and bridging the divergent preferences is interstate coercion. Through the threat or infliction of sanctions, perpetrator governments may be compelled to commit to and comply with a stronger regulatory agreement than they would have preferred. The capacity to exercise coercion, however, is limited to *powerful* victim-governments—those whose resources allow them to impose costs on others for undesirable behavior.[62] Powerful victims can increase the costs of noncooperation and bring weaker perpetrators to suppress illicit trade that they previously tolerated. What coercive means can powerful governments employ?

Although military coercion is a possibility, its costs for the coercing government are so high as to be prohibitive in most cases. Only in extreme circumstances will governments seek to curb illicit trade through the coercive use of military force. A more viable tool for establishing cooperation is economic coercion: the imposition of punitive economic measures on governments that are reluctant to suppress illicit trade. Suspension of aid, trade sanctions, and other economic penalties may be painful to the target government; for the coercing government, however, such measures are relatively cheap.[63] Reputational coercion—the intentional tarnishing of a government's good name—is another form of pressure that entails minimal costs for coercing governments but can prove costly to target governments. Governments that are complicit in illicit trade—by action or omission—may be publicly censured and rebuked. They could be stigmatized as indifferent to the harmful effects of illicit trade and as tolerant or supportive of the unscrupulous actors involved in the trade. Governments that turn a blind eye to money laundering or sex trafficking, for instance, may be branded as abetting crime; the result would be a blow to these governments' international reputation. Like economic coercion, the tarnishing of reputation may influence governments through negative material consequences. For example, an internationally censured government could see incoming foreign investment shrink.[64] Reputational coercion, however, may also have an effect through mechanisms that do not involve a direct manipulation of cost/benefit calculations. Policymakers may indeed wish to avoid the opprobrium that accompanies the violation of widely accepted rules. If publicly chided for immoral conduct that breaks international norms and abets illicit trade, policymakers might suffer embarrassment and shame.[65]

Powerful governments may exercise coercion on an ad hoc basis, but continued, systematic pressure on target governments is more likely to induce cooperative behavior. This is what the United States has sought to achieve through several processes of monitoring and sanctioning, beginning with the 1986 introduction of the drug certification process. As Chapters 5 and 6 will describe, the United States annually reviews the efforts of governments worldwide against illegal drugs, human trafficking, money laundering, and counterfeiting. Governments deemed to have made insufficient efforts are designated as such in public reports. These blacklisted governments are threatened with economic penalties for their failure to suppress illicit trade; they also suffer embarrassing publicity and damage to their reputation. The regularized nature of the process enhances its coercive impact and magnifies the costs of noncooperative behavior. Continuous monitoring, constant risk of economic penalties, and periodic public shaming all raise the pressure on target governments. Domestic and international audiences are annually reminded about the failure of those governments to improve their conduct. On the other hand, meeting the American demands for action against illicit trade yields immediate rewards: lifting of the economic threat and removal from the blacklist of noncooperative governments.

## What Coercion May Achieve

By punishing noncooperation and rewarding cooperation, coercion can overcome the large preference variation and the absence of shared interest among governments. Absent coercion, perpetrator governments are content with a cost-free status quo. As they do not bear the negative externalities of illicit trade, they have no motivation to suppress it. Furthermore, they are protecting the interests of actors who benefit from the trade. The exercise of coercion disrupts the status quo by imposing costs on these governments and giving them a motive for curbing illicit trade: to relieve the coercive pressure. Since mutual benefits and a shared interest cannot induce cooperation, external pressure has to compensate and provide the missing incentives. Yet coercion is no panacea. First, it might be undersupplied due to conflicting foreign policy goals. Cooperation against illicit trade, after all, does not take place in a vacuum. Governments seek to reconcile the response to illicit trade with broader foreign-relations considerations.[66] They are less likely to threaten and punish allies, key trade partners, or other countries deemed important for strategic, political, or economic reasons.[67] Second, even when coercion is exercised, it might still fail to achieve its goal. To succeed, the sanction has to outweigh the influence of the domestic actors and law-enforcement costs that militate against cooperation. The more influential these domestic actors and the higher the law-enforcement costs, the less likely coercion is to be effective.

With these caveats in mind, what could a coercing government potentially gain from threatening or inflicting penalties on noncooperative governments? By increasing the benefits of cooperation and the costs of noncooperation, coercion may convince reluctant perpetrator-governments to commit to an agreement they had wished to avoid. Furthermore, those governments would be forced to join an agreement that is fairly robust— both in substance and in form. A robust agreement establishes comprehensive, far-reaching obligations and requires governments to take substantial measures against the trade. It also includes legally binding, precise rules and a compliance mechanism—that is, arrangements for monitoring and enforcement.

The compliance mechanism is the most important and distinguishing feature of a robust agreement. Monitoring and enforcement are necessary, since commitment to the agreement does not transform the preferences of noncooperative governments. They maintain their aversion to regulation and have strong incentives to renege on their promise. Given the persistence of incentives for defection that are not counterbalanced by expected gains from cooperation, an agreement lacking third-party monitoring and enforcement would suffer repeated violations. To lessen the temptation to engage in violation, powerful governments may incorporate a compliance mechanism in the agreement, delegating enforcement powers to an international organ. Yet within-agreement mechanisms are unlikely to suffice. Given the strength of noncooperative incentives, the remedy must involve intensive and continued pressure through close monitoring, publicizing of violations, and painful penalties. Such coercive pressure might be difficult to achieve through international organs. Powerful governments may therefore supplement the agreement's compliance mechanism with their own monitoring and sanctioning mechanism, outside the framework of the agreement.[68] "Unofficial," direct enforcement can employ a host of punitive measures which are not in the arsenal of international bodies. It is also free of the costs and constraints that come with action through multilateral institutions.[69] The big stick that powerful governments wield outside the agreement, combined with the mechanisms built into the agreement, could diminish the ongoing incentives to defect and encourage compliance. Governments that have little to gain from suppressing illicit trade may still choose to do so, if their conduct is subject to monitoring and potential punishment.

### Weaker Governments and the Use of Issue Linkage

What happens when it is weaker victim-governments that are pursuing international control, against the wishes of powerful perpetrators? Weaker governments do not have the coercive capacity that would allow them to compel cooperation. They also lack bargaining power due to the nonreciprocal nature of cooperation. It is the powerful perpetrator-governments that hold the bargaining leverage, as their participation in the regulatory agreement is necessary. The purpose of the cooperative endeavor is to induce *them* to curb the trade. Without coercive power or bargaining power, weaker governments may not be able to convince powerful noncooperative governments to join an agreement that is inconsistent with the latter's preferences. If the powerful governments do come on board, the likely price is a diluted agreement that establishes limited regulatory measures through imprecise rules with a qualified obligatory force. Most importantly, weaker governments cannot establish strong monitoring and enforcement mechanisms, either inside or outside the agreement. Since the perpetrators joining the agreement have little motivation to comply, the weakness of enforcement could mean significant noncompliance. Indeed, civil society may then step in and urge compliance. NGOs can perform monitoring, expose violations of the agreement, and embarrass violators. But this is only a partial remedy.

While some governments respond to NGO pressure, others ignore it. Even if their criticism is not entirely dismissed, NGOs might still fail to outweigh the influence of exporters or consumers who favor noncompliance. Governments may choose to be shamed rather than bear the costs of complying with international regulation.[70]

In principle, weaker governments could overcome their power limitations and establish cooperation through issue linkage. They may offer to cooperate on a matter of value to perpetrator governments in exchange for the latter's cooperation on illicit trade. In practice, such linkages are unlikely to be common. First, a linkage requires complementary issues that would reward perpetrators and offset their losses from the suppression of illicit trade.[71] Weaker governments are simply limited in the rewards they can offer. Second, powerful perpetrator-governments—influenced by domestic actors who oppose international control—might resist a proposed linkage. In these circumstances, there is little that weaker governments can do to induce acceptance of the linkage. Powerful governments will find it easier to forge an issue linkage than weaker governments, but they are more likely to establish cooperation through coercion for several reasons. First, economic or reputational sanctions are generally less costly and burdensome for the coercing government than offering a positive reward. Second, coercion does not require direct contact or negotiations between the coercing government and its targets; the latter only need to be informed of the threatened sanction. This advantage of coercion increases in importance with the number of targets. Third, coercion is likely to yield the desired effect sooner than an issue linkage. Forging a linkage and reaping its benefits may require an extended period of time. By contrast, imminent sanctions provide powerful immediate incentives for cooperative behavior. Fourth, identifying an appropriate reward can be challenging, especially when the perpetrators are not a homogenous group. For example, the 2001 State Department list of countries that failed to curb human trafficking included, among others, Israel, South Korea, Belarus, Indonesia, the Democratic Republic of Congo, and Turkey.[72] Such diversity significantly complicates the establishment of an issue linkage. It is difficult to identify an issue of interest to all these countries that would allow a joint linkage. Coercion, by contrast, can change the behavior of a variety of actors, given that they will all have an aversion to the threatened punishment.[73]

## The Role of Power: Two Cautionary Notes

As we have seen, the distribution of power plays a key role in shaping cooperation against illicit trade. In the absence of shared interest, the cooperative outcome likely reflects the preferences of the powerful actors. Weaker governments favoring cooperation cannot bring powerful governments to accept regulation inconsistent with those governments' preferences. The resulting international regulation is thus likely to be weak and, most significantly, not to include a strong compliance mechanism. By contrast, powerful governments favoring cooperation can establish more robust regulation that is accompanied by persistent pressure for compliance. External pressure can offset noncooperative incentives and motivate the cooperation of governments that are insensitive to the trade's negative effects.

Two additional points on the role of power deserve mention.

The first point is that a preponderance of power does not guarantee the ultimate effectiveness of cooperation against illicit trade. Powerful governments may indeed establish far-reaching regulatory measures supported by mechanisms of monitoring and enforcement. But robust international regulation by itself does not ensure the elimination or even substantial reduction of illicit trade. Such regulation might still fail to motivate compliance, and even governments willing to comply could face overwhelming practical difficulties. After a century of U.S.-backed international drug control, the illicit drug trade is far from terminated. But the reverse is also true. Regulatory campaigns led by weaker governments are not necessarily without consequence. In fact, they may have important salutary effects. By raising public awareness, for example, such campaigns can pressure governments and market actors to fight illicit trade, even in the absence of coercive threats. As Chapter 4 will demonstrate, a fairly weak agreement initiated by developing countries raised the standards of behavior in the antiquities market. It made it difficult to keep ignoring the fact that many antiquities on the market were, in fact, looted. The general point is that a power advantage is neither a necessary nor sufficient condition for effectiveness. Campaigns led by powerful governments are not bound to succeed in suppressing illicit trade; campaigns led by weaker governments are not doomed to fail.

The second point is that cooperation against illicit trade is not reducible to a simple realist story, despite the important role of the distribution of power. Indeed, it is the distribution of government preferences *combined* with the distribution of power that shapes cooperation. While power has an important causal effect on cooperative outcomes, it cannot account for them by itself. As the following chapters will describe, the United States has exercised its power to achieve different outcomes in different cases in accordance with its varying preferences. It has favored stringent international regulation of drugs, has opposed the international regulation of small arms, and has supported modest international control of antiquities. Furthermore, powerful governments have sometime been at odds with each other. Unlike the United States, the European Union has been a strong advocate of international small-arms regulation. Britain, Germany, and Japan opposed international antiquities regulation for decades, whereas the United States endorsed it early on. The preferences of powerful governments may also shift over time, changing their willingness to cooperate. Accounting for government preferences is therefore a necessary first step in explaining international cooperation. One must turn to the domestic political arena to understand the goals that governments pursue through their power—and why these goals vary across countries, across trades, and across time. Only with a prior account of preferences can one grasp the dynamic of the international political conflict and the role of power in shaping that conflict's outcome.

## Conclusions

This chapter has offered a two-stage theory of cooperation against illicit trade. In the first stage, governments define their preferences: what regulatory measures they would like to establish to curb illicit flows. In the second stage, governments argue, bargain, and clash over international agreements. I have posited that different constellations of exporter and consumer influence, primary externalities, and secondary externalities yield conflicting government preferences. In the absence of mutual gains, the cooperative outcome typically conforms to the preferences of the powerful governments. The lack of shared interest can be mitigated through the external, coercive manipulation of the incentives of noncooperative governments. A domestically induced change in preferences can also motivate governments to suppress illicit trade that they once tolerated. While criminal groups play a central role in illicit markets, the theory has focused on the legitimate actors that are targeted by international regulation and have a voice in shaping it.

Like any theory, the theoretical framework presented here reduces a complex reality to its fundamentals. Simplification allows theories to show how disparate phenomena are, in fact, similar. It enables them to identify and explain patterns and regularities in the seemingly disordered empirical experience.[74] Indeed, illicit trades—from drugs to arms to counterfeits—are diverse phenomena, each with its own specifics and nuances. But my goal is to cut through this diversity and to reveal the common political core that lies underneath. The theoretical framework thus focuses on the elements that are shared across illicit trades and across countries, while deemphasizing elements that are unique or uncommon. For example, the theory highlights negative externalities as the principal motivation for international regulation, although in some instances there may have been additional motivations. The theoretical focus is on the most recurring societal actors: civil society groups that favor regulation, exporters, and consumers; various actors that appear more rarely are excluded. Another simplification concerns exogenous influences from outside the realm of illicit trade. I have pointed out that a government's willingness to exercise coercion may depend on the nature of its relations with the target government; yet this is but one example. Many other processes and considerations may interfere with policy-making on illicit trade. After all, the international regulatory efforts against illicit trade are nested within a wide array of foreign policy concerns. Yet these broader concerns have been left outside the purview of the theory. In short, the theoretical framework is indeed a *framework* that captures the fundamentals of the political dynamic in order to identify broad, general patterns and to reveal similar causal mechanisms at work. This framework allows us to systematically explain observed variations in government preferences and cooperative outcomes. The chapters that follow supplement the framework with additional actors and influences to produce fuller empirical accounts.

The parsimony of the theoretical framework also means that the empirical chapters will somewhat depart from it. The theory attributes an important role to civil society groups—moral entrepreneurs—that advocate the suppression of illicit trade; yet the American campaign against human trafficking worldwide met with skepticism from civil society actors that considered prostitution a legitimate sex-work. A campaign for international regulation typically stems from the difficulties of national regulation; but it was the United States' push for international drug control that motivated the passage of federal narcotics legislation in 1914. The theoretical framework treats the government as a unitary actor with a single preference; but the antiquities regulation introduced in Britain in the early 2000s fell victim to conflicting preferences and priorities within the government. Such exceptions, however, only highlight the rule. At their core, the empirical cases are fundamentally consistent with the theoretical framework, which suggests that the principal obstacle to cooperation is absence of shared interest among governments. Some governments are strongly interested in international regulation to suppress illicit trade; others, however, are reluctant to join an endeavor that is aimed at helping foreign countries at the expense of domestic actors at home. This tension is at the heart of each of the trades examined in this book, from small arms to antiquities to human trafficking to drugs. In each case, certain governments have concluded that the costs of cooperation to exporters, consumers, or law-enforcement agencies outweigh the benefits of cooperation. Whether it was the commercial interests of arms exporters, the cultural and economic benefits of a thriving antiquities market, reluctance to "waste" law-enforcement resources on rescuing trafficked women, or the employment and revenue provided by the drug trade—governments have privileged their domestic concerns over those of the foreigners suffering the trade's negative effects. Across the sectors of illicit trade and across time, the cooperative efforts have unfolded along similar lines. Governments have varied in their cost-benefit calculations and hence in their preferences on international regulation. An international political conflict has ensued over the necessity, extent, and means of trade control.

The theoretical framework identifies the recurring patterns and dynamics underlying cooperation against illicit trade. The framework's explanatory power makes it possible to shed light on a host of empirical puzzles. Why is the international control of small arms much weaker than international drug control? Why did the U.S. government join the efforts against archaeological plunder in the early 1970s, imposing restrictions on the American art market to save foreign antiquities? What motivated Israel to suppress sex trafficking starting in 2001, after a decade of indifference to this problem? The following chapters solve these and other puzzles by examining how domestic actors and illicit trade's negative externalities shape governments' willingness to cooperate.

# 3

## GOVERNING GUNS

International Cooperation against the Illicit Trade in
Small Arms

The death toll from small arms dwarfs that of all other weapons
systems—and in most years greatly exceeds the toll of the atomic
bombs that devastated Hiroshima and Nagasaki. In terms of the
carnage they cause, small arms, indeed, could well be described as
"weapons of mass destruction."
—*Millennium Report of Kofi Annan, Secretary-General of
the United Nations*[1]

Chapter 2 has developed a theoretical framework for the analysis
of cooperation against illicit trade—a framework that emphasizes the variation in government preferences. The present chapter tests this
framework empirically through an analysis of the international regulatory
efforts against the illicit trade in small arms. I begin with a brief overview of
the failed attempts to control the arms trade during the interwar period,
followed by a discussion of the contemporary international efforts against
small-arms proliferation and misuse. The chapter next operationalizes the
theoretical framework with respect to small arms and derives a set of expectations of government preferences. The expectations are tested through an original survey, based on interviewing officials from 118 countries. Quantitatively
and qualitatively, the survey illuminates the variation in government preferences on international small-arms regulation. This is the first type of preference variation identified in Chapter 1: cross-country variation in preferences
on the regulation of a given trade. The chapter then employs this variation to

explain another variation: variation in the robustness of international regulation across trades. I account for the weakness of international small-arms regulation compared with international drug control and with the agreement against counterfeits (TRIPS). I also explain why small-arms control is weaker than other arms-control regimes, despite the fact that small arms are the deadliest weapons of all in terms of actual death toll.

## International Control of the Arms Trade in the Interwar Period

For centuries, free trade in arms had been a well-established international practice. Yet in the aftermath of World War I it became clear that the arms trade had to be subject to control. The rationale for regulation was articulated by the Convention for the Control of the Trade in Arms and Ammunition, signed in the Paris suburb of Saint-Germain-en-Laye in September 1919 (hereafter the Saint-Germain Convention). According to the preamble, the war "has led to the accumulation in various parts of the world of considerable quantities of arms and munitions of war, the dispersal of which would constitute a danger to peace and public order." Furthermore, "in certain parts of the world it is necessary to exercise special supervision over the trade in, and the possession of, arms and ammunition."[2] This was a veiled reference to the colonial possessions of the European powers that were in danger of instability. In light of these concerns, the convention laid out three key principles. First, the export of arms for military use was banned, unless accompanied by an export license. States "reserve[d] the right to grant . . . export licenses to meet the requirements of their Governments or those of the Government of any of the High Contracting Parties, but for no other purpose."[3] This principle essentially limited the arms trade to a circle of recognized governments that were parties to the convention. A second principle was transparency. States were required to publish an annual report of the export licenses they granted, including the quantities and destination of the arms. The third principle established strict regulation of arms shipments to prohibited areas in Africa and Asia in order to prevent insurgents from acquiring arms.[4] Indeed, "[t]he barely concealed purpose of the convention was to protect the great powers in the possession of their colonies, protectorates, and mandates."[5] The Saint-Germain Convention, however, quickly proved to be a failure, as it was not ratified by the arms-producing countries. Of particular importance was the reluctance of the United States, a major arms exporter, to ratify. The United States' concern was that the convention's ban on arms sales to nonsignatories would stifle American arms exports to Latin America, thereby undermining U.S. national security that relied on a strong private arms industry.[6] As the Saint-Germain Convention became a dead letter, the League of Nations decided to abandon it.[7] In June 1925 a new agreement was signed in Geneva under the auspices of the League: the Convention for the Supervision of the International Trade in Arms and Ammunition and in Implements of War (hereafter the Geneva Convention). This convention accommodated the American sensibilities by allowing arms exports to nonadhering countries. On other counts, it was consistent with the Saint-Germain Convention. In particular, it reinforced the strict regulation of arms shipments to territories in Asia and Africa, which were now labeled "special zones," rather than "prohibited areas."

Although the Geneva Convention raised some concerns among arms-producing countries, its chief opponents were small nonproducing countries anxious to guarantee their arms supply. By replacing the principle of free trade in arms with a general prohibition on arms exports subject to exceptions, the convention threatened to put nonproducing countries at the mercy of producing countries. During the negotiations, small countries therefore voiced concerns about the likely erosion of their security by constraining their ability to acquire arms. They strongly protested the right of producer-governments to decide—through licensing—to whom arms manufacturers could sell arms.[8] The Salvadoran delegate, for example, warned against "render[ing] countries which do not produce arms dependent in some sense on the exporting countries and [creating] . . . two groups, one of which would control the other." The Greek delegate expressed similar sentiments, arguing that under licensing "a kind of condominium of the great States will be set up over the small non-producing States, which will, in reality, come under the control of the great. They will be at their mercy; they will be subjected to such economic and political conditions as may be imposed on them." Turkey maintained that governments should have no discretionary power to limit arms exports and that the "freedom to export . . . should be complete and unrestricted."[9] The small countries also worried that transparency of the arms trade would compromise their national security. The convention, however, failed to allay their fears. It never gained the necessary number of ratifications to enter into force.[10]

International regulation of the arms trade reappeared on the international agenda in the mid-1990s in a more limited form. The 1925 Geneva Convention covered the entire trade in conventional arms.[11] By contrast, the UN efforts beginning in the 1990s have had a much narrower focus: small arms. Nevertheless, there are many parallels between the League of Nations' attempt at arms regulation in the interwar period and the contemporary UN efforts against the illicit trade in small arms. Most notably, both endeavors failed to establish strict international control of the arms trade. I now turn to examining why the UN-led process on small arms produced a weak international regulatory framework. The concluding section compares the contemporary efforts with those of the interwar period.

## International Efforts against the Illicit Trade in Small Arms: Background

A note on terminology: the term "small arms" as used here includes small arms (weapons for individual use, such as rifles and pistols) as well as light weapons (weapons for the use of a small crew, such as heavy machine guns and portable launchers of anti-tank and anti-aircraft missiles). The terms "small arms" and "guns" are used interchangeably.

According to estimates, there are at least 875 million small arms in circulation worldwide; a majority of those—roughly 75 percent—are in the hands of civilians.[12] More than 1,200 companies in over 90 countries are involved in some aspect of small-arms production.[13] In most countries, however, production is on a small scale, mainly for domestic consumption. Only 30–35 countries export small arms with annual sales of more than $10 million. In 2003 the leading exporters were Russia, the United States, Italy, Germany, Brazil, and China. Based on reports to UN Comtrade,[14] the documented value of all small-arms exports for that year was about $2 billion. According to estimates, the total annual value of the legal trade in small arms is at least $4 billion.[15] The *illicit* trade in small arms, however, is very difficult to assess, given the scarcity and poor quality of information.[16] Despite this uncertainty, it is fair to evaluate that the overall value of the illicit small-arms market is very modest compared with that of the illicit drug market.[17] Yet in terms of its negative externalities, the illicit trade in small arms matches if not exceeds the drug trade. Furthermore, the actual toll of small arms—in deaths and other adverse effects—far surpasses that of any other conventional or unconventional weapon.

Small arms are the primary tools of violence in the vast majority of recent and contemporary conflicts, being used extensively by both government forces and by actors outside the reach of the state. The majority of direct conflict deaths—between 60 and 90 percent—result from the use of small arms.[18] As conflict hinders access to adequate food and healthcare, the toll of small arms also includes indirect conflict deaths from malnutrition or disease. According to a conservative estimate, at least 52,000 direct conflict deaths and 200,000 indirect deaths occurred annually worldwide between 2004 and 2007; the real figures are likely much higher.[19] Furthermore, the accumulation and spread of small arms could intensify and prolong armed conflicts, hinder the provision of humanitarian assistance, and impede peace building and conflict prevention efforts. Even in a postconflict environment, gun violence might persist.[20]

The negative externalities of small arms are also manifested in nonconflict situations. Small arms are widely used for criminal violence and are a common tool for committing homicide. The number of annual deaths from gun homicides is approximately 200,000–250,000.[21] As the display of a weapon gives its holder the power to intimidate and coerce, small arms facilitate additional crimes, such as rape and robbery. They are also widely used in terrorism and gang warfare. Human rights violations—such as torture, arbitrary arrest, and abduction—often involve the use of small arms.[22]

Another dimension of the externalities of small arms is their economic and social costs. Rampant gun violence has various direct costs, such as medical treatment and rehabilitation, policing and incarceration, postconflict reconstruction, and care of displaced people. Other costs are indirect: losses in productivity and foreign investment, obstruction of trade and tax collection, and disruption of healthcare, education, and other social services.[23] The decline in social services and the collapse of economic activity that stem from rampant gun violence have a cumulative effect of hindering development. Small arms availability and misuse can also derail development by destroying physical infrastructure, such as roads and ports; undermining the personal security and social trust necessary for healthy economic life; and deterring aid agencies from funding and implementing development projects.[24]

## The UN Small-Arms Process

Gun violence is a global problem with many faces, from civil wars to organized crime to terrorism. Yet in no region has gun violence wreaked greater havoc than in sub-Saharan Africa. The proliferation, availability, and misuse of small arms destabilized the region and played a central role in the civil wars that engulfed it in the 1990s. Post conflict, small arms undermined efforts to rebuild communities and foster development.[25] This toll prompted African governments to pursue international efforts against the illicit trade in small arms. As the theoretical framework has suggested, the purpose of cooperation against illicit trade is to shift the burden of control from the externalities-bearing countries to the externalities-generating countries. This was indeed the goal of the African governments, who sought to make up for their own failure to control guns and suppress gun violence. The means: an international regulatory framework requiring arms-exporting countries to behave responsibly and carefully regulate exports.

This regulatory framework was the product of a political process led by the United Nations. It was Mali that placed small arms on the UN agenda after going through a civil war in the early 1990s. In October 1993, Malian President Alpha Oumar Konaré asked UN Secretary-General Boutros Boutros-Ghali for assistance in collecting the abundant small arms still circulating in the country after the achievement of a ceasefire. The UN responded by dispatching an advisory mission to Mali in August 1994; in early 1995 that mission visited six neighboring countries. In December 1994, a General Assembly resolution—introduced by Mali on behalf of several African countries—welcomed the Malian initiative and the UN response. The resolution invited the UN member states "to implement national control measures in order to check the illicit circulation of small arms, in particular by curbing the illegal export of such arms."[26] The Malian episode triggered a chain reaction, fueling interest in small arms and spurring action. In January 1995, Secretary-General Boutros-Ghali published his *Supplement to an Agenda for Peace* in which he sounded an alarm about a new threat: the illicit trade in and proliferation of small arms "which are probably responsible for most of the deaths in current conflicts."[27] Boutros-Ghali urged the international community to begin searching for solutions. His call found fertile ground in Japan.

Japan had been a leading advocate of arms control—especially nuclear disarmament—as a legacy of its past: the only country ever struck by nuclear weapons. Beyond this longstanding interest, action on small arms allowed Japan to play an international leadership role in the new, post-Cold War security environment. The issue may also have resonated with the Japanese in light of their domestic concerns over gun use by organized criminal groups. Japan's proposal was to establish a high-level group of experts under the UN secretary-general to study the question of small arms. In December 1995, in a resolution introduced by Japan, the General Assembly requested the UN secretary-general to prepare, with the assistance of a panel of governmental experts, a report on ways to tackle the excessive and destabilizing accumulation and transfer of small arms, especially as they cause or exacerbate conflict.[28] In its 1997 report, the panel of governmental experts concluded that the illicit trade in small arms "plays a major role in the violence currently affecting some countries and regions, by supplying the instruments used to destabilize societies and Governments, encourage crime, and foster terrorism, drug trafficking, mercenary activities and the violation of human rights." According to the panel, the illicit trade was facilitated by the absence of adequate national controls on arms production, export, and import; poor training or corruption of border and customs personnel; and lack of international cooperation.[29] The panel recommended a host of measures for the purpose of reducing small-arms proliferation and misuse, such as international cooperation among police, intelligence, customs and border officials and adequate national laws and procedures to control the possession and transfer of small arms. The panel further recommended the convening of an international conference on the illicit arms trade.[30] In December 1997, the General Assembly endorsed the panel's report in a resolution introduced by Japan. The resolution called on member states to implement the report's recommendations and asked the secretary-general for a follow-up report.[31] A group of governmental experts submitted that report in

1999, reviewing the implementation of the 1997 report and recommending further measures.[32]

The two reports and the General Assembly resolutions, including a 1998 resolution to convene an international conference on the illicit arms trade no later than 2001,[33] resonated well outside the UN. They spurred regional and subregional efforts to address the problem of small arms, resulting in a complex web of arrangements. Sub-Saharan Africa, the region most severely affected by gun violence, saw several initiatives: a declaration of a moratorium on the import, export, and manufacture of light weapons in West Africa (1998);[34] a declaration on illicit small-arms proliferation in the great lakes region and the Horn of Africa (2000);[35] a declaration and a protocol on small arms in the Southern African Development Community (both 2001);[36] and a declaration establishing a common African position on illicit small arms (the Bamako Declaration, 2000).[37] Seeking to curb gun violence in Latin America, the Organization of American States adopted a convention against the illicit trade in small arms (1997).[38] The response of the European Union (EU) to the problem of small arms included a tripartite framework: an EU program to enhance law-enforcement cooperation between member states and to assist other countries in combating the illicit arms trade (1997);[39] an EU Code of Conduct on Arms Exports (1998), setting common standards for the transfer of arms by member states so as to minimize arms misuse in countries of destination; and an EU Joint Action on small arms and light weapons (1998), committing to promote a series of principles and measures for reducing gun violence. In 2000, the Organization for Security and Cooperation in Europe (OSCE) established various measures against the illicit trade in small arms in the OSCE Document on Small Arms and Light Weapons. That same year, the Pacific nations established their own framework for controlling small arms.[40]

### The Program of Action on Small Arms

The regional and subregional initiatives facilitated and gave momentum to the global efforts. In 2001 two global agreements for suppressing the illicit trade in small arms were concluded: the Protocol against the Illicit Manufacturing of and Trafficking in Firearms, Their Parts and Components and Ammunition, supplementing the United Nations Convention against Transnational Organized Crime (hereafter the Firearms Protocol); and the Program of Action to Prevent, Combat and Eradicate the Illicit Trade in Small Arms and Light Weapons in All Its Aspects (hereafter the Program of Action, or PoA). The two agreements partly overlap, yet the Program of Action is broader in scope. Whereas the Firearms Protocol focuses on illicit arms used in crime and takes a law-enforcement approach, the PoA is more comprehensive, establishing a large array of measures to stem the illicit trade in small arms. Another key difference is that the legally binding Firearms Protocol has achieved a limited number of ratifications, as I discus later. By contrast, the non-legally binding PoA was adopted by consensus of all member states of the UN. The Program of Action is thus considered the primary global agreement on small arms.[41]

While global in scope and application, the Program of Action is a heavily African document. It grew from and responded to an African problem—large-scale proliferation and misuse of small arms in the context of armed conflict. Indeed, the main purpose of the PoA is to help countries affected by conflict to curb gun violence. African officials thus played a major role in the drafting of this document. The Program of Action was significantly influenced, in fact, by the Bamako Declaration that established an African position on the small-arms problem. Like that declaration, the PoA includes both national measures and regional measures, but focuses on the former: the principal responsibility for suppressing the illicit arms trade is at the national level. Among other national measures, the PoA asks governments to put in place laws and procedures to exercise effective control over the production, export, import, and transit of small arms within the national territory; to criminalize the illegal manufacture, trade, and possession of small arms; to ensure that arms manufacturers properly mark each small arm to allow identification and tracing; to establish an effective system of export and import licensing and to assess applications for export authorizations according to strict regulations consistent with international law; to ensure the security of police and military arms stocks; and to develop public-awareness programs on the illicit arms trade and its consequences. The regional measures that the Program of Action envisions are aimed at coordinating and supporting governments' national efforts. For example, the PoA calls on governments to establish subregional and regional mechanisms for transborder customs cooperation and for information-sharing among law-enforcement agencies. The PoA further establishes global-level commitments, such as cooperation with the UN system to ensure the effective implementation of arms embargoes imposed by the Security Council.

The PoA was adopted by consensus at a UN conference in July 2001.[42] It encompasses a wide range of issues and establishes a host of regulatory standards for controlling small arms and reducing the risk of their diversion to the illicit market. Yet overall, the PoA constitutes a relatively weak regulatory framework. First, it establishes only political commitments and lacks legally binding force. Similarly, an international instrument on the tracing of small arms—adopted in 2005 as an offshoot of the PoA—is not legally binding.[43] Second, the Program of Action uses broad, open-ended language that affords governments considerable discretion in the interpretation and implementation of their commitments. While such language offers flexibility and an ability to adapt the PoA to local realities, it complicates the challenge of ensuring compliance with the PoA, potentially providing a cover for governments wishing to shirk their commitments. Third, the compliance challenge is further exacerbated by the absence of a robust mechanism to encourage governments to comply. Indeed, the PoA does not delegate monitoring and verification authority to an international organ, nor does it establish a dispute-settlement body. It merely asks governments—on a voluntary basis—to provide information on compliance in the form of national reports.[44] In June–July of 2006, a UN Review Conference met to assess the progress made since the 2001 PoA and possibly to establish additional commitments. However, the negotiations failed, and the Review Conference ended with no outcome document.

As the PoA itself acknowledges, the illicit trade in small arms "sustains conflicts, exacerbates violence, contributes to the displacement of civilians, . . . and fuels crime and terrorism."[45] Why, then, did governments choose to address this problem through a non-legally binding regulatory framework that lacks an enforcement mechanism? Furthermore, why is the PoA weaker than other arms-control agreements, which are typically legally binding and include monitoring and verification arrangements? Answering these questions requires an in-depth analysis of the conflicting preferences of governments over international small-arms regulation.

## Government Preferences on International Regulation of Small Arms: Expectations

This section operationalizes the theoretical framework with respect to the illicit trade in small arms. I first consider how government preferences are shaped by the trade's primary and secondary negative externalities. I then examine the influence of small-arms exporters and consumers.

### Primary Negative Externalities

Government support for international regulation against illicit trade is generally expected to increase with the magnitude of the trade's primary externalities—that is, the negative effects of the trade within the national territory. The illicit trade in small arms has various externalities, the most significant of which are violent deaths in conflict and nonconflict situations. While violent deaths in conflict receive much international attention, the majority of violent deaths are, in fact, the result of nonconflict-related homicides.[46] Homicide is thus the indicator used in the following analysis. The expectation is that governments will prefer stronger international regulation of small arms when the homicide rate is higher.

Governments' support for international regulation is also shaped by their own capacity to curb the illicit trade's externalities, and the two should be negatively correlated: the weaker the capacity for national trade-regulation, the greater the government's need for international regulation. Control of gun import and possession requires trained personnel and technical equipment; it entails effective customs, border inspection, police, and licensing authorities. For poor countries with an underdeveloped bureaucratic infrastructure and weak law enforcement, national control of small arms presents an enormous challenge. Struggling to establish and enforce gun controls and suppress the illicit trade, governments of poor countries would much benefit from international regulation. By tackling the problem at the source and curbing small-arms exports, international regulation may relieve poor countries of the burden and allow them to reduce gun violence—a goal they cannot achieve on their own. Governments are therefore expected to prefer stronger international regulation when the gross domestic product (GDP) per capita is lower.

## Secondary Negative Externalities

Secondary externalities are those effects of illicit trade that foreign countries bear. The concern about the secondary externalities of illicit small arms stems from the negative humanitarian impact of gun proliferation and misuse, from killing and maiming of innocent victims to refugee flows to stifled development. For governments with humanitarian foreign-policy agendas—such as the British, Canadian, and Japanese governments—rampant gun violence abroad is a cause for concern and action. Some governments may believe that humanitarian action accords with the public's wishes; others pursue humanitarian action to bolster their international reputation and standing. In some cases, humanitarian action reflects policymakers' personal values and moral beliefs. There may thus be different causes for concern about the secondary externalities of small arms, all of them rooted in humanitarian sentiments. I expect humanitarian-motivated governments to prefer strong international regulation of small arms in order to curb gun violence abroad. The following analysis employs provision of humanitarian aid as an indicator of humanitarian motivation: governments are expected to prefer stronger international regulation when their provision of humanitarian aid is higher.

## Exporters

How might international regulation of small arms affect companies that export those weapons? The theoretical framework has suggested that exporters would typically resist international regulation: they prefer minimal constraints on trade. I expect this to be the case for small-arms exporters, as international control of small arms could adversely affect them. Of much concern for exporters is the possible establishment of transfer controls: common standards for governing the export, import, and transshipment of small arms. For example, the competent authorities would not approve an arms export if the arms might be used for human rights violations, negatively affect regional peace and security, or undermine development. For the exporter, such screening discontinues the practice of indiscriminate arms sales, reduces the likelihood of receiving export authorizations, and hurts business.

International regulation of small arms could also impose administrative requirements that would make the export process slower, more cumbersome, and less likely to result in a successful transaction. Effective regulation would require explicit authorization of the transaction by the exporting, importing, and transit countries; the circulation of information among these countries, such as a detailed description of the goods being shipped; export being allowed only upon receipt by the exporting authority of the necessary certification from the importing and transit countries; on-shipment through transit countries being allowed only upon receipt of official import and export authorizations; pre-export inquiry into the legitimacy and responsibility of end-users; and verification of shipment delivery by the exporting country.[47] Such tightening of export, import, and transit controls does not bode well for exporters. The greater the number of authorities involved and checks and licenses required to complete an arms sale, the more expensive and slower is the transaction, and the more likely it is to be blocked.

Transparency of small-arms transfers is another regulatory measure that could diminish arms sales: it would put pressure on exporters to avoid selling arms that bear a high risk of misuse. Transparency could also lead to a more careful scrutiny of requests for export licenses and a lower rate of approvals. Another possible consequence of regulation is higher production costs. For example, an obligation to mark small arms with laser, intended to facilitate gun identification and tracing, would be burdensome for exporters that use other marking methods.

For exporters, international regulation of small arms could be an undesirable constraint that impedes sales and lowers profits; they would prefer to maintain the trade free from control. To what extent can they influence the preferences of governments? In most countries, the arms industry includes a handful of exporters—often only one or two major firms. This reduces the costs of organizing politically and mitigates the collective action problem that exporters face. Furthermore, given the high certainty of significant harm to their commercial interests, arms exporters have strong incentives to lobby against regulation. Mindful of the economic and security importance of the arms industry, governments have good reasons to be attentive to the concerns of exporters. The arms industry may be seen as an essential part of a country's manufacturing capacity or industrial strategy, as well as an important source of employment and defense procurement. Constraints on arms exports, however, threaten to debilitate the arms industry and undermine its contribution to the national economy and security. Governments reluctant to sacrifice jobs at home, damage their balance of trade, or weaken national defense might be wary of such constraints.

And yet, the extent to which arms exporters elicit government support may vary by ownership structure—that is, whether the exporter is state-owned or in private hands. Indeed, state ownership of the arms industry is prevalent, and this may affect governments' calculations. Most obviously, when exporters are state-owned, the government has a direct stake in the arms trade as a source of revenue. This magnifies the government's incentives to guard exporters' interests and to resist international regulation that would harm them. Furthermore, state-owned enterprises are part of the state apparatus. As "Bureaucrats in Business,"[48] state-owned exporters may enjoy easy access to and close ties with policymakers, which facilitate lobbying. State-owned exporters may also be seen as more tightly linked with national power and sovereignty than are privately owned exporters. In addition, governments sometimes have less legitimate reasons to try to shield state-owned exporters from international regulation. Certain governments use their control of state firms for patronage—that is, the transfer of wealth to constituents in exchange for political support. State-owned enterprises may offer various benefits to the government's supporters, such as excess employment and wages or the location of production in politically desirable regions.[49] Beyond political gains, state ownership may yield personal gains in the form of bribes and channeling of revenues to politicians' pockets. The political and personal benefits generated by state-owned arms exporters could make governments more averse to international regulatory constraints. Governments would likely prefer minimally controlled trade when international regulation threatens state-owned exporters.

In addition to its adverse impact on the industry, international regulation could jeopardize governments' use of arms transfers as a foreign-policy tool. After all, arms sales are far more than ordinary commercial transactions: they are *"foreign policy writ large."*[50] Throughout the Cold War, both superpowers used arms transfers to exercise influence and to bolster friendly regimes or undermine hostile ones. Arms provided access to foreign political and military elites and a means of shaping their political orientation and strategic decisions.[51] Today, arms transfers are still a central tenet of U.S. foreign policy and a tool of statecraft in the hands of other arms-exporting countries, such as China and Israel.[52] International regulation of small arms threatens to curb this political use of arms. Transparency of small-arms transfers might discourage arms supply to repressive governments. A ban on arms supply to unauthorized nonstate actors—such as rebel groups—would also diminish the political utility of arms transfers. Governments of exporting countries that wish to maintain this foreign-policy instrument are unlikely to support international regulation of small arms.

In sum, the two considerations—the commercial interests of the arms industry, reinforced by the political use of arms transfers—should push governments of arms-exporting countries in a similar direction: preference for minimally regulated trade in small arms. Where the small-arms industry is state owned, we would expect governments to be particularly unsupportive of international regulation.


## Consumers

Consumers of small arms are numerous and diverse. Which consumers possess both the motive and the means to influence government policy? Armed groups—such as rebels, criminals, and terrorists—have motivation to resist international regulation that would deny them guns. Yet these are precisely the consumers that governments would like to prevent from obtaining guns. Given that their activity is illegal and is, in fact, the motivation for regulation, armed groups' preference for free trade in arms is unlikely to affect government preferences.

What about law-abiding civilian gun owners? The UN small-arms process targets armed groups, rather than civilians. Nevertheless, civilians may be affected as well if regulation raises prices. Moreover, some countries, such as Mexico, argue that civilians' easy access to guns makes those guns more likely to fall into the wrong hands and increases the risk of violence. These countries would therefore like to establish international standards restricting the possession and use of small arms by civilians (for example, a prohibition on civilian possession of automatic weapons, a limit on the number of weapons that civilians may possess, and background checks and safety trainings for gun owners). Civilian gun owners are therefore likely to oppose the international regulation of small arms as a threat to their use and possession of guns. For the most part, however, gun owners are not politically organized. In only a few countries, most notably the United States, do gun owners operate politically through lobbies that promote their interests. Such lobbies—the National Rifle Association (NRA) being the most prominent—may seek to thwart international regulation and keep the trade in small arms free. They would pressure governments to adopt a similar preference.

Governments themselves are major consumers of small arms for internal security and national defense. Nondemocratic governments are particularly less likely to favor international regulation of small arms for two reasons: their need to maintain the military's support and the centrality of domestic repression to their social control and political survival.

Nondemocratic governments often rely on the military to remain in power. To ensure the military's loyalty and support, these governments must maintain the flow of private goods—resources that the military or other security agencies value. This includes, first and foremost, arms. International regulation of small arms, however, could restrict the supply of guns and ammunition and jeopardize nondemocratic governments' ability to provide arms to the military. As an indirect consequence, international regulation could undermine the military's support for a nondemocratic government and threaten that government's hold on power. Democratic governments, on the other hand, are more reliant on public-policy efforts to maintain power than on the provision of private goods. Hence, they find restrictions on arms supply less threatening than do their nondemocratic counterparts.[53]

Nondemocratic governments are also apprehensive about small-arms regulation in light of the importance of repression to maintaining their rule. Many studies have shown that nondemocracies either engage in actual repression and abuse of personal integrity rights or establish a threat of repression through a state police machinery.[54] Both necessity and opportunity explain the repressive tendency of nondemocratic governments. Unable to rely on noncoercive means of social control, such as widespread legitimacy of the regime, nondemocratic governments must resort to the threat or use of violence to ensure the population's obedience and to stifle dissent. Free from constraints on the domestic use of force—such as free elections, judicial review, and critical media coverage—these governments can engage in repression with impunity.

Since forceful repression—actual or threatened—is vital to the functioning and survival of nondemocratic governments, their dependence on small arms is greater than that of democracies. Democratic governments obviously need small arms as well, but they do not directly link the supply of small arms with the regime's stability and viability; to remain in power, they seek popular support, rather than employ tools of repression. All else equal, the ramifications of international small-arms regulation are less threatening to democracies than they are to nondemocratic governments, whose ability to rule relies on their repressive capacity. It is this reliance that makes nondemocracies more sensitive than democracies to any possible interference with their arms supply.[55] If guns and ammunition become more expensive or less easily available because of international regulation, the survival of a nondemocratic regime may be at risk. Moreover, their dependence on arms leaves nondemocratic governments vulnerable to pressure. External actors may exploit international regulation as leverage and demand policy changes in exchange for arms. In particular, provision of arms could be conditioned on respect for human rights.

Indeed, nondemocratic governments may also have incentives to *support* international regulation. Since they do not enjoy popular legitimacy and rely on forceful repression, these governments may be particularly anxious to deny arms to their domestic opponents. International regulation can help them ensure that only government-authorized actors have access to guns. Nevertheless, I expect the anti-regulation incentives to prevail. The threat of arms in the hands of political opponents is one that nondemocratic governments face at home—within their own domestic arena. International regulation may indeed make it easier for them to tackle that threat, but denying arms to opponents is a task that nondemocratic governments may achieve on their own, often with considerable success. Many nondemocracies, in fact, have tight gun control that allows them to secure the government's monopoly on arms within the national territory; the benefits they may derive from international regulation are thus limited. By contrast, the costs of international regulation for nondemocracies are greater and more certain than the benefits. Nondemocratic governments that rely on arms imports are heavily dependent—for both internal and external security—on their continued access to foreign sources of arms. If international regulation diminishes this access, nondemocracies may not be able to recover, as they cannot make up for lost arms-imports through domestic means. Unlike the threat of arms in the hands of domestic opponents, the cutoff of arms supply is not a problem that nondemocracies can overcome on their own. On balance, we would therefore expect nondemocracies to prefer weak international regulation in order to guarantee their gun supply. Governments will prefer stronger international control of small arms when the level of democracy is higher.

To summarize the expectations: Governments will prefer stronger international regulation of small arms when the homicide rate, humanitarian-aid provision, or the level of democracy is higher. GDP per capita and state-owned arms exporters should be negatively associated with government support for international regulation. In addition, I control for the origin of the legal system. Some studies have shown that common-law countries are more cautious about making international legal commitments.[56] We would therefore expect these countries to prefer weaker international regulation of small arms.

## Empirical Testing

I test the expectations through an original survey of government views on the international efforts against the illicit trade in small arms. The survey included interviews with officials from 118 countries, conducted in June–July of 2006 in New York during and immediately following the UN Review Conference on Small Arms (with the exception of eight telephone interviews and one e-mail interview). Respondents came from ministries of foreign affairs, defense, justice, and interior as well as from police and military forces. In most cases one official was interviewed from each country; in 12 cases two or three officials from the same country were interviewed jointly. All respondents received the questionnaire in advance to allow preparation for the interview. The questionnaire asked respondents to convey their countries' views on the UN small-arms process. The questions addressed the 2001 Program of Action as well as proposed regulatory measures not included in the PoA. See Appendix A at the end of the chapter for the survey questionnaire, the distribution of responses, and the views of key countries. Appendix B lists the countries included in the survey.

Based on the survey data, the following analysis examines government preferences as of 2006. I first paint the overall picture through statistical and geographic methods. I then discuss the survey responses to qualitatively illustrate the variation in government preferences. Respondents were promised anonymity; the text below identifies them only by country.

## Statistical Analysis

As Chapter 2 has explained, government preferences range from weak to strong international regulation. To construct this continuum with respect to small arms, I combine three survey questions that focused on the general characteristics of the UN small-arms process. The first question (Q3 in the questionnaire) addressed the scope of the process, asking respondents whether their countries believed that the UN process should only cover the *illicit* trade in small arms or both the *legal* and the *illicit* trade. A preference for limiting the process to the illicit trade and excluding the legal trade indicated weak support for international regulation; a preference for a comprehensive process, which would include the legal trade as well, indicated strong support for international regulation. The second question (Q4) addressed the PoA's level of obligation. Respondents were asked whether their countries were content with the existing politically binding Program of Action, or whether their countries would have preferred the PoA to be legally binding. The third question (Q6) concerned the PoA's compliance mechanism: governments' voluntary self-reporting. Respondents were asked whether their countries were satisfied with the existing mechanism or whether stronger or weaker mechanisms would have been preferable.

The three questions in combination created a 0 to 5 scale of government preferences on international regulation of small arms (REGULATION). A score of 0 indicates a government preference for weak regulation: a limited scope that covers only the illicit—but not the legal—trade in small arms, political rather than legal commitments, and the existing compliance mechanism. A score of 5 indicates a preference for strong regulation: a comprehensive scope that includes both the legal and the illicit trade, legally binding commitments, and a stronger compliance mechanism.

In addition to the composite variable REGULATION, two individual questions are used as dependent variables. The question on the scope of the UN process (Q3) is the most important question in the survey, since it asked directly whether the small-arms trade should be internationally regulated. SCOPE ranges from 0 to 2: 0 means a preference for limiting the UN process to the illicit trade; 2 means a preference for addressing both the legal and the illicit trade. The question about transparency (Q8) represents the survey questions concerned with specific regulatory measures. Respondents were asked whether their countries would support the establishment of an international transparency mechanism for small-arms transfers. TRANSPARENCY ranges from 0 to 2: 0 = no support for transparency; 2 = full support for transparency.

Measures for the explanatory variables are as follows.

HOMICIDE RATE/GUN HOMICIDE RATE. Gun homicide rates come closest to capturing the primary externalities of small arms, yet they raise two concerns. First, gun homicide data reported by governments are highly inaccurate for various reasons, from difficulties in identifying the cause of death to incentives to misrepresent gun violence statistics. Second, many countries do not report gun homicide data. The use of gun homicide rates therefore reduces the number of observations. Importantly, gun homicide figures are unavailable for most countries in sub-Saharan Africa—a region severely affected by gun violence. Given these concerns, I use total homicide rates to capture the negative externalities of small arms. Roughly 42 to 60 percent of all homicides are carried out with guns.[57] Total homicides are thus an imperfect yet reasonable proxy for the negative effects of small arms. The data are rates of intentional homicide per 100,000 inhabitants in 2004.[58] As a check, I present models that use gun homicide rates: intentional gun homicides per 100,000 inhabitants in 2005 or the most recent year available.[59]

LN GDP PER CAPITA. Log of a country's GDP per capita in 2005.[60]

HUMANITARIAN-AID PROVISION. The share of humanitarian aid in overall bilateral Official Development Assistance that a country provided in 2006.[61]

ARMS EXPORTER. Since the influence of state-owned arms exporters is expected to differ from that of privately owned exporters, I use two dummy variables. The first indicates whether (1) or not (0) a country has state-owned arms exporters; the second indicates whether (1) or not (0) a country has privately owned arms exporters.[62]

DEMOCRACY. The variable ranges from –10 (autocracy) to 10 (democracy).[63]

COMMON LAW. The variable indicates whether (1) or not (0) a country's legal system is based on the common law.[64]

Table 3.1 presents the results of an ordered logit analysis. Models 1–3 use HOMICIDE RATE as a measure of the negative externalities of small arms; Models 4–6 use GUN HOMICIDE RATE. The results are consistent with the expectations. Governments prefer stronger international regulation when HOMICIDE RATE/GUN HOMICIDE RATE, HUMANITARIAN-AID PROVISION, or DEMOCRACY is higher. STATE-OWNED

**Table 3.1** Determinants of Government Preferences on International Regulation of Small Arms

|  | Model 1 | Model 2 | Model 3 |
| --- | --- | --- | --- |
| Variables | REGULATION | SCOPE | TRANSPARENCY |
| HOMICIDE RATE | 0.095*** | 0.082*** | 0.034 |
|  | (0.03) | (0.031) | (0.031) |
| GUN HOMICIDE RATE | — | — | — |
| LN GDP PER CAPITA | −0.319* | −0.323 | −0.482** |
|  | (0.172) | (0.204) | (0.243) |
| HUMANITARIAN-AID PROVISION | 17.518*** | 24.12*** | 31.103* |
|  | (6.395) | (9.282) | (16.777) |
| STATE-OWNED ARMS EXPORTER | −1.052** | −1.185* | −2.78*** |
|  | (0.516) | (0.67) | (0.743) |
| PRIVATE ARMS-EXPORTER | 0.389 | 0.619 | −0.712 |
|  | (0.677) | (0.823) | (1.339) |
| DEMOCRACY | 0.121*** | 0.133*** | 0.191*** |
|  | (0.032) | (0.041) | (0.048) |
| COMMON LAW | −1.269*** | −1.021** | −1.182* |
|  | (0.454) | (0.511) | (0.687) |
| Cut 1 | −4.418 | −2.283 | −6.716 |
| Cut 2 | −3.457 | −1.71 | −5.009 |
| Cut 3 | −2.647 |  |  |
| Cut 4 | −1.796 |  |  |
| Cut 5 | −1.085 |  |  |
| Observations | 118 | 118 | 114 |
| Prob>$\chi 2$ | 0.00 | 0.00 | 0.00 |
| Log likelihood | −156.697 | −85.082 | −50.302 |

|  | Model 4 | Model 5 | Model 6 |
| --- | --- | --- | --- |
| Variables | REGULATION | SCOPE | TRANSPARENCY |
| HOMICIDE RATE | — | — | — |
| GUN HOMICIDE RATE | 0.063 | 0.051 | 0.02 |
|  | (0.04) | (0.043) | (0.052) |
| LN GDP PER CAPITA | −0.132 | −0.112 | −0.508* |
|  | (0.218) | (0.271) | (0.311) |
| HUMANITARIAN-AID PROVISION | 12.599* | 17.461* | 95.483 |
|  | (6.649) | (9.137) | (85.269) |
| STATE-OWNED ARMS EXPORTER | −0.654 | −0.932 | −1.185 |
|  | (0.598) | (0.742) | (0.892) |

**Table 3.1** (*continued*)

| Variables | Model 4<br>REGULATION | Model 5<br>SCOPE | Model 6<br>TRANSPARENCY |
|---|---|---|---|
| PRIVATE ARMS-EXPORTER | 0.28 | 0.43 | −1.529 |
| | (0.689) | (0.837) | (1.55) |
| DEMOCRACY | 0.12*** | 0.118** | 0.168*** |
| | (0.043) | (0.052) | (0.057) |
| COMMON LAW | −1.49** | −1.251* | −1.821** |
| | (0.613) | (0.663) | (0.856) |
| Cut 1 | −3.47 | −1.015 | −6.778 |
| Cut 2 | −2.449 | −0.415 | −5.241 |
| Cut 3 | −1.451 | | |
| Cut 4 | −0.713 | | |
| Cut 5 | 0.211 | | |
| Observations | 77 | 77 | 75 |
| Prob>χ2 | 0.00 | 0.00 | 0.00 |
| Log likelihood | −109.203 | −58.741 | −33.314 |

*Notes:* Ordered logit regressions. Standard errors in parentheses. *significant at 10%; **significant at 5%; ***significant at 1%.

ARMS EXPORTER brings governments to prefer weaker international regulation. LN GDP PER CAPITA is negatively associated with support for regulation, indicating poor countries' need for international cooperation to make up for their low gun-control capacity. As expected, COMMON LAW countries prefer weaker international regulation of small arms.

Table 3.2 shows large substantive effects of the different variables on government preferences. When HOMICIDE RATE increases from China's relatively low rate to Brazil's much higher rate, the expected probability of a preference for strong international regulation (REGULATION = 5) rises by 0.52. For example, when HOMICIDE RATE is at China's level and all other variables are at their mean, Pr(REGULATION = 5) is 0.29; when HOMICIDE RATE is at Brazil's level, Pr(REGULATION = 5) is 0.81. This is a considerable substantive effect. Lowering LN GDP PER CAPITA from that of Switzerland to that of Mozambique leads to an increase of 0.36 in the probability of preferring strong regulation. Raising HUMANITARIAN-AID PROVISION from 0 to Norway's level increases the probability that a government would favor strong regulation by 0.46. STATE-OWNED ARMS EXPORTER reduces the probability of a preference for strong regulation by 0.23. When the DEMOCRACY score changes from fully autocratic to fully democratic, the probability of a preference for strong regulation increases by 0.48. COMMON LAW is associated with a decrease of 0.29 in the probability of a preference for strong regulation.

**Table 3.2** Substantive Effects on Government Support for International Regulation of Small Arms

| | ΔPr (REG.=0) | ΔPr (REG.=1) | ΔPr (REG.=2) | ΔPr (REG.=3) | ΔPr (REG.=4) | ΔPr (REG.=5) |
|---|---|---|---|---|---|---|
| HOMICIDE RATE: | | | | | | |
| China → Brazil | −0.08 | −0.09 | −0.13 | −0.15 | −0.08 | 0.52 |
| | (−0.15, −0.03) | (−0.17, −0.03) | (−0.22, −0.05) | (−0.23, −0.05) | (−0.15, −0.01) | (0.25, 0.72) |
| LN GDP PER CAPITA: | −0.08 | −0.09 | −0.1 | −0.08 | −0.01 | 0.36 |
| Switzerland → Mozambique | (−0.24, 0.01) | (−0.21, 0.01) | (−0.21, 0.01) | (−0.17, 0.01) | (−0.05, 0.03) | (−0.04, 0.66) |
| HUMANITARIAN–AID PROVISION: | −0.05 | −0.06 | −0.1 | −0.14 | −0.11 | 0.46 |
| 0 → Norway | (−0.09, −0.02) | (−0.12, −0.02) | (−0.18, −0.04) | (−0.24, −0.05) | (−0.19, −0.02) | (0.19, 0.64) |
| STATE-OWNED ARMS EXPORTER: | 0.07 | 0.07 | 0.07 | 0.04 | −0.02 | −0.23 |
| No → Yes | (0, 0.19) | (0, 0.17) | (0, 0.15) | (0, 0.1) | (−0.08, 0.02) | (−0.41, −0.01) |
| DEMOCRACY: | −0.18 | −0.15 | −0.13 | −0.06 | 0.04 | 0.48 |
| −10 → 10 | (−0.37, −0.05) | (−0.27, −0.05) | (−0.23, −0.05) | (−0.13, 0.01) | (−0.02, 0.11) | (0.26, 0.65) |
| COMMON LAW: | 0.07 | 0.08 | 0.09 | 0.06 | −0.01 | −0.29 |
| No → Yes | (0.02, 0.17) | (0.02, 0.16) | (0.02, 0.17) | (0.02, 0.12) | (−0.05, 0.03) | (−0.46, −0.1) |

*Notes:* The table reports the change in the expected probability of each value of REGULATION resulting from changes in the explanatory variables. Calculations were conducted using *Clarify* (Tomz, Wittenberg, and King 2003) based on Model 1 in Table 3.1. 95% confidence intervals in parentheses.

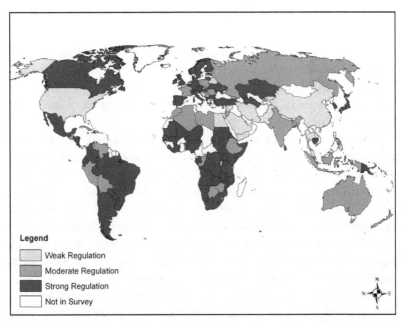

**Figure 3.1** Government Preferences on International Regulation of Small Arms

Robustness Checks

As an alternative measure of small-arms exporters, I used the logged ratio of small-arms exports to total exports.[65] Consistent with the expectation, the higher the ratio of small-arms exports to total exports, the lower the support for international regulation ($p = 0.209$).

Effective gun control requires a significant bureaucratic infrastructure for licensing, registration, and so forth. In lieu of GDP per capita, national capacity for controlling guns was measured through the Bureaucratic Quality indicator from *International Country Risk Guide*. Like GDP per capita, bureaucratic quality is negatively correlated with support for international regulation ($p = 0.116$).

To examine whether a country's general tendency to cooperate affects its preference on regulation, a variable indicating membership in international organizations was included.[66] The variable was not statistically significant and did not affect the results.

Do preferences on international regulation of small arms simply reflect domestic approaches to gun control? Data on civilian gun ownership show this not to be the case. For example, Finland and Switzerland have relatively liberal gun laws domestically and high levels of civilian gun possession,[67] yet they prefer strong international regulation of small arms (REGULATION = 5 for both countries). By contrast, gun control in China and Egypt is very tight, yet both countries prefer weak international regulation of small arms (REGULATION = 0 and 1, respectively).

## Geographic Analysis

To examine cross-regional and intra-regional variation in preferences, REGU-LATION was recoded into a three-level measure: preference for weak, moderate, or strong international regulation of small arms (corresponding to the values 0–1, 2–3, and 4–5 of REGULATION). Figure 3.1 shows government preferences on the world map.

In sub-Saharan Africa and Latin America the illicit trade in small arms creates the largest negative externalities: these are the regions that suffer the most severe problems of gun violence. For example, the gun homicide rate in South Africa in 2002 was 26.1 per 100,000 inhabitants, and the equivalent rate in Colombia was 51.8 (compared to 0.35 in Norway). Heavily affected by gun proliferation and misuse, sub-Saharan Africa and Latin America strongly support the international regulation of small arms. Europe, mainly motivated by humanitarian concerns about gun violence worldwide, is also largely supportive of strong international regulation.

The Middle East, by contrast, prefers weak international regulation. This preference reflects the nondemocratic nature of most Middle Eastern governments, combined with the limited negative externalities of small arms on their territories. For example, the gun homicide rate in Egypt in 2005 was merely 0.14. Furthermore, three countries in the region—Egypt, Iran, and Israel—are major exporters of small arms with state-owned arms industries.

The magnitude of gun violence in East and South Asia is modest compared with sub-Saharan Africa. For example, the gun homicide rate in Thailand in 2002 was 3.22. Moreover, governments in East and South Asia have, on average, greater capacity to curb gun violence than African governments. They therefore take a cautious approach to international regulation. Export interests are another cause for caution: China, India, and Pakistan are major exporting countries with state-owned arms industries.

The Pacific holds an intermediate position. Several countries in the region—especially Papua New Guinea—have suffered gun violence and the resulting social and economic disruptions. Yet overall, the scale of the illicit arms trade and the levels of gun violence and armed conflict in the region are comparatively low. Moreover, stringent regulation might overburden the tiny bureaucracies of the small island states. The common law tradition also weakens the region's support for international regulation.

In addition to cross-regional variation, there is some variation *within* regions as well. Japan and South Korea, both aid donors with humanitarian foreign-policy concerns, are more supportive of regulation than most countries in their region. So are Cambodia and Sri Lanka, two countries that have experienced gun violence and its enormous costs in the form of civil wars. Algeria, Libya, and Morocco are indirectly affected by the gun problems of their African neighbors; hence, they prefer stronger regulation than other Arab countries.

Influence of Primary/Secondary
Negative Externalities

|  | | Low | High |
|---|---|---|---|
| **Exporter/Consumer Influence** | **Low** | **I.**<br>**Bystanders**<br>*Indonesia (3), Peru (3),*<br>*Botswana (3)* | **II.**<br>**Pro-regulation**<br>*Somalia (5), Colombia (5),*<br>*Japan (5), Sweden (4)* |
| | **High** | **III.**<br>**Anti-regulation**<br>*China (0), Egypt (1),*<br>*Syria (1), Belarus (0)* | **IV.**<br>**Cross-pressured**<br>*Austria (5), India (2),*<br>*Cuba (2), United States (1)* |

**Figure 3.2** Variation in Government Preferences on International Regulation of Small Arms

Note: The country's REGULATION score is in parentheses.

France, with a large state-owned arms industry, takes a more cautious approach to international regulation than other Western European countries.

## Qualitative Analysis

The survey reveals a large variation in government preferences on the international regulation of small arms—variation that conforms to the theoretical expectations expressed in Chapter 2's Figure 2.1. Figure 3.2 illustrates this variation. Countries are placed in the matrix according to the corresponding influences on their preferences. Each country's survey-based REGULATION score is in parentheses.

### Pro-regulation Governments

*Primary Negative Externalities*

Governments facing large-scale gun violence, the primary externality of the illicit trade in small arms, are expected to prefer strong international regulation. This is indeed the case with Somalia (REGULATION = 5), Colombia (REGULATION = 5), other countries in sub-Saharan Africa and Latin America that are heavily affected by gun violence, and several affected countries outside these two regions. Respondents from affected countries emphasized the enormous costs of gun violence: loss of human life, crime, political and social instability, and stifled development, among others. According to the Kenyan respondent, the weapon of mass destruction in his country is not a nuclear bomb; rather, it is the Kalashnikov. Additional respondents echoed this sentiment, suggesting that small arms are the "real weapons of mass destruction" that kill and maim on a daily basis. In their view, the solution is stringent international control of small arms. The Liberian respondent, for instance, explained that "by controlling arms, by reducing arms, by ensuring that arms are not in the hands of nonstate actors but in the hands of responsible people . . . Liberia will enhance, protect, and consolidate its peace." Affected countries are especially in favor of regulating the *legal* small-arms trade as a means of curbing the illicit trade. They believe that the legal and the illicit trade are closely interlinked—two sides of the same coin—as most illicit weapons begin their lives as legal weapons. They therefore reject attempts to distinguish between the legal and the illicit trade, arguing that a focus on the illicit trade alone is nonsensical and would serve to undermine the UN process. In the view of affected countries, regulation of the legal trade is imperative in order to hold arms suppliers accountable and prevent the provision of guns to actors who would misuse them.

Respondents from affected countries also expressed disappointment with the political nature of the Program of Action; they argued that a legally binding instrument would have been more effective and less dependent on governments' goodwill. The Brazilian respondent, for example, claimed that an issue as important, complex, and sensitive as small arms should have been addressed through legally binding commitments. Respondents also identified the compliance mechanism—voluntary national reports—as a fundamental weakness of the PoA and one of the main reasons for its limited impact. They pointed out that the voluntary nature of the reports allowed governments to avoid reporting. Moreover, the absence of a standard, mandatory format made it difficult to compare national reports and evaluate overall progress. Respondents further lamented the fact that the UN does not have a formal authority to monitor compliance with the Program of Action. The respondents from Mexico and Tanzania, among others, expressed their governments' interest in a stronger enforcement mechanism that would pressure governments to comply.

Respondents from affected countries expressed strong support for a transparency mechanism for small-arms transfers. They suggested that clear, available information on arms exports and imports would make it easier to control the trade and prevent diversion of arms to illicit channels. The Kenyan respondent expressed his belief that transparency may deter arms sales to "bad guys" and increase the responsibility and accountability of arms manufacturers. A ban on arms transfers to unauthorized nonstate actors is another regulatory measure that enjoys broad support. If arms were sold only to actors duly authorized by governments, it would be difficult for rebels, criminals, terrorists, and gangs to acquire arms. The establishment of such a ban is thus a high priority for affected countries: they consider it essential for suppressing the illicit trade in small arms.

African respondents in particular emphasized their governments' inability to tackle gun violence, making it imperative to restrain arms suppliers through international regulation. The Somali respondent explained that the poor resources of his government and Somalia's large territory hindered the disarming of militias, and therefore international control was necessary. The respondent from Benin argued that exporting countries should assume responsibility for the arms they sell: since those arms are a source of hazard and threat, exporting countries must accept controls. The respondent from Tanzania emphasized that while African countries had made efforts to curb gun violence, the problem could not be solved without controlling the flow of arms from exporting countries. African respondents maintained, however, that the PoA fell short of effectively restraining exporters, especially as it failed to ban arms transfers to unauthorized nonstate actors.

### Secondary Negative Externalities

Governments concerned about secondary negative externalities—gun violence abroad—are expected to support strong international regulation. This is indeed the case with Japan (REGULATION = 5), Sweden (REGULATION = 4), and other countries that provide humanitarian aid. Respondents from these countries explained their governments' motivation in humanitarian and moral terms or as part of their concern for global security or human security. The Norwegian respondent, for example, explained that the UN small-arms process would help her government achieve an important foreign policy goal: improving the humanitarian situation worldwide. Like countries that bear primary externalities, humanitarian-motivated countries tend to prefer comprehensive regulation that would address the legal as well as the illicit trade in small arms. They support legally binding commitments, a stronger compliance mechanism than the existing one, and various regulatory measures, including transparency and international transfer controls.

As the theoretical framework has indicated, governments may be concerned about the trade's impact abroad—secondary externalities—as well as the primary externalities that their own countries bear. Several European respondents indeed indicated such a dual motivation involving both primary and secondary externalities. The Spanish respondent, for example, explained that for his country the efforts to control small arms have two dimensions. First, Spain is "completely committed . . . to combating the humanitarian problems of other countries that are affected by this scourge." As an aid donor, Spain is concerned about the heavy price of small arms in terms of conflict and obstructed development. Second, Spain itself feels the negative effects of small arms in the form of terrorist threats from both Basque separatists and Islamic terrorists. The French respondent similarly indicated that his government is concerned about illegal arms circulation within France that gives gangs access to guns. France is also concerned about the guns that target French troops in peacekeeping missions and hinder the successful conclusion of these missions. At the same time, France harbors broader concerns about global security.

Several respondents, in fact, offered a self-interested rationale for concern about the externalities of small arms abroad. The respondent from New Zealand suggested that gun availability in the Pacific has direct implications for the stability in New Zealand's neighborhood. Furthermore, New Zealand often has to assist its neighbors in restoring law and order and rebuilding economies shattered by armed violence. Similarly, European respondents argued that in a globalized world, instability and insecurity in Africa and the Caucasus threaten the stability and security of Europe. The European respondents emphasized, however, that their principal motivation is moral and humanitarian, rather than self-interested. As the British respondent explained, "the major motivator is a moral motivator . . . proliferation of small arms is causing major havoc in the developing world . . . from a moral position, we want that stopped . . . [we feel that] the world community has to deal with this issue."

The theoretical framework has suggested that while exporters are generally likely to oppose international regulation, they may also derive some benefits from it. Are the humanitarian concerns expressed by European governments merely a cover for commercial motivations? The Syrian respondent indeed offered a conspiracy theory along these lines, maintaining that the real driver of the small-arms process was Europe's pursuit of markets for its arms industry. According to his logic, the global market for European arms has diminished in recent years; international regulation of small arms is a means for Europe to regain its lost market share. By introducing a host of international regulatory measures and insisting on regulation of the *legal* trade, European governments have sought to make their arms industries more competitive. The noble humanitarian concerns were thus only a pretense and a pretext; the real story was about profit and market competition. Consistent with this conjecture, several European respondents identified benefits that the arms industry may reap from international regulation. The German respondent indicated that Germany's arms industry is subject to strict national regulation; it would be to its advantage if arms industries elsewhere were required to comply with similar regulation. The Italian respondent echoed this level-playing-field motivation: "[The view of Italian arms manufacturers] is that we already have high standards [of arms production and export]. So let's try to bring others close to our standards." The Swiss respondent expressed a reputational motivation: arms producers have no desire "to be blamed for doing anything illegal. . . . They have an interest in an environment where they can go along their business, and we [the government] have that [interest] too"; "If there are clear standards, clear guidelines, clear regulations for trade, then it helps us to show that our trade is legal and not illegal." Similarly, the British respondent explained that "many members of the public are slightly distrustful of the arms industry. Unless the arms industry projects a positive and responsible image, they will find it difficult to raise finance." The respondents emphasized, however, that commercial benefits were *not* a significant motivation for their governments' pursuit of international regulation. They vehemently repudiated the argument made by the Syrian respondent.

Commercial interests may indeed have figured into the calculation of European governments. It is unlikely, however, that they were the principal motivation underlying Europe's support for the efforts against the illicit trade in small arms. This conclusion rests on several pieces of evidence. First, European arms manufacturers were not unanimous in their support for the UN small-arms process. Several European respondents indicated that their governments favored international regulation despite concerns voiced by the arms industry. Second, while small arms are the deadliest weapons of all in terms of actual death toll, they are relatively low-tech and cheap and are far less profitable than major weapon systems. Market expansion for an export of declining importance is unlikely to have served as an important European motivation. Third, Europe was not an enthusiastic supporter of the UN small-arms process at its inception. As described earlier, the process began as an African initiative, supported by Japan. Only later did European governments come to embrace international small-arms regulation.

The shift in the British preference is particularly instructive. When small arms first appeared on the UN agenda, Britain was ruled by a Conservative government that considered the arms trade essential to the British economy and security. That government sought to maintain the trade in arms free, and eyed restrictions on arms exports with suspicion. But several arms-scandals—most notably, over arms sales to Saddam Hussein's Iraq—contributed to the Conservative defeat at the polls in 1997. Before the election, Labor exploited the scandals to criticize the Conservative approach to arms sales as ethically deficient. Upon assuming office, the Labor government committed to introducing an ethical foreign policy that would include responsible, strictly regulated arms exports.[68] The government carried out this commitment by issuing new national guidelines for arms sales in July 1997, spearheading the initiative for an EU Code of Conduct on Arms Exports, and playing a leading role in the global efforts to control small arms and to establish an Arms Trade Treaty (discussed later). Critics charge that Britain merely changed its rhetoric, while in practice maintaining a permissive arms-sales policy;[69] yet the leadership position that Britain assumed in international arms-regulation initiatives constituted a major shift. This policy change in favor of regulation was not commercially motivated. Until 1997 Britain judged restrictions on arms sales as antithetical to its economic and security interests. In support of the arms industry, Britain sought to promote and facilitate arms exports, rather than regulate and restrain them. British interest in regulation of arms sales arose only when a new government brought into account human rights and humanitarianism. As will be described in the following chapter, the Labor government also reversed the longstanding British resistance to international control of antiquities. The policy shift on antiquities, as in the case of arms exports, followed embarrassing scandals. More broadly, it stemmed from an ethically minded foreign policy and from concern for Britain's international reputation, which prevailed over commercial interests.

## Anti-regulation Governments

### Exporters

I expected that governments guarding the commercial interests of state-owned arms exporters would oppose international regulation. This expectation finds support in the preferences expressed by China (REGULATION = 0), Egypt (REGULATION = 1), and other non-European countries with state-owned arms exporters. Arms exporters in these countries—unlike some of the European exporters—have little to gain from international regulation. International regulation creating a level playing field would be to these exporters' detriment, subjecting them to stricter control than before. They also do not particularly value the reputational benefits of regulation. Since they are state-owned, these exporters' anti-regulation preference enjoys the support of their governments. As the commercial interest is not counterbalanced by significant concerns about primary or secondary externalities, these governments oppose international regulation as an undesirable shifting of the burden. In their view, international regulation is asking them to compromise strategic and commercial interests for the sake of alleviating other countries' gun problems.

Indeed, respondents representing these governments expressed interest in maintaining freedom of trade and exhibited concern about the implications of international regulation. They objected to what they saw as unnecessary constraints on legitimate arms exports and unwarranted judgment of their export policies. The Pakistani respondent, for example, argued that arms-exporting countries do not bear sole responsibility for arms diversion to the illicit market; they should not be blamed whenever legitimately exported arms end up later in the wrong hands. Respondents therefore insisted that international regulation should be limited to the illicit trade in small arms, leaving the regulation of the legal trade to national authorities. The Iranian respondent, for instance, suggested that devoting time and resources to regulation of the legal trade would detract from the main effort against the illicit trade. Respondents also considered any strengthening of the PoA's compliance mechanism unnecessary, unfeasible, or even counterproductive. The Egyptian and Iranian respondents maintained that stronger enforcement would be unrealistic, since many countries lack the capacity to comply with the PoA. China feels that the current compliance mechanism works well and does not see a need for a stronger one. Israel is concerned that a strong compliance mechanism would be highly politicized and biased.

Respondents from countries with state-owned arms exporters also held strong reservations regarding the proposals to establish a transparency mechanism for small-arms transfers or a ban on transferring arms that might be used for human rights violations. They considered such measures unnecessary or impractical. For example, the Egyptian and Pakistani respondents argued that a human-rights guideline for arms transfers is a noble yet unrealistic idea, since "human rights" is a controversial and subjective concept. They also argued that denying arms to governments on the basis of their human rights record would violate the right to self-defense. Israel similarly believes in maintaining the focus on the illicit trade and considers human rights to be unrelated: human rights violations may exist alongside strict law enforcement and tight control of arms movement.

### Consumers

Governments guarding the interests of consumers are expected to favor weak international regulation. This is indeed the case with Syria (REGULATION = 1), Belarus (REGULATION = 0), and other nondemocratic governments that are anxious to secure their ability to acquire arms and to prevent international regulation from becoming a means of pressure. Respondents representing these governments expressed concern about the implications of the UN small-arms process for their countries' national security. They emphasized that countries relying on arms imports should maintain access to arms. Accordingly, they insisted that international regulation must not violate their countries' right to self-defense, compromise their security, or diminish their ability to maintain law and order. Specifically, respondents expressed a strong preference for limiting the UN process to the illicit small-arms trade, with no regulation of the legal trade. Syria, for example, does not see a necessary link between the legal and the illicit trade and believes that such a link would be misused for political purposes. Zimbabwe worries that regulating the legal trade might impair the government's ability to meet its defense needs and allow external actors to meddle with the country's national security. Belarus believes that the motivation behind initiatives to regulate the legal trade is not necessarily to promote international security, but to create a mechanism of pressure.

Nondemocracies' concerns are also clearly manifested in their positions on transparency and transfer controls. Belarus believes that public information on its arms exports and imports would be misused; for instance, it might bring criticism and demands to conform to the EU standards of arms transfers. The Arab countries would accept transparency on small arms only as part of a comprehensive transparency, which would include weapons of mass destruction as well. Syria and Belarus, among others, are concerned that a human-rights guideline for arms transfers would be misinterpreted and abused for political pressure: denial of arms to governments labeled as "human rights violators." Syria is afraid that its ties with Iran and Palestinian groups might also be a ground for denial of arms.

## Bystander Governments

Bystander governments are expected to support moderate international regulation. Absent strong concerns about the trade's externalities or about exporter/consumer interests, these governments have a small stake in the international control of small arms. Indonesia, Peru, and Botswana are among this group: non-arms-exporting countries that face relatively limited problems of gun violence. For them, the UN small-arms process offers modest benefits and entails low costs. As expected, they favor moderate international regulation of small arms (REGULATION = 3 for all three countries).

## Cross-pressured Governments

According to the theoretical framework, cross-pressured governments with both "victim" and "perpetrator" motivations should vary in their preferences. They may adopt a pro-regulation preference close to that of a victim; resist regulation as if they were perpetrators; or hold an intermediate preference that balances their mixed motives. Consistent with this expectation, cross-pressured governments vary in their preferences on the international regulation of small arms. Certain governments balance the interests of exporters vis-á-vis their countries' gun problem or concerns about gun violence abroad. When the arms industry is private, its concerns carry less weight than those of a state-owned industry. The pro-regulation incentives may therefore prevail over the commercial interests and tilt the balance toward support for regulation. For example, the respondent from Austria (REGULATION = 5) indicated that the arms industry had expressed concerns about international regulation, yet these were dispelled by a government pursuing humanitarian foreign-policy goals. Austria thus adopted a victim preference for strong regulation. By contrast, India balances the desire to mitigate its terrorism problem against the interests of a state-owned arms industry, resulting in a preference for moderate international regulation (REGULATION = 2). On the one hand,

India wishes to limit the regulatory efforts to the illicit trade in small arms; on the other hand, India would have preferred a legally binding PoA to enhance governments' sense of responsibility. Cuba holds a similar preference (REGULATION = 2). The nondemocratic Cuban government seeks international regulation that would curb the inflow of guns, yet not risk the government's own arms supply.

The U.S. government is also cross-pressured. International control of small arms may reduce the risk to American soldiers overseas and is consistent with the humanitarian aspect of U.S. foreign policy. At the same time, international regulation could restrict the American use of arms transfers as a foreign-policy tool; of particular concern for the United States is the proposed ban on arms provision to unauthorized nonstate actors. Most importantly, gun consumers—civilian gun owners represented by the NRA—perceive the UN small-arms process as a major threat to their possession and use of guns.[70] The result of these conflicting incentives, especially the powerful influence of the NRA, is a perpetrator preference: weak international regulation of small arms (REGULATION = 1).[71] On the scope of the UN process, the United States takes an intermediate position, maintaining that the process should mainly deal with the illicit trade, yet recognizing that certain aspects of the legal trade, such as export control, should be addressed as well. The United States believes, however, that the small-arms process should be based on politically rather than legally binding commitments. It is also content with the existing compliance mechanism and sees no need for a stronger one. The rationale: compliance with the PoA depends on governments' political will; legal commitments or stronger enforcement will not necessarily generate such will. The United States particularly opposes the establishment of international rules on civilian possession of arms, seeing this as a domestic matter. It also opposes a complete ban on arms transfers to unauthorized nonstate actors and argues in favor of verifying the legitimacy and responsibility of end-users on an individual basis.

Most significantly, the United States insists that the UN process exclude ammunition. Many respondents, especially from Africa, Europe, and Latin America, expressed the view that the UN small-arms process must cover ammunition, since ammunition is an integral part of the gun. As the respondent from Sri Lanka put it, "a gun without ammunition is just a stick." Therefore, attempting to solve the small-arms problem while excluding ammunition makes little sense and dooms the process to partial failure. Yet ammunition was not explicitly included in the Program of Action, mainly due to the objection of the United States and several Middle Eastern governments. The United States argues that applying small-arms standards such as marking and record keeping to ammunition—a high-volume, expendable commodity—is not cost-effective or feasible, and therefore ammunition should be tackled separately.

Several respondents contrasted the American preference for weak international regulation of small arms with the United States' own advanced system of export control as well as the active U.S. participation in the efforts against gun violence on a bilateral basis or through multilateral frameworks such as the OSCE. They suggested that the cause of this discrepancy is the domestic political controversy over gun control in the United States and the influence of the gun-owners lobby. One respondent tied the U.S. position on small arms to the American skepticism toward arms control in the post-Cold War period (manifested in the failure to ratify the Comprehensive Test Ban Treaty, the refusal to join the Mine Ban Treaty, and the 2002 withdrawal from the Anti-Ballistic Missile Treaty).[72] The unfavorable approach of the George W. Bush administration to the UN and multilateral initiatives further weakened American support for the UN-led efforts to control small arms.

## Additional Evidence

Government statements before and during the 2001 UN conference that adopted the PoA serve as a check on the survey data. These public statements are consistent with the survey responses. Governments in Latin America and sub-Saharan Africa expressed support for the UN process. For example, Senegal (REGULATION = 5) urged giving "absolute priority" to the fight against small-arms circulation and called for a Program of Action that would contain legally binding commitments.[73] Colombia (REGULATION = 5) wanted the PoA to establish mechanisms for ensuring compliance and for regulating and monitoring the entire chain of the small-arms trade, from production to distribution and sale.[74] Humanitarian-motivated governments expressed similar support for strong regulation. For example, Canada (REGULATION = 4) wanted the 2001 small-arms conference to address not only the illicit trade in small arms, but also the interrelationship between the legal and the illicit trade.[75] In line with the survey data, governments guarding the interests of state-owned arms exporters expressed concerns and reservations. China (REGULATION = 0) and Pakistan (REGULATION = 1) wanted the UN process to focus solely on the illicit trade in small arms.[76] Egypt (REGULATION = 1) emphasized that nuclear disarmament remained the international community's utmost priority in the field of arms control.[77] Nondemocracies expressed similar views. Belarus (REGULATION = 0) wanted a non-legally binding PoA that would leave to national governments the primary responsibility for suppressing the illicit trade.[78] Syria (REGULATION = 1) demanded respect for states' right under the UN Charter to secure weapons for national defense.[79] Consistent with the survey, the public American position was less than fully supportive of the UN process. The Unites States indicated its opposition to "measures that would constrain legal trade and legal manufacturing of small arms" and expressed a preference for non-legally binding commitments.[80]

The adoption of the PoA in July 2001 overshadowed the Firearms Protocol that was adopted only two months earlier. As survey respondents noted, the Firearms Protocol had been marginalized in comparison to the PoA. This marginalization comports with the large variation in government preferences documented here. Countries preferring weak international regulation, especially major arms-exporting countries such as China and Egypt, have accepted the non-legally binding PoA. They have refused, however, to make a legally binding commitment by ratifying the Firearms Protocol. Moreover, ratification of the Firearms Protocol follows the cross-regional preference variation depicted in Figure 3.1. It has been ratified primarily by countries in Africa, Latin America, and Europe and has won few ratifications in the Middle East, East and South Asia, and the Pacific. The United States has also not ratified the protocol. Firearms Protocol ratification and REGULATION—the survey-based measure of government preferences—are positively correlated (Spearman correlation coefficient is 0.23, significant at 1%).

The PoA is enmeshed in a web of regional and subregional arrangements that tackle the illicit trade in small arms. As indicated earlier, some of these arrangements were established prior to the PoA and facilitated its development. The 2001 adoption of the PoA, in turn, stimulated and gave further momentum to regional and subregional initiatives.[81] Indeed, the PoA explicitly encourages regional and subregional efforts against the illicit trade in small arms.[82] Such efforts complement the PoA, reinforce it, and facilitate its implementation.[83] Yet the pace and depth of regional and subregional initiatives have not been even. They have exhibited significant cross-regional variation, consistent with Figure 3.1. Sub-Saharan Africa, Latin America, and Europe have developed regional measures and mechanisms to control small arms and suppress gun violence. These are also the regions that prefer strong international regulation of small arms, according to the survey findings. In the Middle East and across Asia, however, regional cooperative action has been much weaker, consistent with the survey-documented preferences of governments in these regions.

In December 2006, five months after the failed Review Conference, the UN General Assembly voted to begin the process of establishing an Arms Trade Treaty (ATT): "a comprehensive, legally binding instrument establishing common international standards for the import, export and transfer of conventional arms."[84] The proposed ATT differs from the PoA in scope and purpose. Whereas the PoA is limited to small arms, the ATT would cover all conventional weapons, from small arms to tanks to battleships. The PoA asks governments to take a wide range of measures intended to combat the illicit trade in small arms; the ATT would set criteria to govern the legal international trade in arms, based on the arms' impact on peace, stability, human rights, and so forth. Notwithstanding these differences, the PoA and the ATT share a fundamental goal—curbing armed violence and the human suffering that it causes. The PoA and ATT also raise similar concerns for arms-exporting countries and for countries dependent on arms imports. This resemblance is manifested in the consistency between the survey's findings on small arms and the December 2006 vote on the ATT. At that time, 153 countries voted to begin working on an ATT; the 24 countries that abstained were either arms-exporting countries with state-owned arms industries (China, Egypt, India, Iran, Israel, Pakistan, and Russia) or nondemocracies (such as Belarus, Libya, Saudi Arabia, and Zimbabwe)—two groups whose survey responses conveyed concern about the international regulation of small arms. The one country that voted against the ATT resolution—the United States—preferred weak small-arms regulation as well. In October 2009, however, the United States reversed its opposition and pledged support for the goal of establishing an ATT. As the theoretical framework has indicated, a change of government may lead to a preference change. The American preference for weak international regulation—as expressed in the small-arms conferences in 2001 and 2006 and in the 2006 ATT vote—was the preference of the George W. Bush administration: an administration with little faith in the UN or in arms control, and also one for which gun owners were an important constituency. By contrast, the Obama administration that agreed to work toward an ATT in 2009 was ideologically committed to international cooperation and institutions and to arms control. It was also less influenced by the gun lobby than its predecessor.

## Explaining the Cooperative Outcome

The foregoing analysis has documented and accounted for a large variation in government preferences on the international regulation of small arms. This section employs the preference variation to explain why the global efforts against the illicit trade in small arms resulted in a weak cooperative outcome: a loose regulatory framework in 2001 and a deadlock at the 2006 Review Conference.

### The Program of Action: An Assessment

The Program of Action is a weak international agreement. First and foremost, the PoA is not legally binding; it is merely a political declaration. Many survey respondents considered the political nature of the PoA to be a fundamental shortcoming that makes compliance voluntary and dependent upon the goodwill of governments. A legally binding agreement, in their view, would have generated a greater sense of government accountability and responsibility. The PoA also uses vague and imprecise language that allows governments to interpret its provisions as they see fit. For instance, the document instructs states to "put in place adequate laws, regulations and administrative procedures to exercise effective control . . . over the export, import, transit or retransfer" of small arms. There is no specification, however, of what constitutes "adequate laws" or "effective control."[85] Finally, the PoA involves no delegation of authority to an international organ for monitoring compliance, let alone for sanctioning noncompliant governments. "Enforcement" is limited to governments' voluntary self-reporting on their compliance with the PoA. As the timing and content of reporting are not formally established, governments vary in the frequency, breadth, and level of detail of their reports.[86] Needless to say, the reports are rarely self-critical. Another mechanism—biennial meetings of states to consider the implementation of the PoA—also lacks the capacity to put pressure on governments.[87] In the absence of enforcement powers, the UN merely plays a facilitating role, such as provision and coordination of technical assistance.

The theoretical framework has suggested that agreements against illicit trade require pressure for compliance, given the persistence and magnitude of noncooperative incentives. Without enforcement, governments favoring weak regulation might commit to the regulatory agreement, but not comply. The absence of a meaningful enforcement mechanism is among the principal reasons for the cross-regional variation in compliance with the PoA. A 2006 analysis by NGOs found that countries in sub-Saharan Africa, Latin America, and Europe had made significant progress toward complying with the PoA and with regional small-arms agreements. By contrast, PoA compliance had been limited in Asia as well as in the Middle East and North Africa.[88] This variation dovetails nicely with the cross-regional variation in preferences on regulation depicted in Figure 3.1.

The PoA's utility as a regulatory framework is further compromised by several critical substantive omissions. First and foremost, the PoA addresses "small arms and light weapons" and does not explicitly address ammunition. The question whether the PoA covers ammunition is thus the subject of a continuing debate. As ammunition is what allows small arms to wound and kill, doubts over its inclusion in the PoA seriously hamper the efforts against gun violence. Another serious flaw is the failure to establish a ban on arms transfers to unauthorized nonstate actors. Nonstate actors, such as rebels, criminals, and terrorists, are responsible for much of the worldwide costs of gun violence. A ban on arms provision to such actors would have contributed to the reduction of gun proliferation and violence. Other major omissions concern transfer controls and the marking of small arms. The 2006 Review Conference could not reach a consensus on international transfer controls. The 2005 International Tracing Instrument[89] failed to establish a universal marking system for small arms that would have facilitated the tracing of guns to their source. Instead, it allows states to maintain their own national marking systems. Finally, the UN small-arms process regulates arms brokering in a fairly weak manner. The idea of an international instrument on brokering was considered early on, since illicit brokering activities fuel the illicit trade in small arms, facilitating arms diversion to conflict-prone areas as well as to criminal and terrorist groups. Yet in 2007 a group of governmental experts merely recommended a set of measures against illicit brokering.[90]

An overall assessment of the PoA must take into account its positive aspects as well. Notwithstanding the gaps, the Program of Action includes most of the regulatory issues related to the trade in small arms. Despite the vague language, it does establish a set of internationally agreed-upon norms and standards for suppressing the illicit trade. There have also been attempts, notably on tracing and brokering, to supplement the PoA. Asked to point out how the UN process had benefited their countries, respondents from different regions noted increased awareness as an important contribution. The UN process and the PoA have shone light on an important problem and created a comprehensive, wide-ranging framework for tackling it. Consequently, government ministries, police and military forces, and customs and immigration authorities have started paying greater attention to the problem and enhanced interagency coordination. The PoA has also set in motion a variety of domestic processes, such as legislative changes, improvement of stockpile security, destruction of surplus weapons, and establishment of national strategies to reduce gun violence. The heightened awareness of donor countries and international organizations has facilitated the provision of financial and technical assistance.

Yet this progress has occurred mainly in countries that, to begin with, were committed to the efforts against the illicit trade in small arms. In countries that lacked such a commitment, it is not clear what, if anything, the UN small-arms process has achieved. It has therefore had only limited added value beyond the regional and subregional initiatives in Africa and Latin America. Cooperative efforts within these regions have enhanced states' capacities to tackle gun proliferation and misuse, yet they provide only a partial remedy. The purpose of *global* regulation through the UN process is to achieve what these limited processes cannot: shifting the burden of control and tackling the problem at the source by constraining arms suppliers and restricting arms exports. The weakness of the UN process, however, means that affected regions cannot count on control at the source and have to rely primarily on their own efforts to curb gun violence.

The limitations of the Program of Action are also evident in comparison to other arms-control agreements. Indeed, the PoA lacks two important features typical of arms control. First, arms-control agreements tend to be legally binding. Whether global (such as the Nuclear Non-Proliferation Treaty (NPT)) or regional (such as the Treaty for the Prohibition of Nuclear Weapons in Latin America and the Caribbean), arms-control agreements usually take the form of legally binding treaties. Second, arms-control agreements rely on mechanisms for monitoring and verification of compliance that may involve international organs, such as the International Atomic Energy Agency. Yet unlike arms-control agreements, the PoA is a political declaration that lacks monitoring and verification arrangements. It neither grants states the authority to monitor compliance, nor does it delegate verification authority to an international organ.

## The Cooperation Problem

The key to explaining the relative weakness of the PoA is the cooperation problem. Arms-control cooperation typically resembles a prisoners' dilemma:[91] states can reduce the likelihood and costs of war by mutually lowering their arms levels, but they also have incentives to defect. Arms-control agreements allow states to realize joint gains by countering the incentives for defection; hence their emphasis on verification arrangements. Indeed, arms-control cooperation is often controversial. The NPT, for example, has been the subject of controversy since its inception, as it formally established and perpetuated the distinction between nuclear-weapon states and non-nuclear-weapon states.[92] Nevertheless, the premise of the NPT is joint gains and a shared interest: averting the danger of nuclear war is of much benefit to all countries. Cooperation against the illicit trade in small arms, however, presents a different challenge. Unlike the control of nuclear weapons, international control of small arms does not offer joint gains and does not build on a shared interest. Rather, it leaves certain governments worse off.

The beneficiaries of cooperation on small arms are primarily countries suffering rampant gun violence in sub-Saharan Africa and Latin America. Their inability to control small arms through national means is the principal motivation for international control, and the UN process therefore enjoys their full support. Other countries, however, are more ambivalent about the international regulation of small arms. The terrorism problem afflicting India, for example, is relatively small compared with the gun problem in war-ravaged African countries. In addition, India guards the interests of its state-owned arms industry against burdensome regulation, and therefore favors moderate international regulation, rather than the stringent control advocated by African countries.

On the anti-regulation side are countries that would have preferred noncooperation. Consider China and Syria. Both countries have tight internal security and low levels of gun violence. They therefore have little to gain from an international process intended to reduce gun violence. Since the small-arms problem is not *their* problem, the process has very limited utility from their point of view. Moreover, regulating the small-arms trade could impose significant costs on both countries. International regulation threatens China's commercial interest as a major arms exporter and might establish a means of pressure on nondemocratic Syria. In addition, regulation could entail various financial, administrative, and law-enforcement costs. Syria, for example, opposes an obligation to require the marking of arms by importing countries—a requirement that, Syria argues, would have substantial financial implications.[93] These calculations have led the Chinese and Syrian governments to resist the international regulation of small arms. Both governments chose, however, to participate in the UN small-arms process. Nonparticipation would have been difficult to justify, given the enormous worldwide costs of the illicit trade in small arms. China's attempts to establish its image as a "responsible major power" would have been difficult to reconcile with an absolute refusal to address an acute humanitarian problem. In 2001 anti-regulation governments thus accepted the PoA—a document that reflected concern about the problem of small arms but lacked teeth due to the absence of legally binding force, detailed and precise commitments, or delegation of authority to international organs. Since 2001, however, these governments have opposed further regulatory initiatives, such as the establishment of international transfer controls.

Several survey respondents indeed highlighted the divergence of government preferences as a primary obstacle to the success of the UN small-arms process. They pointed out that governments vary dramatically in their interests, priorities, and expectations. Affected governments are concerned about the daily killing of innocent victims, while governments of arms-exporting countries protect their commercial interests. For the African governments, the small-arms process is an important priority, while some Arab governments consider it to be a distraction from *their* priority—nuclear disarmament. Many governments would like to address the issues of civilian possession and nonstate actors; for others, these issues are taboo. African respondents lamented the refusal of arms-exporting countries to take full responsibility for the harm they generate and their reluctance to accept international controls. The respondent from Tanzania put it bluntly: the Program of Action "does not force anyone to do anything."

## Preference Variation, Power Distribution, and Cooperation

Heterogeneity of government preferences may sometimes be overcome and does not necessarily result in weak cooperation. Yet for small arms, preference variation has posed an insurmountable obstacle, leading to a weak international regulatory framework in 2001 and a deadlock at the 2006 Review Conference. Why was this the case? There are several reasons. The purpose of international regulation is to reduce the negative externalities of illicit trade by restraining the externalities-generating countries. In the case of small arms, the goal of international regulation is to restrain arms-exporting countries, which requires their cooperation. Since international regulation rejected by arms-exporting countries would be nearly futile, these countries enjoyed a bargaining advantage. The regulatory framework had to be weak enough to satisfy their preferences and secure their participation. Moreover, the small-arms conferences in 2001 and 2006 were consensus-based: an agreement required the consent of all participating countries. This decision rule further enhanced exporting countries' bargaining leverage. Arms-exporting countries favoring weak regulation effectively held veto power and could secure regulatory outcomes consistent with their preferences. Survey respondents noted the benefit of a consensus-based approach—having all countries on board—alongside a major drawback: outcomes reflected the lowest common denominator.

Most importantly, the distribution of power precluded the use of rewards or coercive punishments to establish cooperation. In the case of the NPT, rewards were fundamental to the bargain. The treaty promised to facilitate the transfer of peaceful nuclear technology to countries that agreed to forgo nuclear weapons. The African governments, however, could not offer an equivalent reward to overcome resistance to small-arms cooperation. It is difficult to imagine what they could have offered to regulation opponents, such as the United States, China, and Iran. Domestic opposition of powerful interest groups—arms manufacturers and the U.S. gun lobby—would have made successful use of rewards even less likely. Nor was coerced cooperation a realistic option given the power differential. The African governments could not punish more-powerful governments for their reluctance to estab-lish stringent regulation. Thus, they had to settle for a cooperative outcome that did not fulfill their wishes and expectations.

The distribution of power also accounts for the variation in the robustness of international regulation across illicit trades. Small arms are the primary means of violence in most civil wars; they kill many more people worldwide than any other weapon. The toll of small-arms proliferation in terms of human life as well as social, political, and economic disruptions is at least as high as the toll of drugs, if not higher. The negative externalities of counter-feit goods, while significant, are nowhere near the deleterious effects of small arms. Yet the robustness of international regulation does not match the se-verity of the problems. The Program of Action on Small Arms is a non-legally binding agreement that lacks a monitoring and enforcement mechanism. By contrast, the international drug regime is based on three legally binding treaties that delegate monitoring authority to the UN drug organs. Similarly, the legally binding TRIPS establishes mechanisms to foster compliance with anti-counterfeit obligations.

The greater robustness of the regulatory frameworks for drugs and counterfeits is a product of the American leadership of the cooperative efforts. As will be described in Chapter 6, governments of drug-exporting countries have been ambivalent or outright hostile toward international drug control from its inception in 1909. Since the 1980s, the international efforts against counterfeits have met with resistance from developing countries. In both cases, American power and influence have been crucial to overcoming the heterogeneity of preferences and establishing cooperation. The prohibition on the trade in drugs other than for medical and scientific purposes became a global norm thanks to relentless American efforts; worldwide endeavors against counterfeiting were the result of continuous U.S. coercion. American pressure brought reluctant governments to commit to and comply with agreements against drugs and counterfeits—agreements that were inconsistent with these governments' preferences.

By contrast, the United States did not pressure reluctant governments to accept international controls on small arms. Rather, the United States itself was among those who favored weak regulation. With the United States resisting—rather than leading—the regulatory efforts, they were bound to achieve very modest success. No country could bring a reluctant United States to accept far-reaching, legally binding commitments on small arms. Without U.S. support for and promotion of such commitments, they could not materialize.

## Cooperation against the Illicit Trade in Small Arms: Conclusions

This chapter successfully tested the theoretical model of government preferences on international regulation. Consistent with the theoretical expectations, preferences on the international regulation of small arms vary widely. Governments influenced by primary or secondary externalities favor stringent regulation; governments that give priority to the anti-regulation interests of exporters or consumers favor weak regulation; and cross-pressured governments take a variety of positions. The strongest proponents of regulation are governments inferior in power—governments incapable of overcoming the large variation in preferences. The result is a weak international regulatory framework.

The analysis has focused on the variation in government preferences as the chief obstacle to international cooperation against the illicit trade in small arms. The principal difficulty is that certain governments would benefit considerably from regulation of the small-arms trade, whereas others would benefit very little and, in fact, have much to lose. Yet preference variation is not the only obstacle to the international efforts against gun violence. Lack of capacity may also hinder these efforts: many developing countries lack the human, financial, or technical resources necessary for enforcing their laws and guarding their borders. Informational problems present another challenge. For example, governments may lack reliable data on the quantity or origin of illicit arms in circulation. International coordination between law-enforcement agencies also raises challenges, such as incompatibility of national databases and inadequate information exchange.[94] And yet the key problems are the large variation in preferences on international regulation and the reluctance of certain governments to seriously tackle the illicit trade in small arms. When a common interest exists, governments can work together to enhance capacity, overcome uncertainty, and coordinate action. However, if some governments identify only costs and no gains from international regulation and if the linchpin of cooperation—shared interest—is absent, joint international action is infinitely harder to establish.

The theoretical framework has identified moral entrepreneurs—domestic or transnational civil-society groups—as actors that stimulate governments' concern about illicit trade and promote international regulation. Civil society was indeed involved in the UN small-arms process. Established in 1999, the International Action Network on Small Arms (IANSA)—an umbrella organization of several hundred civil-society groups—raised awareness to the threat of small arms and advocated regulatory solutions. Yet pro-control moral entrepreneurs had only a small impact on the negotiations at the 2001 UN small-arms conference, and the resultant PoA failed to fulfill their expectations;[95] nor were they able to prevent the deadlock at the 2006 Review Conference. The role of civil society in the UN small-arms process was minor compared with its important role in the historical and contemporary campaigns against human trafficking—the subject of Chapter 5. Civil society's modest contribution to the small-arms process was also far from its great success in the landmine campaign.[96]

That campaign—which culminated in the 1997 Mine Ban Treaty—was more conducive to NGO advocacy and influence. First, landmines are a single category of weapons. By contrast, "small arms" is a broad spectrum that ranges from pistols to shoulder-fired missiles and also includes ammunition. Second, the landmine norm was a simple one: complete prohibition. Small arms, however, serve legitimate civilian, law enforcement, and military purposes. Regulation to allow legitimate uses and prevent illegitimate ones presents a more complex challenge than an outright ban. The limited scope—one type of weapon—and the simplicity of the norm allowed for a clear, focused anti-landmine advocacy that could not be replicated in the case of small arms. Third, the NGOs' landmine campaign did not meet significant resistance, since the military and commercial importance of landmines was small.

By contrast, the NGOs advocating control of small arms faced formidable counterforces: the arms industry, governments concerned for their ability to acquire arms, and NGOs *opposed* to the control of small arms—most significantly, the NRA. As a result, pro-control NGOs were highly circumscribed in their ability to shape international regulation. They could also do little to bring reluctant governments to comply. This experience demonstrates the limits of moral entrepreneurs' influence in the face of resistance from powerful regulation opponents. It further shows that civil-society groups may have competing, even rival, agendas. Whereas IANSA promoted strict gun control, the NRA identified the UN's regulatory efforts as a threat to civilian gun ownership. But in terms of impact, the NRA enjoyed a decisive advantage through its significant influence on the U.S. government. The weakness of the PoA and the failure of the Review Conference were consistent with the NRA's goals, to IANSA's disappointment.[97] Chapter 5 will examine another conflict between civil society actors, this time over human trafficking.

This chapter opened with an overview of the attempts to control the arms trade during the interwar period. How does contemporary cooperation on small arms resemble and differ from these early attempts? Most notably, both the contemporary and the interwar efforts failed to produce meaningful international cooperation. The interwar Saint-Germain and Geneva Conventions received few ratifications and never went into effect. The Program of Action on small arms, as a political declaration, does not require ratification and is indeed in force; but the absence of legally binding force, lack of an enforcement mechanism, and substantive omissions significantly circumscribe the PoA's utility and effectiveness. Yet the parallels between the contemporary and the interwar efforts stretch beyond the weakness of the cooperative outcome.

The motivation for controlling the arms trade has seen both persistence and change. The primary goal of the interwar efforts was to prevent insurgents in Africa and Asia from acquiring arms. Preventing arms from falling into the hands of insurgents and rebels in the developing world, especially in Africa, is also a principal goal of the contemporary attempt to control small arms. Yet the actors pursuing that goal have changed. During the interwar years, Africa was under colonial rule. The control of the arms trade served the European colonial powers who sought peace and order in their colonies. By contrast, the contemporary efforts to control small arms have been spearheaded by African governments concerned about the enormous costs of gun proliferation and misuse in their countries. European governments are indeed supportive of small-arms regulation, but their support is not primarily motivated by self-interest as it was in the interwar years. The European concern for Africa today is in large part moral and humanitarian.

Both the contemporary and the early efforts to control the arms trade were based on a similar principle: regulating the export of arms to ensure that the arms reach legitimate actors. Such tightening of the control over exports makes it more difficult to sell and acquire arms. It is therefore potentially detrimental to both exporters and consumers. Indeed, during the interwar period the interests of arms exporters and of arms-importing governments posed a major obstacle to international regulation, as they do today. In their 1934 study of the international arms industry, H. C. Engelbrecht and F. C. Hanighen concluded that

> the basic problem of international control of the arms makers [is] that *few governments, if any, really want international supervision of the traffic in war materials.* Most governments believe that the unhindered international sale of arms would insure their military preparedness, especially since most of them are entirely dependent on imports for their war materials. The great arms producing countries, on the other hand, are averse to harming one of their industries on which they themselves so largely rely for their "national defense."[98]

This explanation for the failure of the interwar efforts still largely holds today. Resistance to small-arms regulation comes from arms-exporting countries protecting the commercial interests of their arms industries. Yet the identity of the exporting countries that oppose regulation has changed. The targets of the regulatory efforts in the interwar period were arms producers in Europe, the United States, and Japan. By contrast, the exporting countries averse to regulation today are countries such as China, Pakistan, and Egypt where the arms industry is state-owned and where small arms—low-tech weapons—are an important export.

As in the interwar period, opposition to small-arms regulation also comes from arms-importing governments determined to secure their access to arms and to prevent arms regulation from becoming a means of pressure. Today, this camp of opposition predominantly includes nondemocratic governments that feel threatened and vulnerable in an increasingly democratic international system. An additional similarity between the interwar and contemporary efforts is the pivotal role of the United States. The American concerns and hesitations were an important cause of the failure of the interwar efforts. In 2001 and 2006, the U.S. preference for weak international regulation of small arms posed a critical obstacle that regulation proponents were unable to overcome.

The survey data presented in this chapter provided a snapshot in time: government preferences on the international regulation of small arms as of 2006. Yet the picture painted by the survey and the political dynamic it captured are not unique to that specific point in time, nor are they exclusive to small arms. Exporters' and consumers' resistance to international regulation and the international political conflict that such resistance can fuel were evident in the interwar efforts to control the arms trade. As will be shown in the following chapter, a similar controversy hobbled the efforts to stem the trade in looted antiquities.

# APPENDICES

## APPENDIX A

# SURVEY QUESTIONNAIRE
# AND RESPONSES

The survey included both open questions and closed questions. For each of the closed questions, the overall distribution of responses is shown alongside the responses of 14 key countries: the most influential countries in each region in terms of military and/or economic power. While most closed questions were phrased as yes/no questions, some answers were in between yes and no; therefore, a middle category of responses was coded. The responses "do not know" and "do not have a position on this issue" are excluded.

Q1. The small-arms process led by the UN attempts to stop the illicit trade in small arms and light weapons. How does [country name] benefit from this process?

Q2. Does the UN small-arms process in any way create difficulties for [country name], such as economic or administrative burdens? If so, what are they?

Q3. Some believe that the UN small-arms process should address only the illicit trade in small arms. Others believe that the process should address both the legal and the illicit trade. What is [country name] position?

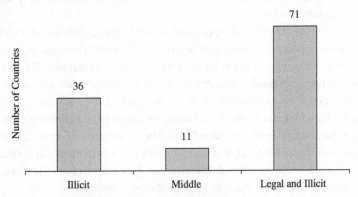

**Figure 3A.1** Q3. Scope of the UN Small-Arms Process

**Table 3A.1** Q3. Scope of the UN Small-Arms Process (Key Countries)

| Country | Illicit | Middle | Legal and Illicit |
|---|---|---|---|
| United States | | √ | |
| Russia | | √ | |
| China | √ | | |
| Britain | | | √ |
| France | √ | | |

**Table 3A.1** (*continued*)

| Country | Illicit | Middle | Legal and Illicit |
|---|---|---|---|
| Germany | | | √ |
| Japan | | | √ |
| India | √ | | |
| Pakistan | √ | | |
| Brazil | | | √ |
| Mexico | | | √ |
| Egypt | √ | | |
| Iran | √ | | |
| South Africa | | | √ |

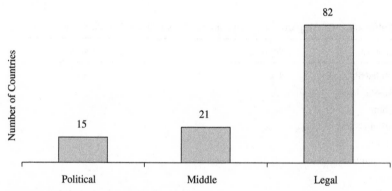

**Figure 3A.2** Q4. Level of Obligation

**Table 3A.2** Q4. Level of Obligation (Key Countries)

| Country | Political | Middle | Legal |
|---|---|---|---|
| United States | √ | | |
| Russia | | √ | |
| China | √ | | |
| Britain | | | √ |
| France | | √ | |
| Germany | | | √ |
| Japan | | | √ |
| India | | | √ |
| Pakistan | | √ | |
| Brazil | | | √ |
| Mexico | | | √ |
| Egypt | | √ | |
| Iran | √ | | |
| South Africa | | | √ |

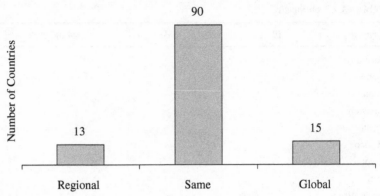

**Figure 3A.3** Q5. Importance of Regional vs. Global Efforts

**Table 3A.3** Q5. Importance of Regional vs. Global Efforts (Key Countries)

| Country | Regional | Same | Global |
|---|---|---|---|
| United States | √ | | |
| Russia | | √ | |
| China | | √ | |
| Britain | | √ | |
| France | | √ | |
| Germany | | √ | |
| Japan | | | √ |
| India | | √ | |
| Pakistan | | | √ |
| Brazil | | √ | |
| Mexico | | √ | |
| Egypt | | √ | |
| Iran | | √ | |
| South Africa | | √ | |

Q4. The Program of Action is a political—rather than legally binding—document. Is [country name] content with the PoA being a political document, or would [country name] have preferred a legally binding PoA?

Q5. Some believe that the illicit trade in small arms should be addressed through regional frameworks. Others think that the efforts against the illicit small-arms trade should be conducted as a global process. Does [country name] see greater importance in the regional process or in the global process?

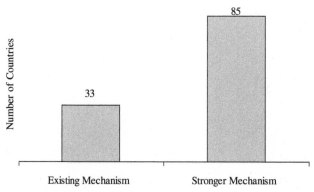

**Figure 3A.4** Q6. Compliance Mechanism

**Table 3A.4** Q6. Compliance Mechanism (Key Countries)

| Country | Existing | Stronger |
|---|---|---|
| United States | √ | |
| Russia | √ | |
| China | √ | |
| Britain | | √ |
| France | | √ |
| Germany | | √ |
| Japan | | √ |
| India | √ | |
| Pakistan | √ | |
| Brazil | | √ |
| Mexico | | √ |
| Egypt | √ | |
| Iran | √ | |
| South Africa | | √ |

Q6. The Program of Action includes a mechanism for compliance and implementation that is based on biennial meetings of states to consider the Program's implementation and on voluntary submission of national reports. Is [country name] content with the existing mechanism, or would [country name] have preferred a stronger mechanism or a weaker one?

Q7. Does [country name] consider the efforts against the illicit small-arms trade more important, less important, or as important as nuclear arms control?

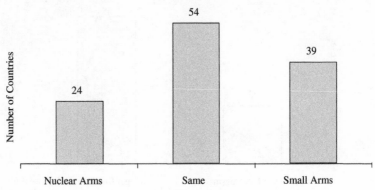

**Figure 3A.5** Q7. Priority: Nuclear or Small Arms

**Table 3A.5** Q7. Priority: Nuclear or Small Arms (Key Countries)

| Country | Nuclear | Same | Small Arms |
|---|---|---|---|
| United States | √ | | |
| Russia | | √ | |
| China | √ | | |
| Britain | √ | | |
| France | | √ | |
| Germany | | √ | |
| Japan | √ | | |
| India | √ | | |
| Pakistan | √ | | |
| Brazil | √ | | |
| Mexico | | √ | |
| Egypt | | √ | |
| Iran | √ | | |
| South Africa | | | √ |

Q8. Does [country name] support the establishment of a transparency mechanism for small-arms transfers, such as the expansion of the UN Register of Conventional Arms to include small arms?

Q9. On a scale of 1 to 5, how would [country name] rate the effectiveness of the UN small-arms process in achieving its goal: "to Prevent, Combat and Eradicate the Illicit Trade in Small Arms and Light Weapons in All Its Aspects?" Why?

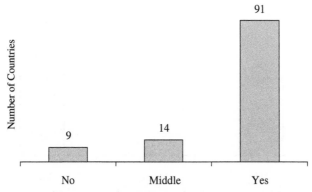

**Figure 3A.6** Q8. Transparency Mechanism

**Table 3A.6** Q8. Transparency Mechanism (Key Countries)

| Country | No | Middle | Yes |
|---|---|---|---|
| United States | | | √ |
| Russia | | √ | |
| China | √ | | |
| Britain | | | √ |
| France | | | √ |
| Germany | | | √ |
| Japan | | | √ |
| India | √ | | |
| Pakistan | √ | | |
| Brazil | | | √ |
| Mexico | | | √ |
| Egypt | | √ | |
| Iran | √ | | |
| South Africa | | | √ |

Q10. Does [country name] support the establishment of international rules on civilian possession of arms, such as an international rule prohibiting civilian possession and use of all light weapons, automatic rifles, and machine guns?

Q11. Does [country name] support the establishment of an international rule prohibiting small-arms transfers to unauthorized nonstate actors?

Q12. Does [country name] support the establishment of an international rule prohibiting the transfer of small arms when there is a clear risk that the

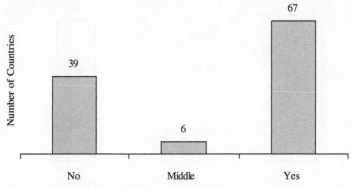

**Figure 3A.7** Q10. International Rules on Civilian Possession of Small Arms

**Table 3A.7** Q10. International Rules on Civilian Possession of Small Arms (Key Countries)

| Country | No | Middle | Yes |
|---|---|---|---|
| United States | √ | | |
| Russia | √ | | |
| China | | | √ |
| Britain | √ | | |
| France | √ | | |
| Germany | | | √ |
| Japan | √ | | |
| India | | | √ |
| Pakistan | √ | | |
| Brazil | | | √ |
| Mexico | | | √ |
| Egypt | | | √ |
| Iran | | | √ |
| South Africa | | | √ |

transfer will violate sanctions of the UN Security Council or other multilateral sanctions?

Q13. Does [country name] support the establishment of an international rule prohibiting the transfer of small arms if the arms might be used for violation of human rights?

Q14. Does [country name] support the establishment of a universal marking system for small arms that allows the identification of the manufacturers and of serial numbers?

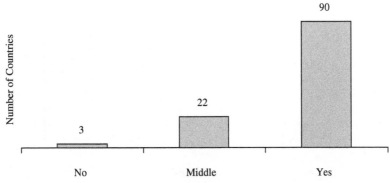

**Figure 3A.8** Q11. Prohibition on Arms Transfers to Unauthorized Nonstate Actors

**Table 3A.8** Q11. Prohibition on Arms Transfers to Unauthorized Nonstate Actors (Key Countries)

| Country | No | Middle | Yes |
|---|---|---|---|
| United States | √ | | |
| Russia | | | √ |
| China | | | √ |
| Britain | | √ | |
| France | | | √ |
| Germany | | | √ |
| Japan | | √ | |
| India | | | √ |
| Pakistan | √ | | |
| Brazil | | | √ |
| Mexico | | | √ |
| Egypt | | √ | |
| Iran | | √ | |
| South Africa | | | √ |

Q15. The UN small-arms process may have consequences for the security forces. How have the security forces in [country name] responded to the small-arms process?

Q16. The UN small-arms process makes demands from and imposes constraints on the arms industry. How have the arms producers in [country name] responded to the small-arms process? (This question was presented only to countries that are major exporters of small arms.)

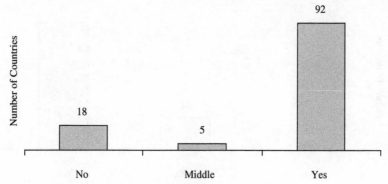

**Figure 3A.9** Q12. Transfer Controls: Security Council Sanctions

**Table 3A.9** Q12. Transfer Controls: Security Council Sanctions (Key Countries)

| Country | No | Middle | Yes |
|---|---|---|---|
| United States | | | √ |
| Russia | | | √ |
| China | √ | | |
| Britain | | | √ |
| France | | | √ |
| Germany | | | √ |
| Japan | | | √ |
| India | | | √ |
| Pakistan | √ | | |
| Brazil | | | √ |
| Mexico | | | √ |
| Egypt | √ | | |
| Iran | √ | | |
| South Africa | √ | | |

Q17. Does [country name] intend to ratify the Firearms Protocol of the UN Convention against Transnational Organized Crime? (This question was presented only to countries that had not ratified the protocol at the time of the survey.)

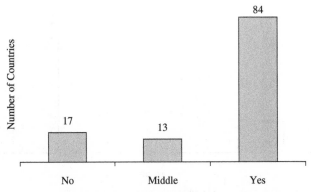

**Figure 3A.10** Q13. Transfer Controls: Human Rights

**Table 3A.10** Q13. Transfer Controls: Human Rights (Key Countries)

| Country | No | Middle | Yes |
|---|---|---|---|
| United States | | | √ |
| Russia | | √ | |
| China | √ | | |
| Britain | | | √ |
| France | | | √ |
| Germany | | | √ |
| Japan | | | √ |
| India | | | √ |
| Pakistan | √ | | |
| Brazil | | √ | |
| Mexico | | √ | |
| Egypt | √ | | |
| Iran | √ | | |
| South Africa | √ | | |

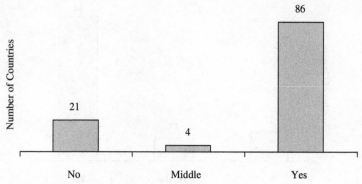

**Figure 3A.11** Q14. Universal Marking System

**Table 3A.11** Q14. Universal Marking System (Key Countries)

| Country | No | Middle | Yes |
|---|---|---|---|
| United States | √ | | |
| Russia | √ | | |
| China | √ | | |
| Britain | | | √ |
| France | | | √ |
| Germany | | | √ |
| Japan | | | √ |
| India | | | √ |
| Pakistan | | | √ |
| Brazil | | | √ |
| Mexico | | | √ |
| Egypt | √ | | |
| Iran | √ | | |
| South Africa | √ | | |

# COUNTRIES INCLUDED IN THE SURVEY

| | | | |
|---|---|---|---|
| Albania | Ecuador | Lithuania | Serbia |
| Algeria | Egypt | Macedonia | Sierra Leone |
| Angola | Eritrea | Malawi | Slovakia |
| Argentina | Estonia | Malaysia | Slovenia |
| Armenia | Ethiopia | Mali | Somalia |
| Australia | Fiji | Malta | South Africa |
| Austria | Finland | Mauritania | Spain |
| Bangladesh | France | Mexico | Sri Lanka |
| Belarus | Gabon | Moldova | Sudan |
| Belgium | Gambia | Morocco | Sweden |
| Benin | Georgia | Mozambique | Switzerland |
| Bolivia | Germany | Namibia | Syria |
| Botswana | Guatemala | Nepal | Tanzania |
| Brazil | Haiti | Netherlands | Thailand |
| Britain | Honduras | New Zealand | Togo |
| Bulgaria | Hungary | Nicaragua | Turkey |
| Cambodia | India | Niger | Turkmenistan |
| Canada | Indonesia | Nigeria | Uganda |
| Chile | Iran | Norway | Ukraine |
| China | Ireland | Pakistan | United States |
| Colombia | Israel | Papua New Guinea | Uruguay |
| Congo, Democratic Republic of | Italy | Paraguay | Venezuela |
| Congo, Republic of | Japan | Peru | Yemen |
| Costa Rica | Jordan | Philippines | Zambia |
| Cote d'Ivoire | Kazakhstan | Poland | Zimbabwe |
| Croatia | Kenya | Portugal | |
| Cuba | Korea, Republic of | Qatar | |
| Cyprus | Kyrgyzstan | Romania | |
| Czech Republic | Lesotho | Russia | |
| Denmark | Liberia | Saudi Arabia | |
| Dominican Republic | Libya | Senegal | |

# 4

## PREVENTING PLUNDER

International Cooperation against the Illicit Trade
in Antiquities

The illicit trade in looted antiquities—antiquities that were illegally excavated and exported—badly damages the world's archaeology.[1] As part of this ongoing trade, archaeological sites and monuments worldwide are plundered, and the loot comes to rest in museums and private collections in Europe, North America, and, increasingly, East Asia. While some maintain that the looting of antiquities "has grown out of all control,"[2] neither the problem itself nor the international efforts against it is new. At the center of these efforts is a 1970 UNESCO convention intended to stem the flow of looted antiquities from poor countries to rich market-countries: the Convention on the Means of Prohibiting and Preventing the Illicit Import, Export and Transfer of Ownership of Cultural Property (hereafter the UNESCO Convention). While this convention was embraced by developing countries facing archaeological plunder, the majority of market countries—including Britain, Germany, and Japan—rejected the convention. From their point of view, it imposed a law-enforcement burden and limited the ability of art dealers, museums, and collectors to acquire antiquities—all to the benefit of foreign countries. Yet, the United States, the largest market country, took a different approach. Soon after the adoption of the convention, the United States began the process of ratification and implementation. Other market countries took more than 30 years to reverse their opposition and accede to the UNESCO Convention.

This chapter examines the domestic and international political conflicts underlying the cooperative efforts against the plunder of antiquities. The first section introduces the reader to the illicit trade in antiquities. The second section explores the battle between source countries, who have advocated stringent international regulation of antiquities, and market countries, who have questioned the desirability and feasibility of such regulation. In the third and fourth sections I examine how domestic politics shapes government preferences and why preferences may shift over time. The third section explains why the United States reversed its liberal approach to the movement of cultural material, joined the international efforts against looting, and established controls on antiquities—to the benefit of foreign countries facing archaeological plunder and to the detriment of the U.S. art market. The fourth section explores Britain's surprising accession to the UNESCO Convention in 2002, after having rejected it for more than three decades. The American and British cases both demonstrate how temporal changes in preferences can bring previously reluctant governments to cooperate against illicit trade.

## The Illicit Trade in Antiquities: Background

The motivation for cooperation against the illicit trade in antiquities is the negative externalities of the looting that feeds the trade. Three types of externalities stem from the looting of antiquities. First, and most obviously, the plunder of antiquities results in archaeological destruction. The clandestine excavation and removal of the objects cause enormous and irreparable damage to the looted sites and monuments, often leaving them in ruin. At times, the destruction caused by the looting itself is accompanied by purposeful destruction intended to eliminate evidence. In many cases the antiquities themselves are damaged as well due to the inexpert excavation and lack of appropriate conservation.[3] Second, looting destroys the archaeological context and thus results in loss of historical information and knowledge. Context, considered by some as "the essence of archaeology,"[4] is "the physical space in which an artifact is discovered in relation to other artifacts and features in the earth."[5] Archaeologists maintain that coherent historical information "comes about only through the systematic study of *context*."[6] Antiquities, in their context of discovery, can shed light on past cultures. Archaeologists thus carefully record the contextual information of objects they excavate—information that looters erase. Wrenched out of their context of discovery, looted antiquities add little to the understanding of history. These may be beautiful objects that please the collector and the museum visitor, but from the archaeologist's viewpoint they are meaningless and worthless.[7] Third, negative externalities are borne by the plundered communities. The illegal removal of antiquities and the accompanying destruction eliminate a part of the people's history and heritage and at times damage sites and monuments that are sacred. Moreover, looting deprives the community of a possibly lucrative economic resource. Had the antiquities been on display at the archaeological site or a nearby museum, they might have attracted tourism and generated profits for the local economy.

From the looting of Mayan sites in Belize and robbing of ancient tombs in Peru to the plunder of archaeology in Mali and Niger to destructive temple robberies in Cambodia, looting takes places in archaeologically rich countries, most of them in the developing world.[8] Archaeologists, however, identify the demand of rich market-countries as the engine of looting and draw a direct link between the two parts of the antiquities market: the legitimate and respectable world of museums and art collectors, who are viewed as patrons of culture and public benefactors, and the underworld where tombs are raided in the dark of night and sculptures are chain-sawed from the walls of temples. Archaeologists maintain that the worlds of culture and criminality are seemingly antithetical, yet in fact are closely intertwined: looted objects obtain a veneer of legitimacy and become museum exhibits or collector items. Such a transformation is possible, as most antiquities—roughly 80-90 percent—"surface" on the market and are sold without *provenance*: there is no accompanying information as to where they have been found and in what circumstances; nor do they carry information about their previous ownership history.[9] Nevertheless, archaeologists believe that an antiquity without provenance is most likely looted. In the strong words of Kathryn Walker Tubb and Neil Brodie: "There can be little doubt that the majority of antiquities without demonstrable provenance which are now flooding the market have been looted from archaeological sites of one form or another. They are illicit and it is foolish to pretend otherwise."[10] Archaeologists further charge that looted antiquities are effectively laundered as they pass through the trading network, so they can be offered for sale legally in a reputable outlet and be purchased by a respectable consumer. The laundering is facilitated by the absence of a requirement to reveal a record of ownership history or the original findspot of an object on the market. The secrecy that typically shrouds the identities of buyers and sellers obstructs any attempt to identify a chain of ownership and trace an antiquity to its source.[11] Illegally excavated and exported, antiquities often change hands several times before dealers and auction houses sell them to museums or private collectors. Any details of the objects' illegal origin are erased or lost in the process: they cannot be recognized as looted.[12]

Trade practitioners—antiquities dealers and auctioneers—vehemently dispute these charges. They repudiate the concept of "guilty until proven innocent"—the assumption that unprovenanced antiquities are looted—and maintain that "thousands of items have lost their provenance for perfectly good reasons."[13] Some antiquities came on the market ages ago, and their provenance was lost over time. War, migration, and sheer indifference have also resulted in loss of provenance.[14] Trade practitioners further argue that many objects come from old collections or are the product of chance finds, discovered in the course of construction projects or agricultural activity.[15]

Archaeologists assign much blame to the dealers and their no-questions-asked approach: the willful neglect to inquire about provenance and failure to verify that the antiquities traded have been legally excavated and exported. Yet archaeologists believe that the ultimate responsibility lies with the end-consumers, whose appetite for antiquities drives the market and fuels the looting that supplies it. Indiscriminate acquisition of unprovenanced antiquities by museums and private collectors is, in the archaeologists' view, the root and ultimate cause of looting: "[N]o informed, rational person can deny that market demand, and therefore collecting is directly responsible for the looting of the world's cultural heritage."[16] By collecting unprovenanced objects, museums and private collectors provide funds "which both reward the looters and underwrite their further depredations."[17] More specifically, archaeologists consider art museums in the United States to be primary culprits in creating demand for looted antiquities. The number of American art museums that collect archaeological material increased steadily throughout the 20th century, and so did the size of their collections. The rising demand of museums met with a diminishing supply of legitimate objects, as more and more countries took measures to prevent the flow of antiquities abroad. As a result, museums seeking to enlarge their collections had to acquire unprovenanced antiquities.[18] Indeed, museums received many such unprovenanced antiquities as gifts or bequests from collectors. Yet archaeologists still consider museums—the final repositories of private collections—as the bearers of ultimate responsibility for the unethical standards of indiscriminate acquisition prevailing in the market and for the looting that results from them.[19]

While consumers—dealers, museums, and private collectors—bear much of the culpability for looting, the blame also rests with the source countries from which the antiquities originate. The chain of illicit trade begins with the looters. Those may be professional bandits, such as the *tombaroli*—Italy's tomb raiders. But oftentimes looters are "subsistence diggers": poor locals who plunder antiquities to supplement their paltry income, in the absence of viable economic alternatives.[20] The compensation these looters receive is, in fact, very modest. Usually, more than 98 percent of an antiquity's final sale price ends up in the hands of middlemen.[21] Moreover, as antiquities are a finite resource, looting is not economically sustainable. Nevertheless, it has persisted and provided much needed income not only to individuals, but to whole communities.[22]

In most archaeologically rich countries, the law prohibits the unauthorized excavation and export of antiquities. In fact, many countries have na-
tionalized their entire archaeological heritage through laws that vest
ownership of archaeology in the state.[23] National ownership is usually accompanied by a stringent export control regime that often amounts to a
near-absolute ban on the export of antiquities. Even when private ownership of antiquities is allowed, their export, in most cases, is highly circumscribed.[24] Yet law-enforcement authorities have overwhelmingly failed to
enforce the laws that protect the archaeological heritage; plunder takes
place as if the law did not exist. The problem often lies in inadequate bureaucratic and law-enforcement capacities. Guarding archaeological sites
and monuments is a demanding task in terms of funds and personnel. A
serious effort to curb looting also requires action by the police, customs,
and border officials. Yet law-enforcement agencies in developing countries
are often understaffed and underfinanced. Moreover, protecting the archaeological heritage ranks low on their priorities.[25] The result is a systematic failure to curb the looting and outflow of antiquities. Another cause of
this failure is corruption. In exchange for a bribe, poorly paid officials may
be willing to turn a blind eye to the illegal excavation and export of antiquities. Allowing the plunder of cultural heritage may also be an easy way
for the authorities to provide income to poor peasants, whereas anti-looting
efforts could cause social unrest.

The looter is the first link in the chain. Looted antiquities then pass on
to regional dealers and metropolitan dealers. At this stage, organized
criminal networks are involved, given the need for movement on a regular basis of illegally obtained objects. The antiquities are then smuggled
out of the source countries in various ways, including tourist luggage,
container ships, and even diplomatic pouches. They typically make their
way to transit countries[26] that perform a legitimate function as markets,
but also facilitate the concealment of the antiquities' real identity. The
change of hands makes it difficult to establish where the items came from
and how long they have been in circulation. Loose regulation of the movement of antiquities is the key to the laundering function of transit countries. These countries have traditionally exhibited little concern about the
way archaeological material reaches their jurisdiction. They have easily
allowed the legal export of antiquities that had been illegally removed
from the source countries. Once the antiquity has passed through a transit country, where it receives an export license, it then enters the marketplace as a legitimate object to be openly sold by dealers and legitimately
purchased by museums and private collectors.[27] Note that the following
analysis employs the term "market countries" to mean both transit markets, such as Britain and Switzerland, and destination markets, such as
the United States and Japan.

## The International Political Conflict over Antiquities Regulation

The theoretical framework has highlighted the role of international regulation in shifting the burden of control from the countries that bear illicit trade's externalities to the countries that generate those externalities. This is precisely the purpose of international antiquities regulation. Source countries fail to enforce their own controls and cannot curb the illegal excavation and export of antiquities; through international regulation, they attempt to induce market countries to control the inflow of antiquities. By restraining market countries' demand—the driver of looting—source countries seek to reverse the outflow of antiquities and retain them. If market countries establish import controls and seize looted antiquities at points of entry, those antiquities may be returned and incentives for further looting should decline. Import control in market countries would thus compensate for the weakness of export control in source countries.

As the following analysis will demonstrate, the international political conflict over antiquities unfolded along lines consistent with the theoretical expectations. The push for regulation came from antiquities-rich countries attempting to curb archaeological looting and its negative externalities. By contrast, market countries showed little enthusiasm for international regulation that would require them to control imports in order to tackle other countries' problem. Market countries were reluctant to assume a law-enforcement burden and limit consumers' acquisition and enjoyment of antiquities while source countries reaped the benefits. The conflicting preferences of market countries and source countries and the absence of shared interest resulted in vehement disagreements not only over the extent and design of regulation, but over its desirability in the first place.

### The 1970 UNESCO Convention

The 1970 UNESCO Convention—the most important international instrument regulating the antiquities trade[28]—was not the first attempt to set rules for the trade in cultural material. The League of Nations made a failed effort to control the movement of cultural objects, inspired by the considerable destruction of cultural property during World War I and an increasing illegal trade.[29] The League's International Museums Office (IMO, or OIM) prepared a draft Convention on the Repatriation of Objects of Artistic, Historical or Scientific Interest, Which Have Been Lost, Stolen or Unlawfully Alienated or Exported. The draft was submitted to the member states of the League in 1933 and met with objections from three major market-countries:

Britain, the United States, and the Netherlands. The OIM continued its attempts to draft a convention that would win the approval of market countries, but the outbreak of World War II terminated the project.[30]

Cooperation against the illicit antiquities trade reappeared on the international agenda in the 1960s. The spread of higher education had heightened the demand for cultural and artistic experiences; the number of museums and private collectors had been growing. With booming demand, rising prices, and an expanding world market, looting reached unprecedented levels. Furthermore, decolonization sharply increased the number of sovereign countries wishing to curb the trade. As long as plunder took place in colonial territories, local populations could do little to protest. With independence and membership in international organizations, postcolonial governments could initiate international action against looting.[31] Preservation of the cultural heritage was of much concern in a postcolonial environment, which was often rife with nationalist sentiments and where antiquities were deemed a part of the new nation's identity.

Mexico and Peru—two countries that had suffered large-scale archaeological plunder—brought up the illicit trade in cultural property during the 11th General Conference of UNESCO in 1960.[32] In response to their appeal for an international convention, the General Conference authorized the director-general of UNESCO to issue "a report on appropriate means of prohibiting the illicit export, import and sale of cultural property, including the possibility of preparing an international instrument on this subject."[33] That report concluded that a multilateral convention was desirable, yet premature: "[A]n international convention creating strict legal obligations identical for a large group of States would stand very little chance in the present circumstances, of being ratified by States in considerable numbers."[34] This grim assessment relied on several factors, including the failed attempts of the League of Nations to establish a convention and post-World War II consultations indicating that "States were not prepared to bind themselves by an international convention in a field of this kind."[35] The report thus proposed issuing a nonlegally binding recommendation that would be acceptable both to source countries "which were determined to take action to prevent illicit exports" and to market countries "which were less whole-hearted about the matter."[36]

In that spirit, the 12th General Conference resolved in 1962 that while an international convention would be more effective, it was advisable to adopt a recommendation first: such a recommendation would improve the international moral climate and foster international solidarity.[37] In 1963 UNESCO circulated a draft recommendation among member states. Among other provisions, the draft recommendation stipulated that "[a]ll imports of cultural property from another State should be subject to control."[38] The responses clearly reflected the expected source countries-market countries cleavage. Source countries were largely content with the draft. Syria, for example, emphasized that the recommendation should be a steppingstone to a legally binding convention:

> Syria has been, and still is, the victim of these thefts; and it is no satisfaction to her to see the pick of her cultural heritage being taken out of the country in defiance of her laws and regulations, just to stock foreign museums illicitly. What we need at this stage of our history is surely an international convention to prohibit and prevent the export, import and illicit sale of cultural property. If this is unfortunately impossible at present, Unesco, pending the adoption of such a convention, ought to prepare a viable and effective recommendation which will denounce these thefts at the international level and even put them down, and herald the day when every country will be in full and undisturbed possession of its own heritage.[39]

By contrast, the draft recommendation drew sharp criticism from market countries. Britain, for example, identified "insuperable practical difficulties in defining and physically distinguishing 'cultural property' for the purposes of an effective import or export control"; it also maintained that "[t]he burden of control should not be shifted to the importing countries."[40] Similarly, Switzerland and the United States questioned the need for and utility of international regulation. Switzerland asserted that source countries were responsible for preventing undesirable export. If those countries "are not able to prevent such exports, which they consider undesirable, by measures prompted by their own domestic legislation, it is not easy to see how international co-operation . . . can be any more successful in removing the main difficulties which are inherent in this very intricate problem."[41] The United States argued that the draft recommendation was "unworkable" and expressed skepticism "regarding the practicability of controlling illicit traffic in cultural property at the international level." The U.S. view was "that the problem of illicit traffic of cultural property cannot best be solved through an international agreement." Rather, the onus was on source countries "to control the export from their territory of materials which they believe should be retained."[42]

The Recommendation on the Means of Prohibiting and Preventing the Illicit Export, Import and Transfer of Ownership of Cultural Property was adopted by the 13th General Conference of UNESCO in 1964. Source countries, however, persisted in their pursuit of a legally binding convention. A 1968 preliminary study by UNESCO brought them closer to this goal, concluding that "[t]he time seems to have come to envisage the drawing up of an international convention . . . [which] would be likely to gain the approval of a considerable number of Member States."[43] In August 1969 UNESCO submitted a preliminary draft convention to member states for comment.[44] As expected, the draft convention elicited favorable responses from source countries. Cambodia, for example, noted that

[f]or a long time it has ardently desired the conclusion of an international Convention on means to prohibit and prevent the illicit import, export and transfer of ownership of cultural property, which has always been to the detriment of the country and its artistic and archaeological heritage. For this reason, the Royal Government of Cambodia unreservedly approves the introduction of such a Convention. The competent authorities have examined the preliminary draft item by item and consider it perfectly adapted to cover all aspects of the problem with which they are concerned.[45]

Market countries, by contrast, exhibited a far less positive attitude and heavily criticized what they perceived as an unjustified shifting of the burden. Japan, for instance, asked for a reexamination of the draft convention to make it acceptable to a large number of countries and cautioned against "the hasty adoption of the convention."[46] Sweden maintained that "a control system of such a complicated and expensive nature as the one proposed in the present version cannot be accepted by the Swedish authorities."[47] West Germany held that "essential parts of the Preliminary Draft Convention are not feasible."[48] Britain asserted that it "could not adhere to a Convention on the lines of the present draft, which conflicts at so many points with the well-established principles on which the subject is dealt with in this country."[49] The United States argued that the international efforts should not only seek to suppress the illicit trade, but also promote legitimate "international movement, exhibit, and study of artifacts and art objects of cultural importance." The United States further argued that international cooperation must be realistic and should not displace the primary responsibility of source countries.[50] Specifically, the United States expressed little appetite for establishing import controls to enforce foreign countries' sweeping export controls:

[T]he Preliminary Draft Convention would require each party to give effect through its own customs laws to whatever export controls may be imposed by any other party. . . . Every State has the right to establish whatever export controls it may choose, but it is difficult to expect a State to give effect through its legislation and administrative processes to foreign legislation that may not take into account in any respect the interests of that State or of the international community. It is one thing to seek international co-operation for the recovery and return of stolen art treasures of national importance, or to stem a flood of exports that threatens seriously to damage the cultural heritage of a people. It is quite another thing to expect States to enforce foreign laws that could lead to the elimination of all significant international movement of art objects of cultural importance and thus diminish the cultural experience of all peoples. The United States does not rule out appropriate international co-operation in the enforcement of reasonable regulations controlling the export of cultural property in cases of demonstrated gravity. However, the United States would be reluctant to agree in advance to undertake this responsibility for any and all export control systems of unknown character and scope.[51]

A related U.S. concern was that import controls would entail "the investment of substantial resources in the customs service. Even with the addition of the necessary trained personnel, the examination of personal baggage and of freight for all of the hundreds or thousands of items that might be classified as cultural property . . . would represent a considerable administrative burden." In light of the difficulties presented by the draft convention, the United States concluded that "consideration should be given to alternative arrangements for international co-operation," such as a statement of principles or cooperative measures on a bilateral or regional basis.[52]

Market countries' hostility to the idea of international antiquities regulation translated into action or, more precisely, inaction. Britain and Switzerland—two major market-countries—did not even attend the meeting of governmental experts that negotiated the final text of the convention in Paris in April 1970. Both countries did not bear the primary externalities of the illicit antiquities trade and were not particularly concerned about secondary externalities—archaeological damage in foreign countries. They did, however, want to avoid a bureaucratic burden and to protect their art markets, and therefore adopted an uncompromising anti-regulation position. Britain and Switzerland—as well as other market countries that did attend the negotiations—ultimately declined to ratify the convention after its adoption by the 16th General Conference of UNESCO in November 1970. Nonratifying countries cited incompatibility of the convention with national legislation (Denmark and the Netherlands); federalism (Switzerland); or the European Community's Treaty of Rome (France and West Germany).[53] Other concerns were the large administrative costs that the convention entailed and the implications of its ratification for the art market. France expressed the fear that strengthening customs control might result in border delays.[54] The Netherlands maintained that import "checks by customs officials have appeared impractical, if not impracticable. . . . In fact, examining shipments on such a large scale as to allow for a deterring effect is regarded neither practically possible nor desirable, because it would considerably hamper the flows of trade."[55] Switzerland worried about the need for a "complicated and costly administrative apparatus."[56] Britain asserted that import controls "would not be practicable" and "would be difficult to operate." Rather, the responsibility for controlling cultural treasures could be most effectively exercised by the source countries.[57] West Germany argued that the convention "may create considerable uncertainty for all persons concerned in trading in works of art" and that "the practical implementation of the

Convention with regard to the maintenance of inventories, frontier controls, customs investigation, accounting and control of the art trade would require the establishment of an administrative machinery of untenable proportions." Germany's view was that "no country with a liberal legal system is likely, on account of legal and practical difficulties, to be able to implement the Convention."[58]

Source countries, by contrast, were quick to join the UNESCO Convention. Mexico, Egypt, and Cambodia, for example, did so within less than three years of the convention's 1970 adoption. Yet by their own means, and in the absence of market countries' cooperation, source countries could not curb the plunder and illegal outflow of antiquities. In 1983 a report prepared for UNESCO thus concluded: "[I]t will have to be accepted that a very large amount of cultural material will be illicitly exported."[59] Given that "exporting countries are in many (if not most) cases unable to prevent illicit export" and that "importing countries neither can, nor are they altogether willing, to do so either,"[60] the report recommended attacking the problem from a different angle: by providing a legal foundation to facilitate the return of illegally exported antiquities to the source countries and removing legal obstacles to such return, such as cross-national variation in systems of limitations. To achieve this goal, the report proposed a convention to unify the rules of private law on the protection of cultural property. The authors of the report hoped that the new convention would appeal to market countries that had declined to join the UNESCO Convention.[61] This hope proved false.

## UNIDROIT Convention on Stolen or Illegally Exported Cultural Objects

The 1970 UNESCO Convention works through public law, administrative procedures, and state-to-state action. Requests for the return of cultural objects are passed through diplomatic channels; the authorities who receive the requests then seize the objects and take the legal actions required to return them. The 1995 UNIDROIT Convention, by contrast, operates through private law. The owner of a stolen cultural object or the foreign state from which the object was illegally exported may sue the holder in the courts of the country where the object is located. That country is then obligated to provide a legal remedy for the theft or illegal export of cultural property.[62]

Following the 1983 report, UNESCO commissioned the task of establishing a convention on private-law rules for cultural property to UNIDROIT, the International Institute for the Unification of Private Law. A study group established by UNIDROIT in 1988 drafted a convention that was subsequently revised by a committee of governmental experts. In June 1995 the draft convention came before a diplomatic conference in Rome. Government comments on the draft revealed the expected fault line: source countries versus market countries. Source countries were content with the proposed convention, which was aimed at facilitating the return of their looted antiquities. China, for example, found the draft convention "generally acceptable."[63] By contrast, Germany, a major market-country, sought to limit the planned convention:

> The Federal Republic of Germany understands the desire expressed by many countries to protect objects which are of cultural significance for the State of origin from transfer abroad by means of appropriate regulation. However, such limitations may seriously impair the legal trade in such items . . . The Federal Republic does not pursue the goal of comprehensively limiting international trade in cultural objects. The global circulation of such objects also serves to promote understanding of cultural diversity and thus also to strengthen cross-border relations between peoples and nations. Past experience has repeatedly shown that even far-reaching restrictions cannot prevent an exchange of goods that is undesirable for the State in question, but rather promote the formation of black markets. Such a development is more likely to be prevented if the duty to return is limited to objects of outstanding cultural significance.[64]

Members of the U.S. art community—dealers, museums, and collectors—warned that the draft convention would eliminate the private art market and empty American museums.[65] They foresaw an outcome that, to them, was unacceptable: the opening of American courts to claims based on violation of foreign export-controls—a reversal of the principle that foreign export-controls are generally not enforceable in the United States.[66]

Given such conflicting views, the 1995 diplomatic conference opened with little hope for the prospects of even achieving a convention. When the delegates "finally got down to the business at hand, it became clear that the little optimism that existed was overstated—it quickly became apparent that UNIDROIT was dying."[67] European market-countries pushed for various revisions that they considered vital if the convention was to win ratification. Those revisions, however, proved unacceptable to the source countries. The numerically superior source countries began winning vote after vote on key issues, heightening market countries' concern that the convention would be rejected at home. In the third and final week of the negotiations, an unofficial working group was formed, comprised of delegates from both source and market countries, to try to reach a compromise. On the final day of the conference, the market countries walked out of the meeting of the working group. Twenty-four hours after the conference was scheduled to end, a conciliation draft was achieved, and the convention was ultimately adopted by the conference.[68] The 1995 UNIDROIT Convention, however, has gained few ratifications (only 32 as of December 2011). No major market-country—including the United States, Britain, and Switzerland—has been among the ratifiers. Given the unpopularity of the UNIDROIT Convention, the UNESCO Convention has remained the principal international agreement on antiquities.

## *The International Political Conflict over Antiquities: Conclusions*

The theoretical framework has identified the large variation in government preferences and absence of shared interest as obstacles to cooperation against illicit trade. This indeed has been the case with the UNESCO and UNIDROIT Conventions. Source countries—the "victims" of the illicit antiquities trade—have supported these international regulatory agreements, which sought to help them curb looting by shifting the burden of control to market countries. Market countries—the "perpetrators"—have opposed the shifting of the burden on practical and principled grounds: the high administrative costs of import controls and their complexity, questionable effectiveness, and disruptive effect on trade, as well as the cultural value inherent in free movement of antiquities. Underlying these objections was the fundamental fact that international regulation has asked market countries to compromise the interests of their own art markets and incur bureaucratic costs *to the benefit of foreign countries*. Market countries have thus been reluctant to shoulder the burden of protecting the archaeological heritage.

Consistent with the theoretical framework, the large variation in preferences, coupled with a power distribution that favors market countries, has resulted in fairly weak international regulation. Most importantly, the UNESCO Convention lacks significant mechanisms for monitoring or enforcement. It merely asks states to report on implementation and gives UNESCO the authority to make implementation proposals. The UNESCO Convention has also suffered from limited membership. For three decades following its establishment, market countries persisted in their repudiation of an agreement that they considered inimical to their interests. The developing countries supporting the convention could do little to foster its acceptance by market countries that were superior in power. The United States, however, has been an exception. While skeptical of international antiquities regulation through much of the 1960s, the United States broke ranks with other market countries in the early 1970s and embarked on the process of ratifying and implementing the UNESCO Convention. Why did the United States join a convention that imposed costs on the American art market and law-enforcement agencies, with no apparent benefit to the United States itself? To explain this puzzle, the next section examines the domestic politics of international cooperation.

## The United States and the Efforts against the Looting of Antiquities

The late 1960s and early 1970s constituted a period of radical change in U.S. policy. The United States joined the international efforts against the plunder of archaeology, and its traditionally liberal approach to the antiquities trade gave way to the acceptance of regulation. Granted, the transformation was far from complete. The United States did not come to embrace antiquities regulation wholeheartedly and did not adopt the pro-regulation view of source countries. In fact, it established limited controls on the international movement of antiquities by implementing merely two of the UNESCO Convention's provisions. Nevertheless, the United States made a conscious choice to reverse the laissez-faire attitude that had allowed the import of looted antiquities into the country. Even the modest measures taken by the United States were significant, given its status as the world's largest art market. Moreover, the American endorsement of the UNESCO Convention contrasted sharply with the adamant refusal of other market countries to accept international regulation. Indeed, U.S. policymakers saw the shift in the American position as an exercise of moral leadership that would show the way to other antiquities-importing countries.

### *The Transformative Period: 1969–1983*

It was not self-interest that primarily motivated the American efforts against the illicit antiquities trade. U.S. policymakers did not consider the looting of American antiquities to be a major problem. Rather, they sought to help foreign countries protect their archaeological heritage. What inspired them to tackle plunder *abroad?* In the course of the 1960s, the antiquities market flourished and expanded along with the looting required to feed it. An increase in the number of collectors provided growing demand for antiquities; on the supply side, new roads and new means of transportation opened up previously inaccessible areas.[69] Yet a conscious effort was necessary in order to place looting on the national agenda. As the theoretical framework has suggested, concern about secondary externalities—the trade's negative effects on foreign countries—may be stimulated by moral entrepreneurs. Through their knowledge and expertise, these actors educate policymakers and urge them to curb illicit trade. The moral entrepreneurs advocating action on antiquities were archaeologists concerned about the plunder and loss of historical knowledge. The initial American interest in tackling looted antiquities can be attributed largely to the work of a single archaeologist: Clemency Coggins. Coggins was a doctoral student at Harvard University, specializing in pre-Columbian art and archaeology, and a research associate at Harvard's Peabody Museum. In 1969 she published an article entitled "Illicit Traffic of Pre-Columbian Antiquities" in *Art Journal*. The article opened with the following forceful words:

> In the last ten years there has been an incalculable increase in the number of monuments systematically stolen, mutilated and illicitly exported from Guatemala and Mexico in order to feed the international art market. Not since the sixteenth century has Latin America been so ruthlessly plundered.[70]

The article examined the illicit removal and export of stelae, large stone slabs carved with Mayan inscriptions and figures, erected in front of pyramids and temples. It explained how looters had been using power saws and other tools to cut the stelae into small segments and sell the pieces separately. Coggins was by no means the first archaeologist to complain about looting, yet her article raised more awareness of the problem than any previous publication and "played an important role in giving credibility to the contention that the illegal traffic in art treasures is a problem that has to be taken seriously."[71] Coggins did not expect the article to have a political impact. Her main goal was to make museums aware of the dubious source of the antiquities they had been acquiring.[72] Why, then, did the article resonate so strongly well beyond the museum community?

First, the article "was not the usual impressionistic account and denunciation of illicit pot hunting."[73] Coggins did not protest the looting of obscure objects from little-known sites, but documented the theft of acknowledged archaeological masterpieces, some registered as national monuments. Second, the article provided detailed evidence of the looting in the form of a two-page fine-print list of specific stone sculptures and reliefs stolen from Guatemala and Mexico. The list dramatized the problem and cast the breaking into pieces and sawing off of monuments in tangible terms that were difficult to ignore. Third, Coggins exposed the tragic consequences of looting. The cutting, sawing, and smashing of stelae sacrificed much of their aesthetic value and compromised their possible contribution to science and scholarship. As stelae were broken into moveable, saleable pieces, information necessary for studying them and deciphering their inscriptions, such as the original location of a stela and its placing within a site, was lost. Coggins thus demonstrated that archaeological looting was much more than ordinary theft. It destroyed historical treasures and the knowledge they carried. Fourth, and most importantly, Coggins pointed to American museums as the primary beneficiaries of looting, since the stolen and mutilated archaeological remains came to rest in their collections. Eminent institutions such as the Cleveland Museum of Art, the Houston Museum of Fine Arts, and the

Minneapolis Institute of Arts were implicated, along with dealers, private collectors, and European museums.[74] Identifying plundered pieces in respectable museums brought an end to their pretense of having no involvement with the trade in looted antiquities. "The cat was thus out of the bag."[75]

In her following publications in the early 1970s, Coggins tried to reach a broader audience, outside the scholarly and museum communities.[76] With the establishment of the UNESCO Convention in 1970, looted antiquities became a political issue and educating policymakers was essential. In articles published in *Smithsonian* and *Science*,[77] Coggins reiterated the charge against the U.S. art world in more emphatic terms, asserting that archaeological "plunder has been financed by the international art market, by collectors and by most museums." She explained the motivations of the various actors: the looter who seeks money with which to buy food; the art dealer who "has tempted the digger to destroy a part of his own past in order to offer" antiquities for sale, while at the same time whetting the appetite of collectors for those antiquities and marketing them as a wise investment; collectors who see antiquities as beautiful objects, symbols of their own wealth, and ultimately—once donated to a museum—as tax deductions; and American museums, whose educational goals had resulted, perversely, in "omnivorous" conduct and willingness to acquire looted material. Coggins maintained that a recklessly excavated antiquity loses its historical meaning and can only be "beautiful but dumb."[78]

Coggins is an ideal example of a moral entrepreneur using her expertise to sensitize policymakers and educate them about the harmful effects of illicit trade. Yet the public atmosphere also stimulated policymakers' concern about secondary externalities, as highly publicized scandals revealed the questionable conduct of museums and collectors and their involvement with stolen art. One notable scandal involved the Metropolitan Museum of Art's 1972 acquisition of a Greek vase known as the Euphronios Krater. The museum was vague about the object's origin. The official story was that the vase had been in a private family collection since circa World War I and that the owner's identity could not be revealed. In February 1973, however, *The New York Times* published a completely different account, charging that the vase had been looted from a tomb in Italy in 1971. Italian authorities made a similar charge shortly thereafter. The Metropolitan, however, defended its acquisition and vehemently denied the looting story.[79] Only in 2008 did the Metropolitan return the vase to Italy.[80] Another scandal erupted after the Boston Museum of Fine Arts announced a sensational acquisition of an unknown portrait by Raphael in December 1969. According to the museum, the portrait had been purchased from an old European private collection in Switzerland. Italian authorities, however, revealed that the portrait had been secretly removed from Italy, where the museum had purchased it. The seller was a criminally convicted dealer who had been barred from art dealing. Moreover, U.S. Customs discovered that the museum had brought the portrait into the United States without declaring it. The painting was seized by Customs and returned to Italy.[81] Yet another scandal followed the 1972 purchase by a California collector of an important Hindu sculpture that had been stolen from a temple in India. Under pressure from the Indian government, the Metropolitan canceled a planned exhibition of the sculpture, and India took legal action to recover possession.[82]

These scandals and others received wide media coverage, triggering further journalistic investigations into looting and the role played by the U.S. art market.[83] Of particular importance was the account by Karl Meyer in several *New Yorker* articles and in his 1973 book *The Plundered Past*. The book was a comprehensive exposé of the American art world and its involvement in "one of the world's sadder problems, the destruction and theft of the remains of the human past."[84] According to Meyer, "no one who makes even a cursory inquiry can doubt that the great majority of antiquities offered for sale is indeed smuggled goods."[85] Coggins's work, the public scandals, and the journalistic accounts placed looted antiquities on the national agenda and paved the way for the introduction of antiquities regulation.

## Regulatory Precursors: the U.S.-Mexico Treaty and the Pre-Columbian Act

President Lyndon Johnson and Mexican President Gustavo Díaz Ordaz discussed the illicit antiquities trade during their meeting in October 1967. It was agreed to explore possible means of controlling the unauthorized movement of antiquities between Mexico and the United States.[86] Cooperation began in earnest in May 1969, when Mexico sought to establish an issue linkage. The Mexican government requested U.S. assistance in the protection of its archaeological heritage in exchange for continued Mexican cooperation in the recovery and return of stolen American cars.[87] The Mexican request introduced Mark Feldman, then assistant legal adviser for inter-American affairs at the State Department, to the problem of looted antiquities. Feldman would later negotiate the UNESCO Convention and design the U.S. legislation implementing it.

Maintaining cooperation in the return of stolen cars was only one reason to meet the Mexican request and extend cooperation on antiquities. The other reason was genuine interest in helping Mexico conserve its archaeological heritage. As Feldman recalls:

> The issue was first brought to my attention by the Mexican government. When we looked into it, I was shocked at the extent to which pillage of archaeological sites in Mexico and Guatemala threatened both the sites

themselves and the record of human civilization, and I became persuaded that international art markets, including the U.S. market, were part of the problem. Heretofore, the U.S. government had resisted the concept of providing legal mechanisms in this country to enforce foreign legislation, but I thought it important to do something. My clients in the State Department agreed, and [we undertook] a series of measures intended to balance the national interest in cultural exchange with the national interest in preserving the world's cultural heritage.[88]

Feldman was influenced by the "pretty dramatic testimony of the extent of the destruction" provided by Clemency Coggins, archaeologist Ian Graham (in his photographs of damaged Mayan ruins), and journalist Karl Meyer. Another influence was the media scandals involving museums, which made looted antiquities an issue of public attention.[89] All these led Feldman to realize that the United States should reverse its liberal policy and take measures to control the antiquities trade. After receiving a first-hand impression of the problem in several trips to Mexico, he negotiated a bilateral treaty on the recovery and return of stolen archaeological material.[90] Signed in July 1970, the treaty was quickly ratified upon the strong recommendation of the Senate Foreign Relations Committee, whose report expressed concern about looting and cited Coggins's 1969 article.[91] Although antiquities dealers were skeptical of this first attempt at regulating the trade, the State Department ultimately received their support for what was a very limited undertaking.[92] Yet despite its narrow scope and bilateral nature, the treaty broke new ground by signaling American interest in fighting archaeological plunder and, for the first time, establishing a measure of control, even if circumscribed, over the movement of antiquities into the United States.

In October 1972 Congress enacted a more comprehensive unilateral regulatory measure: the Regulation of Importation of Pre-Columbian Monumental or Architectural Sculpture or Murals. This statute responded to the growing demands to protect the pre-Columbian heritage in countries beyond Mexico, especially Guatemala. The key to the statute's successful passage was a consultative mechanism convened in 1969, at the State Department's request, under the auspices of the American Society of International Law: the Panel on the International Movement of National Art Treasures (hereafter the ASIL Panel).[93] The 22 members of the panel represented the dealers, the museums, the collectors, the archaeological community, and the State Department; international law experts were also included. Through this panel, the State Department sought to reach a consensus among all relevant stakeholders and, in particular, obtain the crucial support of the dealers for the introduction of regulatory measures. As Mark Feldman observes: "If we had not had the private sector's support from that panel, we would not have gotten anywhere with this program."[94]

Apparently, the dealers saw the handwriting on the wall and recognized that the mounting concern about looting could result in far-reaching regulation. They therefore agreed to a specific measure limited to the vulnerable pre-Columbian market, in the hope of deflating the issue and halting the regulatory momentum. Following the recommendation of the ASIL Panel, the 1972 statute prohibited the import into the United States of pre-Columbian monumental art that had been illegally exported from the (Latin American) countries of origin. This statute, alongside the bilateral treaty with Mexico, was the initial round in the domestic debate over antiquities. These two early episodes foreshadowed the much more intense controversy over the UNESCO Convention and established the contours of the political battle in years to come: support for regulation from the archaeological community; opposition from the trade (that is, the dealers); and in the middle, the State Department—pushing for regulation, yet mindful of the need to secure the trade's approval.

## The United States and the 1970 UNESCO Convention

For most of the 1960s the United States was skeptical of UNESCO's efforts to regulate the antiquities trade. Following its traditionally liberal approach to the movement of cultural property, the U.S. government sought to encourage, rather than limit, the international exchange of antiquities. As late as 1968, the American view was that "further study was necessary before a practicable international convention could be developed."[95] In terms of the theoretical framework, the U.S. government was at that stage an anti-regulation government, mindful of the free-trade interests of American consumers of antiquities and indifferent to the trade's externalities borne by source countries. Yet in the late 1960s and early 1970s, accounts of archaeological destruction and public scandals engendered concern about looting abroad. At that point, the U.S. government became cross-pressured, looking to strike a balance between the interests of the U.S. art market and those of foreign countries facing plunder. The result was a more favorable approach to international regulation. Given the cross-pressures, however, the United States supported only modest regulation and rejected the draft convention prepared by the UNESCO secretariat as a basis for the 1970 negotiations (hereafter the Secretariat Draft). The United States found the Secretariat Draft "unacceptable," as it sought to establish a "blank check system of import controls" and other "sweeping obligations."[96] While acknowledging that international cooperation against the illicit antiquities trade was necessary, the United States insisted that the convention must not impose an impracticable administrative burden or create obligations that governments could not discharge.[97] The primary goal of the U.S. delegation at the 1970 negotiations was therefore to establish limited commitments that would curb the plunder of antiquities without closing down the U.S. art market. The United States favored narrow import restrictions that would address sensitive items of major importance, where a link between the U.S. market and looting could be demonstrated.[98]

As an alternative to the Secretariat Draft, the State Department prepared a comprehensive draft of its own. The Secretariat Draft, however, constituted the basis for the negotiations; alternatives had to be introduced piecemeal as amendments to specific provisions. Certain source countries like Ghana and Iraq, joined by the Communist countries, favored tight international control and resisted the attempt to weaken the Secretariat Draft. Other countries, most notably Mexico, supported the Secretariat Draft while acknowledging the need to reach a compromise document that the United States would accept.[99] The purpose of the convention was to constrain market countries and their demand for antiquities. If rejected by the largest market country—the United States—the convention would have lost much of its value.

Through joint work with other delegations—especially those of Mexico, France, and West Germany—the United States ultimately managed to dilute the Secretariat Draft. Most important was the deletion of the provision requiring states to prohibit the import of any item of cultural property not accompanied by an export certificate. Other provisions were modified through language allowing each state to determine what measures are appropriate for it or by limiting obligations to measures consistent with states' existing legislation.[100] According to Paul Bator, a member of the American delegation to the negotiations, "[t]he text of the UNESCO Convention was the product of U.S. leadership in persuading a majority of UNESCO to adopt a moderate and compromise position. The position of the Soviet bloc countries and many third-world countries, which would have effectively ended all international trade in cultural objects, was rejected."[101] Yet while the United States fashioned a convention suited to its preference for limited regulation, its support for even modest international control was revolutionary. For the first time, a major market-country recognized a certain responsibility for archaeological looting and expressed willingness to share the burden of addressing this problem. "The big change was the recognition that the U.S. art markets were contributing in a significant way to this looting."[102]

This recognition was also manifested in the State Department report that accompanied the submission of the UNESCO Convention to the Senate for ratification in February 1972. The report did identify several American self-interests in ratification: improving U.S. relations with foreign countries—relations that had experienced tensions due to "the appearance of important art treasures of suspicious origin in the United States"; creating a climate more conducive to the work of American archaeologists abroad; and allaying the anxieties of source countries and encouraging them to relax their restrictions on the export of antiquities. Yet the State Department report indicated that the principal motivation for supporting the convention was an authentic, morally inspired concern about the secondary externalities of the illicit antiquities trade: the depredation, mutilation, and robbing of archaeological sites abroad, intended to feed a thriving international art market. The United States was "sympathetic to this effort to help other countries stem the illegal outflow of their national art treasures" and had an "honest desire to deal with the problem."[103] Throughout the ensuing debate over the convention, the State Department maintained that the United States had a "moral obligation to act," even by going it alone, and that the previous "U.S. position was no longer viable in the face of increasing international consciousness of the importance of archaeological objects." Since "[t]he U.S. art market is a major consumer of pillaged treasures," "the United States has a responsibility to put its own house in order to the extent that the American art market is a major, if not the single most important, incentive for this despoliation."[104] Furthermore, in the State Department's view, the UNESCO Convention contained a "realistic allocation of burdens" between source and market countries.[105]

The State Department report identified Articles 7(b) and 9 as the convention's main operative provisions.[106] Article 7(b)(i) requires states to prohibit the import of cultural property *stolen from a museum, public monument, or similar institution* in a state party to the convention, provided that such property is documented in the inventory of that institution. This prohibition is limited to a small subset of objects—those stolen from an institution where they were inventoried—and excludes the vast majority of looted antiquities, which have been illegally excavated and smuggled and do not appear in any inventory. Article 9 addresses situations in which a state party finds its cultural heritage "in jeopardy from pillage." In those circumstances, other states parties are required to participate in a concerted international effort to carry out necessary measures, including export and import control. Singling out these two provisions reflected the American view that "only a small fraction of the Convention was intended to have serious operative consequences; the rest has only rhetorical existence."[107] Articles 7(b) and 9, both originally from the State Department's alternative draft, are thus "the heart of the Convention and contain its major substantive provisions."[108] This interpretation, however, is by no means the only one possible; the rest of the convention is "empty only if one chooses to make it so."[109] The narrow reading espoused by the United States reflected its mixed motivations that yielded a preference for modest international regulation.

Upon the favorable recommendation of the Foreign Relations Committee, the Senate gave its advice and consent to ratification by a vote of 79 to 0 on August 11, 1972, subject to one reservation and six understandings. Those were established together with the State Department and significantly limited the application of the UNESCO Convention in the United States.[110] The instrument of ratification, however, was to be deposited after the passage of the legislation implementing the convention. Due to the prolonged debate over implementation, the United States joined the convention officially only in 1983.

## The Battle over the UNESCO Convention's Implementation

The State Department was well aware of the need to gain the support of the relevant stakeholders, especially the dealers, for the convention's implementation. The ASIL Panel was the vehicle used to obtain initial support. In the run-up to the 1970 negotiations of the convention, the panel studied the drafts circulated by UNESCO; the sharp U.S. criticism of these drafts was influenced by the panel's advice. Yet in April 1970, immediately before the negotiations in Paris, the panel recommended to the secretary of state that the United States enact legislation to prevent the import of illegally exported antiquities, while at the same time working with other countries to expand legitimate art exchanges. A lawyers subcommittee of the ASIL Panel considered the final text of the convention and recommended its approval by the United States, subject to certain reservations and understandings.[111] Throughout the legislative process, the State Department continued to consult extensively with the relevant constituencies, seeking to gain support for the implementing legislation and reach a consensus.[112] The legislation was originally proposed to Congress in 1973. The State Department believed that its proposal protected all the relevant interests and conformed to the understandings with the dealers. But the consensus quickly dissipated. The dealers, initially on board, soon began to voice concerns and skepticism about the proposed legislation, which, they claimed, far exceeded the restrictions that the ASIL Panel had originally foreseen and "would tend to remove the United States from the flourishing international art market."[113] The dealers' vigorous opposition managed to delay congressional action, and the State Department thus revised its original legislative proposal and resubmitted it in 1975—the first of multiple revisions and resubmissions.

Consistent with the American reading of the convention, the proposed legislation focused on implementing Articles 7(b) and 9. Moreover, the convention's Article 9 did not require further agreements for implementation. Yet the proposed legislation required the conclusion of bilateral agreements between the United States and source countries as a prerequisite for the imposition of import controls, thereby creating a hurdle for cooperation. When import controls are established, antiquities from the relevant country may be imported into the United States only if accompanied by documentation certifying that their export was legal; antiquities lacking such documentation are confiscated by customs. U.S. import controls thus enforce foreign export-controls.

The following analysis examines the main contenders in the political debate over the implementing legislation (hereafter the implementation debate): the archaeologists, the dealers, and the museums. I also examine the opposite attitudes of the House of Representatives and the Senate toward the UNESCO Convention's implementation.

### Archaeologists

The theoretical framework has suggested that support for international regulation should come from moral entrepreneurs seeking to curb illicit trade that they consider harmful. The advocacy of the U.S. archaeological community for the UNESCO Convention's implementation conforms to this expectation. As early as December 1970, the Archaeological Institute of America (AIA), a major archaeological association, expressed wholehearted support for the convention and urged its earliest possible ratification.[114] Throughout the implementation debate, from 1976 onward, professional archaeological organizations[115] and individual archaeologists were the most ardent supporters of the proposed legislation: they expressed alarm over the attempts to weaken it and delay its passage. In their statements before Congress, the archaeologists argued that American dealers and collectors sponsored the looting and destruction of archaeological sites in poor countries worldwide; the result was a depletion of those countries' national heritage as well as loss of tourism income. Implementation of the convention, in the archaeologists' view, was "an important first step toward redressing a cultural and economic drain the United States has long imposed on many of these countries." Yet the archaeologists argued that action against looting would not benefit foreign countries alone: it was in the interest of mankind, since antiquities are a vanishing resource that is a part of the *world's* cultural heritage. Furthermore, implementation of the convention would curb the loss of historical knowledge that resulted from the looting—looting fueled by American demand for antiquities.[116]

The archaeologists also tried to appeal to those unmoved by the damage to archaeology. They argued that "the image of the United States and the question of our good faith in cultural relations are at stake. . . . This is a matter of great importance not only to professionals concerned with preservation of cultural heritage."[117] Another line of argument attempted to undermine the legitimacy of the dealers' and collectors' opposition to the bill. The archaeologists portrayed the dealers as a small, well-financed, and powerful special interest group "protecting the continued financial profit of a few individuals." They characterized private collectors as interested in antiquities for "private delight," for investment purposes, or out of "a keen appreciation of the tax benefits that come the way of donors to museums."[118] By contrast, the archaeologists presented themselves as a large constituency—far outnumbering the dealers—that is motivated not by narrow self-interest, but by the desire to protect the archaeological heritage and promote scientific knowledge. The archaeologists further contrasted their own advocacy efforts with the dealers' use of professional lobbyists.[119]

The archaeologists also rebutted the arguments made by the legislation's opponents. They repudiated the argument that source countries did not protect their own antiquities and that these antiquities were better off in the United States, where they would be cared for, enjoyed, and studied. According to the archaeologists, such a paternalistic argument reflected an imperialist attitude and was more at home in 19th century England than in 20th century America.[120] To the argument that since the context had already been destroyed we might as well buy the looted objects once they are out of the ground, the archaeologists retorted:

> [S]uch an argument overlooks the fact that the purchase is what finances the thievery, the smuggling, the destruction. The argument itself, in fact, must give encouragement to those prepared to plunder ancient sites, for they know that if they can just get the material out of the ground and out of the country, there are people in America and other countries ready to buy.[121]

The archaeologists also repudiated the dealers' argument concerning the diversion of the trade to other market countries if the United States alone implemented the convention. Arguing that "if we Americans do not buy the objects, the Japanese, or Germans, or others will buy them" was irrelevant and cynical, the archaeologists maintained, and it ignored the ethical considerations involved. "Somewhere, sometime, somebody ought to say stop. Just because everybody else is doing it, . . . because the materials are still going to go to other countries, does not mean that we might as well throw up our hands and join in the crowds." It would be "shameful to avoid unilateral action simply because it might remain unilateral. . . . Someone must take the first big step. . . . the U.S. [should] be the one."[122]

The archaeologists' response to the argument concerning the right of Americans to enjoy and own antiquities was that there was no "right" to purchase stolen goods and that "wealth and a desire . . . of some Americans to own ancient art objects [are not] a proper substitute for the sovereign rights of other nations." To the claim that source countries themselves were to blame for not protecting their own cultural heritage, the archaeologists' response was that "few of these nations can afford the great expense involved in guarding all their sites; and the logistical problem is over-whelming. Moreover, it is intolerable for the United States to tell these nations that if they do not—or cannot—protect all their sites it naturally follows that we have a right to plunder them." The archaeologists also rejected the dealers' contention that the implementing legislation would end the trade in art: "[P]assage of the bill will allow the free flow of art, art honestly and honorably acquired, to continue to come to the United States."[123]

As the legislative process slowly progressed, the archaeologists protested the delays, the revisions of the implementing legislation to meet the dealers' demands, and the dealers' persistent pressure despite the revisions in their favor. In the archaeologists' view, the legislation had become "a highly selective, and relatively weak tool."[124] Nevertheless, they urged its passage as a necessary step toward preventing plunder and as an assertion of U.S. leadership that would motivate other market countries to follow suit.

### The Archaeologists' Methods of Advocacy

Two factors facilitated the archaeologists' organizing in support of the implementing legislation. First, as the destruction of archaeology threatened their ability to study the past, archaeologists had a direct professional stake in political action to stem the looting of antiquities. Second, professional archaeological organizations provided an institutional foundation for the advocacy efforts.

In oral and written statements and in letters to individual members of Congress, the archaeologists sought to convey the magnitude of archaeological devastation for which the U.S. art market bore some responsibility. For this purpose, they used verbal descriptions as well as photographs of looted sites—photographs that vividly demonstrated "the mindless breakage, widespread trenching, and more sophisticated sawing techniques of looters."[125] The statements and letters also attempted to generate urgency, as Congress was dragging its feet on the legislation. Clemency Coggins, who led the advocacy efforts on behalf of the AIA, expressed urgency in a letter to Senator Abraham Ribicoff (D-CT), chairman of the Senate's Subcommittee on International Trade: "A decade has passed since it has become obvious that there is a crisis situation and we have no more time to hear from the proponents of the status quo—every moment that is lost brings us closer to the total loss of mankind's cultural heritage."[126] Another letter described the looting Coggins had witnessed in Guatemala, "the direct result of the years of [Congressional] inaction on this Convention."[127]

The archaeologists also held personal meetings with members of Congress to enlist their support. Coggins recalls that members of Congress were initially uninformed about the subject and open to persuasion. They were overall receptive to the archaeologists' views and came to recognize the importance of curbing archaeological plunder: "Our position was obviously motherhood and apple pie."[128] However, members of Congress who came under counter-pressure from the dealers ultimately gave their support to the latter. Whereas the dealers were represented by a Washington, D.C. law firm, the archaeologists did not have a permanent presence in Washington, and this hindered their advocacy efforts.

Beyond making principled arguments, the archaeologists tried to appeal to legislators as voters. In a July 1982 Public Action Alert, the Archaeological Institute of America encouraged legislation supporters to send letters to members of the Senate Finance Committee, who were considering the legislation at the time, to "demonstrate clearly that we out-number [the dealers] as voters." Supporters were asked to urge a favorable vote on the bill, oppose all weakening amendments, and—if their senator was running for reelection that year—state that they would be considering his stand on this issue come election day.[129] Writing to the Senate Finance Committee, Coggins noted that the AIA represents "10,000 professional archaeologists and lay enthusiasts . . . [It] is a grass roots organization with its membership in 81 chapters across the United States, in addition to the 50,000 subscribers to its magazine *Archaeology*."[130]

### Antiquities Dealers

The theoretical framework has suggested that consumers would tend to oppose international regulation and pursue minimal regulatory constraints. Indeed, the dealers, consumers of antiquities, staunchly opposed the UNESCO Convention that threatened their ability to buy antiquities, import them into the United States, and sell them to collectors and museums. The dealers also did not face significant obstacles to political organization. The relatively small number of dealers precluded a collective action problem; unlike some of the consumers in other illicit trades, antiquities dealers are legitimate actors whose commercial and political activity is legal; and the adverse impact of regulation on their business was sufficiently large to justify political action. The dealers thus launched a vigorous lobbying effort against the implementing legislation. While professing support for the goals of the UNESCO Convention, they opposed the legislation as "an extraordinarily ill-advised means of implementing that Convention—a means which needlessly poses severe hazards to the enjoyment of art in the United States."[131] They denounced the legislation as a "Draconian" measure that constituted an "extremely shortsighted cultural policy" and "a cultural disaster to the United States."[132]

The dealers aimed their criticism at the implementation of Article 9 of the convention through import restrictions on antiquities. They maintained that the proposed legislation gave the executive branch—effectively, the State Department—sweeping authority: a "blank check" that could be used to terminate the import into the United States of almost all antiquities. The legislation did require the executive branch, prior to the establishment of import restrictions, to reach certain factual findings. The dealers argued, however, that this would be "ritualistic and pro forma in nature."[133] Of particular concern was a presumed State Department bias in favor of foreign countries:

> The Department of State, however, is not primarily interested in fostering the enjoyment of art by citizens of the United States. On the contrary, its primary responsibility is to foster better international relations. This overriding interest of the Department makes it almost inevitable that the powers conferred upon it by the proposed legislation will be employed . . . for purposes unrelated to the preservation of art . . . Indeed, the State Department could and undoubtedly would employ its powers under the proposed legislation as a counter in diplomatic negotiations on matters far removed from the protection of art objects and archaeological sites.[134]

U.S. action on antiquities, the dealers argued, would be "a sop to any Third World nation for more immediate important goals, trade goals, such as oil or arms." The State Department would simply be "bartering and regulating the import of art in exchange for cotton quotas, military bases, help in drug legislation, and the like."[135]

The dealers also maintained that the legislation, which contained no references to multilateral cooperation, was inconsistent with the convention's Article 9 that called for a "concerted international effort" in response to plunder. In fact, at the time of the implementation debate in Congress, no major market-country but the United States had shown any intent to join the convention. By acting alone in imposing import restrictions, the dealers argued, the United States would not contribute to the saving of archaeology; it would merely divert the flow of antiquities to other market countries. "The delighted beneficiaries of the legislation will thus be the museums and collectors of Switzerland, West Germany, France and Japan" who "can hardly wait for the United States to enact such legislation," their responses ranging from "condescending disbelief to unmitigated glee." All that unilateral U.S. import restrictions would guarantee "is that the art works will go to the Tokyo museum, not the Toledo museum. The American public will have made a costly and yet totally unnecessary sacrifice in terms of the cultural enrichment of this country."[136]

In another line of attack, the dealers asserted that source countries themselves were responsible for the destruction of their own cultural heritage through construction and industrialization that disregarded archaeology and through their failure to protect archaeological sites. By implementing the UNESCO Convention, the United States would be doing for source countries what they would not do for themselves. "[M]ust we always become the enforcers and policemen in the world???" This shifting of responsibility was not only unfair, the dealers argued, but also ineffective: only local policing by source countries themselves could prevent the looting. Furthermore, museums in source countries were filled to overflowing with poorly preserved antiquities that would be "invaluable and instructive additions to the collections of many American museums."[137]

In the dealers' view, the U.S. art market was not fueling the destruction of archaeology. By endowing antiquities with high monetary value, the market, in fact, ensured their preservation.[138]

### The Dealers' Goals and Methods of Advocacy

The dealers—led by the American Association of Dealers in Ancient, Oriental, and Primitive Art—hired the Washington, D.C. law firm of Arnold & Porter to represent them and lobby on their behalf. Lawyer James Fitzpatrick, who led the lobbying effort, describes the dealers' goal in the UNESCO implementation battle as "avoiding harm"—that is, minimizing the interference with the traditional working of the art market based on the principle of free trade.[139] Specifically, the dealers pursued the following main objectives:

1. Involving experts in decision making on foreign countries' requests for import restrictions in order to give voice to the art community and to U.S. cultural interests.

2. Insulating the decision-making process from political considerations and, specifically, from the State Department's influence. The dealers had in mind the precedent of American cooperation on antiquities in exchange for Mexican cooperation in returning stolen cars. Since "the State Department is not in the business of saying no to foreign countries,"[140] the dealers sought to grant the authority over import restrictions to another agency that would make decisions on cultural—rather than diplomatic—grounds.[141]

3. Making U.S. action part of a multinational endeavor. The dealers argued that sharing the burden with dealers abroad was imperative as a matter of business competition and fairness. The same applied to museums: "If a museum in Omaha cannot import these goods, why should the Louvre and the British Museum" be able to import them?[142] They therefore sought assurances "that the United States will act cooperatively and meaningfully with other art-importing nations . . . and will not fruitlessly determine to go it alone." They proposed that the legislation make U.S. action conditional upon ratification of the UNESCO Convention and enactment of implementing legislation by a significant number of art-importing countries.[143]

In addition to these three primary goals, the dealers wished to toughen the requirements for the imposition of import restrictions. They wanted the legislation to "make clear that such an embargo is indeed an exceptional measure and is designed to meet exceptional circumstances." They also proposed that the powers of the executive branch to enter into bilateral agreements on import restrictions would expire after five years, and that the agreements themselves would be limited in time.[144] Another goal was to overturn the *McClain* decision.[145] In 1977 the U.S. government prosecuted several dealers under the National Stolen Property Act (NSPA) for conspiring to import and trade in looted archaeological objects from Mexico. A Mexican law enacted in 1972 vested ownership of all unexcavated antiquities in the Mexican nation. The Fifth Circuit Court of Appeals examined that law and found it to have established Mexican ownership of the looted antiquities in question. The court concluded that the defendants had deliberately ignored Mexico's ownership claims and convicted them under the NSPA.[146] Before Congress, the dealers maintained that the "oppressive and extreme" *McClain* decision was inconsistent with the implementing legislation, which required "a careful, case by case and item by item negotiation and determination by our officials to determine what materials in particular should be barred entry." Recognizing and enforcing all-encompassing foreign ownership laws, as the *McClain* decision did, would undermine the legislation's purpose. The dealers therefore asked that the NSPA be amended to exclude acts of alleged stealing from a foreign country where the ownership of the property is based only upon a declaration of national ownership.[147]

The dealers quickly realized, however, that their commercial concerns would be a poor basis for campaigning against the implementing legislation. "The winning argument would not have been: 'Well, I am being put out of business.'"[148] In their oral and written statements, the dealers therefore presented themselves as acting in the interest of the "United States public—a public which has increasingly grown to appreciate the value of art" and would now face cultural impoverishment as a result of the implementing legislation. Furthermore, the dealers argued that the legislation would deprive the American public of its *right* to enjoy and own foreign art. One justification for that right was that Americans are descendants of immigrants from many countries, including those of Africa and Latin America, and are morally entitled to a share of the art of their ancestors. Another justification was that antiquities are the legitimate cultural heritage and property of all mankind, not exclusively of the countries where those objects were found.[149]

The dealers also emphasized the importance of free trade in antiquities for museums. They pointed out that two centuries of free movement of antiquities had allowed the great American museums to enrich the public's understanding of world culture. The dealers further cautioned that restrictions on the import of antiquities would inhibit young museums from developing their collections.[150] Yet despite the close cooperation between the dealers and museums that shared their views, those museums maintained an independent presence to enhance their influence on legislators. Whereas dealers were viewed as "just businessmen," museums were "in a more elevated position because they are representing a much broader, identifiable, supportable public interest. . . . The museums had more moral suasion. They were not just representing commerce; they were representing culture."[151]

The dealers attempted to win over legislators with persuasive arguments, but the key to their influence was their ties to Senator Daniel Patrick Moynihan (D-NY). Moynihan, who served on the Senate Finance Committee and its Subcommittee on International Trade, was the dealers' main ally in the legislative process, as he was committed to the free flow of cultural property. Moynihan had learned much about the issue as the U.S. ambassador to India. As senator, he represented the State of New York. Since the center of the art trade is in New York City, the dealers were Moynihan's own constituency and enjoyed his support. This support proved critical, given that the senator "had the 'go-no go' power."[152] With Moynihan holding veto power over legislation considered detrimental by his constituency, the legislative process suffered repeated delays and came to a conclusion only when the bill was revised to the dealers' satisfaction. Moynihan was, in fact, the architect of the final draft of the legislation.

### Private Collectors

As consumers, collectors tend to oppose international regulation that threatens their ability to acquire antiquities and to enjoy them as aesthetic objects, sources of social status, or a financial investment. However, collectors are not inclined to organize politically. Unlike the dealers, whose commercial livelihood depends on the import of art, rich collectors inhibited from purchasing antiquities would channel their money elsewhere; therefore, they have relatively weak incentives to act against regulation.

Indeed, collectors did not mobilize to lobby Congress and had no independent presence in the debate. They were represented by surrogates: museums, which acquire most of their antiquities as gifts or bequests from collectors; and the dealers, from whom collectors purchase.[153] Collectors did, however, send letters to Congress protesting the implementing legislation. One collector argued that the legislation represented "a cultural tragedy of the greatest significance to the present and future generations of the American public." Furthermore, maintained the collector, archaeological destruction resulted from lack of interest, ignorance, and corruption in source countries. "It is not the job of the American government to act as police for other countries." Another collector asserted that the legislation would deprive American citizens "of the opportunity of improving the quality of their lives by the study and appreciation" of antiquities. He saw "no pressing reason why the United States should, in effect, either through misguided idealism or some kind of governmental masochism, put itself in the position of enforcing the laws and export regulations of other countries." Furthermore, unilateral U.S. action, without other market countries on board, would be ineffective. "The material will be lost to the 'countries of origin' as before, but it will also be lost to American scholars and collections to no purpose whatever. . . . [T]he only lasting effect to be achieved will be to hold the United States up to ridicule for having stupidly cut off its cultural nose to spite its face."[154]


## Museums

American museums are major consumers of antiquities through purchase, gift, or bequest. In fact, as recipients of private collections, museums are the final repositories of most antiquities. One would expect museums to oppose regulation that might curb their acquisition of antiquities and hinder the development of their collections. Yet museums are unique consumers. They are organized as public trusts whose mission is to serve and educate the public. Such a mission means that museums "must take affirmative steps to maintain their integrity so as to warrant public confidence. They must act not only legally but also ethically."[155] Acting in public trust and committed to ethical conduct, museums do not operate solely on the basis of narrow self-interest; they must also consider the normative implications of their conduct. Acquisition of looted material and encouragement of archaeological destruction undermine the public-trust responsibility of museums. Such practices also betray museums' commitment to values such as knowledge, education, and cultural preservation. Museums therefore have normative reasons for endorsing regulatory restraints on the trade in antiquities. They also have practical reasons for supporting regulation. Acquisition of looted material could deal a blow to museums' reputation as respectable institutions and threaten their lifeblood: public and government support through grants, donations, tax exemptions, and so forth. Inappropriate acquisition of antiquities could also embroil museums in prolonged legal battles, and—if the antiquities are ultimately returned—it could bring financial loss.

The important point for the purpose of the following analysis is that museums have more complex incentives than other consumers of antiquities (dealers and private collectors) and consumers in other illicit trades. Museums are *cross-pressured* consumers: their desire to acquire and display the most valuable objects would likely lead them to oppose regulatory constraints, yet that desire is tempered by normative and practical considerations that pull museums toward ethical restrictions. As I discuss below, the balance of these conflicting incentives has varied across museums and over time. Furthermore, museums have organized politically and actively participated in the debate over antiquities, since regulation goes to the heart of their existence, affecting both title to existing collections and the acquisition of new objects.

Museums' acquisition policies became a matter of open debate for the first time in the early 1970s, when several museums adopted ethical acquisition policies. In April 1970 the University of Pennsylvania Museum announced it would no longer purchase antiquities unless accompanied by a pedigree, including information about the place of origin and the legality of export.[156] In 1971 Harvard University barred the acquisition by its museums of illegally exported objects.[157] Several other museums followed suit.[158] The main proponents of these voluntary self-regulatory policies were archaeologists serving in those museums, whose goal was to stop the plunder of antiquities. But there were other considerations as well. As noted earlier, that period saw several public scandals that embarrassed major museums. Committing to ethical policies was thus a precautionary measure and a means of maintaining public trust in museums. Another concern was that source countries might respond to university museums' inappropriate acquisitions by suspending cooperation with other branches of the universities involved.[159] Finally, the new acquisition policies constituted a preemptive measure. The 1970 UNESCO Convention; the shift in the U.S. approach to antiquities; the mounting criticism of museums' conduct—all these did not bode well for museums, which anticipated growing public scrutiny and possibly increasing governmental regulation of their conduct. Museums' self-policing initiatives were meant to preempt governmental control: "If museums fail to stem the tide of criticism by their own acts, legislators may take the initiative away from them."[160] Not all museums, however, adopted ethical acquisition policies. Some, especially art museums that acquired antiquities on the market rather than through archaeological fieldwork, were reluctant to hinder the expansion of their collections by accepting ethical constraints.[161] This split foreshadowed museums' participation in the implementation debate.

The two museum associations, the American Association of Museums (AAM) and the Association of Art Museum Directors (AAMD), believed that museums' concerns transcended their institutional self-interest in acquiring antiquities and the interest of the American public in enjoying art. As custodians of human heritage, museums could not condone the looting of antiquities and the concomitant archaeological destruction and loss of knowledge. They could not fulfill their educational mission by displaying stolen property.[162] The AAM thus voiced support for the UNESCO Convention and the implementing legislation and protested suggested legislative changes that "may lessen the United States participation in the goals of the UNESCO convention." The AAMD expressed similar support, noting the cross-pressures on museums: "We have been particularly anxious to see that the legitimate needs of the American people and their educational and cultural exposure to the art of the world be satisfied, but without continuation of the indefensible and growing destruction caused by robbery and the pillage of cultural property under the protection and regulation of other countries." The AAMD also criticized the dealers and collectors for attacking the implementing legislation, maintaining that the legislation "is clearly right and desirable, even mandatory for the preservation of the world's cultural heritage . . . a matter of honor and integrity."[163]

Individual museums also took part in the debate and expressed a variety of views. Museums of archaeology, dedicated to archaeological knowledge, expressed support for the implementing legislation. Harvard's Peabody Museum of Archaeology and Ethnology was particularly active, arguing that "the majority of illegally exported antiquities eventually end up in the United States," and that the "physical destruction by looters of archaeological sites of incalculable scientific value is the end result of this illegal traffic."[164] By contrast, the major art museums were less supportive of the legislation. While they did not endorse plunder, art museums viewed antiquities as *art* objects and were less sensitive to the destruction of archaeological context. For them, antiquities without context were still valuable and worth bringing into the public domain.[165] Yet given the evidence on the involvement of the American art world with looted material, art museums could not afford to be seen as pursuing the uninhibited expansion of their collections, released from any ethical constraints. The position of the Metropolitan Museum of Art reflected this ambivalence. The Metropolitan expressed "full support for the objectives of this legislation" and "urge[d] its enactment in slightly modified form." Yet the Metropolitan's suggested modifications were not, in fact, slight. As a major museum acquiring antiquities on a regular basis, the Metropolitan had strong anti-regulation incentives, which were manifested in its proposals. It proposed, for example, that bilateral agreements with source countries take the form of treaties requiring Senate ratification. This, of course, would have made the establishment of import controls infinitely more difficult.[166] The Metropolitan also proposed that, notwithstanding import restrictions, antiquities would be legally imported if shown to have left the country of origin at least 10 years before entering the United States. The State Department argued that this could create "a serious loophole for the flow of illicit traffic to the United States."[167] The Minneapolis Institute of Arts expressed similar ambivalence, supporting the legislation while sounding an alarm about "overzealous sanctions" that would "act to our own detriment."[168]

The most vehement opposition came from small, young art museums, especially outside the Northeast. Those museums feared that implementation of the UNESCO Convention would prevent the development of their nascent collections. They therefore shared the anti-regulation preference of the dealers. In their letters to Congress, young museums expressed support for maintaining "[t]he open door policy pursued by the United States Government [which] has had the long range effect of enriching our museums with the culture created throughout the world." They denounced the implementing legislation as a "hasty expedient for the interests of the Department of State." They also claimed that antiquities were better off preserved in American museums than "rotting away in tropical jungles or lying unused, unseen and neglected in some basements and warehouses of different countries."[169]

In summary, the variety of positions taken by museums reflected the conflicting pressures they came under. Archaeology museums' top priority was to curb archaeological plunder; accordingly, they supported the implementing legislation. Art museums placed less emphasis on historical knowledge; hence, their pro-regulation incentives were weaker than those of archaeology museums. Within the art-museum community, however, established art museums had stronger incentives to support regulation than did young art museums. Already possessing rich collections, established museums were less hungry for antiquities than were young museums; they were also more likely to come under public scrutiny and criticism. Young art museums were therefore the strongest opponents of the legislation within the museum community.

## Congress

The opposite positions of the House of Representatives and the Senate exemplified the cross-pressures on the U.S. government. The House was sympathetic to the archaeologists' view and supported the legislation out of concern about looting abroad. The Senate, by contrast, privileged the interests of consumers—dealers, museums, and collectors—and was highly skeptical of the UNESCO Convention and its implementation.

The most ardent supporter of the legislation was Representative Abner Mikva (D-IL).[170] Mikva rejected the arguments against the legislation, particularly the argument concerning the diversion of antiquities to other market countries as a result of unilateral U.S. action:

> What [the diversion argument] says is that since other nations and other people are going to be immoral, we have to keep up with the other immorals in order to preserve our role in the world. Clearly, the United States is the major art importing nation in the world, and if we do not exercise

this kind of moral leadership, who will? If we do not create an example for other countries to implement this convention, who will implement it? If we don't engage in those preliminary actions to put us on the side of the convention which we have already ratified, how can we expect other countries to do it? Clearly, we cannot eliminate pillage or prevent illicit traffic in antiquities alone. Closing the American art market, however, to illegal trade should create a significant deterrent and take a meaningful step toward real international cooperative effort. Let me say again what we are talking about here is art and objects that are illegally taken from the country of origin and it seems to me that as a leader of the civilized world, as a country that proclaims its own morality, we ought to do whatever is necessary to help those countries that want to help themselves.[171]

In a similar spirit, the House Ways and Means Committee argued "that international cooperation to combat pillage and illegal trade in cultural property requires that the United States, as the major art-importing nation in the world, exercise moral leadership and create an example through implementation of the Convention." In the committee's opinion, the legislation established "an appropriate and satisfactory balance" between assisting foreign countries in the protection of their cultural heritage and continuing to import antiquities to the United States.[172]

The Senate, by contrast, was more attentive to the concerns of the dealers. Senators Moynihan and Ribicoff in particular considered the implementing legislation to be a grave threat to the legitimate interests of the United States as an art-importing country. Moynihan argued that "[n]othing has been more striking than the respect which Western countries have shown for the archaeological and ethnological artifacts of other countries." He praised the dealers "as respected and honored members of a profession which has done more, perhaps, to conserve and preserve the art objects of this world than all the museums put together." For Moynihan, the UNESCO Convention was "a self-denying ordinance" that the United States should not be joining "with the sense of our own guilt." Unlike Congressman Mikva, who rejected the dealers' argument against unilateral U.S. action, Senator Moynihan embraced that argument: "We are not going to gain the respect of anybody by being the only ones to do this. . . . [U]ntil we can persuade the other importing countries to act in this matter, we ought not to do so unilaterally."[173] Senator Ribicoff claimed that government authorities in source countries were complicit in the plunder of antiquities and that those antiquities would be better preserved in American museums. Yet Ribicoff also saw the legislation from a broader perspective. His hostility toward the UNESCO Convention had much to do with his apprehension and anger about the diminishing influence of the United States in international organizations. Ribicoff argued that international organizations had become politicized and "invariably against the basic interests of the United States." He considered

UNESCO in particular to be "one of the worst of all of the international organizations in its attitude toward U.S. policy," a "moribund" institution that "is invariably against the United States on everything."[174]

## Convention on Cultural Property Implementation Act

After multiple revisions and delays, the Convention on Cultural Property Implementation Act (hereafter the CPIA, or the Act) was ultimately signed into law in January 1983. The Act authorizes the establishment of import restrictions on antiquities through bilateral agreements or on an emergency basis without an agreement. As the dealers effectively held veto power over the legislation through Senator Moynihan, the CPIA met most of their concerns:

1. Authority to examine the requests of source countries and to recommend the establishment of import controls was given to a body of experts: the Cultural Property Advisory Committee (CPAC). The 11 members of the Committee represent the interests of museums, archaeologists, dealers, and the general public.

2. Most of the decision-making authority that the CPIA confers upon the president was delegated to the United States Information Agency (USIA),[175] rather than the State Department. The dealers' victory in minimizing the State Department's involvement was temporary, however. With the dissolution of the USIA in 1999, the State Department assumed responsibility for implementing the Act.

3. The CPIA requires that import restrictions be established through bilateral agreements "in concert with similar restrictions implemented" by other market countries.[176] The Act thereby met the dealers' request to make U.S. action conditional upon a broader international effort.

The CPIA included several other compromises favorable to the dealers. The bilateral agreements with source countries were to have a limited duration of five years that could be extended by additional five-year periods. The Act allows import of material even in the absence of documentation of legal export, if the material had left the source country at least 10 years prior to the date of entry and the importer had not contracted for the material more than a year before that date. The Act also requires the United States, when granting a country's request for import restrictions, to endeavor to obtain that country's reciprocal commitment to allow the legitimate exchange of antiquities. The dealers failed, however, to overturn the *McClain* decision. Overturning the decision was part of the compromise that led to the passage of the CPIA, but had to be achieved through separate legislation. Senator Moynihan therefore introduced legislation to that effect, but it ultimately failed to pass.[177]

## Antiquities Regulation: The Post-legislative Debate (1983–2010)

El Salvador was the first country to request the imposition of import controls under the CPIA. The Salvadoran request, reporting the large-scale looting of antiquities primarily destined for the U.S. market, was an easy first case: the destruction was evident, the looted area was definable, and the low market value of Salvadoran antiquities did not generate significant opposition from the dealers. Acting upon CPAC's recommendation, the USIA established emergency import restrictions on artifacts from El Salvador's Cara Sucia region in September 1987.[178] In 1995 the United States and El Salvador signed a bilateral agreement, imposing import restrictions on El Salvador's entire pre-Hispanic heritage. As of 2011, the United States had signed bilateral agreements for the imposition of import restrictions with 14 countries.[179]

Litigation has provided another avenue for combating plunder with an even more profound impact than import controls under the CPIA. One case in particular had far-reaching implications: *United States v. Schultz*.[180] Frederick Schultz, a prominent art dealer, was indicted in 2001 for conspiring to import, deal in, and possess antiquities stolen from Egypt in violation of the Egyptian law that vested ownership of antiquities in the Egyptian nation. The Second Circuit Court of Appeals followed the *McClain* doctrine and convicted Schultz. For supporters of the *Schultz* decision, the case sent a warning signal to those who transact in antiquities: a foreign law establishing national ownership of antiquities is enforceable in U.S. courts; trading in looted antiquities may result in criminal sanctions.[181] For its critics, the *Schultz* decision nullified the intent of the CPIA and "cast a cloud over title to every cultural object otherwise lawfully imported into the United States, including objects imported and subsequently exhibited in compliance with the Implementation Act."[182]

The operation of the CPIA itself has also been controversial. The dealers argue that the Act struck a fair compromise and could have done much good, if implemented faithfully—as a tailored response to specific situations of archaeological crisis. They believe, however, that the U.S. government has breached the fundamental principles of the legislation and established excessive, burdensome import restrictions to the detriment of the American art market. This was not always the case. The dealers consider the statutory process to have worked reasonably well over the first 15 years of the CPIA's existence, when foreign countries' requests for import restrictions were specific and narrow. Things changed dramatically in the late 1990s when the U.S. government, according to the dealers, undermined the Act's delicate balance by signing several over-restrictive agreements heavily tilted in favor of source countries. Import restrictions, far from being limited to significant objects, were extended to cover countries' entire cultural heritage and were established even when the evidence of looting was shaky.[183] In the dealers' view, import restrictions have become an "all-you-can-eat buffet."[184] Furthermore, the dealers argue that the United States acted alone in establishing import restrictions, all but ignoring the CPIA's requirement of a joint international effort. They also maintain that their long-held fear has been realized: restrictions on the import of antiquities have become a means of improving relations with foreign countries and eliciting their cooperation on other matters.[185]

The dealers charge that the U.S. government has undermined the congressional intent and devastated the art market by aggressively blocking the import of legitimate material.[186] Furthermore, the *McClain* and *Schultz* decisions established a threat of criminal sanctions for actors transacting in antiquities, causing demand to shrink. The cumulative impact of these developments has weakened the dealers, who are not nearly as organized and politically active today as they were during the legislative process. Moreover, the dealers sense that the public climate has shifted against the antiquities trade. They attribute this change to the advocacy and educational efforts of the archaeological community, which established the perception that museums and dealers fuel looting. The ascendancy of the archaeological viewpoint is also the result of general changes in public morals. Today, people are more inclined to perceive developing countries as defenseless victims of plunder by "rich white guys"—American collectors.[187] Dealers consider this perception to be false, yet its popular appeal has put them on the defensive. The anti-trade shift has also to do with scandals involving museums. Unscrupulous conduct of museums placed looted antiquities on the national agenda in the 1970s and continued to raise concerns in following years. Major scandals, like the J. Paul Getty Museum's acquisition of looted material,[188] tarnished the reputation of the entire market and fostered an anti-trade, pro-source countries mindset.

The pendulum having swung against the dealers is consistent with the theoretical framework, according to which both interest groups and the public's views influence government preferences. During the congressional debate, the dealers acted as a highly organized interest group and exploited their ties with Senator Moynihan to weaken the implementing legislation. In the post-legislative period, the dealers have not enjoyed the same influence over the agency implementing the CPIA—the State Department—as they had over the Senate; the diminution of the trade has further diminished their political influence. At the same time, the public has become more sympathetic to source countries,[189] and the State Department is naturally attentive to foreign countries' concerns, thereby increasing the weight of the trade's secondary externalities. The waning influence of consumers—the dealers— and the growing weight of secondary externalities have tilted American policy toward stronger regulation. This echoes another theoretical observation, namely, that government preferences may change over time.

Archaeologists and other members of the cultural-heritage community[190] consider the CPIA to have worked reasonably well. If they have any complaint, it is that the process of establishing import restrictions is too long and cumbersome and imposes too heavy a burden on requesting countries. They would have liked to ease the process, for example, by concluding bilateral agreements of indefinite duration rather than the current practice: an extendable five-year period. In their view, limited duration is an unnecessary and self-defeating obstacle to cooperation. If looters believe that the agreement will expire, they still have an incentive to plunder.[191]

Whereas the dealers' and the archaeologists' current positions are consistent with their respective views during the implementation debate, the major art museums have since moved further in the anti-regulation direction. Their qualified support for the implementation of the UNESCO Convention has turned into harsh criticism of antiquities regulation. In fact, the major art museums and the Association of Art Museum Directors have taken on the role—previously played by the dealers—of leading the battle against extensive antiquities regulation.

Why do American art museums oppose antiquities regulation? First, art museums focus on the artistic and aesthetic value of antiquities, rather than their contribution to understanding the past. Acquiring and displaying antiquities devoid of archaeological context is thus quite consistent with art museums' goals and philosophy.[192] Second, most American museums hardly acquire antiquities and see little difficulty in ethical restrictions on acquisition. By contrast, the wealthy art museums are active consumers of antiquities, and regulation hinders the enrichment of their collections. Furthermore, museums like the Metropolitan and the Art Institute of Chicago see themselves as *encyclopedic museums*: "they comprise collections meant to represent the world's diversity, and they organize and classify that diversity for ready, public access."[193] The ambition to represent the entire world's art has led to the constant pursuit of new objects and to a preference for liberalization of the antiquities trade.[194] Third, art museums acquire many antiquities as gifts or bequests from collectors; collectors also provide monetary donations to museums and serve as trustees. By adhering to strict acquisition guidelines and declining collectors' gifts that fail to meet those guidelines, a museum risks alienating an important source of support.

During the congressional debate, the major art museums supported the legislation with little enthusiasm. The actual operation of the CPIA, however, has not conformed to their original understanding. Whereas museums envisioned modest, narrowly defined import restrictions, the extent of restrictions has in practice far exceeded their expectations. In addition, the temptations facing museums have increased as they have become wealthier and as the market has expanded to include new supplying countries. The growing incentives to resist restrictions on acquisition have engendered vocal criticism, such as that of James Cuno, director of the Art Institute of Chicago. Cuno argues that in executing the CPIA, the U.S. government has effectively given a blank check to source countries and has been influenced by political considerations. Cuno further denounces the principle of national retention of antiquities, which national ownership laws and the UNESCO Convention promote: "We should all work together to counter the nationalist basis of national laws and international conventions and agreements and promote a principle of shared stewardship of our common heritage."[195] The Association of Art Museum Directors similarly disapproves of U.S. practice, especially what it perceives as disregard of the Act's requirement of a joint international effort. The AAMD believes that unilateral American action does little to curb looting and merely reroutes the trade to other market countries. The Association would have liked the State Department to urge source countries to release antiquities to the legal market.[196]

In recent years, the acquisition of antiquities by American art museums has diminished. Extensive restrictions on export from source countries and growing demand for objects with clean provenance have driven prices up. Acquisition today also carries the risk of legal battles, either over civil claims for return or over criminal charges. Museums caught in unlawful possession of antiquities pay a hefty price in terms of tarnished reputation and loss of the acquisition funds. The chilling effect of litigation has increased their reliance on loans of antiquities and has made them more cautious about accepting objects from collectors.[197] Archaeologists, however, believe that American museums are not yet fully committed to avoiding the acquisition of looted antiquities.[198]

The debate over antiquities regulation has been raging in the United States since the late 1960s with little progress. Do antiquities belong to source countries or to mankind? Should unprovenanced objects be considered looted? Is archaeology best protected through strict control or through the release of antiquities to the open market? The archaeological and art communities give very different answers to these fundamental questions, and the debate between them is still far from resolution.

## Britain and the Efforts against the Looting of Antiquities

Unlike the United States, Britain declined to participate in the 1970 negotiations of the UNESCO Convention and did not ratify the convention for over three decades. Given that both the United States and Britain are major market-countries for antiquities, why did their preferences on international antiquities regulation diverge so sharply? Furthermore, why did Britain reverse its opposition to the UNESCO Convention and join it in 2002? The following analysis examines the American-British divergence and explains the change over time in Britain's preference on the international control of antiquities.

## 1970–2000: Resisting International Regulation

Britain is an important transit country for antiquities. Antiquities from around the world flow into London and are reexported to markets of final destination. The traditional British approach to antiquities of foreign origin was one of lax regulation. Antiquities could be imported freely; licenses for their export were issued more or less automatically.[199] The 1970 UNESCO Convention, which sought to change this reality and strengthen the control over the movement of antiquities, received little sympathy in Britain. As British antiquities were not the target of looting, the British government did not face the primary externalities of the illicit antiquities trade. For reasons explained below, the British government—unlike the U.S. government—was also not particularly concerned about secondary externalities, that is, archaeological destruction abroad. The British government did, however, have powerful incentives to oppose regulation. Foremost on the government's mind were the interests of consumers: antiquities dealers and auction houses (note that the term "dealers" in the following analysis includes auctioneers as well). There were obvious motivations to shield these actors from regulation. The antiquities trade was part of the larger UK art market—a market of considerable importance that employed thousands of people and generated substantial tax revenue. Beyond its economic benefits, the art market significantly contributed to the cultural enrichment of Britain. The British government therefore saw the international regulatory efforts against looting as unacceptable constraints on the art market.[200] Throughout the 1960s, the government expressed much skepticism of these efforts. Upon the 1970 establishment of the UNESCO Convention, and under pressure from the trade, the government adopted a hostile attitude toward this agreement.[201]

As the theoretical framework suggests, governments may also fear the costs that international regulation imposes on the bureaucracy and on law-enforcement agencies. Such concerns clearly contributed to Britain's repudiation of the UNESCO Convention. For example, the convention's requirement of a national inventory of protected cultural property was deemed a heavy bureaucratic burden.[202] The obligations concerning imports were thought to require substantial administrative resources, burdening customs and the police.[203] Yet another concern was the presumed legislative changes that the convention entailed.[204] The traditionally skeptical approach of the British civil service to treaties and the work they create further intensified the perception of the convention as excessively onerous.

From the government's point of view, the UNESCO Convention was inimical to Britain's interests: it threatened to constrain the market and burden the dealers[205] and the government, while offering no benefits in return. In the 1990s, the government maintained that the convention was "unrealistic and totally disproportionate to the end . . . which it is designed to achieve"[206] and that its implementation "would involve a formidable bureaucracy."[207] As late as February 2000, the government stated that it would not join the convention "because significant practical difficulties remain in implementing its provisions into UK law."[208]

The United States was in a similar position to that of Britain: enriched both financially and culturally by a thriving art market. Why, then, did the U.S. government support modest international regulation of antiquities, whereas the British government vehemently opposed it? In the early 1970s the U.S. government came under cross-pressures: concern about looting abroad counteracted the interests of the art market. In Britain, however, the issue was not on the agenda at that point in time. Only in the late 1990s did the British government face the same influences that sparked the American concerns about plunder abroad: public scandals and archaeologists' advocacy. The problem of looting was also prominent in the United States early on given the initial focus of concern: Latin America. Mexico and Peru initiated international action against looting in 1960; Clemency Coggins traced antiquities displayed in American museums back to plundered sites in Mexico and Guatemala. As the primary market for pre-Columbian antiquities, the United States bore greater responsibility for the looting in Latin America than the British market, where pre-Columbian archaeology had a much smaller presence. Moreover, Latin America was an important area of study for American archaeologists, who were thus more concerned about looting than their British counterparts and more motivated to advocate for regulation.

Another distinction between the United States and Britain concerned the ministry involved. In the United States, the State Department led the regulatory efforts, from negotiating the UNESCO Convention to pushing the implementing legislation through Congress. The State Department—the foreign-affairs arm of the U.S. government—was favorable to international cooperation, concerned about the United States' international image, and receptive to foreign countries' pleas. In Britain, by contrast, antiquities regulation was not the domain of the Foreign Service. In the 1990s, the ministries involved were the Department of National Heritage and its successor—the

Department for Culture, Media, and Sport. These departments were less foreign-minded than the State Department and less conducive to international cooperation.

Self-regulation of the trade marked another difference between the United States and Britain.[209] Art dealers in Britain had collectively established codes of conduct since at least 1984.[210] These codes may not have satisfied archaeologists, yet they made the British government less inclined to accept international regulation. The government believed that "the trade should monitor its own activities, regulate itself and take appropriate steps against those who do not abide by its code of practice. Doing this effectively ensures its reputation."[211]

Finally, the colonial legacy made antiquities a thorny issue to tackle in Britain. Britain's belief in the free movement of antiquities was inspired by a long history of removing antiquities from its colonies. Accepting source countries' claims of ownership over antiquities clashed with the colonial legacy of unfettered amassing of antiquities from the world over. Furthermore, although the problem of ongoing looting was separate from the controversy over antiquities taken during the colonial period, the British government may have seen them as linked. Assuming responsibility for ongoing looting would have opened a Pandora's Box by validating foreign countries' claims for the return of objects taken during the colonial era.

## 1990s: Antiquities on the Agenda

The British government had rejected the UNESCO Convention since its inception as an unnecessary burden on the art market and the bureaucracy. Yet several developments in the 1990s came together to put the looting of antiquities on the agenda, counterbalance the anti-regulation incentives, and turn the British government into a cross-pressured government, in a position similar to the one in which the U.S. government had found itself some 30 years earlier.

The emergence of primary externalities was an important part of the change in incentives. Britain had long considered looting to be a problem afflicting foreign countries. In the 1980s and 1990s, however, Britain's own cultural heritage fell victim to plunder and theft. A prominent example is the plunder at Wanborough, Surrey. Treasure hunters looted the site after the 1985 discovery of Iron Age and Roman coins. They removed approximately 5,000 coins, many of which were later spotted in Europe and the United States. Raiding of the site continued thereafter, causing heavy damage to the remains of a temple.[212] A threat to British archaeology also came with the rise of metal detecting as a popular hobby—one that resulted in the massive removal of antiquities.[213] Additionally, Britain experienced a severe hemorrhaging of nonarchaeological cultural objects stolen from churches, local museums, and historic houses. While of little financial value, these objects were considered potent and irreplaceable tokens of British heritage, and their loss stirred considerable concern.[214]

Having failed to curb the outflow of material stolen from archaeological sites and other locations, Britain joined the ranks of countries suffering the primary negative externalities of the illicit trade in cultural property. Once the loss of cultural objects became Britain's own problem, international regulation was no longer seen as serving foreign countries at Britain's expense. Rather, it was an enterprise that Britain itself could benefit from. More specifically, the British government sought to join an international consortium that would oblige foreign countries to return cultural objects illegally removed from Britain.[215] This is an important distinction between the British and American cases. Looting of American archaeology was *not* among the motivations for the U.S. participation in the efforts against the illicit trade in antiquities. The British and American cases are, however, similar in terms of the sources of concern about the trade's secondary externalities: public scandals and archaeologists' advocacy.

Public Scandals

A series of public scandals in the early 1970s shed light on the unethical conduct of American museums and their involvement with looted material. Years later, high-profile scandals brought attention to looted antiquities in Britain and changed the public atmosphere. In 1994 the Royal Academy of Arts displayed antiquities from the collection of George Ortiz. Most objects on show lacked verifiable provenance, and the exhibition therefore created controversy. A second dispute erupted in 1995, this time concerning the Royal Academy's exhibition *Africa: The Art of a Continent*. Several scholars and museums, including the British Museum, criticized the Academy's decision to borrow from private collectors and display plundered terracotta figurines from Mali and Nigeria. The museums decided to withhold objects they had intended to lend to the exhibition, unless the African governments in question agreed to the display of the looted antiquities. It soon became a matter of confrontation between the British Museum and the Royal Academy and received wide coverage. A third scandal concerned the Sevso Treasure, a collection of richly decorated Roman silver objects. Lord Northampton purchased the collection, and his attempt to sell it set off a legal battle in the early 1990s. Before an American court, both Croatia and Hungary argued that the treasure had been illegally removed from their territories. A lord's involvement with material suspected as looted captured the media's attention.[216]

The most important scandal followed Peter Watson's exposé of Sotheby's, one of the world's largest auction houses. In his 1997 book *Sotheby's: Inside Story* and on television, Watson provided an unprecedented glimpse into the illicit antiquities trade, based on documents leaked by a former Sotheby's employee. Watson's investigation showed that many of the antiquities sold by Sotheby's in London without provenance had come from a dealer in Switzerland who was, in fact, a "front" for an Italian dealer, Giacomo Medici. Medici smuggled illegally excavated antiquities in bulk from Italy to Switzerland, where it was legal to import and export antiquities without documentation. From Switzerland the antiquities were sent to London, allowing Sotheby's to claim that they had arrived at the auction house legally. The leaked documents further showed that in certain cases, involving very valuable antiquities, Sotheby's staff was either aware that they had been illegally exported from Italy, or participated in the arrangements. The exposé triggered an investigation by the Italian and Swiss police, leading to Medici's trial and conviction and to the discovery of several warehouses in Geneva that contained thousands of antiquities.[217] Most importantly, the British art market was exposed as an accomplice in the trade in looted antiquities. The Sotheby's scandal exploded the myth, cultivated by the trade, that unprovenanced antiquities were legitimate objects coming from old private collections or discovered in attics. Many unprovenanced antiquities, it now became clear, were illegally excavated and exported and then laundered to erase their illegal source.

The cumulative impact of the scandals was to generate public debate and concern, and to put looted antiquities on the national agenda. "People began thinking: We need to do something about this. It's not just a small problem. It's coming up all over the place. . . . The Royal Academy [displaying] loot; Sotheby's selling loot; English lord buying loot. . . . So the issue was really live. . . . You got the feeling a little bit of a crusade going on, that something had to be done."[218] But as in the United States in the early 1970s, to further stimulate concern about plunder abroad and induce government action required agents who would capitalize on and reinforce the changing public climate: the archaeologists.

### Archaeologists

Until the mid-1990s, the British archaeological community's public voice against looting was Colin Renfrew, an eminent archaeologist and a member of the House of Lords. Throughout his career, Renfrew fiercely criticized the London art market, which he saw as a major clearing house for looted antiquities. He also rebuked the British government, denouncing the freedom to import looted material as a "thieves' kitchen" and labeling the British rejection of the UNESCO Convention "a scandal."[219] Over the years, Renfrew persistently pressed the issue in the House of Lords by posing questions, which the government was required to answer.[220] By the mid-1990s, however, the archaeological community at large became concerned about the plunder of antiquities for various reasons: the looting of archaeology in Iraq in the aftermath of the 1991 Gulf War; the expanding geographical scope of the problem, as stolen cultural objects from China and Eastern Europe began appearing on the market; improvements in transportation that facilitated plunder in hard-to-access territories, such as the Himalayas and the Sahara Desert; technological innovations, such as the metal detector and power tools, which made digging and robbing easier; and new methods of marketing, such as Internet auctions.[221] The aforementioned scandals provided further impetus for the archaeological community to respond.

The archaeologists' response came in the form of the Illicit Antiquities Research Center, established in 1997 under Renfrew's directorship at the McDonald Institute for Archaeological Research at the University of Cambridge. As the theoretical framework has explained, moral entrepreneurs use their knowledge and expertise to educate policymakers and the public about the harmful effects of illicit trade and to foster an ethical terrain that is conducive to regulation. Indeed, through lectures, conferences, exhibitions, and publications, the Illicit Antiquities Research Center sought to "raise public awareness of the problems caused by this trade [in looted antiquities] and seek appropriate national and international legislation . . . to place restraint upon it."[222] The Center's most influential publication was a 2000 report entitled *Stealing History: The Illicit Trade in Cultural Material.* The report examined the causes and consequences of the trade in looted antiquities and the role played by the British art market. It called upon the government to ratify the UNESCO and the UNIDROIT Conventions in order to "prevent the United Kingdom [from] being used as a market place for material which was, in the first instance, obtained illegally." "By failing to ratify," the report warned, "it can be argued that the United Kingdom condones criminal behaviour abroad."[223]

The role of *Stealing History* in fueling the national debate in Britain was akin to that of Coggins's article in *Art Journal* three decades earlier. Both publications brought attention to the illicit antiquities trade, raised awareness of looting outside the small circle of archaeologists, and prompted further investigation and coverage of the issue. Both publications linked plunder in developing countries to consumers of antiquities in rich countries. An important distinction between the two publications, however, was the role of museums. American museums were the primary target of Coggins's criticism; *Stealing History*, by contrast, was commissioned by Britain's Museums Association.

Whereas the U.S. archaeological community has sought to strengthen controls on antiquities, American art museums have fought to weaken them. The museum community in Britain, by contrast, is allied with the archaeologists and shares their support for regulation. That support was manifested early on. The decision of the British government not to ratify the 1970 UNESCO Convention led the British Academy, the Standing Commission on Museums and Galleries, the British Museum, and the Museums Association (MA) to issue a joint statement in 1972. The statement reaffirmed that museums in Britain would not acquire cultural material believed to have been exported in violation of the laws of the country of origin.[224] Successive codes of conduct promulgated by the MA since 1977 required museums in Britain to conform to ethical acquisition guidelines, yet the issue did not rank high on the MA's agenda. Things began to change in the mid-1990s, as looted antiquities received national attention. With the pressure from archaeologists growing, and after the Sotheby's scandal demonstrated that self-regulation is prone to failure, the MA took a more serious look at the issue. It was discovered that museums had been formally adopting ethical acquisition policies but had no procedures in place to implement them. To raise museums' awareness and establish practical recommendations for avoiding the acquisition of looted material, the MA commissioned the Illicit Antiquities Research Center to produce a report. The result was *Stealing History*.[225]

During the public debate in 2000, which is examined later, the MA expressed views consistent with those of the archaeologists: preservation of the archaeological record and context is of great importance; unprovenanced antiquities are most likely looted; demand from dealers and collectors stimulates looting. Accordingly, the MA urged the government to "work to create a climate in which dealing in—or possessing—illicitly obtained cultural property is seen as unacceptable." Whereas American museums have been heavily critical of the UNESCO and UNIDROIT Conventions, the MA urged the British government to ratify both.[226] The sharp contrast between the museum communities in the United States and in Britain is also evident through a comparison of the two countries' most prominent museums: the Metropolitan and the British Museum. During the implementation debate, the Metropolitan expressed an ambivalent position on the UNESCO Convention; in the years since, it has become a vociferous critic of regulation. Philippe de Montebello, director of the Metropolitan (1997–2008), was "puzzled by the zeal with which the United States rushes to embrace foreign laws that can ultimately deprive its own citizens of important objects useful to the education and delectation of its own citizens"; he was "highly skeptical of recent international trends that have drastically reined in museums' antiquities collecting"; and he saw source countries' demands for the return of their antiquities as a "resurgence of nationalism and misplaced patriotism."[227] The British Museum, by contrast, has shared the archaeologists' concern about the loss of knowledge caused by looting and has supported strict ethical guidelines for museums.[228]

Why have the U.S. and UK museum communities taken such different paths? The prominent UK museums—most notably, the British Museum—are museums of *archaeology* and, furthermore, are surrounded by local archaeology. As such, they are concerned for archaeological preservation and see great importance in the provenance of antiquities.[229] By contrast, the American museums dominating the debate are museums of *art* that are less sensitive to questions of provenance and preservation of the historical record. Britain's museums are also not very active consumers. Due to their limited acquisition budgets, they acquire relatively few objects, and these typically are not high-profile antiquities.[230] Furthermore, they already possess many of the world's most important antiquities, obtained during the colonial period. The major U.S. art museums, by contrast, are endowed with large acquisition funds and actively purchase antiquities; they also receive antiquities from private collectors. As active consumers, American museums are more constrained by antiquities regulation than are Britain's museums. Finally, Britain's museums lack some of the attributes that have fueled American museums' resistance to regulation: encyclopedic aspirations, a persistent drive to attract the public, and close ties with collectors.

### Antiquities Dealers

Britain's antiquities dealers, like their American colleagues, prefer weak national and international control of the trade in antiquities. The British dealers reject the archaeologists' assumption that unprovenanced objects are looted. They also repudiate the argument that the demand for antiquities is the culprit, arguing that the "Draconian laws" of source countries are to blame for archaeological plunder. The dealers would have liked source countries to relax their regulation of antiquities and allow legal export.[231] American dealers share these views. On other matters, however, the American and British dealers diverge. American dealers believe that the United States is *not* bound by foreign export controls. In their view, an illegally exported object can and should be imported legally to the United States, with the narrow exception of foreign export controls enforced under the CPIA. Furthermore, they vehemently argue that the United States should not enforce foreign ownership laws that nationalize antiquities. British dealers, while holding serious reservations, do consider themselves bound by foreign export laws.[232] They are also resigned to the fact that foreign ownership laws may be enforced under British law.[233] The British dealers did criticize the UNESCO

Convention for failing to provide a workable solution to the problem of the illicit antiquities trade and for burdening both the government and business.[234] Yet, as described below, in 2000 the dealers supported the Illicit Trade Advisory Panel's recommendations that included British accession to the UNESCO Convention and a set of measures more restrictive than anything the American dealers would have endorsed.

Why have the British dealers been more accepting of regulation? The dealers were concerned for their reputation following the scandals that engulfed the UK art market in the mid-1990s. The association of the market with looted antiquities meant tarnished reputation and "a polluting effect which would be very hard to extirpate once it had taken root."[235] Loss of reputation and credibility, in turn, would have harmed business. In the late 1960s and early 1970s, amid growing scrutiny and criticism of the U.S. art market, the American dealers joined the ASIL Panel and agreed to modest regulation. Similarly, the British dealers were willing to accept regulation in order to protect the reputation of the legitimate trade and prevent loot from leaching into the market, while at the same time guarding against an onerous bureaucratic burden. They also saw government regulation as a means of eliminating the unfair competition from small dealers who operated outside the trade's self-regulatory codes, undercutting the established dealers and tarnishing the good name of the entire market.[236] Furthermore, by accepting a solution that targeted the antiquities problem specifically, the dealers sought to preempt more extensive regulation of the art market as a whole.[237] Given the public climate and the government's desire to take action, the dealers chose to adopt a cooperative position, join the Illicit Trade Advisory Panel, and forge a compromise with the archaeologists. Between the UNESCO and UNIDROIT Conventions, the dealers saw the former as the lesser evil, and supported the recommendation to accede to it.

Several additional factors eased the British dealers' acceptance of regulation. One factor was the position of museums. To a large extent, the ethical standards in the market are set by museums because of their social status and since they are the final repositories of most antiquities. The anti-regulation views of the American dealers have been backed by the major art museums. In Britain, by contrast, museums are on the pro-regulation side, making it harder for the dealers to take an outright anti-regulation approach. Another factor was the introduction of EU legislation on antiquities in the early 1990s: Regulation 3911/92 on the export of cultural goods (1992) and Directive 93/7 on the return of cultural objects unlawfully removed from the territory of a member state (1993).[238] At the time of its negotiation, the trade opposed the proposed Regulation as harmful to the London art market and burdensome to the civil service. Voicing arguments similar to those heard during the implementation debate in the United States, the British dealers insisted that they did not bear responsibility for preserving foreign countries' heritage: source countries should bear the onus of enforcing their own laws. In response, the British government obtained a provision that excluded objects of limited archaeological or scientific significance from the Regulation's licensing requirements.[239] Even with this exclusion, the EU legislation created a precedent. Following its adoption, the dealers started moving along a learning curve of compliance with regulatory requirements, and this eased their acceptance of a more comprehensive regulation in 2000. Furthermore, the experience with the EU legislation demonstrated that international regulation need not deal a deathblow to the trade. In fact, regulation's impact may be limited, given that British authorities do not vigorously enforce it. This was indeed an important difference between Britain and the United States. In the United States, antiquities regulation had teeth: dealers were criminally convicted, and U.S. Customs made attempts to seize looted material. But given the British dealers' social status and political ties, they could expect Britain's authorities to be less determined in their enforcement efforts, and that any new regulation would not require radical changes to the trade's practices.

## The Government

Britain had resisted the international regulation of antiquities since the onset of UNESCO's efforts against plunder in the 1960s. In the British government's view, regulation brought only costs and no benefits. By the late 1990s, the British government had become cross-pressured with the loss of cultural objects of UK origin and amid growing concern about unethical conduct in the London art market. Still mindful of the costs of regulation to business and the bureaucracy, the government finally recognized the value of regulation for curbing the illicit antiquities trade and its negative effects. Yet it was not only the government's incentive structure that changed. *The government itself changed.* In 1997 a Labor government came to power, ending 18 years of Conservative rule. Upon assuming office, Tony Blair's government announced a new foreign policy that had an ethical dimension. That ethical dimension would later be manifested, for example, in British support for the International Criminal Court and the humanitarian intervention in Kosovo.[240] The moral emphasis in its foreign policy also sensitized the government to plunder abroad. As a legacy of Britain's colonial past, the government recognized a certain responsibility for protecting global heritage, and was thus willing to join the efforts against the looting of antiquities.[241] The Labor government was also more committed than the previous Conservative government to international institutions and cooperation, as demonstrated by its decision to rejoin UNESCO. In 1985, shortly after the American withdrawal from UNESCO, Britain also had withdrawn because of concerns about the organization's politicization and anti-Western bias. In July 1997, soon after the Labor government came to power, Britain returned to UNESCO. Criticism of UNESCO was among the causes of the U.S. Senate's skepticism toward the UNESCO Convention during the implementation debate. In Britain, the Labor government's more favorable approach to the organization than its Conservative predecessor's increased its willingness to join the UNESCO Convention.

The ethical and internationalist orientation of the Labor government's foreign policy magnified the weight of the secondary externalities of the illicit antiquities trade. The result was a new balance between the conflicting influences and a new government preference that leaned toward regulation. With its emphasis on moral responsibility and international cooperation, the new government could not ignore the role of the British art market in fueling plunder abroad. The relevant member of government, Minister for the Arts Alan Howarth, was particularly concerned and determined to act. Presentations by archaeologists Neil Brodie and Colin Renfrew of the Illicit Antiquities Research Center convinced Howarth that the problem was serious and that a British response was necessary.[242] The government also found the accusations of Britain's involvement in plunder detrimental to the country's reputation and wanted to reassure foreign countries that Britain would not knowingly be complicit in looting.[243] Commitment to combat the illicit antiquities trade was meant as a signal: a demonstration of British engagement in international affairs, cooperativeness, and willingness to act in a respectable and moral manner.

Another distinction between the Labor and Conservative governments was Conservatives' more extensive ties to the business community and greater dependence on business support.[244] This made them less favorable to market regulation. Indeed, Blair's Labor government also committed to market liberalization and deregulation, but recognized that an ethical foreign policy may require regulatory constraints on business.[245] In July 1997 the government introduced new guidelines for arms exports that took into account respect for human rights. Yet the government was still hesitant to impose regulation on the art market and favored cooperation with the trade, rather than coercion. By the end of the 1990s, the trade came on board. In a public atmosphere rife with scandals and finger-pointing at the art market, the dealers had to salvage their reputation by accepting regulatory constraints. Like the U.S. government three decades earlier, the British government recognized that such constraints required a formal domestic consensus to which the trade would be a part. In both the United States and Britain, the vehicle for forging that consensus was a panel that included all stakeholders and issued policy recommendations. The U.S. government had initiated the ASIL panel in 1969; the British equivalent was the Ministerial Advisory Panel on Illicit Trade (known as the Illicit Trade Advisory

Panel or ITAP)—a body whose members represented the archaeologists, the museums, and the trade.

## Illicit Trade Advisory Panel

The British Parliament provided the final impetus for the establishment of ITAP. In response to the scandals and the archaeologists' pressure, the House of Commons' Culture, Media, and Sport Committee launched its own inquiry into the illicit trade in cultural property in February 2000. The Committee did not have formal powers vis-à-vis the government, but it could raise questions, issue a critical report, and embarrass the government. The government felt the heat; addressing the antiquities problem became urgent. In May 2000, even before the Parliamentary committee issued its report, the minister for the arts appointed the Illicit Trade Advisory Panel under the chairmanship of Professor Norman Palmer. In addition to the chairman, ITAP had eight members who represented a spectrum of views, from archaeologist Colin Renfrew, the harshest critic of the British art market, to representatives of that market. Their mission was "to consider the nature and extent of the illicit international trade in art and antiquities, and the extent to which the UK is involved in this"; and to consider how "the UK can play its part in preventing and prohibiting the illicit trade, and to advise the Government accordingly."[246]

Both the archaeologists and the dealers serving on ITAP realized that a compromise was in their interest. Their pragmatic approach was manifested in the panel's report, submitted in December 2000. The report's opening propositions captured the conflicting incentives facing Britain. ITAP recognized the contribution of a market in cultural objects to the economy and to cultural institutions in Britain. At the same time, the panel was mindful of alarming reports of cultural depredation both within and beyond the United Kingdom, the obliteration of the historical record caused by illicit archaeological excavations, and the need "to ensure that the UK is not used as either a repository or a transit point for [looted] material."[247] On that basis, ITAP made four principal recommendations:

1. After examining both the UNESCO and UNIDROIT Conventions, ITAP recommended that Britain join the former, but not the latter.

The panel did recognize certain virtues of the UNIDROIT Convention. By establishing a direct right of recovery of stolen cultural objects without need for government intervention, the convention "could substantially stem or reverse the national outflow of stolen cultural objects from the UK." Furthermore, the UNIDROIT Convention deals expressly with antiquities obtained through the illicit excavation of sites, and subscribing to it "would signal to both domestic and overseas interests a national determination to curb the unlawful removal of cultural objects."[248] Yet the panel concluded that the drawbacks of the UNIDROIT Convention outweighed its benefits. The convention does not allow for reservations; and the long limitation periods it sets were judged as unduly onerous, as they would have left dealers vulnerable to legal claims for an extended period of time. The fact that the convention had won few ratifications—only 12 at the time of ITAP's deliberations—detracted from its attractiveness as well. Most importantly, the trade was implacably opposed to the UNIDROIT Convention.[249]

By contrast, ITAP recommended that Britain accede to the UNESCO Convention. Compared with the sweeping UNIDROIT Convention, the UNESCO Convention seemed modest and circumscribed—a gentler and more attractive convention. Unlike the UNIDROIT Convention, the UNESCO Convention allows for reservations and affords contracting states considerable discretion in implementation to reflect local conditions and preexisting obligations, including EU law. Furthermore, the possibility of entering reservations allowed Britain to limit the range of objects covered. The panel recommended that in acceding to the convention, Britain state that the term "cultural property" would be confined to objects listed in the Annex to the EU Regulation on cultural goods. This also made things easier for the trade, which was accustomed to the EU definitions.[250]

Most importantly, ITAP found the UNESCO Convention attractive since it believed that compliance would not be onerous. Britain's longstanding rejection of the convention had been based on the presumed burdens it would impose on the British bureaucracy and the trade. ITAP, however, conducted the first serious—and favorable—examination of the convention's implications for British law and practice and exploded the myth of an excessive burden. The panel concluded that Britain was already in compliance with the convention's requirements and could accede without bureaucratic or legislative changes. For example, one of the major stumbling blocks identified by previous governments had been the convention's requirement of a national inventory of protected cultural property. The panel concluded that Britain's existing export-licensing system, with its list of categories of relevant objects, satisfied this requirement.[251]

Widespread membership in the UNESCO Convention—91 countries at the time of ITAP's deliberations—further increased its appeal compared to the unpopular UNIDROIT Convention. First, the panel assumed that "that many countries can't be wrong." Second, accession to an agreement that commanded worldwide support would give Britain "the patina of respectability."[252] At the same time, the failure of other European market-countries to join the convention would magnify the political dividends of British accession, positioning Britain as a leader.[253] Third, the widespread ratification of the UNESCO Convention enhanced its value as a means of recovering objects unlawfully removed from Britain. Of particular importance was the news about an impending Swiss accession to the UNESCO Convention. The panel realized that if Switzerland, a major market-country for antiquities, was about to accede, Britain ought to consider accession as well. Moreover, if Switzerland were to close its doors to looted material, that material might be rerouted to London—an outcome that the panel wished to prevent.[254]

ITAP did recognize certain drawbacks of the UNESCO Convention. For example, the convention depends on government intervention and gives no direct right of action to the former possessors of stolen objects. Yet the panel ultimately endorsed the convention in light of its benefits in terms of recovering "objects removed from the UK and of the message which accession would send to interested parties across the world," and based on "the understanding that accession requires no further legislative commitment."[255]

2. ITAP proposed a new criminal offense of dishonestly importing, dealing in, or possessing any cultural object, knowing or believing that the object was stolen, illegally excavated, or removed from a monument contrary to local law. The offense was to apply irrespective of the country in which the theft, excavation, or removal occurred, including Britain. The panel further proposed to enhance the relevant powers and resources of British law-enforcement agencies.[256]

3. Under the 1992 EU Regulation, applications for export licenses for cultural objects imported from another EU country are checked to ensure that the export from that country was legal. ITAP considered this system of export control to be a workable model for curbing the movement of objects illegally exported from non-EU countries. It was recommended that with respect to objects recently imported into Britain for which an export license is sought, the same checks would be performed as for objects imported from another EU country.[257] The panel judged that the imposition of import controls by Britain was not feasible; hence the recommendation to employ export control instead.

4. A major challenge facing those who transact in antiquities is to ascertain that objects were removed legally from their countries of origin. To facilitate this task, the panel recommended the institution of a comprehensive database of international legislative information and a database of cultural objects unlawfully removed from any place in the world.[258]

### Implementation of ITAP's Recommendations

ITAP achieved an unprecedented consensus between the archaeologists and the trade on a set of regulatory measures.[259] The trade's endorsement of these measures was especially critical. As the chairman of ITAP acknowledges, "If the trade had opposed the [ITAP] report, the report would have been dead."[260] The government accepted the panel's main proposals, yet momentum dissipated quickly. Britain did accede to the UNESCO Convention in August 2002, 32 years after its establishment. This, of course, was the easiest recommendation to implement, since accession, as per ITAP's conclusions, did not involve changes to British law or practice. For the government, accession was a low-cost signal of commitment to the efforts against looting. It was trumpeted as an indication "that the UK is serious about joining the international effort to stamp out illicit trade in cultural objects."[261] The government, however, dragged its feet on the new criminal offense.[262] Only in 2003 was there a rush to enact the Dealing in Cultural Objects (Offences) Act, following the looting of the Baghdad Museum in the aftermath of the invasion of Iraq. As part of the invading coalition, the British government could not allow objects of Iraqi origin to appear on the London market. Yet the impact of the new offense—dealing in tainted objects—has been small. To accommodate the trade's interests, the legislation's provisions were diluted.[263] Furthermore, the government did not implement the panel's recommendation to provide law-enforcement agencies with additional resources and has shown little enthusiasm for actually prosecuting dealers.

The government failed to carry out ITAP's two other recommendations. Citing incompatibility with EU legislation, the government's lawyers thwarted the implementation of the export licensing system to curb the outward movement from Britain of cultural objects unlawfully removed from foreign countries.[264] The databases recommendation was also abandoned due to cost and complexity. The failure to establish the unlawfully removed objects database was particularly upsetting to the dealers. They had accepted the sticks—accession to the UNESCO Convention, export control, and a new criminal offense—in exchange for a carrot: a database that would facilitate due diligence. Yet the government ultimately failed to deliver the promised carrot.[265] A follow-up report by ITAP warned that "[i]f a substantial period elapses between accession [to the UNESCO Convention] and the adoption of the panel's other main proposals, there is a risk that this will be interpreted (both within and beyond the UK) as an exercise in heel-dragging, or as a desire to enjoy the benefits of UNESCO without any of the burdens. It would be unfortunate if the substantial goodwill generated by the announcement that the UK is to accede to UNESCO were to be dissipated by later inaction, or if the lead given by the UK government to other countries were to become tarnished by a perception that form usurps substance."[266]

Why was momentum lost? To a large extent, ITAP's recommendations fell victim to divergent interministerial priorities. While curbing the trade in looted antiquities may have been a goal of the Department for Culture, Media, and Sport, it was a low priority for the Home Office that is in charge of law enforcement. Moreover, the civil service was not keen to spend money and create more work for itself. Beyond these specific obstacles, the

fundamental problem was that the transformation of the British preference, although significant, was only partial. Britain did not shift from the
anti-regulation pole to the pro-regulation side; rather, it became cross-pressured. While interested in curbing the plunder of antiquities, the government favored only modest regulation that would neither burden the trade
and the bureaucracy nor divert efforts from more pressing law-enforcement
priorities. Furthermore, after the scandals of the 1990s subsided, the illicit
antiquities trade was again a relatively marginal political issue with little
presence in the public debate. As the government no longer faced demands
for action on this problem, the incentive to allocate the necessary resources
diminished considerably. The long-term impact of the scandals on the
dealers' image was also limited. The dealers managed to maintain their
high social status and esteem as well as political ties. They were not seen as
complicit in crime, and the government had little interest in enforcement
against them.[267]

What, then, was the impact of the change in the British government's
preference? One could argue that it had no real effect on the ground. While
the UNESCO Convention seeks to enhance the control over the movement
of antiquities, Britain failed to establish import or export controls and to
enforce criminal justice measures. Its accession to the convention can thus
be seen as an empty gesture. On the positive side, the establishment of ITAP
and the scandals preceding it, the accession to the UNESCO Convention,
and the enactment of the new criminal offense all served as a warning sign.
These developments signaled government, media, and public concern
about the looting of antiquities. This had at least a marginal effect on the
dealers, who were anxious to maintain their reputation and to prevent
looted material from tarnishing their name and harming their business.
The dealers realized that turning a blind eye to the dubious origin of antiquities may not be as easily forgiven as in the past: the trade was now
expected to act more responsibly. As a result, the dealers started paying
greater attention than before to the provenance of antiquities in an effort to
ensure their legitimacy. This by no means amounted to a complete transformation of the trade's practices, but some modest changes have been made.

In addition to its domestic implications, Britain's accession to the UNESCO
Convention reverberated internationally and generated a snowball effect.
Prior to Britain's accession, the convention had been rejected by all major
market-countries, with the exception of the United States. The accession of
Britain, an important market-country that had opposed the UNESCO Convention since its inception, made other market countries take a fresh look.
Switzerland, Japan, Germany, the Netherlands, and other market countries
followed Britain's example and joined the convention. The British accession
proved to be a turning point.

# The United States, Britain, and the Efforts against Looting: Conclusions

The participation of the United States and Britain in the efforts against looting is consistent with this book's theoretical framework. Moral entrepreneurs—the archaeologists—used their knowledge and expertise to stimulate concern about and to urge action against the secondary externalities of the illicit antiquities trade: plunder abroad. The information provided by the archaeological community—especially Clemency Coggins's 1969 article in the United States and *Stealing History* in Britain—brought national attention to the problem, raised policymakers' and public awareness, and exposed the complicity of the art market. Consistent with the theoretical framework, consumers of antiquities—the dealers—have opposed regulation and have lobbied governments against the acceptance of international control. The behavior of museums, however, only partially conforms to the theoretical framework. The major American art museums, especially in recent years, have taken an unequivocal anti-regulation position, as expected from consumers. Other museums, however, have balanced their public-trust responsibility and commitment to cultural preservation against their self-interest in acquiring antiquities. They have therefore expressed more moderate views and in some cases have actually favored regulation. Furthermore, even the British dealers tempered their resistance to regulation in the changing normative environment of the late 1990s. When scandals tarnished the art market's reputation and threatened to harm business, the trade had to distance itself from archaeological plunder and drive a wedge between legitimate and looted objects. This demonstrates that while consumers typically favor uncontrolled trade, under certain circumstances they may come to support regulation.

The case of antiquities further shows how governments form their preferences on international regulation by balancing the competing influences; it also demonstrates that this balance is dynamic and may change over time. Policymakers were clearly influenced by a well-connected interest group: the dealers. The United States resisted international regulation until the late 1960s and Britain persisted in its rejection of regulation until 2000 so as not to constrain a lucrative and thriving market. As long as the main motivation of the U.S. and British governments was to avoid burdening the trade and the bureaucracy, they had little interest in cooperation against looting. But the anti-regulation pressure of the trade and the concerns about a law-enforcement burden were ultimately offset, at least in part, by a changing public atmosphere. In the United States in the early 1970s, a series of scandals and the work of archaeologists brought looting into the limelight and created a climate conducive to restraints on the art market. A similar shift occurred years later in Britain. The London art-market scandals and the educational efforts of archaeologists in the 1990s generated a public demand for government action against looting abroad. Amid growing concerns about the art market's complicity in plunder, both the U.S. and British governments became cross-pressured; these concerns also weakened the resistance of regulation opponents, who realized that a more constructive approach would be in their interest. At that point, government indifference to archaeological plunder and the repudiation of international regulation were no longer tenable. Both governments sought to signal—domestically and internationally—their determination to address the problem of looting. This was to be achieved through cautious acceptance of international antiquities regulation.

In Britain, additional developments over time prepared the ground for regulation: the loss of Britain's own cultural objects and the change of government. According to the theoretical framework, different governments in the same country may vary in their preferences. The Labor government was indeed more committed than its Conservative predecessor to international cooperation and more concerned for Britain's moral standing. The result was a more favorable approach toward the efforts against looting. But a relatively positive approach should not be mistaken for enthusiastic endorsement. Policymakers were still very much aware of the dealers' concerns and tried to accommodate them. Even after deciding to join the efforts against looting, the U.S. and British governments sought a regulatory solution that would only minimally interfere with the working and profitability of the trade. Furthermore, both governments realized that any viable regulation must gain the dealers' approval. They struck compromises that would contribute to the prevention of plunder abroad while avoiding an onerous burden at home.

Yet the analysis has also revealed certain differences between the American and British cases. Britain's museums share the archaeologists' views, whereas American museums are closer to the trade in their preference for weak regulation; British dealers hold more moderate views than their American colleagues; and the pro-regulation forces in Britain did not face a hurdle similar to the U.S. Senate's support for the art market. These factors should have pushed Britain toward a more stringent regulation of antiquities than in the United States. Yet today the protection of antiquities of foreign origin is stronger in the United States than in Britain. The CPIA led to actual restrictions on the movement of antiquities, which the U.S. government has enforced; this was not the case with Britain. The cause of this difference was the divergent attitudes of the U.S. and British bureaucracies. The State Department has led the regulatory efforts in the United States, from the negotiation of the UNESCO Convention to its implementation through agreements with source countries. The U.S. Justice Department has prosecuted dealers, and U.S. Customs has taken action against the import of looted antiquities.

By contrast, the British civil service has been reluctant to follow suit. Its budgetary constraints and favorable attitude toward the dealers have resulted in a less-than-wholehearted commitment to the efforts to protect the archaeological heritage. Divergent interministerial priorities have also been an obstacle. The minister in charge of arts and culture had limited influence vis-à-vis a Home Office with more pressing concerns than plunder abroad. The theoretical framework has treated the government as a unified entity with a single preference. While this approximation is useful for analytical purposes, the British case demonstrates that governments may sometimes speak with more than one voice. Tensions between politicians and bureaucrats, as well as rivalries among ministries, might hinder international cooperation. External coercion may be able to overcome such tensions and rivalries; but the efforts against looting have not involved the exercise of coercion. By contrast, the U.S.-led campaign against human trafficking has employed coercive pressure, as described in the following chapter.

# 5

## PROTECTING PERSONS

International Cooperation against Human Trafficking

---

Hundreds of thousands of people are trafficked across borders every year for sexual or labor exploitation; many more are trafficked within their own countries.[1] Sex trafficking typically involves abuse within the commercial sex industry: trafficked women and girls are trapped in abusive and exploitative prostitution, often aggravated by physical and mental brutality. Labor trafficking traps vulnerable workers in an extremely harsh and abusive work environment. Victims toil in sweatshops, fields, and construction sites, kept in submission by threats, violence, exploitative debts, and deprivation of freedom.

Throughout the 20th century, several international agreements tackled human trafficking, starting with the 1904 International Agreement for the Suppression of the White Slave Traffic. This chapter opens with a historical overview of these agreements. Its focus, however, is on the American legislation on human trafficking: the Trafficking Victims Protection Act of 2000 (hereafter the Trafficking Act or the Act). The Trafficking Act is a domestic law rather than an international agreement to which governments have consented. Yet in its purpose, the Act resembles the international regulatory agreements examined in this book: it sets global standards for the elimination of illicit trade and seeks to bring governments worldwide into compliance with these standards. The Trafficking Act thus effectively functions as international regulation, albeit not consensual but imposed by a powerful country. Why, then, focus on this Act, rather than on the international agreements that target human trafficking? As the theoretical framework has suggested, coercion plays a major role in the cooperative efforts against illicit trade. Unlike the international agreements, the Trafficking Act includes a monitoring and sanctioning mechanism and is thus better suited to establishing cooperation. By analyzing the Trafficking Act and its effects, I shed empirical light on several components of the theoretical framework.

The second section of this chapter explores the domestic political process that culminated in the passage of the Trafficking Act. Continuing a theme of Chapter 4, it examines how moral entrepreneurs stimulate government concern about the negative effects of illicit trade abroad. The third and fourth sections explore Israel's policy on sex trafficking and labor trafficking, respectively. Throughout the 1990s the Israeli government was indifferent to human trafficking and failed to take action against it. Only following the 2001 and 2006 Trafficking in Persons Reports, issued by the State Department, did remarkable changes occur in Israel's policy. The Israeli case illustrates how coercion can change government calculations and motivate the suppression of illicit trade.

## Cooperation against Human Trafficking: A Historical Perspective

The late 19th century witnessed the expansion and flourishing of migratory prostitution. Colonialism induced the mobilization and migration of large numbers of single men, who provided a demand for sexual services. This worldwide demand was met by an influx of Asian, European, and American women driven from their countries of origin by political and economic turmoil.[2] These women entered the international sex trade "under a variety of circumstances, ranging from astute entrepreneurial calculation to entrapment. They operated along a spectrum of autonomy, from full control over their labor conditions to the virtual enslavement of locked brothels."[3] Despite this variation, and although many of them were women of color, the phenomenon came to be known as "white slavery" or "white slave traffic." While the term had several interpretations, its popular meaning was the procurement, by force, deceit, or drugs, of a white woman or girl for involuntary prostitution. The number of actual cases that met this definition was apparently small.[4] Yet stories of enslaved women, especially of European origin, circulated widely, generated public outrage, and triggered an international campaign against white slavery.

The initiative for this campaign came from two groups of moral entrepreneurs. British feminists, led by Josephine Butler, saw prostitutes as victims who should be rescued and rehabilitated. In 1886 their efforts led to the repeal of Britain's Contagious Diseases Acts, whose regulation of prostitution resulted in the degrading and mistreatment of women. Next, Butler and her feminist movement turned to agitating against the international trafficking in women and children. They were joined by British social-purity reformers, who sought to cleanse society of immorality and vice. These social reformers established the National Vigilance Association (NVA), which became the foundation for a wide coalition against white slavery. NVA leaders toured Europe in the 1890s and formed national committees in several European countries. In 1899 the NVA established an international bureau to coordinate between national committees and distribute information.[5]

Campaigners against the sex trade argued that organized trafficking networks preyed on unsuspecting white women. To arouse public sympathy, the campaign portrayed the women as innocent, helpless victims forced into the lurid world of sexual slavery.[6] In 1904 these efforts bore fruit with the adoption of the International Agreement for the Suppression of the White Slave Traffic. The agreement established a set of limited measures, such as the coordination of information on the procurement of women "for immoral purposes abroad,"[7] monitoring of train stations and ports for traffickers and victims, and repatriation of victims to their countries of origin. The ineffectiveness of this agreement led to the 1910 International Convention for the Suppression of the White Slave Traffic—a convention that required criminalization and punishment of traffickers.

International efforts against the sex trade continued after World War I under the auspices of the League of Nations.[8] Two new conventions expanded the scope of protective measures and punishable acts; they also replaced the term "white slave traffic" with the colorblind "traffic in women": the International Convention for the Suppression of the Traffic in Women and Children (1921) and the International Convention for the Suppression of the Traffic in Women of Full Age (1933). The League's efforts also included two fact-finding missions that investigated sex trafficking.[9] Yet despite the League's ambition to "vanquish this powerful evil,"[10] the impact of its efforts was limited. As I discuss below, governments often have little motivation to suppress human trafficking; external pressure is thus necessary to compel them to do so. The League's proclamations and agreements, however, were not accompanied by coercive pressure. Ultimately, national restrictions on migration and the decline of migration flows diminished the international market for women and made a greater contribution to curbing the sex trade than the League's endeavors.[11]

Shortly after its establishment in 1945, the UN addressed sex trafficking through a new convention that consolidated and supplemented the four previous ones: the Convention for the Suppression of the Traffic in Persons and of the Exploitation of the Prostitution of Others (1949). This convention required states to take a range of measures against prostitution and sex trafficking; yet like the earlier conventions, it was not accompanied by an enforcement mechanism to foster compliance.

The UN's early interest in sex trafficking quickly dissipated, in large part because the problem seemed to be waning. A 1959 study commissioned by the UN found that trafficking and forced prostitution had not altogether disappeared, but concluded that in most countries the percentage of foreign prostitutes was very low.[12] Yet sex trafficking was not wiped off the international agenda. From the 1950s through the 1980s, the trafficking of women and children from Asia, Africa, and Latin America into Europe, Japan, and the United States continued to raise concerns; so did the travel of rich-country nationals to poor countries for the purpose of sex tourism.[13] This led to some modest steps, such as the inclusion of a provision on sex trafficking in the 1979 Convention on the Elimination of All Forms of Discrimination against Women.[14]

It took the political and economic upheaval of the 1980s and 1990s to revive the international efforts against the sex trade. The collapse of the Soviet Union and economic reforms across the developing world resulted in job displacement and unemployment which, in turn, led to a sharp increase in sex trafficking. The UN responded by adopting a new international agreement in 2000: the Protocol to Prevent, Suppress and Punish Trafficking in Persons, Especially Women and Children, supplementing the United Nations Convention against Transnational Organized Crime (hereafter the UN Protocol). This protocol went further than previous agreements. For example, it provided a definition of trafficking in persons and prohibited labor exploitation in addition to sexual exploitation. Yet the UN Protocol followed its predecessors by failing to establish a mechanism to ensure compliance. Monitoring of compliance and coercive pressure on noncompliant governments were important innovations in the U.S. anti-trafficking legislation and the key to its impact.

## The American Efforts against Human Trafficking Worldwide

The demand for cooperation against illicit trade typically comes from victim countries: those countries that bear the trade's negative externalities. Chapter 3 examined African countries' pursuit of international small-arms regulation to reduce gun violence. Chapter 4 documented the international efforts against the looting of antiquities: the initiative came from countries where the plunder of archaeology was rampant. The United States' global campaign to eliminate human trafficking is different. The main motivation for this campaign, which was launched in 2000, was not to end the victimization of American women and their trafficking across borders. Rather, the U.S. government acted on behalf of, and out of concern for, foreign victims. Its goal was to relieve the plight of men, women, and children worldwide that "were bought, sold, transported and held against their will in slave-like conditions."[15] The United States thus acted as a self-appointed victim, motivated by secondary externalities: the harm that human trafficking causes abroad. What inspired the American concerns? Why would the U.S. government commit "to rallying the world to defeat human trafficking?"[16] Behind this international campaign stood an unlikely coalition of religious groups and women's organizations. The following analysis explores how these moral entrepreneurs turned their cause—the elimination of human trafficking—into an American foreign policy goal.

## The Moral Entrepreneurs' Motivations

The campaign to eliminate human trafficking came on the heels of the campaign for international religious freedom. Both campaigns owe much of their success to the initiative and relentless efforts of Michael Horowitz, a former Reagan administration official and a think-tank fellow.

In 1995 Horowitz—himself Jewish—launched an international campaign against the persecution of Christians. The campaign was inspired by Horowitz's view of Christianity as a force for modernity and human rights that can make the world's culture and politics more caring and less bloody. Horowitz also believed that the treatment of Christians in societies worldwide was a litmus indicator of freedom generally. Curbing religious persecution and protecting vulnerable Christians abroad would therefore promote respect for the human dignity of all.[17] To this end, Horowitz mobilized a faith-based coalition, with evangelical Christians at its core. He brought the issue to the attention of evangelical leaders and convinced them to champion legislation to combat religious persecution worldwide. This coalition proved to be an effective vehicle for advocacy that overcame the opposition from businesses and from the Clinton administration.[18] In October 1998 President Bill Clinton signed the International Religious Freedom Act into law. This legislation established a State Department office to monitor religious freedom worldwide and authorized the president to take countermeasures against foreign governments that engage in or tolerate severe violations of religious freedom.

By drawing religious groups into the human rights area and catalyzing them into a political force, the campaign against religious persecution prepared the ground for the anti-human trafficking campaign. Even prior to the passage of the International Religious Freedom Act, Horowitz sensed that the coalition he had mobilized was capable of achieving goals beyond religious freedom; he sought to put the evangelical force to further use. His search for a new cause ended upon reading an article on sex trafficking published by The New York Times in January 1998. "As soon as I read it," Horowitz recalls, "I knew that that was Act Two for this coalition."[19]

The article, by Michael Specter, told the story of Irina, a young Ukrainian woman who had left her home country to rescue herself from poverty, only to end up in a brothel in Israel, where her boss burned her passport and said that he owned her. Irina at first refused to prostitute herself, but succumbed after being beaten and raped. Following a police raid on the brothel, Irina found herself in a women's prison, awaiting deportation. Irina's story served as an example of the "international bazaar for women" that involved "selling naive and desperate young women into sexual bondage."[20] Specter's article examined the dire social and economic climate that facilitated this market by impelling young women to flee their homelands; the methods of recruitment into the sex trade, which often involved deception; the complacency of law-enforcement agencies; and the brutalized lives of trafficked women, forced to have sex with a large number of clients every day.

The article exposed a reality of exploitation and abuse that moved Horow-itz deeply. As a Jew, he was particularly appalled by the participation of Israel in sex trafficking. The story also struck a personal chord with Horowitz, reminding him of an event that had taken place more than 30 years earlier. On a rainy night in a Manhattan bar, Horowitz had witnessed a pimp beating up a prostitute. No one had come to the prostitute's help, including Horow-itz. The *Times* article immediately brought back the emotional memory of that personal experience. Horowitz's past failure to help a defenseless prostitute against an abusive pimp strengthened his newborn determination to combat human trafficking. He found it to be a perfect issue around which to mobilize evangelicals—demonstrating that this community was not preoccupied with parochial concerns, but committed to human dignity.[21]

As I discuss later, Horowitz assembled an unusual coalition of religious groups and feminist activists to advocate for anti-trafficking legislation. Different members of the coalition approached human trafficking with related yet distinct views and motivations. Horowitz himself saw human trafficking through the prism of slavery. He considered it to be the slavery issue of our time and drew an analogy between contemporary efforts against human trafficking and Britain's anti-slavery campaign in the 19th century. For him, the contemporary fight against human trafficking continued the legacy of William Wilberforce, a leader of the British movement to abolish the African slave trade.

Religious sentiments motivated evangelical Christians to combat sex trafficking and prostitution—two phenomena that they saw as inherently tied together. Evangelicals explained their efforts as being inspired by the view that all human beings were made in the image of God and that God's image imparts an unspeakable value to each person. This belief led them to confront attacks on human dignity, including sex trafficking. Evangelicals also sought to answer Christ's call upon them to be the light that dispels darkness, where trafficking for sexual exploitation is a form of darkness and oppression, and combating it an answer to Christ's call.[22] Furthermore, evangelicals' condemnation of sex trafficking was consistent with their espousal of traditional family values and their belief that sexuality should only be expressed within monogamous heterosexual marriage.[23] Finally, sex trafficking resonated with the evangelical community because of evangelicals' historical efforts against the commercial sexual exploitation of women. The contemporary efforts of evangelicals against human trafficking followed in the footsteps of Josephine Butler and of Salvation Army founders William and Catherine Booth.

The feminist approach to the efforts against sex trafficking demonstrated a duality that departs from this book's theoretical framework. The theoretical framework has identified moral entrepreneurs as actors that seek the suppression of illicit trade. These value-motivated groups lobby policymakers to curb trade that they deem harmful. Yet moral entrepreneurs do not always agree with each other on how to tackle illicit trade. In fact, they may have fundamental disagreements, as shown by the rift within the feminist community over prostitution and its connection to sex trafficking.

The main contending views in the feminist debate over prostitution are abolition versus sex work. Abolitionists consider the commercial sexual exploitation of women—first and foremost, prostitution—as an inherently oppressive practice that stems from women's inequality.[24] Abolitionists reject the distinction between forced and voluntary prostitution and view the woman's will or consent as meaningless: they see *all* prostitution as exploitative, degrading, and harmful, and do not consider it a legitimate form of labor. Abolitionist groups—such as Equality Now and the Coalition Against Trafficking in Women (CATW)—argue that prostitution and sex trafficking are closely linked, since most prostitutes are victims of sex trafficking. In their view, decriminalization, regulation, or any toleration of prostitution results in greater demand for trafficking victims and increases the number of women trafficked into prostitution.[25] For abolitionists, sex trafficking is a major human rights violation directed primarily against women.

By contrast, sex-work proponents see prostitution as legitimate labor that women may voluntarily choose as a valid livelihood option. They believe that prostitution should thus be decriminalized and, perhaps, regulated by the state. Importantly, sex-work advocates reject the conflation of trafficking and prostitution, and argue that linking them is a ploy to eliminate commercial sex. For them, trafficking is limited to prostitution that involves force or coercion.[26] Whereas abolitionists oppose both sex trafficking and prostitution, sex-work supporters oppose trafficking but would legitimize prostitution.

Abolitionist feminists teamed up with the evangelicals in support of legislation against human trafficking. Sex-work advocates, however, believed the Trafficking Act promoted an anti-prostitution agenda. In the years following the Act's passage, proponents of sex work continued to denounce the efforts of the evangelical-feminist coalition as a misguided moral crusade against the sex industry. They challenged the core claims underlying the "crusade," such as the evilness of prostitution, the inextricable link between prostitution and sex trafficking, and the rapidly growing magnitude of the latter.[27] They also criticized the imposition of American standards on foreign countries through the Trafficking Act.[28]

## The Moral Entrepreneurs' Methods of Advocacy

How did a diverse and fragile coalition of moral entrepreneurs put sex trafficking on the national agenda? How did this coalition convince U.S. policymakers to address a tragic phenomenon abroad that had no real impact on American interests?

Forming a broad right-left coalition of religious groups and abolitionist feminists was in itself essential to the success of the campaign. By the late 1990s some of these actors had already engaged in separate efforts against human trafficking, but these did not achieve any policy traction in Washington.[29] Michael Horowitz realized that a legislative effort would require uniting the disparate activists into one coalition. He found the evangelical community receptive to the anti-trafficking cause, which was a logical follow-up to that community's previous work on religious persecution.[30] Evangelical leaders Chuck Colson, Gary Haugen, and Richard Land were among the most dedicated to the campaign against trafficking; so was conservative politician Bill Bennett. Some Jewish groups joined the coalition as well. Rabbi David Saperstein, director of the Religious Action Center of Reform Judaism, came to play a key role in the campaign, especially in dealing with the Clinton administration. On the feminist side, the coalition was joined by activists such as Laura Lederer and Jessica Neuwirth, both with long experience in fighting the commercial sexual exploitation of women.

Horowitz believed that a broad coalition would increase politicians' receptiveness to the campaign. Since groups on the right and the left had already expressed enthusiasm, politicians themselves had to spend relatively little time galvanizing support. Such an unusual coalition of groups, all committed to the same cause, also signaled the importance and seriousness of the issue and enhanced the legitimacy and credibility of the campaign. As Horowitz recalls, politicians "knew something was very different, and their antennas started to quiver." A broad coalition gave them the opportunity to be "the grand marshals of a parade"[31] of diverse groups from across the political spectrum: Christian groups such as the National Association of Evangelicals and the Southern Baptist Convention, alongside women's groups such as Equality Now. Obviously, the combination of right-wing evangelicals and left-wing feminists was not the most natural of coalitions. There was skepticism and unease on both sides about reaching across the political divide and working with bitter rivals. As a member of the coalition put it, the joint work on human trafficking legislation was not "a big love fest." Nevertheless, "people had the strategic sense that having that kind of coalition was necessary."[32] On behalf of the common cause of combating sex trafficking, the two camps had to rise above their sharp disagreements on other matters.

How did members of the coalition advocate for their cause? While everyone recognized that sex trafficking was morally repugnant, more than that was needed to induce political action: policymakers had to be convinced that the United States could not stand idly by as foreign women were sold into prostitution. The argument for combating human trafficking was essentially about human decency, but the coalition framed it in ways that would have a stronger resonance with politicians. Describing sex trafficking as modern-day slavery was one such way, since slavery's legacy in the United States makes American policymakers sensitive to this issue. By declaring the anti-trafficking efforts "abolitionist"—a term that denotes the fight against slavery—the coalition enhanced the campaign's appeal.[33] The coalition further emphasized that sex trafficking was not a parochial concern, but a cause that transcended the politics of self-interest: one of the great moral issues of the 21st century. The campaign against trafficking was presented as an opportunity for politicians to take part in a history-making initiative, one that would score points with diverse constituencies.[34]

Key to the success of the campaign was the support of several members of Congress, in particular Representatives Chris Smith (R-NJ), Sam Gejdenson (D-CT), and Frank Wolf (R-VA) as well as Senators Sam Brownback (R-KS) and Paul Wellstone (D-MN). The coalition worked extensively with them and with their staffers on the anti-trafficking bill. These members of Congress were deeply moved by the problem of human trafficking, especially after coming face-to-face with victims. Sam Brownback, for example, visited Nepal where he "met with a number of girls who had been tricked, taken against their will into the sex trafficking, into India, two-thirds of them coming back with AIDS and/or tuberculosis, many of them tricked into the trade at ages 11, 12 years of age, coming back at the ages of 16, 17 . . . to die a horrible death."[35] Other members of Congress received a firsthand impression of the brutality of trafficking through victim testimonies in congressional hearings. Disguised for safety reasons, a woman named Inez shared her story with a Senate Foreign Relations subcommittee. She had come to the United States from Mexico ostensibly for a restaurant job, only to end up in a brothel, where she was severely abused by clients and bosses.[36] Similar stories came from Russian women who had been trafficked into prostitution in Germany and Israel.[37] These victims' testimonies educated and touched members of Congress.[38]

Congressional hearings were also an opportunity for members of the coalition to advocate policy solutions. In oral and written statements, Laura Lederer provided information on the magnitude of the problem and explained how foreign countries could tackle it through strict, enforceable laws aimed at the prevention of trafficking, prosecution of traffickers, and protection of victims. She maintained that the "United States is perhaps the only country right now that can play a leadership role in encouraging countries to address the problem of trafficking."[39] Gary Haugen of the International Justice Mission explained how the United States could play that leadership role. He argued that the ease with which forced prostitution operated in certain countries created the financial incentives for traffickers. The toleration of forced prostitution depended, in turn, on the quality and vigor of local, street-level law enforcement. The vigor of local law enforcement was the product of politicians' priorities, and it is here that the United States could enter the picture:

> U.S. policy toward a country can have a very powerful effect upon the priorities of a nation's most senior authorities who sit on top of local law enforcement's chain of command. . . . [T]hese public officials will move an issue from the "good idea" column and into the "urgent priority" column only when they think something bad will happen if they don't. This is why senior government authorities may be pushed to the point of making forced prostitution an "urgent priority" through a sense that something bad is going to happen in their relationship with the U.S. Government if they don't. Let's face it. The victims of forced prostitution generally come from the most powerless and vulnerable sectors of the society. . . . The victims are first and foremost, the poor, the children, and the women. They simply do not constitute a powerful or even significant political constituency. And yet, if the goodies that flow from a country's relationship with the world's only remaining superpower and the world's largest economy are jeopardized by a failure to respond to an issue, then that issue can take on an utterly fresh sense of urgency. This is where the stick of negative consequences in U.S. policy can have a powerful and occasionally decisive impact. It can reorganize the priorities of senior officials. And they in turn will reorganize the priorities of those who report to them.[40]

As we shall see, Haugen accurately predicted the powerful impact of the U.S. anti-trafficking legislation on Israeli policymakers and the resulting change in their law-enforcement priorities.

Another important tool employed by the coalition was letters to policymakers. The most significant of those was a letter sent in June 1999 to the speaker of the House, House minority leader, and the majority and minority leaders of the Senate. The letter carried the signatures of nearly 140 religious leaders—both Christian and Jewish—from around the country. It described the "stark realities of a sinister trade that profits ruthless businessmen, criminals, and corrupt public officials at the expense of millions of women and children." The letter's signatories declared that the "God-given dignity and integrity of each individual compels us to take action to combat this evil." They expressed strong support for the proposed anti-trafficking legislation, and in particular for its enforcement through sanctions. They also drew a comparison "between the actions of our 18th and 19th century forebears against the English slave trade and the modern day cause of abolishing sexual trafficking." The letter concluded by expressing "a moral obligation to act" and pledging to work with Congress through the legislative process.[41] By having so many religious leaders sign the letter personally and express their commitment, the coalition signaled the importance and popularity of the anti-trafficking cause.

Building on their expertise and access to policymakers and employing a variety of tools and techniques, members of the coalition educated policymakers about sex trafficking and shaped the legislation.[42] Yet they had to overcome significant obstacles.

## *Obstacles to the Trafficking Act*

The Clinton administration was not supportive of the legislation advanced by the evangelical-feminist coalition. To be sure, the administration had been working to combat human trafficking independently of the coalition's legislative initiative. The administration's anti-trafficking strategy was set forth in a presidential directive of March 11, 1998, on *Steps to Combat Violence Against Women and Trafficking in Women and Girls.* Pursuant to this directive, the United States engaged in bilateral and multilateral anti-trafficking initiatives, such as economic-alternative programs for victims and law-enforcement training in Ukraine; co-sponsorship, with the EU, of public awareness campaigns to warn Eastern European women about the dangers posed by traffickers; and negotiating the UN Protocol on trafficking in persons.[43] In fact, the United States played an important role in these negotiations, which took place in Vienna in 1999–2000, at much the same time as the congressional process of enacting the Trafficking Act.[44] Appearing before Congress, administration officials conveyed "the message that the entire Administration shares [the congressional] determination that we must stop those who profit from the tragedy of trafficking, and we must help those who are its victims once again find dignity." They also emphasized that the "Administration strongly supports the bill's objective of combating trafficking and appreciates the efforts . . . to try to craft legislation that reflects our shared goals, preventing trafficking, prosecuting those who engage in these terrible crimes and protecting trafficking victims."[45] Nevertheless, administration officials expressed serious reservations about the proposed legislation. The main points of contention were as follows:

1. Labor trafficking—The Clinton administration sought to broaden the legislation to include labor trafficking, in addition to sex trafficking. The administration maintained that trafficking into the sex industry "is merely one form of a broader range of trafficking," and that the United States should not limit its "efforts to one form of trafficking over another form."[46] The coalition opposed this idea as an attempt to create equivalence between labor trafficking and sex trafficking and thereby legitimize prostitution as just another form of labor. Furthermore, the coalition suspected that the inclusion of labor trafficking was intended to kill the legislation by entangling it in debates over labor standards. Michael Horowitz's motto was "Less is more": a narrow bill focused on sex trafficking alone would have better chances of passing and would give the United States leverage vis-à-vis foreign countries; its effects would ultimately spill over into labor trafficking.[47]

2. Sanctions—The coalition advocated legislation that would include mandatory economic sanctions—suspension of nonhumanitarian aid— against countries that failed to combat human trafficking. The goal was not necessarily to impose sanctions in practice, but to use the threat of sanctions as leverage: a signal to foreign governments that the issue must be taken seriously, and a means of ensuring that human trafficking would be discussed in high-level meetings between American and foreign officials. The coalition, in fact, sought to make the president personally accountable for anti-trafficking efforts.

The Clinton administration, however, strongly opposed the inclusion of sanctions in the legislation: "Sanctions simply are not the answer to the problem of trafficking." Sanctions, the administration argued, would exacerbate the root causes of trafficking: they would make the targeted countries poorer, diminish economic opportunities, and leave victims more vulnerable to traffickers. Furthermore, "targeted sanctions against specific states are far less effective when the prime moving force behind the problem are not national government officials or policies, but nonstate actors." Sanctions would merely punish governments and societies without affecting the real perpetrators: organized crime syndicates. The administration also argued that governments might choose to downplay the seriousness of the trafficking problem to avoid sanctions, and their willingness to collaborate internationally on this issue would decline. Governments might also come to see a threat in the work of local NGOs to call public attention to this problem; that could lead to retaliation against those NGOs, which are essential to the fight against human trafficking. The administration further claimed that mandatory sanctions would reduce the flexibility necessary for tackling the diverse situations in which trafficking occurred. The conclusion was that "creating a sanctions regime for this problem would be profoundly counterproductive" and would undermine the international efforts to combat human trafficking: "[T]raffickers would applaud the implementation of such sanctions." Moreover, coercion was unnecessary since "government leaders, as they learn about the issue, want to do something about it." In fact, "[a] unilateral sanctions regime that targets even those countries who are starting to address the issue could end up discouraging rather than encouraging effective international cooperation." The administration believed that the United States should work cooperatively with foreign governments to realize "our shared objective of reducing trafficking" through public awareness and education programs, law-enforcement training, and so forth.[48]

As the case of Israel will demonstrate, the administration's view was misguided. The administration assumed that foreign governments shared the goal of suppressing human trafficking, but lacked the capacity to realize this goal: "A great many affected governments want to deter trafficking but lack the resources to do so."[49] In fact, governments often lack political motivation to suppress human trafficking, and coercion may provide the necessary motivation.

3. Bureaucracy and reporting—The administration opposed the establishment of a new State Department office on human trafficking and a separate human-trafficking report. According to the administration, new reporting requirements were unnecessary, costly, and burdensome. Instead, the administration proposed to report on trafficking in the annual Country Reports on Human Rights Practices. Similarly, it was "unnecessary for Congress to impose upon the Secretary of State or the President an organizational structure . . . for addressing trafficking." The administration maintained that the required tools and mechanisms were already in place and there was no reason to reinvent the wheel: "What we need is not new institutions and new bureaucratic requirements, but sufficient capacity for existing offices that already recognize the problem and have a mandate to deal with it."[50]

4. The definition of trafficking—The administration's view was that human trafficking necessarily involved force, fraud, or coercion.[51] The coalition's concern was that force, fraud, or coercion might be difficult to prove; their inclusion in the definition of trafficking would thus create a high evidentiary hurdle. But when the definition controversy threatened to derail the bill, the coalition proposed a compromise two-tiered definition that distinguishes between trafficking and severe forms of trafficking. The legislation's operative definition was to be limited to severe forms of trafficking: those involving force, fraud, or coercion.[52] A similar controversy occupied much of the UN Protocol negotiations, in which both abolitionist and

sex-work feminists participated. Led by the International Human Rights Law Group and the Global Alliance Against Trafficking in Women, sex-work NGOs sought to limit the definition of trafficking to situations involving force or coercion, thereby excluding voluntary, noncoerced prostitution. Abolitionist NGOs, led by CATW, insisted on a definition of trafficking that did not require proof of force or coercion. The view of the United States and other Western countries was closer to that of the sex-work groups.[53]

Why was the Clinton administration unsupportive of the coalition and of the legislation it advocated? In part, the lack of support stemmed from the same concerns that brought the administration to oppose the evangelicals' previous endeavor: the religious-freedom legislation. The administration believed that both initiatives would unnecessarily elevate specific concerns above others, create problems in U.S. foreign relations, and complicate an already complex array of foreign-policy laws.[54] In addition, both wings of the coalition—evangelicals and abolitionist feminists—had little influence over the Clinton administration. The evangelicals were clearly not a Clinton constituency, but even feminist activists found the administration unresponsive. To advance the cause of suppressing illicit trade, moral entrepreneurs need access to open-minded policymakers; but the Clinton administration did not give the coalition a favorable hearing and was not open to persuasion. Rather, the administration sought input from human rights groups such as Human Rights Watch and Amnesty International, as well as from mainstream women's groups such as NARAL and the Center for Women Policy Studies. Ann Jordan, a leading advocate of sex work, also had the administration's ear. These actors' view was that sexual activity between consenting adults—including prostitution—was legitimate, and that trafficking was limited to situations involving force, fraud, or coercion. This view shaped the Clinton administration's approach to sex trafficking as a form of coerced labor.[55]

In addition to opposition from the administration, the legislation met with resistance from some members of Congress on the grounds of immigration. The bill established a new "T" visa for victims trafficked into the United States. This visa was intended to encourage victims to cooperate with law-enforcement agencies in the investigation and prosecution of trafficking. More broadly, the goal was to bolster U.S. moral authority and leverage in demanding that foreign countries address the problem seriously. Yet certain conservative members of Congress were outraged by what they saw as "green cards for whores."[56]

The coalition responded to these challenges vigorously through strongly worded letters to Congress and to members of the administration. Following are several examples.

- In letters to Congress, evangelical leaders argued that "[e]ffective legislation must include an enforcement mechanism," namely mandatory sanctions that could only be waived by the president. They maintained that weakening the sanctions mechanism, as the administration wanted, "would drastically reduce the priority status of the sex trafficking issue on the part of the senior government officials, and . . . would drastically reduce Presidential accountability for failure to take action against international traffickers." It also "undermines our leverage to pressure [foreign countries] to act against sexual traffickers." Furthermore, the evangelical leaders maintained that sanctions against sex trafficking should not be less aggressive than sanctions against drug trafficking: "Congress should not take the trafficking of women and children any less seriously than they do that of drugs."[57]

- In a letter to President Clinton, ten feminist leaders criticized the administration's support for a limited definition of trafficking at the UN Protocol negotiations. Limiting the definition to *forced* prostitution, they argued, "would not only fail to protect a substantial number of trafficking victims, it would also shield many traffickers in the global sex trade from prosecution." The letter charged that "the Administration's current position on the definition of trafficking is extremely detrimental to women" and inconsistent with fundamental principles of human rights.[58] Bill Bennett and Chuck Colson voiced similar criticism in an opinion piece in *The Wall Street Journal*.[59]
- Members of the coalition, from both the religious and feminist wings, wrote to Congress in an attempt to defeat an amendment to the original bill that would have allowed the granting of U.S. visas only to trafficking victims aged 16 and under. Such an amendment, the coalition argued, would reduce victims' willingness to come forward and assist in identifying and prosecuting traffickers. It would also undermine American moral authority and ability to pressure foreign countries to protect victims and prosecute traffickers. Furthermore, allowing the deportation of trafficked women and children over 16 defied the sense of justice, as it would leave them "liable to literal enslavement, to retribution, perhaps to death" in their countries of origin.[60]

The Trafficking Act was signed into law on October 28, 2000. On most issues, the coalition prevailed. The Act established a sanctions mechanism with presidential determination of the sanctions; it imposed no age limit on victim visas (though their number was capped at 5,000 per year); and it authorized the establishment of a new bureaucracy within the State Department: the Office to Monitor and Combat Trafficking in Persons (hereafter the TIP Office). The Trafficking Act also adopted the two-tiered definition of trafficking proposed by the coalition. The Act did, however, cover labor trafficking, as the administration wanted. Adopted by the UN General Assembly in November 2000, the UN Protocol included a compromise definition of trafficking. Consistent with the abolitionist view, trafficking may involve not only force or coercion, but abuse of a victim's vulnerability; furthermore, the victim's consent is irrelevant. Sex-work advocates, however, heralded the fact that the protocol did not prohibit prostitution.[61]

## Putting the Trafficking Act into Effect

The Trafficking Victims Protection Act of 2000 established minimum standards for the elimination of human trafficking. These apply to governments of countries of origin, transit, or destination. For example, the Act requires governments to vigorously investigate and prosecute acts of trafficking, to protect victims, to take preventive measures, and to cooperate with foreign governments in investigation and prosecution. The sanction against governments that do not comply with these standards and make no significant effort to comply is suspension of nonhumanitarian, nontrade-related foreign assistance.[62] The process of sanctions imposition begins with an annual Trafficking in Persons Report (hereafter TIP Report), issued by the State Department's TIP Office. The report ranks foreign countries into three tiers: *Tier 1*: Countries whose governments are in full compliance with the trafficking-elimination standards; *Tier 2*: Countries whose governments do not yet fully comply with the standards but are making significant efforts to bring themselves into compliance; and *Tier 3*: Countries whose governments do not fully comply with the standards and are not making significant efforts to bring themselves into compliance. Within 90 days following the submission of the report, the president gives notice of his determination with respect to Tier 3 countries. These countries might come under sanctions, or the sanctions may be waived on the grounds of U.S. national interest.

President Clinton signed the Trafficking Act into law, but the task of implementing it fell to the George W. Bush administration. To its disappointment, the coalition quickly realized that the change in administration did not alter the State Department's attitude toward the Trafficking Act. State Department officials who disagreed with the Act's approach maintained their positions under the new administration and showed little enthusiasm for putting the legislation into full effect. From the coalition's point of view, the career personnel at the State Department's TIP Office were paying lip service while, in fact, undermining the Act and sidetracking the issue. The coalition particularly opposed the idea of delegating the presidential responsibility for waiving the sanctions to the assistant secretary of state level. In the coalition's view, only presidential responsibility could ensure that human trafficking would become a foreign policy priority. The coalition was also disappointed with the failure of the TIP Office to exert pressure on foreign governments through the threat of sanctions. In fact, the coalition maintained that the State Department had assured foreign governments that the Act's sanctions provisions should not be taken seriously and would never be invoked. Other concerns raised by the coalition were the continued awarding of federal grants to sex-work groups as well as the State Department's failure to develop interagency coordination against human trafficking. Underlying these failures, the coalition argued, was "the policy idea still prevalent in many government agencies that worldwide prostitution can or should ever become an 'empowering' career option for women."[63]

In personal meetings and in correspondence with administration officials, Michael Horowitz did not mince words. He warned that "the administration is facing a *crisis* . . . and will soon be caught in a horrid crossfire from right and left, dems and republicans, feminists and christians, unless steps are immediately taken."[64] Sabotage of the Trafficking Act, Horowitz predicted, would "seriously hurt the administration's standing with church and women's groups . . . and strip from the president the ability to spectacularly succeed on an issue that he could easily define to soccer moms and evangelicals alike as both the slavery issue of our time and the women's issue of our time."[65] In a similar spirit, a letter to President Bush signed by members of the coalition rebuked the administration, and the State Department in particular, for their "passive acceptance of the world trafficking status quo, mixed with largely rhetorical and low-priority policies that contravene the Trafficking Act." The letter warned that "[c]ontinued administration failure to seriously enforce the Trafficking Act will leave millions of Americans rightly puzzled and angry at its failure to address the worldwide, criminal enslavement of millions of women and children."[66]

The coalition's efforts fell on fertile ground. The Bush administration, starting with the president himself, was receptive to faith-based initiatives and advocacy. The campaign against human trafficking had a moral and religious appeal that was reinforced by its political appeal: the evangelical groups represented a large and important constituency. Furthermore, as the theoretical framework has suggested, governments sometimes show concern about illicit trade abroad to burnish their international image. Amid international criticism over the war in Iraq, the Bush administration sought an issue on which it could win support.[67] Added motivation came from allegations linking U.S. military personnel in South Korea and U.S. government contractors in Bosnia to human trafficking.[68] These allegations caused embarrassment and could have damaged American interests; to counter them, the administration had to take a tough stand on human trafficking and signal its determination to tackle this problem.

The coalition's advocacy efforts, coupled with the administration's need to improve its international image, resulted in significant policy changes. Whereas the Clinton administration had been unresponsive to the coalition's demands, the Bush administration came to endorse its goals and took measures to fulfill them. In December 2002 President Bush signed National Security Presidential Directive 22, which instructed federal agencies to strengthen their efforts to eradicate human trafficking. This directive in effect adopted the abolitionist position, describing prostitution as an inherently harmful and dehumanizing practice that fueled human trafficking.[69] In September 2003 President Bush expressed a commitment to the anti-trafficking cause in an address to the UN General Assembly: he emphasized the brutality of human trafficking and urged UN members to eliminate this practice.[70] The Trafficking Victims Protection Reauthorization Act of 2003 established a Senior Policy Operating Group to coordinate the federal government's policies on human trafficking; the Reauthorization Act also prohibited the use of U.S. funds to support programs or organizations that promote the legalization or practice of prostitution. Also in 2003, the coalition won a major achievement when John Miller—a former congressman—became director of the State Department's TIP Office, replacing a director whom the coalition considered incompetent. Fully committed to the efforts against human trafficking, Miller transformed and reenergized the TIP Office. Under his leadership, the annual TIP Report became a forceful publication carrying dramatic victim stories, best practices from around the world and, most importantly, critical country evaluations that did not pull any punches.[71]

Soon enough, the Trafficking Act turned into a powerful tool for influencing foreign governments, as the coalition had envisioned. Consider the impact of the TIP Report released in June 2003. The months before the report was issued saw a flurry of activity intended to avoid a Tier 3 ranking. Examples included the passage of anti-trafficking laws in the Philippines and Haiti, as well as arrests of traffickers in Serbia. The threat of sanctions also had the intended effect on countries that were ultimately ranked as Tier 3 in that report. Shortly after its release, the State Department drafted work plans for Tier 3 countries, listing the measures they had to take to avoid sanctions. Ten of these countries, including Turkey, Greece, and Kazakhstan, agreed to follow the recommended course of action and took anti-trafficking measures. The State Department thus raised them from Tier 3 to Tier 2, thereby lifting the threat of sanctions.[72] The rest of this chapter examines how the TIP Report induced the Israeli government to curb human trafficking.

The TIP Report is far from a perfect tool. A 2006 assessment by the Government Accountability Office (GAO) noted that the annual report "has increased global awareness about trafficking in persons, encouraged action by some governments who failed to comply with the minimum standards, and raised the threat of sanctions against governments who did not make significant efforts to comply with these standards."[73] Yet while the TIP Report has indeed spurred certain governments to adopt anti-trafficking measures, various flaws have detracted from its credibility and usefulness. For example, the GAO found that the report had sometimes relied on dubious estimates of the number of victims. Furthermore, many of the report's country narratives had failed to provide a clear and comprehensive evaluation of governments' compliance with the trafficking-elimination standards, resulting in incomplete explanations of tier rankings.[74] The GAO also revealed political influences on these rankings. The rankings were often the subject of disagreements between the TIP Office, which was committed to abolishing human trafficking, and the State Department's regional bureaus, which were reluctant to complicate relations with foreign countries over this issue. At times, these disagreements were "resolved by a process of 'horsetrading,' whereby the Trafficking Office agrees to raise some countries' tier rankings in exchange for lowering others. In these cases, political considerations may take precedence over a neutral assessment of foreign governments' compliance with minimum standards to combat trafficking."[75]

Notwithstanding these flaws, the TIP Report is still superior to any other alternative. International organizations, such as the UN and the OSCE, assess governments' efforts against human trafficking; but they cannot be as candidly and publicly critical as the United States, nor can they wield the stick of sanctions. The appropriate criteria for judging the American anti-trafficking efforts are: Do they go further than other endeavors to combat human trafficking? Do they enhance governments' political motivation to address a hitherto ignored problem? Are they bringing this problem any closer to eradication? I would answer these questions in the affirmative. As the theoretical framework has indicated, absence of shared interest among governments is a significant obstacle to cooperation against illicit trade, and coercion may overcome this obstacle. The Trafficking Act's monitoring and sanctioning mechanism has thus been a major improvement over past and contemporary initiatives that did not involve coercion and left compliance to governments' goodwill. The Act has made an important step in the right direction: toward providing noncooperative governments with the incentives to change their behavior and combat human trafficking.

### The American Efforts against Human Trafficking: Conclusions

The American campaign against human trafficking originated in 2000 from concerns about human trafficking worldwide. In the following years, the campaign gave growing attention to the United States' own trafficking problem: the trafficking of U.S. citizens and foreign persons for sexual or labor exploitation in the United States. But for our purposes it is the worldwide campaign that is of interest for understanding cooperation against illicit trade. In particular, this campaign sheds light on the influence of secondary externalities—the deleterious effects of illicit trade abroad. As the theoretical framework has suggested, concern about secondary externalities stems from policymakers' personal values, the wishes of the public, or the pressure of moral entrepreneurs. All three drove the American campaign against human trafficking. Policymakers' values were certainly an important influence. The members of Congress who sponsored the legislation were committed to promoting what they saw as a great moral cause. Human trafficking resonated with their belief in freedom and disgust with slavery. Yet the moral appeal of the issue was, to an extent, a construct of moral entrepreneurs. It was the evangelical-feminist coalition that framed human trafficking as modern-day slavery and as a moral challenge of historic proportions. Through hearings, personal meetings, and letters, the coalition convinced policymakers of their moral obligation to act; it also appealed to their pursuit of popular support. The coalition, especially its evangelical part, represented a large block of voters and used this as leverage. Support for anti-trafficking efforts would be favorably viewed by constituents, the coalition promised; obstructing those efforts could trigger a backlash. Ultimately, both their own values and their desire for public support motivated policymakers to launch a worldwide effort against human trafficking; but it was the coalition that put the issue on the agenda and tied it to moral values and to support from constituents.

The analysis has empirically demonstrated another theoretical observation, namely, that a new government in power may respond to different interest groups than its predecessor and form a new preference. The Clinton administration was influenced by human rights organizations and mainstream women's groups; it was less sympathetic to the coalition of evangelicals and abolitionist feminists and to its demand that human trafficking be prioritized above other foreign-policy concerns. By contrast, the Bush administration was attentive to the evangelical community and showed greater enthusiasm for a faith-inspired campaign against human trafficking. The change of government thus transformed the national preference. Indeed, the Bush administration's commitment to abolishing human trafficking was not always manifested on the ground; it was sometimes trumped by other foreign-policy considerations. Yet the difference between the Bush and Clinton administrations—in rhetoric and practice—was palpable. The coalition's abolitionist views and goals took hold, to the dismay of sex-work advocates who bemoaned the "institutionalization of the anti-prostitution crusade." They regretfully noted that the Bush "administration rejected the Clinton approach and replaced it with a model that is virtually identical to what was being advocated by the anti-prostitution crusade. In a remarkably short time span, the latter's views were accepted, incorporated into official policy, and implemented in agency practices."[76]

There are some similarities between the contemporary U.S. campaign against human trafficking and the campaign against white slavery a century earlier. Both campaigns were initiated by feminists and other morally motivated activists determined to abolish what they saw as a social evil. Both campaigns resulted in a set of international guidelines for combating human trafficking, ranging from protections for victims to the prosecution of traffickers. Both campaigns used a similar advocacy technique: telling the stories of trafficked women as a means of stirring emotions and inducing action. Yet there are also important differences. Whereas the efforts of the late 19th and early 20th centuries focused initially on white women, the contemporary U.S. campaign makes no distinction among victims on the basis of color or gender. In addition, the 19th century activists sought to generate popular concern over the sex trade through such means as newspapers and books, while the contemporary American activists were elite-focused. Their advocacy efforts, especially at the beginning of the campaign, were aimed primarily at policymakers rather than the general public. Most importantly, while the two campaigns shared the same goal—international cooperation against the sex trade—they sought to realize this goal by different means. The early efforts involved international agreements that relied on governments' consent and voluntary participation. Governments could choose to join these agreements and comply with them or refrain from doing so. By contrast, the contemporary campaign is based on *coerced* cooperation and on the unilateral imposition of standards of good behavior by the United States. Government consent—an important element of the earlier agreements on sex trafficking and of international law generally—was replaced by an American dictate and penalties for noncompliance. This change of means—from consensual to coerced cooperation—proved effective, as the case of Israel demonstrates.

## Sex Trafficking in Israel

### Background

The trafficking of foreign women into prostitution in Israel began in the early 1990s. According to official estimates, the number of trafficked women reached 3,000 in the late 1990s and early 2000s, with the number of brothels ranging between 300 and 400.[77] The post-Soviet countries—particularly Russia, Ukraine, Moldova, Belarus, and Uzbekistan—were the main sources of trafficked women. Trafficking of women thrived there for two reasons. First, the collapse of the Soviet Union and the weakness of the rule of law in its aftermath gave a boost to organized criminal groups. Sex trafficking promised these groups high profits at low cost and low risk. Rampant corruption and the common practice of bribing officials facilitated the smuggling of the women from their countries of origin. Second, the difficult social and economic conditions in the post-Soviet period took a heavy toll on women. The deterioration of the economy left many women unemployed or in low-paying jobs, and the state's social safety net no longer provided adequate support. Sharp cuts in state care for children and the elderly imposed a heavy burden on women, who were often the sole breadwinners. In the absence of local economic opportunities, many women had to seek employment in rich countries to support themselves and their families. Some saw no other choice but to join the sex industry.[78]

Based on interviews with trafficked women, a 2003 study by Israeli NGOs found that economic hardship—poverty and unemployment—motivated the women to search for work abroad. A third of the women interviewed had not known they would engage in prostitution: they had been promised jobs such as cleaning, waitressing, and childcare. A majority of the women, however, knew they would be prostitutes, but were unaware of the inhumane and exploitative employment conditions. They had been falsely promised a monthly pay of $1,000, a small number of clients per day, and the freedom to leave once they paid back the cost of their trip to Israel. Most of the women included in the NGOs' study were single women in their 20s with an average 11 years of schooling; a quarter of them had children. Only 9 percent of the women had engaged in prostitution in the past. Twenty-nine percent had been unemployed, with the rest having worked in various occupations, such as secretary, teacher, and hairdresser. Their average wage in the countries of origin had been thirty-eight dollars a month, making the promised monthly wage of $1,000 extremely attractive. The women had been recruited by various means, including newspaper ads, employment agencies, and acquaintances. Until 2000, trafficked women arrived in Israel through the air or sea ports, pretending to be tourists or Jewish immigrants. With the tightening of control over ports of entry, the loosely controlled Israeli-Egyptian border became the main route for transporting women into Israel. Seventy-two percent of the women interviewed for the NGOs' study arrived in Egypt and were smuggled across the border in a journey that lasted up to two weeks. Some were raped during the journey by the Bedouin smugglers.[79]

How did the sex trade in Israel work? Some women had already been bought by Israeli traffickers before leaving their countries of origin. Others were bought upon their arrival in Israel, sometimes through a "public auction." At the auction, women suffered indignities, including touching of their private parts. They were ultimately sold off to the highest bidder. The price paid for a woman in the Israeli sex industry typically ranged between $5,000 and $10,000, depending on her age and looks. At the brothel, the reality of trafficked women's lives included enslavement, violence, and exploitation.

The enslavement of the women, which began with their recruitment and sale, was perpetuated through a "debt" that they incurred. To the original debt—the cost of bringing a woman to Israel and purchasing her—the traffickers added high interest as well as some of the brothel's operating costs, such as rent and contraceptives. This prevented the women from ever paying off their debt. Another manifestation of the women's enslavement was the withholding of their passports or other identifying documents, to prevent their escape.

The women's weakness and their control by the traffickers allowed the latter to impose a highly exploitative work regime. The women typically worked seven days a week, 13 hours a day on average, serving up to 30 clients every day. At best, they enjoyed a single day off a month. Although clients were charged between 100 and 600 shekels ($25–$150), the women received approximately 20 shekels per client. They often gave up even this compensation to pay for "fines." The traffickers fined the women on various grounds, such as going out of the brothel or receiving a telephone call without permission. Women who wished to leave faced physical violence and threats. The most common threat was harm to them or to their relatives in the countries of origin. Another threat was that an attempted escape would result in the woman's sale to a worse brothel, especially in the Palestinian territories, where she would face terrible abuse. In some cases, the deprivation of freedom involved not only threats, but physical confinement of the women behind locked doors and barred windows.

The engagement in prostitution, accompanied by occasional rape and violence at the hands of traffickers and clients, harmed the women's physical and mental health. Nevertheless, many of them received no medical treatment. The women also tended not to turn to the police for help, as they were led to believe that this would result in their own imprisonment.[80]

## Israel's Policy on Sex Trafficking in the 1990s

Throughout the 1990s, Israeli authorities failed to establish any policy against trafficking of women for prostitution and made no effort to address this issue. They did not identify sex trafficking as a problem or even as a new and unique phenomenon. Instead, it was classified into preexisting, familiar categories. Law-enforcement authorities viewed sex trafficking as "just another prostitution-related offense" and treated it with the neglect reserved for prostitution.[81] This neglect was reflected in the 1994 State Attorney Directive on prostitution-related offenses, which limited enforcement against brothels to specific cases, such as those involving prostitution of minors, committing of additional crimes, or creation of a public nuisance.[82] In all other cases, law-enforcement authorities were to avoid action against brothels.

Adherence to these guidelines meant, in effect, overlooking the trafficking of foreign women and not interfering with the operation of brothels that employed them. Brothels did not even hide in discreet locations—clear signs guided clients to "massage parlors" in downtown Tel Aviv—yet law-enforcement authorities all but ignored their existence. The police did not close down brothels and initiated few investigations against them. The authorities could have prosecuted traffickers for a variety of offenses: pimping, false imprisonment, rape, assault, and withholding of passports. Yet, given the general tendency to overlook prostitution-related offenses, only a small number of criminal cases were filed. When traffickers did stand trial, plea bargains with light punishments were often reached for a variety of reasons: difficulties in gathering evidence, to avoid the trouble of a full trial, or in exchange for the traffickers' readiness to provide information on offenses deemed more serious than sex trafficking. Even when full trials were held, courts generally meted out light sentences.[83]

The forgiving attitude toward traffickers resulted from the classification of sex trafficking as prostitution—a negligible issue for law-enforcement authorities. The women themselves, however, were looked upon as offenders. They were classified as illegal aliens or even criminals, having entered Israel illegally, sometimes by using forged documents. Consequently, those women apprehended by the police were deported as soon as possible. They were not encouraged to testify against the traffickers, let alone treated as crime victims deserving of protection and rehabilitation. For the police and the Ministry of Interior, the women themselves were guilty of an offense—illegal entry into Israel.[84]

Why were the Israeli authorities indifferent to sex trafficking? Why was there no serious attempt to fight this problem throughout the 1990s? As the theoretical framework has suggested, governments' motivation to curb illicit trade is higher when the trade's negative externalities are larger in magnitude; their motivation is lower when the consumers are more influential. I first examine the consumers involved in the sex trade and then consider its externalities.

Chapter 4 has shown that politically organized consumers may lobby governments in favor of free trade and against regulation. Yet the failure of the Israeli government to suppress the trade in women was not the result of consumers' lobbying. The sex trade's consumers consisted of two groups: traffickers and clients. The majority of traffickers were Israeli men who had migrated from the former Soviet Union. Fluency in Russian and contacts in the countries of origin facilitated their business of trafficking in women. Whereas in the popular imagination sex trafficking is associated with organized crime, Israeli traffickers did not necessarily have a previous criminal record. Some ran a brothel in addition to having a legitimate job or had turned to sex trafficking after losing their previous job.[85] The traffickers, however, were not politically organized, as their activity was illegal: Israeli law criminally prohibits pimping—living off the earnings of prostitutes—as well as causing a person to engage in prostitution. Even when these prohibitions were not enforced, as was the case in the 1990s, the criminal nature of their business prevented traffickers from organizing politically to lobby politicians. Criminalization also meant that no politician wanted to be associated with the sex industry or to be perceived as catering to traffickers.

The second group of consumers included clients who paid for sex with the trafficked women. The overwhelming majority of clients were Israeli Jews from all sectors of society, including businessmen, soldiers, policemen, and ultra-Orthodox Jews.[86] Whereas Israeli law criminalizes traffickers, it does not criminalize clients. Nevertheless, going to a prostitute is considered an immoral, even shameful, social practice. Clients were therefore reluctant to reveal their use of prostitution services, let alone organize politically in support of prostitution.

What about the negative externalities of sex trafficking? Sex trafficking can potentially have negative effects on society, such as the corruption of immigration and border control officials, violence, and communicable diseases.[87] Such externalities, however, were not evident in Israel. The sex trade did not adversely affect the Israeli public in any significant, tangible way: it posed little threat to public health or to political and social stability. According to Israeli activist Nomi Levenkron, the price of sex trafficking was the moral corruption of Israeli society.[88] Yet this moral price did not particularly bother the Israeli public throughout the 1990s. In the absence of material, tangible negative effects, Israelis were indifferent to sex trafficking. The operation of brothels where foreign women were enslaved did not generate a public outcry or voters' demand for action.

The trafficked women themselves were the ones who bore the negative effects of the sex trade, such as physical and mental abuse and loss of freedom. Israeli law does not criminalize prostitutes, yet for obvious reasons trafficked women could not be politically active. Having entered Israel illegally, controlled by their traffickers, living in a foreign country whose language they did not speak, lacking the knowledge and means necessary for political action, including the right to vote—trafficked women could not organize to change the horrific reality of their lives. Furthermore, throughout the 1990s the women were victims of two biases of Israeli officials. First, they were neither Israeli nor Jewish. In the Jewish state, offenses against non-Jews rank low on the priorities of law-enforcement agencies. Second, as prostitutes, the women belonged in the margins of society and were not seen as deserving of attention and serious treatment. Moreover, officials perceived the women as having received what they wished for. In their view, the women had come to Israel to work as prostitutes and indeed fulfilled their goal; therefore, there was no reason for the authorities to help them.[89]

Given the absence of significant externalities on society, the indifference of the Israeli public, and the marginal status of trafficked women, Israeli authorities had little incentive to take action. From their point of view, sex trafficking was not a problem and its elimination would not yield any benefits. Therefore, there was no reason to tackle this issue. Furthermore, the suppression of sex trafficking entailed a variety of costly measures, such as tightening border control, conducting investigations and raids on brothels, and providing shelter and medical services for victims. This required the allocation of considerable financial and human resources, all for a matter of little concern to Israeli society and authorities. Moreover, in the 1990s fighting terrorism was the utmost priority of Israel's law-enforcement community. Diverting efforts and resources to address prostitution—an issue that had always been at the bottom of law-enforcement priorities—was unthinkable.

## Israel's Policy on Sex Trafficking, 2000–2010

The Israeli government's response to sex trafficking began to shift in 2000 and was transformed in 2001. This transformation had both domestic and international causes. While international pressure was the main cause, domestic developments played an important role as well, at times interacting with international influences to bring about a sea change in policy.

### Domestic Sources of Policy Change

The first domestic development was the growth and escalation of the trafficking phenomenon. In the early 1990s Israeli authorities saw trafficked women as prostitutes who warranted little law-enforcement attention. Yet by the end of that decade, the large number of women and the proliferation of brothels made it clear that sex trafficking was a distinct phenomenon that required a more vigorous response. Consequently, new police guidelines were issued in June 2000, declaring sex trafficking a "subject of interest" and calling for investigations. In September 2000 Israel's attorney general initiated the establishment of an interministerial task force to study sex trafficking and make recommendations. Submitted in November 2002, the task force's report proposed a series of operative measures for tackling this phenomenon.[90]

A second domestic development was the enactment in July 2000 of a new offense that criminalized trafficking for the purpose of prostitution, thereby distinguishing and separating sex trafficking from "ordinary" prostitution. The new criminal offense, an initiative of Member of Knesset (MK) Yael Dayan, at first met with government resistance. The government maintained that trafficking was already covered by existing offenses relating to prostitution, and that the new offense was therefore unnecessary and redundant.[91] The government reversed its position and allowed the establishment of the new offense following an Amnesty International report—released in May 2000—that criticized Israel's failure to curb sex trafficking.[92] This legislative move turned out to be consequential, as it inspired new thinking about trafficking in women. As the subject of a distinct criminal offense, sex trafficking was no longer "only" a marginal issue of prostitution or a matter of illegal entry into Israel. Rather, it became a phenomenon that required an appropriate and unique law-enforcement response.[93] This change of attitude was reinforced by court decisions in cases involving the new offense. These decisions expressed the judiciary's view of trafficking in women as a grave problem that had to be eliminated. Supreme Court Justice Mishael Cheshin called for a war "with no ceasefire or compromise"[94] against sex trafficking.

The third domestic catalyst of change was the activities of several actors: the Parliamentary Inquiry Committee on Trafficking in Women (hereafter the Parliamentary Inquiry Committee), local NGOs, and the Government Coordinator of the Battle against Trafficking in Persons.

The Parliamentary Inquiry Committee was initiated by MK Zehava Galon following a TV report that exposed the auctioning off of women. The Knesset established the committee in June 2000—shortly after the release of the Amnesty International report—to investigate trafficking in women and recommend appropriate measures. As the chair of the committee, MK Galon sought to put sex trafficking on the national agenda and motivate the authorities to combat it. She considered public exposure and media coverage to be critical for achieving these goals.[95] Indeed, the deliberations of the Parliamentary Inquiry Committee and Galon's frequent media appearances did much to dispel the public's ignorance and indifference and heighten awareness of trafficking in women. This, in turn, put pressure on the government and on law-enforcement authorities to tackle this issue. Once sex trafficking came into the limelight and became a matter of public interest and debate, it could no longer be relegated to the bottom of law-enforcement priorities—an appropriate government response was necessary. We have seen a similar phenomenon in the case of antiquities. Media scandals and archaeologists' advocacy exposed the detrimental effects of the illicit antiquities trade, changed the normative environment, and pushed the American and British governments to action. Similarly, public exposure of the brutality of sex trafficking put pressure on the Israeli government to respond.

The Parliamentary Inquiry Committee also served as a watchdog of government action. Law-enforcement officials and representatives of government ministries regularly attended the committee's meetings, where they often met with criticism and had to justify their conduct. Another tool for prodding the authorities into action was the abundance of legislative proposals put forth by the committee. The committee proposed laws on a variety of issues, such as mandatory minimum penalties for traffickers and legal aid to victims. Many of these proposals were ultimately included in the comprehensive 2006 law on human trafficking, which is discussed below.

The local NGO community also played a role in changing the authorities' attitude toward sex trafficking. Whereas the anti-trafficking coalition in the United States included both religious groups and feminist activists, their Israeli counterparts were secular NGOs committed to the rights of women or migrant workers. Among the most prominent organizations were the Hotline for Migrant Workers, Woman to Woman, the Association of Assistance Centers for Victims of Sexual Assault, Awareness Center, and the Women's Lobby. The NGOs fought hard to establish the perception of trafficked women as *victims* deserving of protection and rehabilitation, rather than prostitutes, criminals, or illegal aliens. As the theoretical framework has suggested, moral entrepreneurs employ their knowledge and expertise to educate the authorities and the public about illicit trade. The use of information and expertise was clearly evident in the Israeli NGOs' efforts to raise awareness of sex trafficking and in their calls for the prosecution of traffickers and protection of victims. Through their daily contact with trafficked women, the NGOs obtained a wealth of information on the origins, manifestations, and consequences of trafficking. They disseminated this information in occasional publications, in seminars and training sessions for officials, and in meetings of the Parliamentary Inquiry Committee. The meetings of the committee served as an important vehicle for NGO advocacy. In those meetings, seated at the same table with government and law-enforcement representatives, the NGOs aired their complaints against the authorities, demanded action, and reached understandings.[96]

Another important domestic actor was the Government Coordinator of the Battle against Trafficking in Persons, Rahel Gershuni. Gershuni, an official at the Ministry of Justice, began her unofficial work as a coordinator in 2002. She was officially appointed by the government in May 2006 to coordinate action on human trafficking among government bodies and between the government and actors outside it. Gershuni saw her role as being to catalyze domestic processes to address human trafficking and ensure Israel's compliance with international standards in this area. Among her many activities, Gershuni encouraged cooperation between government bodies and NGOs, held awareness-raising and training sessions for law-enforcement agencies and the bureaucracy, took part in establishing relevant legislation, regulations, and procedures, and maintained contact with international actors, such as the State Department and the United Nations High Commissioner for Refugees.[97] According to the 2006 TIP Report, Gershuni "has led a reform movement within the Israeli government by serving as a catalyst for the development of policies that treat sex trafficking victims as true victims and not as criminals."[98]

International Pressure: The State Department TIP Report

Domestic actors in Israel played an important role in pushing the authorities to eliminate sex trafficking. These domestic actors, however, were greatly assisted by external influences. The first external influence was the publication of the Amnesty International report in May 2000. As noted above, MK Galon's initiative of a Parliamentary Inquiry Committee and MK Dayan's effort to enact a sex-trafficking offense came to fruition in June and July 2000, respectively, shortly after the release of Amnesty International's report. Yet the watershed moment came with the publication of the first State Department Trafficking in Persons Report in July 2001. That report, and the annual reports that followed, exerted heavy pressure on the Israeli government to suppress human trafficking and triggered a complete transformation of the authorities' attitude and actions.

The 2001 TIP Report gave Israel the lowest possible ranking: Tier 3. According to the report, "[t]he Government of Israel does not meet the minimum standards for combating trafficking in persons, and has not yet made significant efforts to combat the problem, although it has begun to take some steps to do so. The Government recognizes that trafficking in persons is a problem, but devotes limited resources to combating it."[99] This criticism came as a bombshell to Israeli officials. The Ministry of Foreign Affairs claimed that it had not been informed of the report prior to its publication, nor had it been asked to respond or to provide information.[100] Local NGOs, in particular the Hotline for Migrant Workers, furnished the State Department with the relevant information.[101]

Israeli authorities responded to the first TIP Report with a mix of resentment and alarm. The resentment was directed, first, toward the NGOs that had been the source of information. Meir Sheetrit, the minister of justice, insisted that "the dirty laundry should be aired at home." He chastised the NGOs: "Slandering Israel before the U.S. Congress is a disgrace, simply a disgrace. You have caused great damage to the State of Israel. . . . If you have anything to say, you should come and say it here, at the Knesset, don't go abroad."[102] Israeli officials also resented what they perceived as unfair treatment of Israel by the State Department. One manifestation of unfairness in the first report—the failure to ask the Israeli government for information or a response—was subsequently rectified. The coverage of Israel in the following TIP Reports relied not only on local NGOs, but also on confidential annual reports submitted by the Israeli government in response to a State Department questionnaire. Yet this did not entirely allay the sense of injustice engendered by the American criticism. Israeli officials continued to believe that the State Department applied higher standards to Israel than to less-developed countries. The result was the lumping together of the Israeli government—that could have done more to combat human trafficking—with governments that actively assisted traffickers. Moreover, the TIP Report may have excluded countries with a worse record than Israel's simply due to lack of sufficient information. By contrast, the openness of Israeli society and the availability of information made Israel an easy target.[103]

Beyond the sense of injustice, the 2001 TIP Report aroused alarm and concern among Israeli officials. Actors who had witnessed the Israeli authorities' response described it as "hysteria" and "fireworks" that resulted in a "frenzy of activity," a "complete turnabout," a "shakeup"[104]—a remarkable reversal of the 1990s' indifference and apathy to sex trafficking. Israeli officials saw the country's bottom ranking as a major problem; they resolved to remove Israel from Tier 3 through serious efforts to eliminate trafficking in women. This determination soon led to action. Israeli authorities began taking operative steps against sex trafficking along the three dimensions of prevention, prosecution, and protection. Prevention included, among other endeavors, efforts against smuggling via the Israeli-Egyptian border and the distribution of information in countries of origin to warn potential victims. As for prosecution, the police and prosecution authorities overhauled their approach to sex trafficking. The elimination of trafficking became a major goal of the police, resulting in heightened investigative work, raids on brothels, and a large number of arrests. Whereas the police launched only one investigation of sex trafficking in 2000 and 25 investigations in the first half of 2001, the number of investigations leapt to 351 in 2002.[105] Prosecutors began seeking heavier sentences for trafficking offenses, and courts abided.[106] In terms of protection, a shelter opened in 2004 to house victims until their return to the countries of origin or until the conclusion of their testimony against the traffickers. Efforts were also made to provide medical services and legal aid to victims.[107] The culmination of Israel's efforts was the enactment of a comprehensive anti-trafficking law in 2006.

Why did the State Department report arouse such alarm and apprehension among Israeli officials? How did it spark such a remarkable policy shift? The theoretical framework has suggested that economic coercion as well as the danger of tarnished reputation can motivate noncooperative governments to curb illicit trade. In this case, while Israeli officials did not entirely dismiss the economic consequences of Israel's poor ranking in the 2001 TIP Report, the adverse implications for Israel's international image were of greater concern.

Countries designated as Tier 3 by the TIP Report could face a serious economic penalty: suspension of American aid. On July 18, 2001, soon after the release of the first TIP Report, the Parliamentary Inquiry Committee gathered for an "Urgent meeting due to concern about economic sanctions following the publication of the U.S. State Department report that includes Israel in a 'blacklist' of countries that traffic in persons."[108] Yet, the withholding of aid was not the main concern on the minds of Israeli officials.[109] While not entirely complacent about this economic threat, they considered it unlikely. First, the Trafficking Act established a two-year grace period. The threat of aid suspension was not to materialize before 2003. Second, Israeli officials believed that the close and special relationship between the United States and Israel and the requirement of a *presidential* determination of sanctions would ultimately prevent the United States from carrying out the economic threat.

Ultimately, it was not economic coercion but reputational coercion that had an impact on the Israeli government, bureaucracy, and law-enforcement agencies. Israeli officials were greatly concerned about the tarnishing of Israel's image as an enlightened, democratic, and law-abiding country that respects human rights. While the desire to enjoy international respectability is by no means unique to Israel, Israeli officials are especially preoccupied with their country's reputation abroad. Since Israel is isolated in its own region and often faces heavy criticism in international forums, the country's acceptance by the international community is a foreign-policy priority. The TIP Report, however, threatened to undermine Israel's efforts to enhance its international reputation. Contrary to Israel's claim of being a rule-of-law country, the State Department report criticized the failure of Israeli authorities to enforce the law against traffickers. Although Israel takes pride in being one of the first countries to establish women's equality, the report revealed that Israeli authorities had been indifferent to the abuse and exploitation of trafficked women.[110] Israeli officials seek to disprove the notion that Israel violates the human rights of Palestinians, yet the report found that the government had done little to protect the human rights of trafficked women. The TIP Report thus dealt a blow to the Israeli efforts to project a positive image and establish a good name. The American criticism could have further complicated Israel's delicate situation in the international arena, potentially putting fresh ammunition in the hands of actors unfriendly to Israel.[111]

In addition to the adverse effects on Israel's foreign relations in general, some voiced specific concern about the possible damage to U.S.-Israel relations.[112] The special bond between the United States and Israel relies on shared values, cultural similarity, and an American appreciation for Israeli society. The TIP Report threatened to cast a shadow over this normative core of U.S.-Israel relations. The report's depiction of Israel as a country that was not making significant efforts to combat human trafficking was at odds with the American perception of Israel as a democratic country committed to high moral standards. Maintaining the tight relationship with the United States is a major priority of Israel's foreign policy; Israeli officials did not want human trafficking to strain that special relationship or damage Israel's image in the eyes of its most important ally.

The TIP Report's impact on Israeli officials stemmed from both instrumental and psychological motivations. As Iain Johnston argues, actors may be interested in maximizing status and reputation for instrumental purposes: a good reputation can build trust as well as foster friendly relations and cooperation. But high status and a positive reputation may also bring psychological benefits. They may generate a sense of accomplishment and fulfillment, satisfy the need for recognition of one's worth in the opinion of others, and reaffirm the actor's self-valuation. By contrast, deviation from widely accepted behavior often results in feelings of shame and social disgrace.[113] Both motivations—the instrumental and the psychological—fueled Israel's efforts to improve its TIP Report evaluation. Instrumentally, Israel's positive reputation as a country that respects human rights is crucial to its foreign relations, especially with Europe and the United States, as well as to its standing in international organizations. Israel's international reputation may also have implications for trade, investment, tourism, and so forth. Yet according to Israeli officials, the *psychological* motivation was no less central than the instrumental.[114] Israel aspires to be an enlightened country and to be perceived as such by others. The TIP Report, however, revealed that Israel had violated behavioral norms expected from an enlightened country. Not only was this a blow to Israel's quest for international legitimacy, it also clashed with Israel's self-identity. Israeli officials consider their country to be a liberal democracy that is sensitive to social injustice. The gap between this self-identity and Israel's reflection in the TIP Report caused embarrassment and shame.

The effect of the 2001 TIP Report was far greater than the limited impact of the previous year's Amnesty International report. The modest response to the Amnesty report—making sex trafficking a criminal offense and establishing the Parliamentary Inquiry Committee—bore little resemblance to the urgency and rush to action that followed the State Department report. As Johnston notes, actors' sensitivity to arguments that their behavior is inconsistent with their self-identity as high-status actors depends on who is making these arguments. The greater the audience's legitimacy, that is, the more its opinions matter, the greater the effect of the disapproval it expresses. "Actors more easily dismiss the criticisms of enemies and adversaries than they do of friends and allies."[115] Whereas Israelis consider Amnesty International biased and even hostile to Israel, they regard the United States as Israel's closest friend and ally and a subject of admiration. Although the American criticism was essentially similar to that of Amnesty International, Israelis considered the former more legitimate, meaningful, and important.

What was the relative contribution of the American pressure and of domestic actors to the transformation of Israel's policy on sex trafficking?

American pressure was likely the main driver of change. The burst of government action starting in 2001 did not follow a sudden increase in the magnitude or effects of the sex trade, nor did it coincide with the establishment of the Parliamentary Inquiry Committee in 2000 or with the activities of local NGOs since the late 1990s. The principal cause of the policy shift was the 2001 TIP Report and its consequences: damage to Israel's international reputation, the threat of aid suspension, and local media attention to sex trafficking. As an activist put it before the Parliamentary Inquiry Committee, "We did a lot prior [to the 2001 TIP Report] and no one heard our voice. Often times, when you turn outside, it shakes things up in Israel. . . . The [TIP] Report changed things, changed the attitude, accelerated processes that had maybe started to occur."[116] Indeed, these internal processes were not inconsequential. The U.S. pressure was so powerful and effective because the ground in Israel had already begun to shift, as domestic actors sought to bring attention to sex trafficking. Most importantly, it was on the basis of information provided by local NGOs that the 2001 TIP Report ranked Israel in Tier 3. But in the absence of the TIP Report, the domestic developments alone would have resulted in some minor policy changes, not a policy turnabout. It was the American monitoring and criticism that reinforced the domestic sources of change and gave them momentum. In fact, Israeli officials started using the specter of the annual report to goad hesitant government bodies into action. Rahel Gershuni, the government coordinator, repeatedly reminded officials that the United States was holding Israel "under the microscope" and scrutinizing its efforts to combat trafficking. The TIP Report turned out to be her strongest weapon vis-à-vis government ministries and law-enforcement authorities.[117] The Ministry of Foreign Affairs became an active participant in domestic policymaking on human trafficking, constantly emphasizing the implications for Israel's foreign relations and international reputation.[118] MK Galon, the chair of the Parliamentary Inquiry Committee, also used the American pressure as a catalyst and leverage, warning government authorities that failure to act could result in American sanctions.[119]

## Sex Trafficking in Israel: Conclusions

Between 2005 and 2010, the trafficking of foreign women for prostitution in Israel diminished dramatically. The number of women smuggled through the Israeli-Egyptian border declined precipitously; sex trafficking in its most severe manifestations—women auctioned off and locked in brothels—was nearly eliminated. In 2010 there were no new reports of foreign victims of sex trafficking. This is not to say that sexual exploitation of foreign women has disappeared altogether. Concerns remain regarding the use of discreet apartments instead of the brothels that had operated in plain sight; the sexual exploitation of mail-order brides; and the bringing of foreign women to provide sexual services to migrant workers residing in Israel.[120] These concerns notwithstanding, the once-flourishing phenomenon of sex trafficking has largely been curbed. This is partly a result of the improvement of economic conditions in Eastern Europe, which has lowered women's incentives to leave. But the more important cause of the sex trade's decline was the vigorous efforts of Israel's law-enforcement agencies and government ministries beginning in 2001. The State Department recognized these efforts: the 2002 TIP Report raised Israel to Tier 2.

Indeed, the Israeli authorities transformed their approach to sex trafficking. Instead of prostitutes, trafficked women came to be seen as victims of serious crimes and human rights violations. No longer an issue undeserving of law-enforcement attention, the elimination of sex trafficking became a law-enforcement priority. This paradigm shift and the actions it triggered owed much to the efforts of MK Galon, local NGOs, and the government coordinator Gershuni. But it was the American pressure that provided the decisive impetus. As MK Galon noted in the urgent meeting of the Parliamentary Inquiry Committee following the release of the 2001 TIP Report, "Unfortunately, [Israelis] are not alarmed unless there's a sword hanging over the head of the Israeli government."[121] The 2001 TIP Report and subsequent reports acted as a sword through economic pressure—the threat of withholding aid—and, more importantly, through social pressure. As Johnston argues, social pressure requires "a forum or institution that makes acting a particular way public and observable."[122] The annual TIP Reports indeed placed the Israeli authorities under periodic evaluation and gave that evaluation worldwide publicity. A negative assessment threatened to undermine Israel's international reputation and its aspiration to be considered an enlightened country. To avoid opprobrium, the Israeli authorities made the elimination of sex trafficking a priority, just as the Trafficking Act had intended. The results on the ground were apparent.

Are these findings generalizable across countries? A possible concern is that Israel might be unique because of its Jewish character and close relations with the United States. Yet these attributes do not necessarily make Israel a special case. Given Israel's Jewish character, the authorities had little interest in curbing the trade in non-Jewish women; but indifference to the trafficking of foreign migrants is prevalent among governments and law-enforcement agencies worldwide. The same applies to U.S.-Israel relations. Israel indeed gives great weight to its image in the eyes of the United States— its closest ally—and is thus particularly amenable to American pressure. Yet other countries would also like the United States to view them favorably and would find it difficult to dismiss American criticism. Moreover, Israel sought to comply with the American demands although the threat to suspend aid lacked credibility, given the special relations; on other governments, the economic threat is likely to have a larger effect. Governments may vary in the weight they give to the reputational versus the economic ramifications of a Tier 3 designation; but the combination of public shaming and the threat of sanctions is one that many governments will find difficult to ignore. As indicated earlier, Serbia, Turkey, and various other countries have also responded to American pressure by launching efforts against sex trafficking.

The case of sex trafficking in Israel is largely consistent with the theoretical framework. The theoretical framework has emphasized the large variation in government preferences and absence of shared interest as obstacles to cooperation against illicit trade. Indeed, the Israeli failure to curb sex trafficking in the 1990s stemmed from a lack of political motivation. The Israeli authorities were not too corrupt or weak to take action against traffickers; they simply saw no reason to do so, in the absence of material externalities on society. The success of American pressure in spurring efforts against trafficking is consistent with the central role that the theoretical framework attributes to coercion as a mechanism for establishing cooperation. Since the Israeli government preferred to overlook sex trafficking, external pressure was necessary in order to motivate anti-trafficking efforts. In particular, this case demonstrates how *reputational* coercion can induce cooperative behavior and motivate governments to suppress illicit trade that they previously tolerated.

## Labor Trafficking of Migrant Workers in Israel

The trafficking of women for prostitution and the labor trafficking of migrant workers share some important commonalities. Both types of trafficking begin with migration in search of economic alternatives.[123] Both sex and labor trafficking involve negative effects that are borne by the trafficked persons themselves—effects to which governments are often indifferent. Therefore, external pressure is required to compel government action against these practices. Yet there are also important distinctions between the two phenomena, most notably the role played by consumers. In the case of labor trafficking, unlike sex trafficking, the interests of consumers— employers of migrant workers—had a major influence on the Israeli government, and it is this influence that the following analysis highlights.

### Background

Migrant workers[124] began arriving in Israel in large numbers in 1993. Subsequently, their numbers rose precipitously, reaching a high point of 243,000 workers in 2001, according to official estimates.[125] Unofficial estimates put the peak number of migrant workers at approximately 300,000—more than 12 percent of the local labor force. This rate of migrant workers was among the highest in any developed country.[126]

Migrant workers were originally introduced as a solution to the shortage of cheap Palestinian labor. After the 1967 War, the Israeli economy came to rely on unskilled labor from the Palestinian territories. Yet with the first Intifada and the Oslo Process, the territories grew increasingly separate from Israel, and frequent closures prevented Palestinian workers from showing up to work regularly. The decreasing availability and reliability of Palestinian workers posed a serious problem to the Israeli economy, especially in the agriculture and construction sectors. In 1993 the government responded by issuing permits for the employment of migrant workers in Israel; by 1996 approximately 100,000 permits had been granted.[127] Over the years, migrant workers became more than a temporary substitute for Palestinian labor, as Israeli employers developed an increasing dependence on and appetite for them. Migrant laborers were hard-working and accepted low-pay and low-status jobs that Israelis were reluctant to accept, including caregiving to the elderly and the disabled. They worked for a much lower wage than did Israelis, often in poor conditions and without employment benefits.[128] Moreover, migrant workers could be easily exploited as they did not speak the local language and were unaware of their rights. Most importantly, as explained below, the employment arrangements made migrant workers entirely dependent on their employers and, hence, docile.

Despite the low wages and often poor working conditions, Israel was an attractive destination for migrant workers. The workers' wage, low by Israeli standards, was typically higher than what they had earned in their countries of origin. Remittances sent by workers were therefore an important source of income for their families back home. According to a 2002 estimate, about half of all migrant workers originated from East Asia (mainly the Philippines, Thailand, and China), with the second largest group coming from Eastern Europe, especially Romania. Migrant workers were employed primarily in the agriculture, construction, and caregiving sectors.[129]

The key to understanding the plight of migrant workers in Israel is the *triangular* relationship, involving not only the migrant worker and the Israeli employer but also middlemen: local and foreign employment-agencies. The process of recruiting workers took the following form. The Israeli government decided on quotas of migrant-worker permits. The Ministry of Labor divided the permits among employers, who then approached private local employment-agencies. The latter recruited the workers through employment agencies in the countries of origin. Virtually all workers who wished to come to Israel were required to pay considerable recruitment fees, typically ranging from $3,000 to $10,000. The highest fees were charged by government-run employment agencies in China. Typically, the fees were split between the Israeli and foreign employment agencies; Israeli employers in the agriculture and construction sectors at times received a share of the fees.[130] The charging of recruitment fees from workers violated Israeli law[131] and resulted in a heavy burden. To afford the high fees, workers were often forced to take loans and mortgage their property, and the debt they incurred made them vulnerable to abuse. A worker who had to pay off a large loan was less likely to risk losing his job and legal status and much more likely to tolerate harsh treatment by the employer. The recruitment fee effectively tied the worker to the employer and became a means of pressure and exploitation.

Another cause of worker exploitation was the Binding Arrangement. This policy allowed a migrant laborer to work only for a specific employer, whose name appeared on the worker's permit to reside in Israel. If the laborer was fired, resigned, found another job, or was transferred to another employer, he was immediately and automatically viewed as having violated the conditions of employment and residence. His permit thereby expired, and he became an "illegal worker" liable to be arrested and deported.[132] Moreover, even if the termination of employment was caused by reasons that were not the worker's fault—such as employer's bankruptcy, nonpayment of wage, or violence—the worker would still lose his legal status and have to leave the country.

For the government, the Binding Arrangement was a means of tightly controlling work migration and preventing workers from overstaying in Israel. Yet this arrangement created a host of problems and difficulties for the workers themselves. As the worker's legal status in Israel depended upon his employer's will, the worker had little bargaining power vis-à-vis the employer and could be easily exploited. Since a worker could lose his residence permit at the first hint of a problem, the Binding Arrangement essentially made employers immune to workers' demands and complaints.[133] Combined with the workers' lack of knowledge of the local language and of their rights, the Binding Arrangement allowed employers to determine the wage and working conditions unilaterally and even to control workers' personal lives. The Binding Arrangement, in effect, trapped the worker. In the words of the Israeli Supreme Court, the Binding Arrangement "leaves [the worker] with no real choice between being compelled to continue working in the service of an employer who may have violated his rights, delayed paying his wages and abused him, on the one hand, and resignation on the other, a choice that means losing the permit to reside in Israel."[134] The employer's power to easily transform a worker from a legal resident into an illegal alien forced workers to accept any conditions and demands made by employers. Yet it was not only the workers who were bound. Employers were bound as well, as they could only employ through the permits issued to them. If a worker left, the employer could face difficulties in obtaining a permit for a new worker. This encouraged employers to severely limit workers' freedom and even conduct manhunts for "runaway" workers.[135]

Withholding of passports further facilitated workers' abuse. Although a criminal offense, passport withholding used to be a very common practice, especially in the agriculture and construction sectors. Upon arrival in Israel, many workers had their passports taken away and held by the employers or employment agencies. This caused various problems and risks for workers. A worker deprived of his passport could not leave the country at will—due to illness, for example. Without a passport, workers were unable to prove to the police that their stay in Israel was legal, and might therefore face arrest. With no passport, workers could not open bank accounts and had to carry large sums of money, making them easy prey for thieves.[136]

The practices described above put pressure on workers and curtailed their basic freedoms, facilitating abuse and exploitation. Most workers' wages were well below the legal minimum wage and far lower than the wages promised to them in the contracts they had signed in their countries of origin. In addition, workers often did not receive their wages in time or at all; they were not paid for overtime, nor did they receive employment benefits granted to them by law. In many cases, their working and living conditions were harsh. In 2000 the Ministry of Labor issued regulations establishing the minimal living conditions that workers should enjoy. These regulations, however, were rarely complied with. Construction workers, for example, often resided at the construction site; in one of the most notorious cases, agricultural workers from Thailand used to sleep in a chicken coop. Some employers limited workers' access to legal advice and medical care or banned the use of cellular phones. In one case, workers were prohibited from leaving the construction site during the week, even after the end of the workday, and roll calls were held three times a day to make sure no one escaped.[137] Faced with such a reality, many workers realized they had been exploited and would not be able to save money or even pay off the debt incurred for the purpose of working in Israel. They would likely have preferred to leave their employer and seek a better-paying job that would not restrict basic freedoms. Such a choice, however, would have meant automatic loss of legal status and possible deportation.

When does the exploitation of migrant workers amount to trafficking? Labor trafficking of migrant workers is more difficult to identify than sex trafficking. Construction, agriculture, and caregiving are all legitimate economic sectors in which migrants may be legally employed. The line that separates labor trafficking from "ordinary" worker exploitation is not always easily recognizable. Labor trafficking is typically identified through the accumulation of several indicators of particularly harsh treatment and abuse, such as violence, insults, threats, excessively long working hours, degraded living conditions, nonpayment of wage, and inability to move freely or leave the work premises.[138] The term "labor trafficking," in fact, encompasses several practices, such as slavery, forced labor, and debt bondage.

Migrant workers are by definition a vulnerable population, given their status as foreigners and their struggle with economic hardship. The Binding Arrangement and recruitment fees exacerbated this vulnerability, making workers easily exploitable by employers and employment agencies. Labor trafficking thrived in this atmosphere, while the Israeli government stood idly by. The next section examines the causes of the government's inaction.

## Israel's Policy on Labor Trafficking, 1993–2005

From the mid-1990s to the mid-2000s, Israeli authorities attempted to lower the costs that migrant workers' employment imposed on the Israeli economy and society. The means to this end was by reducing the number of migrant workers in Israel. The welfare of the workers themselves—protecting their rights and preventing their abuse—was of little concern.

The Israeli authorities identified various negative externalities stemming from work migration—externalities seen as outweighing the benefits to employers. Migrant workers, it was argued, displaced Israeli workers and contributed to unemployment. By providing cheap labor, migrant workers depressed the wages in certain sectors, harming Israelis employed in these sectors. Other externalities included a burdening of the education and healthcare systems as well as emerging social tensions. The Israeli authorities were concerned that the growing number of migrant-worker communities with distinct ethnic and cultural identities could generate hostility and xenophobia among Israelis, leading to conflicts between migrant workers and the local population.[139] Some, especially religious politicians, considered migrant workers a threat to the Jewish character of Israel. The authorities' view of work migration was summarized by the State Comptroller: "The migrant workers, the employers, and the middlemen benefit from migrant workers' employment . . . By contrast, the State and its citizens are harmed by the large number of migrant workers. In addition to the costs of operating a mechanism to grant and implement permits and oversee migrant workers, there are negative externalities to the economy, which are not borne by any of the actors who benefit from the employment of migrant workers."[140]

In June 1997 the government decided to reduce the number of migrant workers by 2002 to a total of 25,000–29,000 (approximately 1 percent of the Israeli labor force). This goal was to be accomplished by increasing the cost of migrant-worker employment, stepping up the deportation of illegal workers,[141] and enhancing enforcement against employers who violated the law, especially those who employed workers without a permit. The government's plan, however, failed miserably. Measures to reduce the gap in employment costs between a migrant worker and an Israeli worker did not come to fruition, the rate of illegal-worker deportation was much lower than the target, and there was little improvement in enforcement against employers.[142] As a result, the overall number of migrant workers soared from 164,000 in 1997 to 243,000 in 2001. In August 2002 the government decided to establish the Emigration Administration within the Israeli police for the purpose of reducing the number of illegal migrant workers. The Emigration Administration indeed managed to reverse the upward trend in the number of migrant workers by deporting tens of thousands of workers; yet the process of arrest, detainment, and deportation often involved serious violations of the workers' rights. Police tended to use excessive force, broke into homes without court orders, and arrested workers in places of worship. Workers were often not informed of their rights during the detention and the legal proceedings leading to deportation. Moreover, these legal proceedings were conducted without interpretation, in some cases using hand signs for lack of a better way to communicate.[143]

In contrast to their toughness toward migrant workers, the police and the Ministry of Labor treated employers gently. Employers' misconduct gave rise to various regulatory offenses, such as employing a migrant worker without a permit, failure to provide proper housing, and nonpayment of minimum wage. Employers also committed criminal offenses, such as the exploitation of a vulnerable population and withholding of passports. Although employer offenses were rampant, law enforcement against delinquent employers was lax. Compared with the staggering number of legal violations, the number of fines imposed was small, and for the most part their amount was too low to deter law-breaking or to offset the profitability of migrant-worker employment. Furthermore, in many cases the fines simply went unpaid. In 2003–2004 the rate of fine collection from employers was a mere 17 percent. The authorities could have instead penalized employers by revoking their permits to bring in workers. Such a penalty would have been far more effective than a fine and easier to enforce. Nevertheless, the Ministry of Labor chose not to revoke employers' permits; nor did it stop employment agencies from charging illegal recruitment fees, although these fees facilitated worker exploitation. The establishment of the Emigration Administration in 2002 did not change this reality. The Administration focused its efforts on worker deportation and failed to act decisively against employers who broke the law. While few employers were held liable, workers were often punished for their employers' legal transgressions. Many workers lost their legal status after they were illegally transferred to a new employer, yet the transferring employer enjoyed impunity.[144]

Another manifestation of the Israeli authorities' indifference to the hardship of migrant workers was the refusal to undertake any international commitment on work migration. Like the vast majority of destination countries for migrant workers, Israel did not join the International Convention on the Protection of the Rights of All Migrant Workers and Members of Their Families. Israel also refused to sign agreements with countries of origin or with the International Organization for Migration concerning the recruitment of migrant workers or their rights in Israel.[145]

How can one reconcile rampant employer law-breaking with the lax enforcement of Israeli authorities? Why did the police and the Ministry of Labor fail to protect migrant workers and curb worker exploitation? There were several causes for the choice to focus on hunting down, arresting, and deporting workers instead of deterring and punishing employers. Israeli authorities cited budgetary constraints and shortage of personnel as reasons for the weak enforcement against employers.[146] Another difficulty was workers' reluctance to complain. Whether out of a desperate need for money, fear of being deported, a culturally ingrained loyalty to the employer and respect for authority, or toleration of working and living conditions not unlike those in their home countries, workers rarely filed complaints.[147]

Yet the roots of employer impunity and indifference to migrant workers' hardship ran deeper. As the theoretical framework suggests, governments seek to curb the negative externalities of illicit trade when they harm the local public. The Israeli government was indeed concerned about the externalities of work migration on Israeli society, such as the displacement of local workers. The means of lowering these externalities was migrant-worker deportation. By contrast, the government had little incentive to eliminate the trafficking of migrant workers—a practice whose negative effects were borne by migrant workers themselves. Migrant workers were an extremely weak population. In Israel temporarily, they neither held voting rights nor spoke the local language; they were also not unionized. Since they lacked electoral power or any other way to wield political influence, their exploitation was of little concern to the government. Moreover, as in the case of foreign women trafficked for prostitution, the Israeli public and authorities were indifferent to the labor trafficking of migrants who were neither Israeli nor Jewish. Far from being seen as a vulnerable population in need of protection, migrant workers were perceived as a demographic problem that threatened the Jewish character of Israel. The result was the authorities' focus on worker deportation and their inaction against the trafficking of workers.

The other factor shaping the government's response to labor trafficking was the employers, who correspond to consumers in the theoretical framework. Consistent with the theoretical framework, the government was protective of employer interests. The various legal arrangements regulating work migration, first and foremost the Binding Arrangement, were heavily biased in favor of employers, to the workers' disadvantage. The lax enforcement against employers was another manifestation of their favored position. Employers won the authorities' sympathy for three reasons. First, they were

Israeli. The police and government ministries had no misgivings about enforcing the law to its fullest against foreign migrants, even without their wrongdoing. Yet when it came to Israelis, the authorities were much more compassionate. Second, notwithstanding their exploitation of migrant workers, employers were largely law-abiding citizens, engaged overall in legitimate economic activities (unlike sex traffickers). Israeli authorities sympathized with disabled and elderly people who were desperate for domestic help and with farmers whose crops would rot unless picked by migrant workers.[148] When those employers turned out to be abusive, the sympathy turned into forgiveness.

The third reason for the authorities' sympathy toward employers was their political power. Farmers and contractors enjoyed significant political influence and ties to policymakers, which allowed them to shape policy on work migration. Employers' lobbying focused primarily on worker quotas. The farmers' and contractors' lobbies persistently demanded more migrant-worker permits in order to save the agriculture and construction sectors from collapse. Employers also opposed the elimination of the Binding Arrangement, which gave them control over workers, ensured that the workers would not seek another job, and prevented competition among employers that might have forced them to offer better wages and working conditions. Employment agencies lobbied as well against proposals to regulate their business and loosen their grip on workers.[149] At least publicly, there was no lobbying to relax law enforcement against abusive employers or against those employing workers without a legal permit. The Association of Contractors and Builders, for example, acknowledged that a small minority of employers had violated their workers' rights and should suffer legal consequences.[150] Nevertheless, there is little doubt that the authorities' tolerance of employers' law-breaking had to do with the political power they wielded. It was much more convenient to treat the powerless migrant worker as the criminal, rather than the powerful employer. Employers' breaches of the law were therefore not seen as serious offenses deserving of severe punishment. They were overlooked as minor regulatory infractions.

## Israel's Policy on Labor Trafficking, 2006–2010

The Israeli policy had been faulty on two grounds: first, police violation of migrant workers' rights (for example, the use of excessive force for arrest); second, nonenforcement against employers and lack of effort against the trafficking of workers. However, 2006 saw a significant improvement in the authorities' own conduct toward migrant workers as well as an increasing willingness to tackle abuse by employers and curb labor trafficking. As with sex trafficking, these policy changes stemmed from a confluence of pressures exerted by domestic actors as well as the United States, with the latter having the most decisive impact. Yet while the authorities made notable progress, their response to labor trafficking was less than determined and yielded mixed results. Labor trafficking was not gone; the efforts to eliminate it were less fruitful than those against sex trafficking.

The most important domestic catalyst of change was the local NGO community, especially the Worker's Hotline—an organization committed to the rights of disadvantaged workers. The NGOs implemented a multipronged strategy, including:

1. Raising workers' awareness of their rights. Importantly, workers were made aware that employers were prohibited from withholding their passports. Worker awareness, combined with police enforcement, nearly eliminated this once-common practice.

2. Sending letters to delinquent employers requesting due payment for workers and urging officials to take action against those employers.

3. Litigation. The NGOs filed numerous court cases challenging the authorities' conduct in specific cases, especially concerning the arrest, detainment, and deportation of migrant workers. They also filed several court cases against work-migration policies in general. In the most important case, six NGOs jointly challenged the legality of the Binding Arrangement before the Supreme Court. In their petition, the NGOs argued that this arrangement violated workers' fundamental rights, turning them, in effect, into employers' property. In its 2006 decision, the Supreme Court determined that the arrangement indeed infringed basic rights, and ordered the government to formulate a new employment scheme for migrant workers that would not bind them to a single employer.[151]

4. The Worker's Hotline enlisting the help of the United States by urging the State Department to address work migration in Israel in its annual Trafficking in Persons Report. I return to this point later.

The Knesset Committee on Foreign Workers played a role, albeit a limited one, in changing the authorities' attitude toward migrant workers. Overall, its influence was smaller than that of the Parliamentary Inquiry Committee on Trafficking in Women. The Committee on Foreign Workers did manage, however, to set boundaries to the authorities' permissible conduct toward migrant workers. At the committee's behest, the police ceased to conduct arrests in churches, schools, and hospitals, and toned down the use of force against workers during their arrest.[152] The committee also sought to bring the authorities to treat the *employer* as the offender, rather than the migrant worker; yet this change did not materialize. While the police did start treating migrant workers more humanely, they did not fully transform their approach to employers. For Israeli authorities, migrant-worker employers—unlike sex traffickers—were legitimate actors with legitimate needs, interests, and constraints. Unlike sex traffickers, migrant-worker employers had ties to and influence over politicians. This posed an insurmountable challenge to the Foreign Workers Committee, one not faced by the Parliamentary Inquiry Committee on Trafficking in Women.

Although domestic actors did affect the authorities' conduct, the single most decisive influence, as in the case of sex trafficking, was American pressure. Whereas the TIP Reports from 2001 to 2004 focused mainly on sex trafficking, the 2005 report expanded the coverage of labor trafficking. This was clearly manifested with respect to Israel. The report criticized the Israeli government for its failure to curb the exploitation of migrant workers, observing that "[s]ome trafficked foreign workers suffer from non-payment of wages, threat, coercion, physical and sexual abuse, debt bondage, and restrictions on freedom of movement, including the withholding of their passports." The report pointed out that Israel "lacks a law against trafficking for the purpose of labor exploitation, although such a law was drafted in 2003 and awaits approval."[153]

Whereas in 2005 Israel was still ranked in Tier 2, as it had been since 2002, The 2006 TIP Report moved Israel down to the Tier 2 Watch List.[154] It noted that "[w]hile the government made noticeable improvement in its law enforcement efforts against traffickers for sexual exploitation, it did little to address the much larger problem of involuntary servitude among foreign migrant workers." Although some employers and employment agencies had been indicted, few "faced jail time as a punishment; most were punished with fines." The report concluded that "[t]he scope of labor trafficking in Israel merits a higher number of investigations, prosecutions, convictions, and manpower agency closures. Israel also failed to enforce bans on charging recruitment fees for employment and withholding workers' passports."[155] This criticism reflected the State Department's growing attention to labor trafficking worldwide; but it was also the result of the efforts of Israeli NGOs. For the Worker's Hotline, it was a priority to have the TIP Report address labor trafficking in Israel. The organization provided information and "lobbied like crazy"[156] in meetings at the U.S. embassy in Tel Aviv. In 2001 the information provided by local NGOs had led to Israel's being ranked in Tier 3 for its failure to suppress sex trafficking; in 2006 the NGOs once again—frustrated by their inability to effect significant change—brought in the State Department to pressure the Israeli government.

The aftermath of Israel's drop to the Tier 2 Watch List in 2006 resembled the dramatic effect of the first TIP Report in 2001. Faced with American pressure, Israeli authorities once again rushed to action. The previous indifference to labor trafficking and weak law enforcement against employers were replaced by significant efforts to tackle labor exploitation. The most important and immediate consequence of the 2006 TIP Report was the enactment of a comprehensive anti-trafficking law.[157] The process of legislation began as early as 2003,[158] yet the government was in no hurry to complete it. With the publication of the 2006 TIP Report, passing the new law became a priority. During the summer of 2006, while Israel was in the midst of a war in Lebanon, weekly meetings were held at the Knesset, culminating in the law's passage in October 2006. The new law established a cluster of criminal offenses, including trafficking in persons for the purpose of slavery or forced labor, holding a person under conditions of slavery, and forced labor. The law also established a series of protections and legal rights for victims. It sent a strong message to the courts by mandating minimal sentences for trafficking and slavery offenses and by encouraging the courts to award compensation to victims.

The changing government attitude toward the trafficking of migrant workers was manifested on the ground in the work of the Emigration Administration. Since its establishment in 2002, the Administration had had two tasks: the deportation of illegal migrant workers and investigation and prosecution of employers' offenses against migrant workers. The Administration, however, had focused almost exclusively on worker deportation. Except for the withholding of passports, a phenomenon that the Administration had managed to reduce, employers' offenses had largely gone uninvestigated and unprosecuted. This changed in the months following the 2006 TIP Report, as offenses against migrant workers came to occupy a much more central role in the Administration's work.[159] Heightened investigative efforts led to several criminal indictments against abusive employers.

Another major step was the establishment in 2007 of a National Plan for the Battle against Slavery and Trafficking in Persons for the Purposes of Slavery or Forced Labor. The National Plan included a set of recommended measures, such as efforts to inform migrant workers about their rights, a policy of encouraging workers to complain against offending employers, enhanced oversight of employers and employment agencies, and improved collaboration among law-enforcement agencies in the investigation and prosecution of labor trafficking.

The timing of these policy changes leaves little doubt that they were indeed prompted by the 2006 TIP Report, and this was also the impression of actors who participated in the policymaking process. Rahel Gershuni, the Government Coordinator of the Battle against Trafficking in Persons, identifies a dramatic shift in attitude following the 2006 TIP report: no longer denying the existence of labor trafficking, Israeli authorities came to acknowledge this phenomenon and took measures to combat it.[160] MK Ran Cohen, chair of the Knesset Committee on Foreign Workers, also considers the American involvement to have been a vital motivating factor: Israeli officials "know in the back of their mind that [the TIP Report] exists, sets the norms, and has to be complied with"; they listened to the Foreign Workers Committee "because they know that if the committee issues a decision against them, the State

Department will then use it and say: 'Someone in Israel is sounding an alarm, and yet the government fails to act.'"[161] Yuval Livnat, legal advisor at the Worker's Hotline, similarly credits the 2006 TIP Report as the single most important cause of the Israeli government's efforts against labor trafficking.[162]

Following these developments, the 2007 TIP Report ranked Israel in Tier 2, where it stayed through 2011. Yet, although much has changed, the policy transformation on labor trafficking was partial and did not amount to the complete turnabout witnessed with respect to sex trafficking. Dozens of sex traffickers were criminally prosecuted, convicted of trafficking for the purpose of prostitution and/or related offenses, and imprisoned for their crimes. By contrast, offending employers of migrant workers were not prosecuted for trafficking crimes under the 2006 anti-trafficking law. They were usually charged with lesser crimes—the exploitation of vulnerable populations or withholding of a passport—and did not receive prison sentences. Whereas the government encouraged victims of sex trafficking to assist in investigations against their traffickers, victimized migrant workers did not receive similar encouragement. In 2009 enforcement against employers diminished further, after the Emigration Administration closed and transferred its authorities to the newly created Population, Immigration, and Border Authority in the Ministry of Interior.[163]

Moreover, the Binding Arrangement and the recruitment fees that made migrant workers vulnerable to exploitation have not been eliminated. In 2006 the Supreme Court declared the Binding Arrangement illegal and ordered the formulation of an alternative employment scheme, yet the government only complied in part. The construction sector underwent reform: manpower corporations became responsible for employing migrant workers and paying their wage. This new scheme was supposed to make migrant-worker employment more expensive and less profitable; it was also meant to guarantee workers' rights and allow them job mobility. Yet violations of workers' rights have persisted even after the reform. In the caregiving sector, the employment scheme was partially reformed, whereas in agriculture no reform was implemented—the binding of workers to employers continues.[164] There has also been little progress concerning recruitment fees. In fact, the fees have kept increasing: each worker who entered Israel in 2010 paid $10,000 on average. Israeli authorities argue that evidentiary difficulties prevent the curbing of this practice: since the workers pay the fees in their countries of origin, it is difficult to prove the complicity of Israeli employment agencies.[165]

## Labor Trafficking in Israel: Conclusions

Objective difficulties clearly hindered the efforts against labor trafficking in Israel. One of the major stumbling blocks was migrant workers' reluctance to file complaints against employers and their inability to provide information necessary for investigation and prosecution.[166] Another persistent problem was personnel shortages within government authorities. Yet the chief obstacle was the indifference on the part of the government and law-enforcement agencies and their unwillingness to tackle migrant-worker exploitation. The main problem was that "migrant workers were treated through the prism of deportation; they were not seen as victims. The Israeli police simply did not consider cases [of offenses against migrant workers] a priority."[167] The Israeli government and public were anxious about the upsurge of migrant workers and its negative externalities on Israeli society, from the displacement of local workers to undermining Israel's Jewish character. By contrast, migrant workers' exploitation and abuse raised little concern. Furthermore, the workers' countries of origin rarely demanded better treatment of their citizens. These countries' utmost priority was to secure their citizens' ability to work in Israel and send remittances back home.[168]

As the Israeli public and the countries of origin disregarded the trafficking of migrant workers, the Israeli government had little incentive to curb this practice. American pressure was therefore necessary in order to provide the missing incentive and change the government's attitude. Yet, despite the American involvement, the Israeli efforts against labor trafficking were less determined than those against sex trafficking. The reason was that combating labor trafficking required the prosecution and punishment of employers—actors who, unlike sex traffickers, enjoyed legitimacy and political clout. The legitimate economic interests involved in migrant-worker employment made labor trafficking a more delicate and sensitive issue for law enforcement than sex trafficking—an area where the interests of "pimps and criminals" were at stake.[169] The efforts against sex trafficking included preventing the women's arrival in Israel and closing down brothels. Such an eradication approach could not apply to migrant workers, who were vital to the Israeli economy. Israeli authorities therefore had to engage in a balancing act, fighting migrant-worker exploitation without interfering with the legitimate employment of migrant workers, and protecting the basic rights of workers while safeguarding the interests of employers and Israeli society. As a result, Israeli authorities adopted a much more restrained approach toward labor trafficking than toward sex trafficking. Although abusive employers of migrant workers no longer enjoy impunity, the law-enforcement authorities have not fully internalized the view of employers as offenders.

The case of human trafficking demonstrates the merit of this book's approach compared with existing approaches to the analysis of illicit trade. Existing accounts identify a range of problems and obstacles that hinder the efforts against human trafficking; yet the government's political motivation to curb trafficking usually receives less-than-satisfactory consideration. Julie Mertus and Andrea Bertone's analysis of the response to sex trafficking in the Balkans in the early 2000s is typical.[170] Mertus and Bertone offer a host of explanations for the limited effectiveness of anti-trafficking efforts, among them the persistence of macro-level problems that fuel trafficking, such as poverty and the lower social status of women; traffickers' change of tactics in response to increased law enforcement; and insufficient cooperation between governmental agencies and between governments and nongovernmental partners. The government's own incentive structure receives little attention in this account. Mertus and Bertone merely note that the failure to prosecute traffickers and protect victims points "toward a general sluggishness on the part of the government to tackle the serious problem of trafficking."[171] In Kathy Richards's account of labor trafficking, official corruption is the culprit: "Corruption can smooth the bumps in the road for the trafficker during the journey, help negotiate transactions for the trafficker, hold trafficked workers in bondage and forced labour, and undermine efforts to prevent labour trafficking." Richards argues that "[e]mployers of the trafficked worker are able to pay bribes to police, prosecutors, or magistrates to have the charges dropped, while the trafficked workers with no funds to pay bribes are frequently abused and deported."[172]

This book's theoretical framework, by contrast, puts the government's political motivation to curb illicit trade at the center of the analysis; in particular, it calls attention to the impact of legitimate societal actors on the government's preference. By focusing on political incentives, the theoretical framework allows us to gain a better understanding of governments' response to human trafficking. The Israeli failure to suppress sex and labor trafficking prior to American pressure was not simply a result of poor coordination between governmental agencies; nor was it primarily caused by official corruption, criminals' skills and adaptive tactics, or the persistence of economic conditions that fuel the influx of migrants. Rather, the Israeli government did not identify any gains from cracking down on human trafficking: the sexual exploitation of foreign women and severe abuse of migrant workers were not seen as social problems that merited law enforcement's attention. As the Israeli public disregarded human trafficking, and since the trafficked persons themselves had no political power, the government lacked any motivation to tackle this issue. In the case of labor trafficking, there was an additional obstacle: Israeli authorities were reluctant to take on otherwise law-abiding employers who enjoyed political influence. Domestic political considerations thus explain Israel's inaction against human trafficking; existing approaches that are unmindful of such considerations would misinterpret the Israeli policy. Furthermore, existing approaches cannot explain the divergent Israeli responses to sex trafficking and labor trafficking in the aftermath of American pressure. The difference in the legitimacy and political clout of the consumers is a key distinction between sex trafficking and labor trafficking that led to more determined government action against the former. This distinction is lost in existing accounts of human trafficking; it is revealed only through an analytical framework that highlights the political conflicts over illicit trade and the impact of societal actors on governments' political calculations.

# 6

## EXTENSIONS

### Opposing Opium, Combating Counterfeits

---

The previous empirical chapters have all demonstrated the key problem hindering cooperation against illicit trade: international regulation aimed at curbing the trade exacts a heavy price from governments with little motivation to pay that price. These governments are not concerned about the trade's negative externalities; rather, they are protecting the interests of domestic actors involved in the trade. They are therefore reluctant to bear the burden and make the sacrifices that international regulation entails. As a result, an international political conflict ensues between governments supportive of regulation and governments opposed to it. The present chapter explores the sources and dynamics of the international political conflicts over three types of illicit trade: drugs, money laundering, and counterfeits. The analysis highlights the commercial interests that have hindered international regulation and the exercise of American coercion to compel cooperation.

## Drugs

The most powerful weapon in fighting the drug trade is an intangible: political will. The best-trained counternarcotics force, equipped with state-of-the-art police and military hardware, cannot succeed without the full commitment of the country's political leadership. When political leaders have had the courage to sacrifice short-term economic and political considerations in favor of the long-term national interest, we have seen the drug trade weaken. Conversely, when they have succumbed to the lure of ready cash, the drug syndicates have prospered accordingly.[1]

The international drug regime is the oldest and most enduring global endeavor against illicit trade.[2] Three international agreements constitute the pillars of the contemporary regime: the Single Convention on Narcotic Drugs, 1961; the Convention on Psychotropic Substances, 1971; and the Convention against Illicit Traffic in Narcotic Drugs and Psychotropic Substances, 1988. These three post-World War II agreements build upon the regulatory foundation established and developed since the inception of international drug control in 1909. Most importantly, the contemporary drug regime enshrines the basic norm that the United States has forcefully advocated from the outset of the international efforts: drugs may be legitimately used only for medical and scientific purposes.

A comprehensive examination of the evolution of international drug control is beyond the scope of the current analysis. Instead, my goal here is to employ the theoretical framework to shed light on the fundamental dynamics and influences that have propelled or obstructed drug cooperation. Today, the chief threat to antidrug efforts comes from criminal groups and their ability to corrupt and intimidate. Yet from a broader historical perspective, the primary challenge to international drug control has been the one highlighted by this book's theoretical framework: *legitimate* commercial interests and attendant political concerns. Governments of drug-exporting countries have been reluctant to bear the burden of tackling the drug trade's externalities; they have shown little enthusiasm for curbing a lucrative trade that benefits domestic constituencies while inflicting harm abroad. Coercion has thus played an important role in bridging the gap between proponents and opponents of international regulation.

A note on terminology: The text distinguishes between two types of drug-exporting countries: producing countries that grow organic raw materials (opium, coca, or cannabis), and manufacturing countries that fabricate drugs in an industrial process. The term "formative period" denotes the early era of international drug control: 1909–1939.

## The Motivation for Cooperation: Negative Externalities

The theoretical framework has suggested that curbing the negative externalities of illicit trade is the main purpose of international cooperation. When governments are unable to curb these externalities or unwilling to pay the price of doing so, they seek to shift the burden elsewhere through international regulatory agreements. Indeed, international drug control has been mainly—though not exclusively—rooted in the negative effects of drugs and their economic and social costs:[3]

- Healthcare costs—Drug abuse involves health risks to the abusers themselves as well as costs to society: the expenses of drug-abuse treatment and prevention, as well as costs relating to the medical consequences of abuse (such as drug-exposed infants and infection with HIV from injection drug use).
- Crime—Beyond drug-specific offenses (such as the production, possession, and consumption of drugs), drugs are associated with various kinds of criminal activity: violence among rival traffickers, crimes committed under drug influence, and crimes stemming from the need of drug addicts to finance their addiction. The crime-related costs of drugs include bodily or property damage and criminal justice costs (policing, judicial resources, and imprisonment).
- Loss of productivity—Drug abuse reduces the labor and efforts available to the legitimate economy through drug-caused premature death, illness, or hospitalization; the difficulties of finding and holding a job; and incarceration.

Much of the contemporary concern over drugs relates to addiction and abuse in Western countries, particularly the United States. The economic cost of drug abuse in the United States in 2002 (including health, crime, and productivity consequences of abuse) was approximately $180.9 billion.[4] In 2000, an estimated 17,000 U.S. deaths resulted from illicit drug use, directly and indirectly.[5] Yet the initial impetus for cooperation against drugs in the early 20th century was the *Chinese* opium problem, "the largest substance abuse problem the world has ever faced."[6] Opium consumption in China, previously reserved to social elites, skyrocketed in the 19th century. The Chinese market was flooded with opium imports, primarily from British India and also from Turkey, Persia (modern-day Iran), Egypt, and the Balkans. Domestic opium production in China itself also grew mightily. The result was widespread opium addiction at all levels of Chinese society.[7] The Chinese government launched a domestic anti-opium campaign in 1906 and engaged in bilateral efforts to stem the inflow of drugs, setting the stage for a U.S.-led multilateral endeavor.[8] In 1909, upon American initiative, met the first international conference dedicated to drugs: the Shanghai Opium Commission.

What spurred American concern over the secondary externalities of the opium trade—that is, the drug's negative effects on China? According to the theoretical framework, government interest in curbing the secondary externalities of illicit trade may stem from advocacy of moral entrepreneurs. Such actors indeed played an important role in inducing the United States to initiate international drug control. To suppress what they regarded as a moral evil, American missionaries in China sought to elicit sympathy for China's drug problem among the American public and to encourage U.S.

government action against the opium trade. The missionaries employed various tools in pursuit of their goals, including petitions, addresses, letters to and meetings with American officials, and reports to the press and to churches in the United States.[9]

The moral dimension of the American concern over China is consistent with the ethical motivations identified in previous chapters. The European interest in curbing gun violence in Africa; American participation in the efforts against the looting of antiquities; and U.S. leadership of the campaign against human trafficking—all of these were fueled mainly by moral concerns. Similarly, the United States presented its efforts for international drug control as a moral crusade on behalf of Oriental peoples.[10] Yet the American concern over China's opium problem was also motivated by economic self-interest: promotion of U.S.-China trade. Seen as responsible for China's social and economic degeneration, opium was thought to reduce the Chinese demand for other goods; by contrast, a China released from the scourge of opium held an enormous potential for American traders and manufacturers. The U.S. government also hoped that American leadership of an effort to relieve the opium problem would signal goodwill, curry favor with China's imperial authorities, and facilitate American access to Chinese markets. The American endeavor was also the product of political and economic calculations relating to great-power competition. By helping to rid China of a problem for which the British bore much of the responsibility, the United States sought to enhance its influence in East Asia at Britain's expense and to bolster China against the encroachments of foreign powers. More broadly, the campaign against drugs allowed the United States to assume international leadership on a moral issue and thereby enhance its international status.[11]

China's opium problem was the main motivation for the U.S. initiative regarding international drug control before World War I. Yet the moral and self-interested concerns over secondary externalities were reinforced by American determination to tackle primary externalities: the drug problems in the U.S.-governed Philippines and in the United States itself.

Upon assuming control of the Philippines in 1898, the United States had to directly confront drug use in the islands, a legacy of the Spanish colonizers who had operated a government monopoly of opium sales to a large ethnic-Chinese addict population. Appointed in 1903, an Opium Committee proposed an ultimate prohibition on opium in the Philippines, except for medical purposes. In 1905 Congress passed legislation that imposed a ban on the import, sale, and use of opium in the islands, to take effect in 1908. Yet the large-scale production of and trade in opium across Asia threatened to undermine the U.S. efforts to suppress opium in the Philippines. The United States believed that solving the Philippine drug problem entailed controlling the opium trade and curbing production in countries such as India, China, Burma, Persia, and Turkey.[12]

Concern about drug consumption in the United States was among the motivations for drug cooperation prior to World War I and became the chief driver of the American efforts following the war, eclipsing China's opium problem.[13] International control was, in fact, part of a broader trend that swept through Western societies at the turn of the 20th century: the replacement of the laissez-faire approach to drugs with nascent regulation. Drug control was supported by various social-reform groups, especially those advocating temperance, and by physicians wishing to gain control over access to the powerful substances. Another impetus for control was the public panic over drug addiction among feared minority groups. Chinese workers in the United States were seen as a threat to American labor, and their habit of opium smoking, a menace to American society. In the South, cocaine supposedly made Blacks violent and prone to rebel against White society and even endowed them with superhuman strength.[14]

Concern over the drug problem in China, fortified by alarm over drugs in the Philippines and the United States, brought the U.S. government to initiate an international campaign for drug control. Yet the relationship between international drug regulation and national regulation at the outset of the campaign reversed the theoretically expected pattern. U.S. advocacy of international drug control did not stem from the insufficiency of federal narcotics legislation; rather, it triggered the passage of such legislation.

State laws were enacted in the last decade of the 19th century to curb morphine and cocaine abuse. These laws were ineffective, but federal anti-narcotics legislation stalled due to the opposition of drug manufacturers and retail pharmacists as well as constitutional limits on the police powers of the federal government.[15] Extensive drug use in the United States, unconstrained by federal legislation, threatened to become evidence of American insincerity and to undermine the credibility of the U.S. ambition to lead an international anti-narcotics effort: How could the United States urge other countries to pass strict drug laws without doing so itself? Leaders of the anti-narcotics movement, especially Dr. Hamilton Wright, were thus anxious to pass federal legislation to save face, avoid international embarrassment, and set an example for other countries to follow. Federal legislation was seen as necessary for bolstering the United States' international leverage and for inducing foreign governments to establish controls on drugs. The American leadership of the international efforts was thus an important motivation for passing the 1914 Harrison Narcotics Act—the law that launched federal involvement in drug control and served as the country's basic drug legislation for decades.[16]

Yet in another important respect the American efforts have echoed one of this book's central themes: international regulation as a means of shifting the burden of control. Since the outset of the international campaign, the United States has advocated the suppression and prohibition of drugs except for medical and scientific purposes, denouncing other uses as abuse that is morally wrong and a menace to society. At the same time, the United States has argued that domestic drug laws could not sufficiently protect Americans from the threat of drugs, making international cooperation necessary for curbing drug *supply*. Consistent with the theoretical framework, the United States has sought to transfer the onus of regulation to drug-exporting countries through *control at the source*: limitation of the production (including cultivation of the raw plant) and manufacture of drugs as the best method for controlling the drug trade and reducing drug abuse within U.S. borders. If foreign countries were to restrict drug production and manufacturing only to medical and scientific needs and curtail excess supply, the illicit trade to and within the United States should dry up.[17] This supply-focused vision, put forth as early as 1909, underpinned the American efforts for international drug control throughout the 20th century and has changed little since its initial articulation.[18]

Why has the United States sought to shift the burden of control abroad? According to the theoretical framework, governments seek international regulation when they lack the capacity or the will to curb illicit trade through domestic measures. Capacity constraints and objective difficulties have indeed hindered American national efforts. For example, the length of the U.S.-Mexico border and the enormous number of people who cross it have posed formidable challenges for drug interdiction; so has traffickers' ability to adapt to law-enforcement pressure. Yet the American pursuit of international regulation has also reflected an unwillingness to bear the full domestic costs of drug control. Blaming the U.S. drug problem on foreign countries and shifting the regulatory burden onto them has relieved the United States of much of its own responsibility as a consuming country, especially the need to seriously tackle the intricate issue of demand for drugs. Suppressing drug consumption in the United States entails substantial costs, such as programs for drug education, prevention, and treatment; law enforcement and incarceration; and social tensions and violations of civil rights. A supply-side strategy that locates the root of the trouble abroad and deflects the costs of drug control has thus been politically expedient and popular.[19]

## Commercial Interests

Illicit drugs inflict enormous harm on societies worldwide; yet for more than a hundred years, cooperation against the illicit drug trade has been mired in international controversy. Consistent with the theoretical framework, the root of the controversy has been the threat that regulatory constraints have posed to commercial interests. The contemporary fight against drugs is largely directed against organized crime; yet from its onset through to the 1960s, the international drug regime was primarily aimed at regulating and supervising *legal* drug activities: suppression of the illicit trade was to be achieved through the prevention of drug diversion from legitimate sources.[20] During the regime's formative period and throughout its subsequent evolution, concerns for the interests of legitimate market-actors have thus fueled government opposition to international control and hindered drug cooperation. As early as 1909, the United States recognized that "private and governmental considerations of revenue constituted the main if not the only barrier to a proper solution of the [drug] problem."[21]

### Producers

In the formative period, governments themselves had a direct commercial stake in the trade. Colonial governments in Asia held monopolies over the production, domestic distribution, and trade in opium—monopolies that generated considerable revenues and served as an important source of income and hard currency for colonial administrations. As a major export, opium was central to colonial economies.[22] Colonial powers—Britain, France, the Netherlands, and Portugal—thus opposed restraints on the drug trade that would have disturbed colonial administrations' profits and threatened their lifeblood.[23] Consider Britain. The heavy reliance of the British Empire on opium profits fueled two wars between Britain and China in the mid-19th century. Yet by the convening of the Shanghai Opium Commission in 1909, Britain had moderated its preference for unrestricted trade in opium. The profitability of the Indian opium trade had been declining; the trade strained London's relations with China and, by weakening the latter, threatened nondrug British economic interests. Importantly, the involvement in the drug trade met with increasing public criticism at home, inspiring a campaign of British anti-opium reformers who considered the trade immoral. Following the Liberal electoral victory in 1906, the British government indicated its willingness to curb the India-to-China opium trade. In the 1907 Ten-Year Agreement, Britain committed to steadily reducing Indian opium exports to China until their elimination after 10 years, provided that China eliminated domestic opium production at the same rate.[24] The pro-regulation impulse, however, was restrained by opium producers and merchants in India and by the Indian government, who wished to carry on the drug trade. Cross-pressured, the British were far from keen about international drug control. During the deliberations of the 1909 Shanghai Commission, they opposed various American proposals, from efforts to limit opium to strictly medical use, to a call on governments to assist each other in the solution of their domestic opium problems, to permission for countries to prohibit the import of opium into their territories except for medical purposes.[25] Britain's ambivalence on the opium trade persisted into the interwar period and led the Americans to charge the British with favoring revenue considerations over morals.[26] Other colonial powers joined Britain's resistance to stringent control in Shanghai. Throughout the interwar era, controls on drugs continued to clash with their economic interests.[27]

While colonial interests no longer hinder drug cooperation, sovereign drug-producing countries have remained ambivalent or hostile toward international drug control to this day. The governments of these countries have often depended upon drug cultivation for a significant share of their revenue; in some cases, politicians themselves have been involved in the drug business. Drug production has also been a major source of employment. Drug-producing countries have therefore considered drugs as an integral part of their economies and a profitable export, the reduction of which would trigger serious economic disorders. Furthermore, by shrinking government revenue and lowering employment, drug control threatened governments' political survival.[28] Consequently, international drug control, from its inception, provoked producing countries' anxiety and resistance.

Consider Persia. In the 1920s opium was cultivated in 18 of Persia's 26 provinces, in many of which it was the only cash crop of significance. Opium was a major export and accounted for about 9 percent of the government's revenue. The wealthy class and many of the influential clergy were opium producers and merchants. From the government's point of view, international controls on drugs threatened to increase the already large deficit, exacerbate unemployment and poverty, and aggravate the country's political instability.[29] Other drug-producing countries, from Turkey to Yugoslavia to Peru, shared Persia's concerns. They saw the curtailing of opium or coca cultivation as an economic peril to the government and to the millions of people dependent on the drug trade for living, an affront to national sovereignty, an obstacle to modernization and self-sufficiency, and a threat to entrenched social habits in which drugs were deeply embedded.[30]

The resistance of producing countries has persisted throughout the life of the drug regime, hindering the international efforts. Today, the drug sector is still a vital source of employment and income in various countries, including Afghanistan, Colombia, and Bolivia.[31] The adverse economic and political implications of drug control—first and foremost, the undermining of the livelihoods of a large sector of the population—lessen these countries' willingness to cooperate.[32] Furthermore, the longstanding noncooperative incentives have been reinforced since the 1980s, as organized criminal groups have used bribery and corruption to penetrate the state and shield the drug trade from legislation, interdiction, or enforcement.[33] Some producing countries, however, have become cross-pressured when the growing criminal influence resulted in substantial negative externalities, including large-scale drug-related violence, undermining of the state's authority and institutions, or the financing of insurgency through drug profits. Consistent with the theoretical framework, the pro-regulation influence of the trade's externalities has tempered governments' resistance to international control and facilitated cooperation. A prominent example is Colombia's aggressive antidrug efforts since the late 1990s as manifested by Plan Colombia—a military and law-enforcement strategy to reduce drug production, implemented with U.S. assistance.[34] We have seen a similar dynamic of preference change in the case of antiquities: the emergence of primary externalities—loss of its own cultural objects—that moderated Britain's longtime opposition to international antiquities regulation.


Manufacturers

Curbing the illicit drug trade at its source by limiting supply also entails restrictions on drug manufacturing. Drugs legitimately manufactured by pharmaceutical companies may be later diverted to the illicit market or abused; pharmaceutical companies may even be knowingly complicit in the illicit trade, as shown by a series of interwar cases implicating European firms.[35] Pharmaceutical companies have thus been key targets of international drug control. Consistent with the theoretical framework, these companies have been wary of—and at times vigorously resisted— international regulatory measures intended to constrain and curtail their business. Governments have sought to defeat or weaken the control of manufacturing, in support of pharmaceutical interests.

The anti-regulation impact of the industry has been evident from the outset. Concerned for its large pharmaceutical industry, Germany opposed the nascent pre-World War I international efforts and sought to avoid interference with the manufacture of and trade in morphine, heroin, and cocaine.[36] Over time, the growing scope and stringency of international control increased the stakes for pharmaceutical companies, which came to wield significant influence over the evolution of drug cooperation. They figured prominently in the calculations of national authorities, shaped governments' preferences, and even participated in international negotiations.[37] The anti-regulation effect of pharmaceutical interests was clearly manifested in the interwar period, as manufacturing countries—most notably, Germany, Switzerland, and France—sought to dilute the substantive control requirements over manufactured narcotics and keep regulatory power vested in national authorities.[38] In the post-World War II era, pharmaceutical companies continued to champion regulatory moderation, resisting what they saw as an undue burden on the trade in manufactured drugs that would diminish their profitability. Regulatory agencies in

Western Europe and the United States, often in cozy relations with the industry and seeking its cooperation, vigorously protected pharmaceutical interests against stringent control.[39]

Yet the theoretical framework has also suggested that market actors may favor international regulation that offers benefits for business. Such benefits, although not the principal driver of regulation, have indeed accompanied international drug control. Alongside their firm resistance to onerous regulation, pharmaceutical companies recognized certain advantages that international regulation may yield and have sought to weaken the drug treaties to the minimum required in order to enjoy these advantages. For example, international drug control established worldwide regulatory standards that many countries would not exceed, thereby facilitating the business of developing, obtaining approval for, and marketing new substances in a global market. The regime's rules and requirements also functioned as barriers, benefiting established pharmaceutical companies and eliminating competition from unscrupulous manufacturers.[40] Furthermore, international drug regulation was a means of leveling the playing field among manufacturers. During the interwar period, American drug companies, which exported relatively modest amounts of opiates and cocaine, argued that the U.S. drug control system had disadvantaged them compared to their European competitors. To improve their position in the world market, they urged the U.S. government to encourage the adoption of similarly stringent controls by European countries.[41] In another manifestation of the competitive dynamic, regulation opponents insisted on broad treaty membership to spread the costs of control across countries, diminish their competitors' advantage, deflect attention from their own culpability, and slow down the regulatory momentum. Aware of the high price that drug control would exact from its Indian colony, Britain wished to share the burden with Germany by demanding that the Hague Opium Conference (December 1911–January 1912) address not only opium, but manufactured drugs as well. At that conference, the Germans, supported by the French, insisted that all producing, manufacturing, and consuming countries—including those not present at the conference—must ratify the International Opium Convention before it entered into force. Germany argued that this was necessary for effective cooperation, but its real goal was to protect the highly profitable trade by delaying or preventing the convention's entry into force.[42]

## Consumers

What has been the impact of consumption concerns on cooperation against drugs? The role of drug consumers has generally been smaller than that of consumers we have encountered in previous chapters. Individual drug users—even where drug use is legal or tolerated—have not enjoyed the same social status, organizational capacity, and political influence that facilitated the anti-regulation efforts of antiquities dealers and museums or of arms-importing governments. In the United States, drug users have been represented by proxies, such as reform-minded lawyers and academics.[43] Yet other drug consumers have been directly involved in the political process, aiming to ensure drug availability and ease the costs of international control. In the United State and Europe, pharmaceutical companies in their capacity as consumers have sought to ensure the adequate supply of raw materials for manufacturing; physicians and pharmacists have opposed administrative burdens and restrictions on their professional prerogatives; and the scientific community has sought to minimize regulation's interference with research.[44] Consumption considerations—guaranteeing access to essential medications at a reasonable cost—have also figured prominently in the calculations of countries that lacked both raw materials and manufacturing capacity.[45] Yet ultimately, consumers' role in shaping the drug regime has been limited. Export concerns have fed the primary opposition to drug control, fueling an international political conflict.

## The International Political Conflict

The greatest political challenges to international drug control have been the large variation in government preferences and the absence of shared interest in cooperation. The large preference variation has repeatedly precipitated political battles along the theoretically expected fault line. Governments concerned about the negative externalities of drug abuse, led by the United States, have sought to strictly regulate the drug trade and to suppress the illicit trade; they have met with vigorous opposition from governments seeking to dilute trade restrictions and to minimize the economic, social, and political costs of international control. The United States, as a primary bearer of the trade's externalities, has had powerful incentives to establish control at the source; yet drug-exporting countries have been reluctant to shoulder the burden of curbing these externalities by curtailing a lucrative trade. This section briefly demonstrates how the political conflict has unfolded in several episodes of drug negotiations.

The fundamental disagreement over the responsibility for tackling the drug problem has been evident from the outset. The 1909 Shanghai Opium Commission issued nine nonbinding resolutions that reflected a compromise between the United States and China, on the one hand, and, on the other hand, the colonial powers engaged in the drug trade, especially Britain.[46] Much skepticism greeted the American invitation to a follow-up conference in The Hague to give legally binding effect to the Shanghai resolutions.

Portugal accepted the American invitation while indicating its intention of protecting the opium trade of Macao and considering only conference decisions adopted unanimously and applicable to all countries, including those not attending the conference. France raised various objections to the tentative program. Britain and Germany sought to delay the convening of the Hague Opium Conference, while two other exporting countries—Switzerland and Turkey—declined to attend altogether.

The International Opium Convention adopted by the Hague conference in January 1912 marked progress for the anti-opium movement. Most notably, the convention required the parties to prevent the export of raw and prepared opium to countries that prohibited the drug's import. Yet the convention had to bridge the preference gap between governments protecting commercial interests and governments seeking to eliminate drug addiction and abuse. The convention's provisions therefore afforded the parties considerable discretion in interpretation and implementation; some obligations were qualified with expressions such as "the contracting Powers shall use their best endeavors"; and there was no delegation of monitoring authority to an international organ. Britain and Persia pushed for weakening the convention on behalf of producing countries, while Germany, guarding the leading market position of its drug manufacturers, managed to reduce the obligations on manufactured drugs to vague promises. Furthermore, as noted earlier, Germany insisted on universal adherence to the convention to prevent it from going into effect, or at least to ensure that Germany would not sacrifice its industry for the benefit of nonadhering countries. The universality requirement was indeed included in the convention to allow its unanimous adoption. Unsurprisingly, this requirement became a major obstacle. The United States failed to overcome other governments' reluctance to cooperate and was unable to secure universal ratification. On the eve of World War I, 18 countries, including Germany, had not announced their intention to ratify; two opium-producing countries—Turkey and Serbia—had refused to even sign the convention.[47]

The international political conflict between regulation proponents and opponents persisted in the interwar period, as manifested by the negotiations of the 1925 International Opium Convention, which institutionalized an international mechanism of control: a system of import certificates and export authorizations to eliminate drug diversion to illicit channels, and a Permanent Central Opium Board to oversee the international drug trade through government-provided statistics of drug production, manufacture, import, export, and consumption.[48] Manufacturing countries, however, managed to limit the Board's powers, and producing countries rejected the cardinal point in the American program: limiting the production and export of raw materials only for medical and scientific needs. Persia maintained that such a limitation would be extremely difficult economically; Turkey similarly suggested the need for financial aid to substitute other crops for the opium poppy; and Yugoslavia argued that further restrictions on production would bring serious economic disorders. Colonial powers repudiated another important American demand: the suppression of opium smoking as a means of shrinking the market for raw opium and curbing production. Disappointed, the United States shocked the participants by withdrawing from the negotiations in Geneva and declining to sign the convention.[49]

This outcome vividly captures the theoretically expected preference variation. In the absence of a significant commercial interest in the drug trade and facing a growing drug-abuse problem, the United States had little to lose and much to gain from stringent international control. Other countries, however, favored weak regulation, as strict drug control threatened them with loss of revenue and domestic instability. The American disappointment with the 1925 convention reflected a failure to grasp the depth and causes of this preference gap. The United States underestimated the economic and political sacrifice that drug-exporting countries were asked to make and did not consider financial gain a legitimate reason for being exempted from drug regulation.[50] As I detail later, subsequent years would see a similar unqualified American commitment to international drug control and insensitivity to the anti-regulation incentives of foreign governments—except now, the United States would be better positioned to impose its regulatory vision on those defying international control.

The international political conflicts over drug control after World War II resembled the controversies that had hindered the earlier efforts to introduce regulation. The idea of consolidating the prewar drug treaties and rationalizing the control system emerged in the late 1940s, but disagreements among governments delayed the process. Only in 1961 did an international conference meet for the purpose of establishing a single convention to control narcotic drugs.[51] The variation in government preferences manifested at this conference was consistent with the theoretical framework (see Figure 2.1). Victim countries such as Sweden and Brazil—which were suffering the negative externalities of drugs and lacked an economic interest in the trade—advocated a pro-regulation approach. These countries saw stringent international control as necessary for curbing drug abuse within their boundaries. Bystander countries—those with neither a significant drug problem nor an economic interest in the drug trade—took an intermediate position. Members of this group—primarily from Africa, Central America, and sub-Andean South America—generally remained passive and favored compromise to ensure wide acceptance of the resulting agreement.

As expected theoretically, regulation met with resistance from perpetrators: the producing countries. Led by India, Turkey, Pakistan, and Burma, the anti-regulation group also included the coca-producing Andean countries of South America, the opium- and cannabis-producing countries of

South and Southeast Asia, and the cannabis-producing countries in the Horn of Africa. These countries had been the longstanding targets of the regulatory efforts and, from their point of view, had been paying a heavy price in terms of economic and social dislocation to the benefit of foreign countries. They therefore sought to dilute obligations and loosen controls by inserting exceptions and loopholes or by threatening to enter reservations or decline ratification. Presaging the arguments made by small-arms exporting countries years later,[52] producing countries advocated control at the *national* level that would suit local conditions. In their effort to weaken international control, they found allies in the Soviet Union and its satellites. Lacking a direct stake in the trade, the Soviet-bloc countries nevertheless opposed the sovereignty costs of international drug control and the outside interference in a matter that they saw as purely domestic.

Lastly, manufacturing countries—including the United States, Britain, Switzerland, the Netherlands, West Germany, and Japan—were caught in a web of cross-pressures. Suffering drug-abuse problems of varying degree, these countries sought tight control over the production of organic raw materials and suppression of the illicit trade. At the same time, they were protective of pharmaceutical interests and opposed heavy restrictions on medical research and on the fabrication and distribution of manufactured drugs. Their goal was to retain maximum commercial freedom and shift the regulatory burden to countries producing the raw materials, while avoiding an overly stringent agreement that producing countries would not join.[53]

The outcome agreement—the Single Convention on Narcotic Drugs, 1961—reflected a compromise among the conflicting preferences that was tilted in favor of manufacturing interests. Producing countries defeated provisions that would have required them to nearly eliminate the production of raw materials; yet the controls on raw material production and movement continued to be stricter than those on manufactured drugs. The pro-regulation camp achieved a relatively stringent document that retained the primary pillars of the previous treaties and somewhat strengthened the international control apparatus. The Single Convention required the parties to submit estimates of drug needs and statistical returns of drugs produced, manufactured, imported, exported, kept in stocks, and consumed. Merging two preexisting international-control organs,[54] a new International Narcotics Control Board was empowered to use that data for overseeing the legal drug trade, with the goal of limiting drug distribution and use only to medical and scientific purposes. The Single Convention also maintained the system of import/export authorizations and import certificates intended to prevent drug diversion to the illicit market; it instructed governments to require that drug manufacture, trade, and distribution be performed under license; it obligated government authorities, manufacturers, traders, hospitals, and scientists to keep drug records; and it mandated the criminalization of several drug-related activities.[55]

## Psychotropics

While narcotic drugs had been the longstanding focus of the international drug regime, a new threat became a matter of public concern after World War II: psychotropics—synthetic drugs made from nonorganic raw materials, such as amphetamines, barbiturates, and tranquilizers. Pharmaceutical companies and their government backers initially opposed any international control of these substances that would reduce their profitability. Yet as the negative effects of psychotropics abuse became apparent, and as national controls proved insufficient, manufacturing countries began to face domestic and international pressures for setting international restrictions. In the late 1960s, pharmaceutical companies recognized the inevitability of a treaty; furthermore, they realized that standardizing the regulatory terrain through a weak agreement might actually work to their advantage. Together with their government allies, pharmaceutical industry representatives sought to establish a least-restrictive environment for psychotropics, arguing that stringent regulation would limit access and deny the therapeutic benefit of the drugs to those in need.[56]

The international political conflict that unfolded at the 1971 treaty negotiations in Vienna conformed to the expected pattern of preference variation, reflecting the interplay of concerns about drugs' negative externalities and commercial interests. A pro-regulation coalition sought to incorporate stringent controls in the new treaty, equivalent to those on narcotics. This coalition included, as before, countries that were suffering severe drug abuse, especially in Scandinavia. They were joined by the Soviet-bloc countries that, while guarding against interference in their internal affairs, saw an opportunity to score political points against the West. Producing countries—especially Turkey and India—were also members of the pro-regulation camp, reversing their position on narcotic drugs. To avenge the burdensome controls imposed on them in the 1961 Single Convention, producing countries sought to subject manufacturing countries to similar regulation.

Protecting pharmaceutical interests, manufacturing countries now advocated weak control and loopholes—the same position espoused by producing countries and opposed by manufacturing countries in the 1961 negotiations. Ironically, manufacturing countries offered arguments similar to those they had rejected when made by producing countries concerning narcotics: tight international control would bring economic hardship and undermine sovereign prerogatives. Among manufacturing countries, the United States expressed a relatively moderate position: its drug abuse problem somewhat counteracted the anti-regulation influence of pharmaceutical companies, scientists, and physicians. Other manufacturing countries, including Switzerland, West Germany, Denmark, the Netherlands, Belgium, and Austria, were more forceful in their resistance to regulation and did their utmost to avoid stringent controls.

The outcome agreement—the Convention on Psychotropic Substances, 1971—reflected the power and dominance of manufacturing countries, subjecting them to relatively limited regulation replete with loopholes and safeguards. By exercising political pressure and threatening nonagreement, manufacturing countries narrowed the reporting requirements and import/export controls for some categories of drugs, inserted provisions that would make it difficult to add new substances over time to the original list of regulated drugs, and, most importantly, limited the convention's application to a small number of compounds by omitting derivatives—the majority of the substances manufactured by pharmaceutical companies. The pro-regulation camp, anxious to secure the acquiescence of pharmaceutical companies and reach an agreement, accepted an outcome that fell far short of the standard set by the Single Convention. Nevertheless, a principle of international control over psychotropics had been established. In the following years, pro-regulation governments, together with the UN secretariat and drug organs, would fill some of the Psychotropics Convention's gaps.[57] It would take more than two decades for Belgium, Switzerland, the Netherlands, and Austria to ratify the convention.

## The International Political Conflict Mitigated

In the last quarter of the 20th century the international political conflict somewhat abated and drug control came to enjoy a larger consensus. The early years of the drug regime had seen a sharp distinction between an anti-regulation camp of drug-producing and drug-manufacturing countries and a pro-regulation camp of countries suffering rampant drug abuse. This distinction was now eroding. As producing countries acknowledged that their own societies were threatened by drug abuse and drug-related crime and violence, they tempered their aversion to regulation. At the same time, the explosion of demand for drugs made Western countries recognize, to some extent, that control at the source is not a cure-all and that they must curb illicit demand. These changes partially mitigated the large preference variation that had plagued international drug control, allowing for relatively rapid completion of the international regulatory framework and the tackling of a new challenge: the emergence of an enormous illegal black market dominated by organized criminal groups. The 1988 Convention against Illicit Traffic in Narcotic Drugs and Psychotropic Substances—an agreement focused on criminal measures and cooperation in law-enforcement efforts—was negotiated in a more favorable international climate than earlier treaties and entered into force in less than two years. A further boost to antidrug efforts came in 1998 with the unanimous adoption by the UN General Assembly of a Political Declaration denouncing drugs as a threat to the health and wellbeing of all mankind. This declaration was linked to several other documents, including a Declaration on the Guiding Principles of Drug Demand Reduction.

But rhetorical changes and growing consensus notwithstanding, the drug regime maintained its longstanding focus on curbing excess supply, and producing countries still bore most of the burden. The blame game that had characterized the regime from its inception persisted: governments kept seeking to shift the responsibility for the drug problem elsewhere.[58] The international political conflict at the heart of the regime was alleviated, but not resolved. Coercion thus remained as necessary for establishing cooperation as it had been since the outset of the international efforts.

## Drug Cooperation and the Role of Coercion

The theoretical framework has suggested that the distribution of power plays a crucial role in shaping cooperation against illicit trade: powerful governments may coerce weaker governments into cooperating, contrary to the latter's preference. The history of international drug control provides ample evidence in support of this proposition. In the early years of the drug regime, the United States had not yet amassed the requisite power to overcome resistance to international regulation. The rise of American power and influence, especially after World War II, allowed the United States to promote its vision of drug control through coercive means.

Yet even before reaching superpower status, the United States exploited its limited international influence to bring pressure to bear on drug-exporting countries. Pressure was necessary, for example, to convene the opium conference in The Hague in 1911, after the American invitation initially met with general nonenthusiasm. To induce participation, the State Department sent repeated notes to the reluctant powers and pressed the British, German, and Dutch ambassadors to the United States to appeal to their governments. The victory in World War I gave the United States temporary leverage and allowed the imposition of drug control on noncooperative countries—first and foremost Germany—that had refused to ratify and implement the 1912 International Opium Convention. Following its military defeat, participation in the drug regime was forced upon Germany in the Treaty of Versailles. Article 295 of the treaty required the parties to bring the 1912 Opium Convention into force and enact the necessary legislation; ratification of the peace treaty was deemed equivalent to ratification of the Opium Convention. Peace treaties with other defeated powers included a similar article—a clear manifestation of coerced cooperation.[59]

The mixed record of the interwar years demonstrates the challenge of establishing cooperation in the absence of significant coercive power. Unable to impose its preference for stringent control and dictate the outcome of negotiations, the United States ultimately refused to join agreements that it deemed too weak: the 1925 International Opium Convention and the 1936 Convention for the Suppression of the Illicit Traffic in Dangerous Drugs.[60] Willingness to compromise allowed the United States to achieve greater success with the 1931 Narcotics Limitation Convention.[61] Adopting a pragmatic approach aimed at a practical treaty that would gain wide adherence, the American delegation fashioned an agreement that established restrictions on the manufacture of narcotic drugs.[62]

Yet the United States did apply what limited means of pressure it had during the interwar period. As a key manufacturing and consuming country, the United States could threaten to prohibit legitimate drug imports from countries involved in illicit trade. Turkey faced such an American threat in 1931 because of overproduction and illicit trafficking in manufactured drugs. The United States also warned Turkey that shipments from countries not party to the 1912 Opium Convention would be searched for illicit drugs. The prospect of Turkish goods delayed in American ports brought Ankara to ratify the 1912 and 1925 conventions and close several illicit factories. The United States also channeled its pressure through the League of Nations' Opium Advisory Committee (OAC). At American behest, the OAC created a Subcommittee on Illicit Traffic that monitored drug-smuggling trends. During the 1930s, the United States could thus pressure noncooperative countries by documenting and threatening to reveal violations. The United States also used OAC sessions to publicly criticize and embarrass countries that did not comply with their obligations, at times successfully motivating them to take action.[63]

The persistent U.S. pressure throughout this period bore fruit, winning adherence to American ideas of drug control and bringing governments to adopt measures they would not have otherwise. After three decades of drug-control efforts, one key goal was achieved: setting a boundary between the legal and the illicit trade and regulating the former. Yet by the end of the 1930s, the system was unraveling. Perversely, international controls exacerbated illegal manufacturing, excess production, and illicit international trafficking; colonial drug interests continued to hamper the regulatory progress; and the League's international control organs—the Permanent Central Opium Board and the Drug Supervisory Body—proved weak, unable to overcome growing resistance. The primary weapon they wielded was the publication of violations—a tool with little impact on defiant countries such as Japan (a major trafficker of manufactured drugs) and Persia.[64] For the United States, the lesson of that period was that drug cooperation necessitated coercion. This lesson guided the American efforts in following years, when the

United States finally held the power and influence necessary for tightening international drug control.

## U.S. Coercion in the Post-World War II Era

Even before the end of World War II, in late 1943, the United States exploited the realigned distribution of power, successfully pressuring two colonial powers—Britain and the Netherlands—to suppress opium smoking and government opium-monopolies. In the immediate postwar years, the provision of reconstruction aid gave the United States further leverage over the traditional opium powers and dampened their opposition to the U.S. supply-control approach; American-style drug control was also imposed on occupied Japan, curbing its narcotics trade. In 1944 the United States launched a short-lived carrot-and-stick strategy that combined economic and political pressure with inducements for compliance. Countries that failed to join the existing drug treaties and avoid excess production risked retaliatory legislation, including careful inspection of goods imported from these countries. The United States also threatened to rely only on compliant countries to fill its raw-material needs. The ultimate threat was to step up the development of synthetic narcotics, thereby eliminating the need for legal opium production. To cooperative countries, the United States offered financial aid and crop substitution assistance.[65]

Further coercive efforts in the latter 1940s encountered practical and political difficulties. Pressure was of little help against Burma, which lacked control over opium-growing areas, or against the corrupt Thai government. The exercise of coercion against Iran had to be restrained for fear of destabilizing the government and bringing leftists to power. The United States therefore decided to exploit its predominance within the United Nations and channel its efforts through the new organization and its primary policymaking body on drugs: the Commission on Narcotic Drugs (CND). From the early postwar period through the mid-1960s, the United States dominated the CND and its formulation of control policies. By linking drug control to economic and political support, the United States gained the acquiescence of CND members and brought them to accept stringent regulation. Developing countries, especially those of Latin America, faced pressure tactics aimed at aligning their votes on drug resolutions with the United States and compelling them to implement strict control policies; threats to withdraw aid were a favorite weapon. [66]

Few nations were willing to stand up to American pressure and allow drugs to damage their relations with the United States. In 1954 and 1955, the U.S.-dominated CND adopted the American prohibitionist approach to cannabis and denounced coca leaf chewing as a harmful drug addiction, although in many countries cannabis use or coca chewing were deeply rooted cultural practices. Perhaps the most significant imprint of the overwhelming U.S. influence was the 1961 Single Convention—an agreement that consolidated and fortified the drug regime based on the strict regulatory approach advocated by the United States. The key provision of this convention—Article 4(c)—enshrined the basic American principle: drugs may be legitimately used only for medical and scientific purposes. In 1972 the convention was further strengthened upon American initiative with the adoption of an amending protocol.[67]

The American vision of drug control still permeates and guides the UN drug control system. Writing in 2009 and reflecting on a century of international drug control, the executive director of the UN Office on Drugs and Crime maintained that "illicit *drugs continue to pose a health danger* to humanity" and rejected economic, health, and security arguments for relaxing controls on drugs.[68] The UN's espousal of strict control has a threefold effect. First, the UN drug apparatus directly fosters drug control by monitoring control practices worldwide. The International Narcotics Control Board evaluates governments' compliance with the drug-control treaties and can call international attention to violations.[69] Second, by designating drugs as a threat to humanity and requiring their stringent regulation, the UN endows antidrug norms with legitimacy and moral force, delegitimizing actors who deviate from these norms. A view that carries a UN imprimatur seemingly enjoys a global consensus and is more difficult to challenge. Third, multilateral antidrug norms established under the auspices of the UN and enshrined in its conventions have, at least in part, legitimized the American unilateral efforts *outside* the organization since the 1980s. While not formally authorized by the UN, the U.S. coercive campaign has drawn some justification from its goal: enforcing a UN-backed regulatory framework. Consistent with its approach since 1909, the United States' unilateral endeavors have been supply-driven, identifying drug-producing and drug-transit countries as the root of the problem and aiming for control at the source.[70]

A precursor of the turn to unilateralism came in the late 1960s. Soon after entering office in 1969, the Nixon administration decided to launch an international offensive against foreign sources of heroin and marijuana and designated Mexico as a primary target. This was not the first time that Mexico's drug policy had come under American pressure. Disapproving of Mexico's approach to treating drug addiction in the late 1930s, the United States helped oust the head of Mexico's Federal Narcotics Service, and in 1940 embargoed the export of medicinal drugs to Mexico. Some 30 years later, American pressure on Mexico took the shape of Operation Intercept: a 20-day effort, beginning September 21, 1969, of heightened inspections along the U.S.-Mexico border, coupled with enhanced air and sea surveillance. While the stated goal of the operation was to seize drugs at the border, its real purpose was to compel the Mexican government to tackle drug cultivation and trafficking. The intensive inspections indeed created massive border delays that disrupted legitimate trade and tourism and wreaked economic havoc on Mexico's border communities. The result was Mexican anger, frustration, and protest, and ultimately—willingness to cooperate. Operation Intercept forced the Mexican government to confront the drug problem and accelerated the previously lagging Mexican campaign against narcotics. With American assistance, Mexico implemented a supply-side program focused on the eradication of opium poppies and marijuana and escalated its efforts with the 1975 launch of Operation Condor—an antidrug offensive involving extensive use of herbicides and massive military participation.[71]

Dissatisfaction with the modest progress achieved through the multilateral framework and alarm over a rise in consumption, crime, and drug-related deaths prompted the United States to launch an aggressive unilateral campaign against drugs worldwide in the mid-1980s. This campaign responded not only to a truly escalating problem, but also to a public *perception* of a catastrophic drug crisis.[72] Beyond the intensifying rhetoric—identifying drug trafficking as an evil and a grave threat to American and regional security[73]—the U.S. campaign combined military and economic duress in pursuit of control at the source. The most prominent instance of military coercion was the American invasion of Panama and overthrow of accused drug trafficker Manuel Noriega in 1989. In the late 1980s and early 1990s, Peru, Colombia, and Bolivia consented to the involvement of U.S. military forces in counternarcotics operations on their soil—for fear of losing American economic aid.[74]

The intensification of U.S. pressure also involved the systemization and formalization of economic coercion with the 1986 introduction of the drug certification process. This process, as reformed in 2002, requires the president to submit an annual report identifying the major illicit drug-producing countries and drug-transit countries. The report also designates any of the named countries that, over the previous 12 months, have failed to demonstrably make substantial efforts to comply with international counternarcotics agreements and to take other antidrug measures specified in U.S. law. Designated countries are penalized by suspension of American assistance, unless the president determines that provision of assistance to a designated country is vital to the U.S. national interest or that the country has made substantial efforts to adhere to its obligations subsequent to the designation.[75] The September 2009 presidential report identified 20 major drug-producing or drug-transit countries; three of those—Bolivia, Burma, and Venezuela—were designated as having failed to fulfill their antidrug obligations. The president issued a national-interest waiver to Bolivia and Venezuela to allow support for development and democracy-building programs.

The drug certification process has a dual punitive impact. Not only do noncooperative countries bear the adverse economic, political, and social consequences of U.S. aid suspension, but they also suffer a blow to their international reputation following their branding by the United States as complicit in drug trafficking. This negative reputational effect was amplified after the terror attacks of September 11, 2001. With the rhetorical conflation of antidrug efforts and counterterrorism, a country that fails to meet antidrug standards is also potentially labeled a friend of terrorists.[76]

But has the certification process enhanced drug cooperation? In specific cases, the pressure generated by the process indeed brought foreign governments to engage in antidrug efforts.[77] Yet overall, there is no clear, systematic evidence to suggest that the process has achieved its goal.[78] Critics have also charged that the certification process is unfair, as it punishes supplying countries while neglecting demand, and often overlooks the poor record of U.S. allies. Furthermore, the process may be counterproductive, as loss of American aid exacerbates the difficulties of enforcing drug control and increases the economic importance of the drug trade.[79] Despite the criticism, the U.S. government remains convinced of the effectiveness and necessity of coercion, given the source of noncompliance with drug obligations. Failure to comply may indeed stem from lack of capacity or low technical expertise, but often it is willful and deliberate. In exporting countries the authorities "were content to ignore local drug production . . . not enforcing local laws [and] international agreements." Only American coercion, the U.S. government believes, can make noncooperation costly and painful enough to overcome countervailing influences and bring governments to comply; hence "the critical importance of the certification process in winning cooperation."[80] As we have seen in Chapter 5, a similar logic inspired the sanctioning mechanism for human trafficking. Drug coercion, however, has served an additional goal: satisfying public demand for vigorous action against drugs.[81]

## Exogenous Influences

The elements highlighted by the theoretical framework—negative externalities, commercial interests, and coercion—go a long way toward explaining drug cooperation. Yet as the theoretical framework has indicated, these are not exhaustive and may be complemented by influences outside the purview of the theory. Some such exogenous influences have been noted in previous chapters. Hostility toward UNESCO, for example, dampened the U.S. Senate's enthusiasm for UNESCO-led cooperation against the looting of antiquities. Yet the history of international drug control is particularly replete with exogenous influences that sometimes strengthened the regulatory efforts, but more often weakened them.

In the interwar period, international drug control was under the League of Nations' mandate; the United States' leadership of antidrug endeavors was hindered by its nonmembership in and ambivalence toward this organization.[82] By contrast, arms-control negotiations during the same period reinforced the efforts for drug control: many believed that these are similar issues requiring similar solutions and hoped that successful drug regulation would provide a model for tackling the arms-control conundrum.[83] Since the early days of the Cold War, the United States' exercise of pressure to promote drug control was in constant tension with broader foreign policy goals: maintaining good relations with foreign countries, supporting friendly governments, and preventing the rise to power of leftists. Facing this tension, the United States often gave precedence to nondrug concerns over the promotion of drug control, restraining its criticism and coercion of governments that did not toe the American line on drugs.[84] U.S. policy toward Afghanistan, for example, has consistently manifested the subordination of drug control to more pressing political concerns. To prevent an Afghan move toward Soviet influence, the United States backed Afghanistan's request to become a legitimate opium producer in the 1950s; years later the United States would also tolerate the opium ties of the anti-Soviet Mujahedin and of warlords allied in anti-Taliban efforts.[85] In the Western hemisphere, security interests often led the United States to overlook the drug links of its allies, such as the Nicaraguan Contras. Another stark example is the aforementioned application of the national-interest waiver to avoid sanctions against friendly countries that have failed to meet their antidrug obligations.[86]

This prevalence of exogenous considerations serves as a reminder that cooperation against illicit trade is situated within a broader political and economic context. The analyst must be sensitive to this wider context as an added layer that supplements and refines the theory-based understanding of cooperation.[87]

## Cooperation against Illegal Drugs: Conclusions

The efforts against the illicit drug trade are overall consistent with this book's theoretical framework. The main goal of these efforts has been to lower the negative externalities of drug abuse. In particular, they have sought to establish control at the source and shift the burden of curbing drugs' externalities from consuming countries to exporting countries. The burden-shifting goal of the drug regime has given rise to the theoretically expected conflict of government preferences. Whereas the primary bearer of the externalities—the United States—has favored stringent control, drug-exporting countries have resisted regulatory constraints that harm their commercial interests, threatening the livelihood of peasants or the profits of pharmaceutical companies. Like arms-exporting countries and antiquities-importing countries, drug-exporting countries have been reluctant to bear the costs of control to the benefit of other countries, and it is this reluctance that has been the most significant and persistent challenge to drug cooperation. Indeed, the efforts on behalf of drug control have also been hindered by official corruption, criminal influence, and the capacity constraints of governments; but the foremost obstacle has been the one that this book highlights: lack of political motivation and insufficient shared interest in cooperation. From Germany in 1912 to Burma a century later, governments have weighed the costs and benefits of drug cooperation and concluded that it would make them and their constituencies worse off. For these governments, commercial interests and concerns for political survival trumped the negative effects of the drug trade abroad.

Consistent with the theoretical framework, the outcome of the international political conflict reflects the distribution of power. The limited international influence of the United States during the drug regime's formative period resulted in a modest regulatory framework that fell short of the American ambition. Following World War II, the United States was better equipped to overcome the conflict of government preferences and establish cooperation. U.S. power and leadership thus produced a robust international regulatory framework. The contemporary drug regime is based on three legally binding conventions that establish relatively precise and comprehensive regulatory standards. These conventions enjoy nearly universal membership, including all major drug-exporting countries. Most importantly, international drug control is accompanied by strong pressures for compliance: the limited powers of the UN drug organs are complemented by unilateral U.S. enforcement. Overall, the U.S.-led international drug control is significantly more robust than the international regulation of small arms and antiquities, spearheaded by developing countries. Both the Program of Action on Small Arms and the 1970 UNESCO Convention lack monitoring and enforcement mechanisms—a critical omission given the persistence and strength of incentives for noncompliance.

The theoretical framework has identified two mechanisms for resolving the political conflict over illicit trade: change in government preferences, and coercion. Some governments have indeed moderated their anti-regulation preference over time. The transformation of Britain's position in the formative period of the drug regime is a prime example; so is producing countries' declining resistance to control in the last quarter of the 20th century. Yet the establishment of drug cooperation has more often involved the use of coercive means. These allowed the United States to impose its preference for strong regulation on governments with markedly different preferences. The exercise of U.S. coercion has, in fact, been two-pronged. Given the lucrative nature of the drug trade, governments have powerful incentives to oppose the establishment of stringent regulation; they are also motivated not to comply with regulation they have committed to. Through economic and political pressure, the United States has sought both to forge robust regulatory agreements and to enhance compliance with them. The goals of the drug control system, the control apparatus, the range of drugs under control, the regulatory means, and the general international policy—all of these bear the clear mark of American influence.[88]

The theoretical framework has highlighted the central role of legal, legitimate actors in the efforts against illicit trade, and this emphasis dovetails with the case of drugs. International drug control originally focused on the regulation of legitimate drug activities, and the drug regime as it exists today is the product of decades of influence by legitimate societal actors. Moral entrepreneurs—social-reform advocates, religious groups, and antinarcotics associations—served as catalysts for drug cooperation. They put drugs on the national agenda in the United States, fueled interest in the subject, and pushed the U.S. government to tackle the drug menace in China and in the United States. Yet while the moral entrepreneurs played an indispensable role early on, their influence waned by the 1930s.[89] By contrast, the general public has exerted a pivotal influence throughout the life of the drug regime: public concern has motivated the U.S. government to tackle drug abuse by deflecting the blame overseas and pursuing control at the source. The livelihood of peasants has been another persistent concern, which led producing countries to resist international control. Yet the societal actor most heavily and directly involved in shaping drug cooperation has been the pharmaceutical industry. A major goal of the drug regime is to control the legal trade and induce more responsible conduct on the part of pharmaceutical companies, which were therefore key targets and stakeholders from the outset. Like arms exporters and antiquities dealers and museums, pharmaceutical companies have viewed the regulatory efforts unfavorably and sought a least-regulated trade. To realize this goal, they have lobbied governments and participated in domestic political processes and international negotiations.

As noted earlier, policymakers in the interwar period believed that arms cooperation is fundamentally similar to drug cooperation. The foregoing analysis has substantiated this similarity. Both small-arms cooperation and drug cooperation have been beset by political conflicts between governments concerned about the externalities of trade and governments protecting commercial interests. At the center of these conflicts has been a disagreement over a basic question: who should shoulder the responsibility for and costs of curbing illicit trade and its negative effects? The same dilemma has plagued the international efforts against money laundering.

## Money Laundering

The international campaign against money laundering (AML) was launched in 1989 with the establishment of the Financial Action Task Force (FATF) and the publication the following year of the Forty Recommendations: the international standards for combating money laundering. This campaign grew from the efforts to control drugs. The difficulties of and disillusionment with drug control led to the pursuit of a different means of attacking crime: curbing its financial profitability.[90] AML efforts soon took on a life of their own: the goals have expanded, as have the institutional infrastructure, geographic coverage, and the variety of actors they regulate. Yet at their heart remains the fundamental problem that hinders cooperation against illicit trade: certain governments find cooperation inimical to their interests; they have no motivation to join a cooperative endeavor that requires much cost and offers little gain. The efforts against money laundering have thus involved pressure and coercion to induce governments to cooperate.

### The Motivation for Cooperation: Negative Externalities

Money laundering is the conversion of criminal profits into assets that cannot be traced back to their illegal source. This conversion process is conventionally divided into three phases: (1) *Placement*—the proceeds from illegal activity are moved to a place or into a form that is less suspicious to law-enforcement authorities and more convenient to the criminal; typically, the proceeds are deposited in a bank account; (2) *Layering*—the proceeds are separated from their illegal origin through multiple complex financial transactions, such as wire transfers or buying and selling of investment instruments; and (3) *Integration*—the illegal proceeds reenter the legitimate economy through normal financial or commercial operations, such as real estate investments, business ventures, and the purchase of luxury assets.[91]

What negative externalities are associated with money laundering? First and foremost, money laundering encourages and facilitates crime. The ability to launder funds and protect them from possible confiscation makes crime more profitable and provides further incentive for criminal activity; the laundering of criminal proceeds also makes it harder for law-enforcement agencies to detect and suppress crime. AML efforts are aimed at creating a less hospitable environment for criminal organizations and making criminal activities more difficult, more costly, and less profitable. In short, the principal goal of these efforts is to control and reduce crime. At its inception, the AML regime targeted drug trafficking; since then, it has expanded to address other forms of serious organized crime and various offenses that can generate demand for money laundering, such as bribery, extortion, and embezzlement.[92]

Following the terrorist attacks of September 11, 2001, the AML regime became an important pillar of the efforts to combat the financing of terrorism. Indeed, there are certain differences between money laundering by criminals and the financing of terrorism. Terrorists, for example, are not primarily motivated by financial gain. Furthermore, funding for terrorism may come from both legitimate and illegal sources. Yet terrorists, like criminals, seek to obscure the link between the source of funds and their ultimate purpose. Terrorist-financing techniques are essentially the same as those used for laundering criminal proceeds. Given this similarity, the AML regime was expanded for the purpose of blocking and seizing funds intended to finance terrorism.[93] The term AML in the following text also applies, with the necessary changes, to CFT: combating the financing of terrorism.

The negative externalities of illicit trade diverge significantly across countries, and this variation is clearly apparent in the case of money laundering and terrorist financing: countries vary tremendously in the magnitude of the crime and terrorism threats they face. As Chapter 3 has documented, certain countries and regions suffer high homicide rates, whereas in others homicide rates are relatively low. Rates of illegal drug use also exhibit cross-national variation;[94] so does terrorism. While considered a global problem, terrorist attacks have been heavily concentrated in a handful of countries.[95]

This book has highlighted secondary externalities—the trade's negative effects abroad—as an influence on international cooperation. As we have seen, secondary externalities have led the United States to combat the plunder of antiquities and to launch a worldwide campaign against human trafficking. In the case of money laundering—as well as that of counterfeits—the impact of secondary externalities is less pronounced. It was *primary* externalities that motivated the American leadership of international efforts against money laundering and counterfeits. The United States was deeply concerned about these phenomena because of their negative effects on itself, rather than their effects abroad.

## Market Actors

The international regulatory efforts against illicit trade are often aimed at constraining and setting rules for *legitimate* market actors, so as to lower the negative externalities associated with their business. This is indeed the premise of AML efforts. The AML regime seeks to shape the conduct of market actors who provide the service of money laundering or are otherwise involved in the process. Responsible behavior on the part of these actors would make it more difficult and more costly to launder money, thereby making crime less profitable. Governments and criminal justice systems still play an important role in the efforts against money laundering; yet from the outset it was clear that exclusive reliance on criminal law and government action would be insufficient. The suppression of money laundering requires a broader range of measures to be implemented by a variety of market actors, banks first and foremost. Banks are the financial institutions most vulnerable to being used for money laundering, as they play a central role in all stages of the process: from the entry of the funds into the financial system, to the concealment of the funds' illicit source through complex financial transactions, to the integration of the funds into the legitimate economy.[96] Banks have therefore been at the heart of AML efforts: they have been required to implement measures to disrupt the laundering process.

Launderers have adapted by increasingly diverting their activities to nonbank financial institutions that are less regulated and supervised than banks. These include, among others, bureaux de change, securities brokers, and insurance companies. Bureaux de change are useful for cash placement, whereas the securities and insurance sectors allow the layering and integration of criminal proceeds. Yet the risk of abuse for the purpose of money laundering is not limited to financial institutions: various nonfinancial businesses have also become vehicles for money laundering. Illicit funds can be commingled with those generated by retail stores and restaurants; casinos can launder money by representing criminal proceeds as legitimate winnings; art dealers, auction houses, and sellers of luxury goods and precious metals are also possible channels for laundering money. Another concern is professionals—such as lawyers and accountants—who often assist in providing a legitimate cover for criminal profits. For example, they can create complex legal arrangements to confuse the link between the crime and its proceeds, buy and sell property as the final investment at the integration stage, or perform financial transactions.[97]

Given that nonbank financial institutions and nonfinancial businesses and professions play an important role in laundering criminal proceeds, they have assumed growing importance in AML efforts. Yet among all market actors involved in AML initiatives, the largest role is still reserved to banks, and they are the focus of the following analysis.

According to the theoretical framework, exporters typically oppose international regulation that threatens to constrain their business and diminish its profitability. In the case of money laundering—a service—the equivalents of exporters are the service providers: banks that, knowingly or unwittingly, launder criminal proceeds. The expectation of resistance to international regulation certainly applies to banks, as AML measures could prove costly to them. First and most obviously, banks bear operating costs: the direct costs of implementing and complying with AML measures. The Forty Recommendations require banks to undertake customer due-diligence measures, such as identifying and verifying the identity of customers and beneficial owners. The Recommendations also subject banks to recordkeeping rules, such as maintaining for at least five years all necessary records of domestic and international transactions and providing them to the authorities upon request. Banks are also asked to pay special attention to and carefully examine complex, unusually large transactions and transactions with no apparent lawful purpose. They are also obligated to report suspicious transactions to the authorities.[98] Compliance with all these requirements—from verifying customer identity to submitting reports—imposes costs on banks. The estimated cost of compliance with AML measures to U.S. banks in 2003 was $1.5 billion.[99] Beyond direct compliance costs, AML measures entail indirect costs: loss of business due to the rerouting of international financial flows and declining demand for banking services. Some of this loss is the intended consequence and goal of AML efforts: the elimination of "dirty" money from the financial system. Yet in addition to losing business in handling illicit funds, banks might also lose legitimate business. AML measures involve cumbersome administrative requirements that even law-abiding, legitimate customers would rather avoid. Implementation of AML regulation could motivate these customers to redirect their business to less heavily regulated financial centers.[100]

The theoretical framework has suggested that while international regulation tends to adversely affect exporters, it may also offer them some benefits, especially in the form of competitive and reputational effects. Indeed, due diligence, recordkeeping, and reporting requirements, while burdensome, may benefit banks by mitigating the risks that money laundering poses to them. Banks involved in money laundering run several risks. The corrupt employees who launder criminal proceeds may ultimately defraud customers or the institution itself, possibly leading to a bank failure. In extreme cases, banks could become controlled by criminal interests. Yet the most immediate risk that money laundering presents is that of compromising banks' integrity and reputation. Reputation for integrity and public trust are essential for a viable financial institution: the nature of the banking business requires the confidence of depositors, creditors, and the marketplace. Money laundering undermines this essential confidence. By turning criminal proceeds, in particular drug revenue, into legitimate funds, banks lose their image as honest, law-abiding institutions and become implicated in crime. The blow to a bank's reputation is particularly heavy when money-laundering allegations lead to investigations of the bank's management and staff, and possibly to indictments and prosecutions. Tarnished reputation, in turn, makes customers reluctant to entrust the bank with their money. Other financial institutions might also avoid business with the disreputable bank for fear of contaminating their own reputations. AML regulation offers a remedy for these risks. By complying with regulation, banks can insulate themselves from ties to criminal activities, maintain their integrity and reputation, and avoid legal and financial liability.[101] Furthermore, international efforts against money laundering may serve a competitive motivation. Banks constrained by national AML measures see financial flows redirected to loosely regulated foreign banks; international regulation could eliminate the latter's advantage and level the playing field, bringing all banks into compliance with uniform regulatory requirements.

AML regulation thus imposes costs on banks while holding the promise of rewards. In that sense, it is akin to antiquities regulation and its impact on museums. As explained in Chapter 4, the international regulation of antiquities harms museums by limiting their acquisition of new objects. At the same time, regulatory compliance allows museums to maintain their reputations and reduces the risk of scandals and legal battles that might result from acquisition of looted material. Most importantly, ethical standards aimed at preventing archaeological plunder are consistent with museums' public-trust responsibility and their commitment to knowledge and cultural preservation. For these reasons, I have characterized museums as being cross-pressured. Yet while AML regulation may have both salutary and detrimental effects on banks, banks are closer to the anti-regulation pole; they are not as conflicted as museums in their approach to regulation. Unlike museums, which have normative reasons to support regulation, banks' considerations are pragmatic and self-interested. As commercial, profit-driven entities, they are not committed to a set of values that would motivate them to embrace regulation. Moreover, the costs of AML measures to banks are tangible and immediate: loss of business due to the redirection of funds to jurisdictions with loose supervision, and the onus of due diligence, record-keeping, and reporting. By contrast, the benefits of AML regulation in terms of reputation and public trust are more remote and less easily quantifiable than the costs. To the extent that banks are interested in averting the risks associated with money laundering, they can do so through self-regulation, without governmental interference. Banks therefore do not necessarily consider AML regulation to be in their best financial interest. Nevertheless, in some cases banks may support such regulation. Banks subject to national AML laws may wish to impose similar constraints on foreign competitors through international regulation. An embarrassing scandal may also spur banks' interest in action against money laundering. Yet banks' ultimate preference is for minimal regulatory restrictions and requirements. They may be willing to participate in AML efforts, but will remain on guard against an onerous burden.

According to the theoretical framework, the strongest resistance to international regulation should come from governments that do not face the negative externalities of illicit trade, but are protecting the interests of exporters or consumers who might be harmed by regulation. With respect to money laundering, the governments with the strongest incentives to resist international AML efforts are those that are protecting lucrative financial sectors and do not face serious problems of crime or terrorism. For these governments, money-laundering cooperation means significant costs with no gains. Beyond the costs to banks, governments themselves are asked to bear costs. AML cooperation requires government regulators to put in place regulations to prevent money laundering, monitor financial and other institutions to ensure compliance, maintain systems of suspicious-activity reports, and punish individuals and institutions that fail to execute required preventive measures. Government agencies are also responsible for the enforcement pillar of the AML regime: detection and investigation to identify specific instances of money laundering and, in appropriate cases, prosecution and punishment.[102] While the costs of AML measures to governments are difficult to assess with any accuracy,[103] they can clearly amount to a real burden, especially for small, developing countries. By resisting international AML efforts, governments wish to ease the burden on regulatory and law-enforcement agencies; even more importantly, they seek to secure the interests of banks and, by extension, protect the national economic interests. Indeed, "the vigour with which a country tackles the problem of money laundering, may have repercussions for its competitiveness as a financial centre."[104] The loss of banking business that results from stringent AML measures could undermine the sector's contribution as a source of income and employment.

Within this category of governments that are protective of banks' interests, two groups can be distinguished. One includes well-established financial centers, such as Switzerland, Liechtenstein, and Luxembourg. In these countries, private banking and the management of international assets constitute a prosperous financial niche and significantly contribute to the high standard of living. The appeal of these financial centers and their ability to attract business have relied on secrecy and loose supervision. AML measures would have ended precisely these practices, thereby driving funds, including legitimate ones, offshore. Although governments within this group have similar noncooperative incentives, their behavior has varied. Swiss banks already established a self-regulatory code of conduct on due diligence in 1977, in the wake of a banking scandal; they have had a large stake in maintaining the reputation and credibility of the banking system. Switzerland has thus participated in the international AML campaign and in the FATF's work since their beginning in 1989.[105] By contrast, Liechtenstein was designated by the FATF as a noncooperative country.

The most vigorous resistance to money-laundering cooperation, however, came from a second group: governments of resource-poor countries for which bank secrecy and light regulation were an attractive development strategy and a source of international competitiveness. These countries attracted legitimate funds as well as criminal proceeds through easy rules of incorporation, the absence of recording requirements for large cash transactions, and limited capacity for asset seizure or confiscation. Nauru is a prime example of countries in this group. A small island in the Pacific, Nauru established an offshore financial center to replace its traditional and declining source of income: phosphate mining. To enhance its attractiveness and overcome its remote location, the government of Nauru enacted financial-secrecy laws that protect banks and companies registered in Nauru from investigation by foreign law-enforcement agencies. This strategy achieved its goal, prompting approximately 400 banks to establish a presence in Nauru. These banks, however, were shell banks that existed on paper only for the purpose of erasing money's origin and obscuring the paper trail.[106]

A policy of lax regulation and willful ignorance of money laundering does not necessarily constitute a successful development strategy. Such a policy may not yield the anticipated economic benefits; in fact, it could prove harmful, as money laundering erodes financial institutions, undermining the trust of customers and fellow institutions. These effects are particularly damaging to developing economies, where growth depends on sound financial institutions.[107] Nevertheless, certain governments in the developing world have treated bank secrecy and loose supervision as attractive policies. They feared that stringent AML regulation would prevent them from establishing a niche in the global financial markets, and placed far less weight on any benefits that such regulation could yield. Accordingly, they expressed an anti-regulation preference and opposed the requirements and constraints imposed by AML standards. The incentive structure of these governments was similar to that of anti-regulation governments we have encountered in previous chapters. The governments of China and Egypt, among other arms-exporting countries, have been reluctant to curb arms exports for the purpose of reducing gun violence in sub-Saharan Africa. The antiquities-importing countries of Western Europe had little desire to limit the economic and cultural benefits of their art markets and to incur law-enforcement costs, all for the sake of protecting the archaeological heritage of foreign countries. Similarly, governments guarding a lucrative banking sector but not facing significant crime or terrorism had little interest in cooperation. They perceived AML measures as a costly and undesirable burden that was being unnecessarily shifted onto them by foreign governments.

Major financial centers, such as the United States, Britain, and France, were more strongly motivated to cooperate against money laundering. Their governments came under cross-pressures: while safeguarding the interests of the financial sectors, they pursued AML cooperation in order to curb crime and, later on, terrorism. Of the cross-pressured governments, it was the U.S. government that took the lead. Not only was the United States facing an enormous drug and crime problem, but U.S. law enforcement that was investigating criminal finances increasingly found money trails leading to noncooperative foreign countries.[108] Getting these countries to cooperate was imperative. Furthermore, the U.S. government had already established national regulation against money laundering prior to the initiation of international regulation: American banks had come under AML requirements with the passage of the Bank Secrecy Act in 1970. International regulation promised to level the playing field and distribute the burden borne by American banks and regulators among their foreign counterparts as well.[109] For the United States, an international campaign against money laundering served to spread the costs of AML efforts and to make these efforts more effective by enlisting the participation of financial centers worldwide.

## The Establishment of Cooperation

Consistent with the theoretical framework, the problem at the heart of the efforts against money laundering is a large variation in government preferences and in their willingness to cooperate. Certain governments view AML cooperation as beneficial, while for other governments it is a net loss. Even governments favoring cooperation have to tread carefully to avoid an onerous burden on law enforcement and banks. Given these tensions and noncooperative incentives, the campaign against money laundering has relied on international political pressure, primarily from the United States, as the driving force.[110]

An early American attempt to internationalize money-laundering efforts through coercion did not meet much success. The 1988 "Kerry Amendment"[111] required the Treasury to negotiate with foreign governments in order to have foreign banks record large U.S. currency transactions and provide the information to U.S. law enforcement for narcotics investigations. Noncomplying banks were threatened with denial of access to any U.S. dollar clearing or wire-transfer system. Fear of encouraging foreign alternatives to U.S. clearing facilities and concerns about retaliation against American banks, among other reasons, led to the failure of this unilateral initiative; the United States then turned to a multilateral approach. Yet the principle underlying the Kerry Amendment—coerced cooperation—has persisted and guided the following, more successful efforts against money laundering.

The first multilateral measure initiated by the United States was the criminalization of money laundering in the 1988 UN Convention against Illicit Traffic in Narcotic Drugs and Psychotropic Substances. Another U.S.-led effort was a statement of principles on the Prevention of Criminal Use of the Banking System for the Purpose of Money-Laundering, issued in December 1988 by the Basel Committee on Banking Regulations and Supervisory Practices.[112] Yet the most significant step was the establishment of the Financial Action Task Force at the G-7 summit of 1989. The FATF is the primary source of multilateral pressure to secure action against money laundering. An independent intergovernmental body, FATF membership more than doubled from the original 16 members to 36, as of 2011. Yet the FATF is not a formal international organization with a fully developed bureaucratic apparatus and an unlimited life span. Rather, it is a policy forum that brings together officials from government ministries, law-enforcement authorities, and regulatory agencies to establish AML rules and to monitor compliance with them.[113] In April 1990, less than a year from its creation, the FATF issued a set of Forty Recommendations, which quickly became the international standards for the fight against money laundering. Originally an initiative to combat the laundering of drug money, the Forty Recommendations have been since revised to reflect the evolution of money laundering techniques. They were also supplemented by a set of Nine Special Recommendations to suppress the funding of terrorism.

The Forty Recommendations are comprehensive in scope: they ask governments to put in place various measures within their criminal justice and regulatory systems; they make the private sector a key participant in the efforts against money laundering, imposing a host of obligations on financial institutions and other businesses and professions; and they lay out steps to enhance international cooperation, such as the provision of mutual legal assistance. Yet, as their title indicates, the Recommendations are non-legally binding measures that governments and nongovernmental actors are called upon to implement, but are not required to do so as a matter of law. The non-binding nature of the Recommendations is also demonstrated by the repeated use of the voluntary term "should" rather than the mandatory "shall" and the absence of need for ratification.[114] Furthermore, the Recommendations only set minimum standards, allowing "countries to implement the detail according to their particular circumstances and constitutional frameworks."[115] As such, the Recommendations are closer to open-ended benchmarks than to strict, determinate rules.

Why did the FATF opt for a non-legally binding, imprecise instrument as the foundation of the campaign against money laundering? One reason is practical necessity. Given the diversity of legal and financial systems, mandatory obligations that are detailed and precise could have raised serious difficulties of implementation and might even have been unworkable. Nonbinding standards that governments can interpret and apply in accordance with their unique circumstances were preferable. Another advantage of a nonbinding document is its flexibility and adaptability to evolving financial practices and to innovations in money-laundering techniques. Revising the Recommendations is easier and faster than the amendment of a treaty.

Politically, nonbinding standards facilitated compromise between governments that varied in the magnitude of the crime problems that they faced and thus in the benefits they derived from cooperation. Nonbinding standards also made regulation more palatable to the financial sector. Given the prominent role of financial institutions in the suppression of money laundering, their cooperation had to be secured. Yet, "[i]t is difficult to imagine gaining the cooperation of private financiers with a binding international agreement that forces change in the way they conduct much legitimate business and alters, for many, their fundamental relationship with their clients."[116] In many countries where money laundering was a concern, the financial sector enjoys significant political clout and is closely allied with regulatory authorities. Given the political influence and economic significance of financial institutions, strict legal requirements seen as adverse to their interests might have been met with fierce resistance; a set of nonbinding recommendations was easier to swallow. We have already encountered similar instances of softening of regulation to make it acceptable to legitimate and influential market actors, from arms manufacturers to antiquities dealers to pharmaceutical companies.

A further motivation for choosing a non-legally binding instrument was the tradeoff with the compliance mechanism. Nonbinding standards made it easier for governments to accept a strong mechanism that included monitoring and peer pressure.[117] FATF members' compliance with AML standards is assessed through a mutual-evaluation process. The evaluation is conducted by a team consisting of four to six experts from different countries with legal, financial, or law-enforcement background as well as two members of the FATF secretariat. In the course of the process, the team makes an on-site visit to the evaluated country and meets with government officials and the private sector. The evaluation examines whether the necessary laws, regulations, and other required measures are in force and in effect; whether all necessary measures have been fully and properly implemented; and whether the system in place is indeed effective. For each Recommendation, the evaluation rates the country's compliance on a scale that runs from Compliant through Largely Compliant and Partially Compliant to Noncompliant. The draft mutual-evaluation report is shared with all FATF members and, following discussion and adoption by the FATF plenary, is published online. Upon the completion of the mutual evaluation, the evaluated country enters a follow-up phase in which the FATF monitors its progress in addressing deficiencies in its AML system.[118]

The mutual-evaluation monitoring process generates peer pressure through "naming and shaming." The distribution of the reports to FATF members, their discussion in open session in the FATF plenary, and their public release have the potential to embarrass countries identified as failing to comply with AML standards. Consider the following criticism of Greece in its 2007 mutual-evaluation report:

> Greece's legal requirements in place to combat money laundering and terrorist financing are generally inadequate to meet the FATF standards and there are some serious concerns about the effectiveness of the AML/CFT system in place. . . . In general, it appears that the ML offence is not effectively implemented. . . . The preventive system that deals with customer identification is generally insufficient and not in line with the international standards. . . . [T]here are serious concerns regarding the level of awareness and commitment to implementation of effective AML/CFT measures by the non-financial businesses and professions.[119]

Beyond a critical report and the resulting embarrassment, noncompliant countries risk additional penalties, the most severe of which is suspension of FATF membership. In 2000 the FATF threatened to suspend Austria unless it eliminated anonymous passbook savings accounts that could be used for money laundering. After the Austrian government took the required measures, the threat of suspension was lifted.


## Countermeasures against Noncooperation

The FATF had to take a tougher approach toward nonmember countries that were reluctant to apply AML standards to their loosely regulated financial systems. The means of obtaining their cooperation was coercive countermeasures: painful penalties to make action against money laundering more attractive. The primary manifestation of the FATF's coercive efforts was a process aimed at Non-Cooperative Countries and Territories (NCCTs): countries and territories "whose detrimental practices seriously and unjustifiably hamper the fight against money laundering."[120] In 2000–2001, the FATF identified 23 NCCTs and made this designation public. Among the designated countries were Egypt, Israel, Liechtenstein, Marshall Islands, Nauru, Philippines, and Russia. Inclusion on the NCCT blacklist had significant adverse consequences. One consequence was reputational: a country labeled as an obstacle to the international endeavors against money laundering suffered a blow to its international reputation. A second consequence, with immediate, tangible effects, was the application to all NCCTs of Recommendation 21,[121] which asks financial institutions to "give special attention to business relationships and transactions with persons, including companies and financial institutions, from countries which do not or insufficiently apply the FATF Recommendations." Such attention could mean higher costs and legal uncertainty in business relations with NCCTs. Heeding the Recommendation, banks from FATF countries began reviewing their relationships with banks from NCCTs, leading in some cases to the breaking of business ties. Some NCCTs also complained about difficulties in processing international wire transfers.[122]

The FATF threatened to employ further countermeasures against NCCTs that still failed to make adequate progress toward complying with AML standards. Such countermeasures included stringent requirements for identifying clients before establishing business relationships with individuals or companies from these countries; enhanced reporting of financial transactions with these countries; taking into account the fact that a bank is from an NCCT when considering requests for establishing subsidiaries or branches of that bank in FATF countries; and warning nonfinancial businesses that transactions with entities within NCCTs could carry the risk of money laundering. To qualify for removal from the NCCT list, countries were required to enact laws and regulations, especially in the areas of criminal law, financial supervision, customer identification, suspicious-transaction reporting, and international cooperation. Countries that enacted appropriate legislation had to report on its implementation; effective implementation was also confirmed in on-site visits to the NCCTs. When the FATF was satisfied that a country had taken sufficient steps to ensure the continued effective implementation of AML measures, that country was delisted, yet remained subject to monitoring for an additional period.[123] The pressure on NCCTs indeed achieved its intended goal. In response to economic coercion, these noncooperative jurisdictions made progress toward adopting and complying with AML measures. In some cases officials explicitly stated that the purpose of passing AML legislation was to escape the FATF's blacklist.[124] By October 2006 all NCCTs had been delisted. In three cases—Nauru, Ukraine, and Myanmar—the FATF had to apply countermeasures beyond Recommendation 21 to compel anti-money laundering reforms.

The NCCT process engendered controversy, as it imposed AML standards on countries that had not agreed to them.[125] The FATF therefore halted the process, yet remained committed to its coercive approach toward noncooperative countries. Between 2007 and 2009, the FATF issued statements expressing concern about the deficient AML measures in several countries; against Iran, the FATF took the additional step of calling for countermeasures. In June 2009 the FATF adopted new procedures for identifying noncooperative and high-risk jurisdictions, including a review of AML practices and public identification of jurisdictions found to be noncooperative or high risk; a call for enhanced scrutiny of transactions involving these jurisdictions; and, ultimately, a call for the application of additional countermeasures to protect the financial system.[126]

The FATF's pressure managed to turn the efforts against money laundering into a worldwide endeavor. By the FATF's 2009 count, its AML standards had "been endorsed by more than 180 jurisdictions around the world."[127] This number included FSRBs: FATF-style regional bodies whose member jurisdictions have committed to the implementation of the Forty Recommendations and have agreed to submit their AML systems to mutual evaluations.[128] The International Monetary Fund and the World Bank also evaluate countries' AML systems. Moreover, the UN Convention against Transnational Organized Crime (2000) and the UN Convention against Corruption (2003) contain money-laundering provisions drawn from the Forty Recommendations. The Recommendations have thus become a regulatory framework with global application and membership. They have, in fact, attained a more mandatory status than their title indicates. Most significantly, the mechanisms of monitoring and enforcement make the Recommendations a fairly robust regulatory framework, as might be expected of one led and backed by powerful countries.

The United States plays a dual role in the efforts against money laundering, as in international drug control. We have seen earlier that the United States has been the driving force behind the multilateral drug regime and has complemented that regime with coercive unilateral action. Similarly, it has led the multilateral efforts against money laundering in addition to engaging in unilateral monitoring and enforcement. Every year, U.S. agencies with AML responsibilities jointly assess the money laundering situation in countries worldwide. Among the issues assessed are the significance of financial transactions in the country's financial institutions that involve proceeds of serious crime, the conformity of national laws and policies with international standards, the effectiveness with which the government has acted, and its political will to take needed action. In its annual International Narcotics Control Strategy Report, the State Department identifies "Jurisdictions of Primary Concern" whose financial institutions conduct transactions involving a significant amount of criminal proceeds (this designation is based on the significance of the amount of laundered proceeds, rather than the AML measures taken). Section 311 of the USA Patriot Act authorizes the Treasury to find that foreign jurisdictions or financial institutions are of primary money laundering concern. The Treasury may then require domestic financial institutions to take special measures, such as recordkeeping and reporting of transactions, with respect to the designated foreign jurisdictions or institutions.

## Cooperation against Money Laundering: Conclusions

The establishment of cooperation against money laundering is consistent with the theoretical framework and with the previous empirical cases. Cooperation has been motivated by a desire to spread the burden of fighting crime. As with small arms, antiquities, and drugs, the attempt at burden-spreading resulted in an international political conflict: certain governments were ambivalent or hostile toward AML efforts. These governments were safeguarding *legitimate* actors—banks—against the administrative burden of AML measures and an expected loss of business. Given the powerful noncooperative incentives, money-laundering cooperation has required persistent pressure. The FATF's monitoring and countermeasures have provided that pressure, escalating the costs of noncooperation enough to bring governments to cooperate. The FATF would not have been able to generate that pressure without the United States' support and leadership. American leadership has been indispensable to the campaign against counterfeits as well.

## Counterfeits

One of the major challenges facing the contemporary global economy is the proliferation of counterfeits—goods produced and distributed in violation of intellectual property rights: copyrights, trademarks, and patents. Moisés Naím has aptly described the magnitude of this problem:

> Whether you call them knockoffs, replicas, bootlegs, copies, or simply fakes, counterfeits are everywhere. Think of any product in any industry, and in all likelihood it has suffered the onslaught of copycats. Weapons and perfumes; cars, motorcycles, and running shoes; medicines and industrial machinery; watches, tennis rackets, golf clubs, video games, software, music, and movies—none is immune.[129]

The international protection of intellectual property rights dates back to the 1883 Paris Convention for the Protection of Industrial Property and the 1886 Berne Convention for the Protection of Literary and Artistic Works. But only in the 1980s did the United States launch an international campaign against counterfeits that culminated in the 1994 signing of TRIPS: the Agreement on Trade-Related Aspects of Intellectual Property Rights. What fueled the American endeavor? The motivation for cooperation against counterfeits stems from their negative externalities that are borne primarily by industrialized countries. The direct bearers of these externalities are the producers of the legitimate goods, who suffer losses in sales volume, downward pressure on prices, and damage to the value of the brand and to the reputation of the firm. Yet counterfeiting also imposes externalities on society as a whole. One such externality is the inhibition of future innovation. If creators of literary and artistic works or technological inventions are unable to reap the fruits of their labor, their incentives to innovate may be dampened; society would lose the social, cultural, and economic benefits that come with creative works and products. Other externalities may include loss of jobs to counterfeit-producing countries and forgone tax revenues; lower consumer utility as a result of inferior product quality; and health and safety risks to consumers, especially from substandard food, medicine, cosmetics, and electronics.[130] The question, however, is why these externalities became a matter of great concern to the United States in the 1980s.

According to the theoretical framework, government support for international regulation increases with the magnitude of the trade's negative externalities and with their perceived severity. Indeed, in the late 1970s and early 1980s the magnitude of the counterfeits problem was increasing, as advances in technology made counterfeiting an inexpensive and lucrative business. American companies suffered significant losses owing to the fierce competition from counterfeits of their goods in both domestic and foreign markets.[131] Furthermore, the broader economic troubles plaguing the United States at the time magnified the perceived severity of the counterfeits problem. Concerns about rising trade deficits, diminished U.S. competitiveness, and loss of the manufacturing base escalated the counterfeits threat in the eyes of policymakers; tackling this threat offered the hope of a partial remedy for America's economic difficulties. The labeling of the issue as piracy and theft further aggravated the perception of the threat. The morally loaded language fostered a sense of indignation toward the wrongdoers and narrowed the room for compromise.[132]

The linking of counterfeits to America's economic predicament and the use of evocative language were, in fact, part of a conscious effort by American corporations to construct counterfeits as a threat, place the threat on the agenda, and motivate international action against it. Indeed, the impetus for an international regulatory campaign against counterfeits came from private businesses that had been suffering the negative effects of this trade. Beginning in the late 1970s and increasingly throughout the 1980s, adversely affected American industries lobbied the U.S. Congress and the executive branch in pursuit of enhanced intellectual property protections worldwide. They sought to make their cause—combating counterfeits abroad—a U.S. foreign policy goal and to harness American economic power to achieve this goal. Underpinning this lobbying effort was the industry's realization that only U.S.-government pressure could compel foreign governments to curb the trade in counterfeits. The strongest, best organized lobbies were several industry associations and coalitions, especially the Pharmaceutical Manufacturers Association; the Motion Pictures Association of America; the

International Intellectual Property Alliance (IIPA) that represented a variety of copyright interests; and an ad hoc Intellectual Property Committee (IPC, discussed later). These groups, and several key executives in particular (most notably, Pfizer's Edmund Pratt and IBM's John Opel), used various means and channels to vigorously press their case. They educated policymakers about the failure of foreign governments to curb counterfeiting, the losses to the industry, and the negative implications for U.S. trade and competitiveness. They framed action against counterfeits as a boost for American exports and a solution to the perceived economic decline of the United States, advocating the use of trade measures against noncooperative governments.[133] As I describe later, the extensive lobbying effort bore fruit and galvanized congressional and administration support. The U.S. government launched a campaign against counterfeiting through unilateral and multilateral trade-based mechanisms.

The American campaign met with fierce resistance from developing countries that produce counterfeits for export or domestic consumption.[134] Consistent with the theoretical framework, this resistance stemmed from governments' calculation that the costs of cracking down on counterfeits far outweighed the limited benefits. From developing countries' point of view, there was little they could gain from addressing a problem that was not *their* problem: the trade's externalities were borne primarily by industrialized countries and by the foreign firms whose goods were the subject of counterfeiting. The costs of cooperation, on the other hand, were large. First, efforts against counterfeits entail considerable law-enforcement costs. Courts, the police, customs, and administrative agencies all play a role in enforcing intellectual property rights and combating counterfeits. Judicial proceedings, raids, customs inspections, and administrative hearings consume precious resources, often at the expense of more pressing law-enforcement priorities.[135] Second, counterfeits can generate large profits to the counterfeiters themselves and are of significant value to developing economies as a source of jobs and an important export. Anti-counterfeiting measures hurt a lucrative business, result in labor displacement, at least in the short run, and may cause the loss of a significant source of income. As we have seen, drug-exporting countries feared similar adverse consequences from international drug control. Third, curbing counterfeits limits the access of the poor to low-cost goods of much value, such as medications, books, and software. It also limits the ability to obtain technological knowledge through uncompensated imitation, thereby slowing economic development.[136]

Developing countries discounted or overlooked certain benefits that they may reap from cooperation against counterfeits. Intellectual property protections and elimination of counterfeits may stimulate local invention and innovation, encourage foreign direct investment and the international transfer of knowledge, and thus *enhance* economic development.[137] Yet for politicians with short time-horizons, these long-term benefits have failed to counterbalance the immediate costs. Displaced entrepreneurs who suffer tangible losses in the present are a powerful political influence against reform, while future beneficiaries are less likely to mobilize politically.[138] As a result, developing countries exhibited significant concern about the costs of eliminating counterfeits and showed much less appreciation for the future gains they may enjoy. Consistent with the theoretical framework, they did not identify a shared interest in cooperation against counterfeits. Rather, they viewed the U.S.-led efforts as threatening to impose on them a costly, unjustified, welfare-diminishing burden. Their cooperation had to be achieved through coercion.

## The International Political Conflict and the Role of Coercion

Divergence of national preferences constituted the primary obstacle to the anti-counterfeit campaign from its inception. Industrialized countries, first and foremost the United States, championed stringent international regulation that would require vigorous action by developing countries. Developing countries, however, were reluctant to accept regulatory constraints that burdened them to the benefit of foreign corporations. This tension was already evident in the failed attempt to revise the 1883 Paris Convention in the early 1980s. Industrialized countries sought to modify this convention so as to improve anti-counterfeit enforcement, whereas developing countries wished to adjust patent protections in their favor. The result was a deadlock. By the mid-1980s, as American companies faced increasing competition from counterfeits of their goods, it became clear that the preferences of industrialized and developing countries were irreconcilable. The efforts against counterfeits had to shift their focus from consensus-based measures to unilateral, coercive means.[139]

In response to industry pressure, Section 301 of the U.S. Trade Act was amended in 1984 and 1988 to make it a potent tool for fighting counterfeits by threatening foreign countries with penalties for noncooperation. The amended legislation empowered the United States Trade Representative (USTR) to determine whether foreign governments had failed to adequately protect intellectual property and to retaliate against such failure through trade sanctions. Industry lobbying also made the Generalized System of Preferences (GSP) a weapon in the American war on counterfeits. Under the GSP program, the United States waived tariffs on many imports from developing countries on a nonreciprocal basis. The 1984 amendment of the Trade Act established the protection of intellectual property rights as a requirement for GSP benefits eligibility.[140] The private sector saw the GSP as an "attractive trump card"[141] and an effective form of leverage to compel cooperation against counterfeits.

Once the means of pressure had been established, the industry sought to put them into effect. In 1985 industry complaints brought the USTR to launch a Section 301 case against South Korea concerning a range of goods, from pharmaceutical and chemical products to books to films. Following the threat of trade sanctions and GSP benefits withdrawal, Korea pledged to strengthen its anti-counterfeit legislation and enforcement. In 1987 the USTR filed a case against Brazil over pharmaceuticals. The following year, Brazil's refusal to change its policy brought the United States to carry out its Section 301 threat for the first time. A $39 million retaliatory tariff was imposed on Brazilian imports; it was lifted after Brazil agreed to comply with the American demands.[142] The industry also urged the U.S. government to follow through on the threat of withdrawing GSP benefits. A 1986 report by the IIPA surveyed 10 countries, most of them GSP beneficiaries, and suggested that "the United States Trade Representative should make it known to these countries that . . . unless significant improvements are made . . . their GSP beneficiary status is in jeopardy."[143] The Advisory Committee for Trade Negotiations—a committee of business executives appointed by the president to provide private-sector advice on trade policy—similarly pressed for the deployment of GSP benefits as part of a carrot-and-stick strategy. In 1987 the United States exercised the GSP leverage for the first time, denying Mexico benefits worth $500 million for failure to provide pharmaceutical patent protection.[144]

In 1985, simultaneously with the expanding unilateral U.S. efforts, American businesses set a new goal: incorporation of anti-counterfeiting into the multilateral trade regime. They achieved the support of the USTR, who asked for the industry's help in placing the issue on the agenda of the Uruguay Round. In March 1986, six months before the beginning of that negotiations round, the industry formed the Intellectual Property Committee: a group of 12 CEOs of U.S.-based multinational corporations, especially pharmaceutical companies. The IPC quickly established its vision of a multilateral anti-counterfeiting agreement that would set minimum standards of intellectual property protection, render violations more transparent, and, most importantly, include an enforcement mechanism. The next goal was to build a consensus among industrialized countries. IPC members met with their peers—European and Japanese business associations—and received their support for pursuing a multilateral regulatory agreement. By the launching of the trade round, the European and Japanese associations had obtained their governments' approval for the initiative.[145] The speedy formation of a pro-regulation bloc consisting of the United States, Europe, and Japan was made possible by the fact that all three were suffering the negative effects of counterfeits and stood to benefit from cooperation against them.

Developing countries, by contrast, bore the costs of cooperation and were reluctant to join the anti-counterfeit bandwagon.

Between 1986 and early 1989, an anti-regulation group of 10 developing countries, led by India and Brazil, managed to stall the discussion of counterfeits in the trade negotiations. This group strongly protested the inclusion of the issue on the agenda and denounced the basic framework of the agreement, as proposed jointly by the American, European, and Japanese industry representatives.[146] Unilateral U.S. coercion through Section 301 and GSP actions proved an effective tool for softening the resistance to the emerging TRIPS and for bringing recalcitrant countries on board. As mentioned earlier, Brazil and South Korea were the targets of Section 301 measures; India came under intense pressure that involved suspension of GSP benefits for its pharmaceutical products in 1992; Thailand's GSP benefits were revoked as well (1989); and other developing countries found themselves on the USTR's blacklist, became the subject of investigation, or faced the threat of trade penalties. The message was clear: countries that resisted the U.S. multilateral efforts would pay a price. Given the large costs of noncooperation, developing countries accepted the regulatory agreement they had initially resisted. TRIPS indeed held many troubling implications for them, but American trade penalties were costlier. Anxious to maintain good trade relations with the United States and preserve their access to the U.S. market, developing countries capitulated and reversed their opposition to the agreement. The inclusion of a dispute settlement mechanism in TRIPS facilitated its acceptance as a means of relieving the American pressure.[147]

Alongside coercion, issue linkage played a key role in overcoming the defiance of developing countries. Among the items on the Uruguay Round's agenda was the liberalization of the trade in textile and agricultural products, which developing countries stood to benefit from. The simultaneous discussion of the issues and their inclusion in one final package—a "single undertaking"—allowed a linkage: the losses that developing countries incurred in TRIPS were offset by their anticipated export gains from the liberalization of textile and agricultural trade. Accepting TRIPS as part of the Uruguay Round bargain also allowed developing countries to be among the founding members of the new World Trade Organization (WTO).[148]

By the end of 1989, the resistance of developing countries had waned, but the American threat of coercive trade measures persisted through the successful adoption of TRIPS at the end of the Uruguay Round in 1994. Spearheaded by powerful countries, TRIPS establishes a fairly robust regulatory framework. It is a legally binding agreement whose substantive scope is broad, covering the entire spectrum of intellectual property rights; it specifies minimum standards for the protection of intellectual property, and delegates monitoring and enforcement powers to international organs: the TRIPS

Council that oversees compliance with the agreement and the WTO Dispute Settlement Body.

### After TRIPS

The signing of TRIPS did not bring the international political conflict over counterfeits to an end. Cooperation against illicit trade requires sustained post-agreement pressure to ensure compliance, given the persistence of noncooperative incentives. Such pressure is typically beyond the capacity of international organizations and has to be provided outside the multilateral framework. We have seen this logic at work in the case of drugs; a similar logic has guided the U.S. government in the post-TRIPS era. Encouraged by industry, the USTR has indeed made considerable use of the multilateral enforcement mechanisms. TRIPS Council's meetings have allowed the USTR to pose questions to developing countries and to engage with them on issues surrounding TRIPS implementation; the USTR has also aggressively pursued WTO dispute settlement for the resolution of counterfeit-related concerns.[149]

Yet contrary to the hopes of developing countries, the United States has not forsaken the coercive means that had proved so effective for establishing TRIPS. Far from disappearing, threats of Section 301 and GSP actions have been routinely utilized by the USTR to compel action against counterfeits. In the annual Special 301 Report, published since 1989, the USTR identifies those countries whose practices have an adverse impact on U.S. goods and designates them as "Priority Foreign Countries" (the worst offenders), "Priority Watch List," or "Watch List." The USTR may then engage in bilateral efforts to change the offending policies and practices, and can ultimately wield the stick of trade countermeasures against noncooperative countries. For example, Ukraine suffered suspension of GSP benefits in 2001 and trade sanctions in 2002; the sanctions were lifted in 2005 and the GSP benefits were restored in 2006, after Ukraine passed new legislation and improved enforcement. Industry plays a key role in this process by providing the USTR with assessments of anti-counterfeit policies worldwide and by pressing for the use of Section 301 and WTO dispute settlement to achieve compliance with TRIPS.[150]

Industrialized countries have exerted additional forms of pressure to remove the loopholes and ambiguities of TRIPS and to strengthen anticounterfeit rules and enforcement. The United States has employed its trade leverage to bring developing countries to commit to higher standards than those mandated by TRIPS by including "TRIPS plus" rules in preferential trade agreements, starting with the 2000 agreement with Jordan; the EU has similarly secured anti-counterfeit commitments in bilateral trade agreements. The United States has also raised counterfeit concerns with foreign officials through diplomatic channels, launched STOP!—a Strategy Targeting Organized Piracy—in 2004, and in 2007 announced, jointly with other industrialized countries, an initiative for a new Anti-Counterfeiting Trade Agreement.

Governments of developing countries, already dissatisfied with TRIPS, resented the pressure to boost anti-counterfeit commitments and enforcement.[151] Some governments stood up to American pressure and persisted in their practices, especially if they believed that the United States would not actually impose trade penalties or if the anticipated economic damage of these penalties was small. India, for example, found itself on the Priority Watch List every year from 1995 through 2010. Yet in other cases, the pressure bore fruit. Ukraine, mentioned earlier, is a case in point; Pakistan is another. From 2001, Pakistan faced U.S. demand for action against copyright infringements. In 2005 that demand was accompanied by a threat to suspend GSP benefits. This threat, and Pakistan's hope of concluding a bilateral investment treaty with the United States, resulted in improved enforcement efforts. The United States responded in 2006 by withdrawing its threat and moving Pakistan from the Priority Watch List to the Watch List.[152]

American coercion also proved effective vis-à-vis China. In its bilateral intellectual property negotiations with China over the period 1991–1996, the United States repeatedly wielded the threat of trade sanctions. Beyond their direct economic costs, the looming sanctions could have adversely affected foreign direct investment in China, diminished the prospects of congressional approval for the renewal of China's most-favored-nation status, and tarnished China's reputation as a responsible trading partner. The American pressure prompted China to enhance its anti-counterfeit efforts by promulgating relevant laws and regulations, and launching enforcement actions.[153] This by no means led to the elimination of the problem. In 2010 the USTR still placed China on the Priority Watch List, criticizing the rampant counterfeiting and the "largely ineffective and non-deterrent" enforcement. At the same time, the USTR acknowledged that China had made some progress in its anti-counterfeit efforts.[154] Chinese cooperation, partial and hesitant as it was, would not have been achieved without persistent U.S. pressure.

## Cooperation against Counterfeits: Conclusions

The foregoing analysis has suggested an important distinction between cooperation against counterfeits and other cooperative endeavors examined in this book. From arms exporters to antiquities dealers to banks, the market actors we have previously encountered resisted the international efforts against illicit trade, as those posed a threat to their commercial interests. By contrast, the international campaign against counterfeits was the product of the relentless efforts of market actors: American industries that bore the negative externalities of the trade in counterfeits. Industry worked closely with the U.S. government throughout the process of establishing TRIPS, shaping the American positions and proposals at the negotiations.[155] Thereafter, industry has pressed the USTR to employ the means in its arsenal to achieve compliance with TRIPS and obtain foreign countries' commitments beyond TRIPS. The role of civil society in the counterfeits case is also unique. In the campaigns against illicit antiquities and human trafficking, civil society was at the forefront of the regulatory efforts. By contrast, shortly after the conclusion of TRIPS, civil society groups began voicing *opposition* to stringent anticounterfeit regulation that might impede access to vital medications.

Yet in terms of the obstacles to cooperation, anti-counterfeit efforts are fundamentally similar to other campaigns against illicit trade. As in other campaigns, the involvement of criminal groups and the use of bribery and threats of violence have hindered action against counterfeits;[156] yet these have not been the primary obstacle. The main problem has been absence of shared interest in cooperation. From developing countries' point of view, anti-counterfeit efforts require them to bear a significant burden for the purpose of enriching foreign corporations. They were asked to suppress a thriving commerce that provides employment and income and hence economic and social stability; to adopt policies that threaten a host of legitimate actors, such as retail stores, pharmaceutical industries that manufacture generic medications, and farmers concerned about patents on seeds;[157] to sacrifice various public policy goals such as speedy technological progress and the provision of cheap medications to the populace; and to expend lawenforcement resources at the expense of more pressing priorities. Perceiving action against counterfeits as being inimical to their interests, developing countries adopted an anti-regulation preference and resisted the U.S.-led regulatory efforts. Coercion was therefore essential for the purpose of establishing TRIPS and compelling governments to curb counterfeiting thereafter.

# 7

## CONCLUSION

---

From civil wars sustained by the supply of small arms to human trafficking to the social costs of widespread drug abuse, illicit trade has dire consequences for human welfare. The need for effective multilateral cooperation against illicit trade has been evident since the beginning of the 20th century, when the first international agreements on drugs and sex trafficking were signed. It has become all the more acute, however, in the present era of globalization, which has boosted illicit trade and aggravated its deleterious social, economic, and political effects.

Despite its importance, illicit trade has received little attention in the literature on international cooperation and institutions, and it is this gap that motivated the present study. Having identified illicit trade as a distinct area of cooperation, I sought to uncover the political logic underlying governments' joint endeavors in this area. My goal was to develop a systematic, unified account of the international regulation aimed at curbing illicit trade, focusing on the conflict of government preferences as the key obstacle to such regulation. More specifically, this book set out to explain three types of variation in government preferences on international regulation: across countries, across trades, and across time. It also sought to explain a fourth variation: differences in the robustness of international regulation across trades.

To account for these variations, the theoretical framework examined how domestic political pressures shape government preferences on international regulation. Certain governments seek to suppress illicit trade in response to public concern or to the advocacy of moral entrepreneurs. These governments seek strong international regulation so as to curb the trade's negative externalities at home or abroad. Yet their regulatory efforts meet resistance. Other governments vehemently oppose regulation, as they are protecting the interests of exporters or consumers who wish to avoid international control. The problem that stems from the large variation in preferences is absence of shared interest in cooperation. In the absence of shared interest, the robustness of international regulation typically reflects the distribution of power: powerful governments can exercise coercion to establish robust regulatory agreements and ensure compliance. Change in government preferences over time may also alleviate the absence of shared interest and facilitate cooperation.

The empirical chapters were largely consistent with the theoretical framework and employed it to shed light on observed variations. Chapter 3 focused on cross-country variation in government preferences, explaining why governments varied in their preferences on international small-arms regulation and why they failed to identify a shared interest in cooperation against the illicit trade in small arms. On one side stood governments that were concerned about rampant gun violence in their own countries or in foreign countries. On the other side were governments protective of a variety of interests: their own interest in acquiring arms, the commercial interests of arms exporters, or the interests of civilian gun owners. As the distribution of power favored regulation opponents, a weak international regulatory framework for small arms was adopted in 2001. In the absence of interstate coercion or a temporal change in preferences, the international political conflict was left unresolved, leading to a deadlock at the 2006 UN Review Conference on Small Arms.

Chapter 4 first analyzed the cross-country variation in preferences on the international regulation of antiquities. Throughout most of the 20th century, source countries and market countries failed to identify a shared interest in suppressing the illicit trade in antiquities. The most important market-countries—the United States and Britain—believed that international control of antiquities would be to their detriment. Yet temporal changes in government preferences ultimately mitigated the international political conflict. As explained in the chapter, the American and British preferences on antiquities regulation reflected a compromise among the conflicting influences of archaeologists, public scandals, antiquities dealers, and museums. Changes in these influences over time—or a change of the government itself—transformed government preferences, making these countries more cooperative. The United States reversed its opposition to the international control of antiquities and joined the efforts against looting in the early 1970s; it would take Britain three decades to follow suit.

Chapter 5 examined how an evangelical-feminist coalition initiated a U.S. government campaign to rescue foreign women and children sold into the sex industry. The analysis explained the change in the American preference over time, namely, the greater determination of the Bush administration to combat human trafficking worldwide compared to the Clinton administration. But the chapter's focus was on the exercise of coercion for the purpose of establishing cooperation against illicit trade. The chapter examined how

American pressure induced a dramatic change in Israel's policy on human trafficking, demonstrating that coercion can overcome the absence of motivation to cooperate. American coercion as a means of compelling cooperation was further highlighted in the extension cases analyzed in Chapter 6: drugs, money laundering, and counterfeits.

The theoretical framework has identified four principal influences on government preferences: primary externalities, secondary externalities, exporters, and consumers. These building blocks make it possible to systematically explain variation in government preferences across illicit trades. Most importantly, they account for the different positions that the U.S. government has taken in different cases. In the case of human trafficking, the main influence on the U.S. government was secondary externalities. Following the advocacy efforts of a coalition of moral entrepreneurs, the United States became concerned about the trade in persons and its victims abroad. The concern about secondary externalities was not counterbalanced by any pressure from exporters or consumers; as a result, the United States adopted a strong pro-regulation preference, seeking to eliminate human trafficking worldwide. Similarly, in the cases of drugs, money laundering, and counterfeits the American preference was largely shaped by pro-regulation incentives. The United States bore the primary externalities of these illicit trades and led the international regulatory campaigns to suppress them. In the antiquities case, by contrast, the United States came under cross-pressures, making it necessary to balance secondary externalities—looting abroad—against the interests of American consumers: antiquities dealers and museums. The result was an American preference for moderate international regulation of antiquities. In the case of small arms, the U.S. government's concern about gun violence abroad was overwhelmed by the concerns of highly influential and vocal consumers: civilian gun owners represented by the NRA. Consequently, the United States has favored weak international control of small arms.

Alternative explanations fail to account for the observed variations in government preferences. One might expect democratic countries with a commitment to the rule of law to be at the forefront of the regulatory efforts against illicit trade. This expectation seems to be supported in the small-arms case: democracy is indeed associated with greater support for international regulation of small arms. Yet overall, preferences on international regulation have not varied systematically with the level of democracy. The United States—a democratic, rule-of-law country—has favored stringent international regulation against certain illicit trades; in other cases, it has been ambivalent or hostile toward international regulation. Democratic governments have also disagreed among themselves. They have not manifested a uniform approach to the international control of small arms, as shown by the conflicting preferences of the U.S. and European governments.

Another rift among democracies emerged in the case of international antiquities regulation, which the United States endorsed long before the Western European countries did. In fact, the strongest supporters of the international efforts against looting were nondemocracies; established democracies, such as Britain and Switzerland, staunchly opposed these efforts. The Israeli failure to suppress human trafficking also demonstrates that democratic countries are not necessarily committed to the elimination of illicit trade. Nor is such commitment or lack thereof explained by economic development. Poor countries whose antiquities had been plundered initiated the efforts against looting—efforts that rich countries opposed. Yet poor countries resisted international agreements against drugs and counterfeits—agreements that threatened important sources of employment and income. In the case of small arms, international regulation enjoyed support from the poor countries of sub-Saharan Africa as well as from the rich countries of Europe and from Japan. Economic development and democracy also fail to account for changes in preferences over time, such as the shift in the American and British attitudes to the efforts against looting. The three preference variations—across countries, trades, and time—are better explained by combining illicit trade's externalities and the interests of exporters and consumers.

Government preferences in combination with the distribution of power account for the variation in the robustness of international regulation across trades. Given the absence of shared interest in cooperation, it is the preferences of the powerful actors—first and foremost the United States—that have determined the robustness of regulation. In cases where the United States has favored cooperation—such as drugs and counterfeiting—international regulation establishes clear rules and enforces them through agreement-based mechanisms and outside-agreement pressures. By contrast, the international control of small arms is based on a weak, non-legally binding agreement that lacks monitoring and enforcement mechanisms. To a large extent, this weakness was the result of American and Chinese resistance to regulation.

I now turn to examining the broader ramifications and insights that this study offers for the analysis of illicit trade, for international relations, and for policy.

## Implications for the Study of Illicit Trade

The literature on illicit trade has examined various aspects of this phenomenon, including the efforts to curb illicit trade through global prohibition regimes. The dynamics of these regimes have been studied in detail in specific cases, especially drugs, money laundering, and human trafficking. The literature, however, has not offered a comprehensive and unified account of the domestic and international political conflicts over these regimes; nor has it systematically addressed questions such as: What is the cooperation problem that makes it difficult for governments to establish and maintain prohibition regimes? Why do some governments support these regimes while others oppose them? Why do certain governments change their views over time? The literature has provided case-specific answers to these questions. The purpose of this book, however, has been to answer them in a broader, more general manner. The international efforts against gun violence, the looting of antiquities, human trafficking, drugs, money laundering, and counterfeits indeed vary in different ways, but they also share many important commonalities. Similar patterns run through these cases in terms of the actors involved, the motivations for cooperation, the cooperation problem—absence of shared interest—and the cooperative outcomes. My goal has been to highlight and explain these patterns in an account that integrates domestic and international processes.

More concretely, this book offers four contributions to the literature on illicit trade: it offers an alternative explanation for the difficulties of suppressing illicit trade; it broadens the scope of investigation to include noncriminal measures against illicit trade and noncriminal actors; it calls attention to the role of weaker countries in spearheading campaigns against illicit trade; and it identifies and accounts for variations that the literature has thus far overlooked or not thoroughly explained.

## The Persistence of Illicit Trade

Illicit trade persists despite the existence of international regulatory agreements against it. As H. Richard Friman points out, the most prominent explanation for this reality contrasts the growing power and capacity of criminal networks in the era of globalization with the capacity constraints of governments.[1] This explanation has been articulated most clearly by Moisés Naím. Naím argues that "illicit trade has reached a point it had never reached before—in terms of geography, profits, and the share of the world's population that it touches."[2] This dramatic expansion of illicit trade is a result of innovations in technology, communication, and transportation as well as the lowering of barriers to trade and investment. It is also a result of the flexible and highly adaptive nature of trafficking networks that allows them to avoid detection and suppression.[3]

But globalization has not only made it easier for criminals to engage in illicit trade and escape law enforcement. Naím argues that it has empowered criminals politically, allowing them to achieve "political influence in direct proportion to their enormous profits. The political influence . . . includes the prolonged 'capture' of certain state and local governments, almost sovereign control over territories that may or may not coincide with political boundaries, and in extreme cases control of crucial decision-making centers within national governments."[4] While the scale of illicit trade and the threat it poses have grown mightily, Naím suggests, governments' response has been hamstrung by their bureaucratic nature. Unlike the flexible criminal networks, government bureaucracies are hierarchical entities in which establishing coordination and collaboration among units is a constant struggle. Governments can only operate within the limits of the public budget and of the law; criminal networks are free from such constraints.[5] Since the enforcement capability of governments has not increased to match the enhanced capacity of criminals, "*governments are failing*"[6] in the fight against illicit trade.

Another explanation for the persistence of illicit trade emphasizes societal resistance to and noncompliance with criminal prohibitions.[7] Activities that the law proscribes may be seen as legitimate and acceptable by the participants and by large segments of the population; at times they reflect deeply rooted social practices.[8] According to Peter Andreas and Ethan Nadelmann, "[m]ost difficult to suppress are those activities that require limited and readily available resources and no particular expertise to commit, those that are easily concealed, those that are unlikely to be reported to the authorities, and those for which consumer demand is substantial, resilient, and not readily substituted for by alternative activities or products."[9]

Both the criminal-capacity and the societal-resistance explanations implicitly assume that policymakers are committed to the elimination of illicit trade: the political will to suppress the trade is taken as given.[10] The problem is not that governments do not wish to suppress illicit trade, these explanations suggest; rather, they are unable to do so. This book, by contrast, has put the political motivation to curb illicit trade at the center of the analysis. I have argued that the principal obstacle to the international regulatory efforts against illicit trade is absence of shared interest in cooperation. Certain governments identify only costs and no gains from international regulation; hence, they see no reason to sign on to such regulation and to comply with it. The absence of political motivation to cooperate has three causes. First, noncooperative governments view illicit trade as a problem that is of little interest or consequence to them. Since the negative externalities of the trade are not borne by their own countries or other countries they care about, these governments do not consider illicit trade to be a threat, nor do they value the welfare gains that would come from mitigating the trade's externalities Therefore, they lack the essential motivation for cooperation: the expectation that cooperative behavior will yield rewards. Second, international regulation entails law-enforcement costs. Governments that, to begin with, are not particularly concerned about the trade are asked to invest in combating it. For example, they may be required to set up systems of export or import licensing, strengthen customs and border control, or enhance policing. Such efforts could come at the expense of more pressing law-enforcement priorities without offering any benefits to the countries making the effort; the beneficiaries are the foreign countries harmed by the trade. Third, international regulation threatens exporters or consumers, which in many cases are *legitimate* societal actors. Noncooperative governments privilege domestic constituencies over foreign countries: they are unwilling to hurt the former for the sake of assisting the latter.

These three factors have been the prime obstacles to international cooperation in the cases that this book has examined. In the small-arms case, the key problem was the reluctance of arms-exporting countries such as China and Egypt to seriously tackle a problem that did not affect them. Both countries had no need for international control of small arms, given their low levels of gun violence. From their point of view, international control would only constrain state-owned arms exporters. The obstacle to cooperation was not criminal infiltration and capture of the Chinese and Egyptian governments, nor was it lack of bureaucratic capacity: both governments had the ability to tighten the control over the production and export of guns, *given the political motivation to do so*. The problem was that they had no such motivation, as they judged that cooperation would impose costs without bringing any gains.

The international efforts against the looting of antiquities encountered the same problem: absence of political motivation. For many years, Britain saw the looting of antiquities as other countries' problem. Measures to tackle this problem were seen as a burden on the London art market as well as on Britain's bureaucracy and law-enforcement agencies. Britain was thus complicit in the trade in looted antiquities not because of criminal influence on policymaking and enforcement, limitations and pathologies of government action, or societal resistance to criminalization. Britain was complicit simply because *it did not care* about the damage that looting caused abroad. Furthermore, the trade in looted antiquities enriched Britain both culturally and financially. From the British government's point of view, efforts to suppress the trade were highly undesirable and there was no reason to join them. Only when Britain began losing its own cultural objects and when scandals engulfed the London art market, did the government find the requisite motivation to accede to the 1970 UNESCO Convention.

Indifference to illicit trade and absence of motivation to suppress it also hindered the Israeli response to human trafficking. Trafficked women were seen as prostitutes who did not merit law-enforcement attention rather than victims of severe abuse and exploitation. The problem was not criminal influence on the Israeli government and police; it was also not the capacity of criminals and the difficulty of fighting an underground activity—brothels used to operate in the open; nor was it unrelenting demand for sexual services or a social norm that legitimized these services. The problem was that trafficking of foreign women was seen as harmless to Israeli society and that the women's own plight was overlooked. For the Israeli government, sex trafficking was not a problem and there was little need to fight it; there was definitely no incentive to shift law-enforcement resources to this "marginal" issue. Only the coercive effect of the State Department's TIP report managed to generate motivation for action.

The general point is that illicit trade often persists because governments are reluctant to combat it. These governments may be well positioned to curb the trade, but they have no desire to do so, given that the trade poses no threat to their own countries and that its suppression would entail law-enforcement costs and could harm domestic actors. The political motivation of governments to tackle illicit trade should therefore be problematized, rather than assumed. The capacity and influence of criminals can obstruct the efforts to suppress illicit trade, but sometimes governments have no interest to engage in these efforts in the first place.

## Noncriminal Measures and Actors

This book has examined the international endeavors against illicit trade as regulatory in nature. By contrast, the existing literature typically frames the efforts against illicit trade as *criminalization*: certain cross-border activities become the subject of criminal prohibitions, and the state uses its policing powers to enforce these prohibitions. Andreas and Nadelmann explain the centrality of criminal sanctions to the suppression of illicit trade:

> International prohibition regimes resort to force in the form of criminal justice (and, in some cases, military) measures in part because the violators—whether pirates, slave traders, or elephant poachers—are themselves armed and reliant on violence to perform their illicit deeds; in part because efforts to prohibit anything that many people desire are bound to require some degree of coercion; and in part because criminal justice measures are the principal, and typically most punitive, means of dealing with those who defy the norms of developed societies.[11]

This book has demonstrated that the focus on criminalization is overly narrow. International regulatory campaigns against illicit trade do not rely solely on criminal prohibitions. Rather, they include a wide array of civil and administrative means. To curb the illicit trade in small arms, the 2001 Program of Action calls on states to adopt a host of administrative measures, such as effective systems of export and import licensing, regulation of arms brokering, and procedures to secure national arms stocks.[12] Indeed, the PoA does ask states to criminalize the illegal manufacture, possession, stockpiling, and trade of small arms;[13] but the majority of measures that the PoA advocates do not involve criminal justice. Similarly, cooperation against the looting of antiquities relies on the regulatory efforts of market countries. At the center of these efforts are import controls: an administrative measure implemented by customs and accompanied by a civil sanction—seizure and confiscation of the illegally imported antiquities. To stem the trade in conflict diamonds, the Kimberley Process establishes a set of administrative measures intended to certify shipments of rough diamonds as conflict-free. The key here is not a criminal prohibition, but standardized certificates that must accompany diamond shipments. In the case of money laundering, the Forty Recommendations require governments to put in place criminal as well as administrative measures. Financial institutions themselves are asked to take various steps to prevent money laundering.

The existing literature focuses on criminal prohibitions because it is driven and dominated by a single case: drugs. Indeed, the international drug regime has shaped much of the thinking about illicit trade. The efforts against illicit trade are often equated with criminalization since contemporary drug control is largely based on criminal prohibitions. Undoubtedly, the case of drugs is a very important one. Yet the focus on this case leads to the neglect of the multifaceted nature of the efforts against illicit trade. In these efforts, criminal prohibitions play an important role, but so do a range of noncriminal regulatory means. Furthermore, even the drug regime is not purely about criminalization. Today, and especially since the 1988 Convention against Illicit Traffic in Narcotic Drugs and Psychotropic Substances, criminalization is at the heart of international drug control. Yet from a broader historical perspective, criminalization has been only one component in the regulatory edifice of the drug regime. During the regime's formative period (1909–1939), the goal was to confine the movement of drugs to legal trade channels through controls on supply and distribution. The early drug treaties had penal provisions, and the 1936 Convention for the Suppression of the Illicit Traffic in Dangerous Drugs adopted a penal approach; but overall, the focus was on administrative control measures, rather than criminal prohibitions.[14] A similar focus characterizes two of the central pillars of the contemporary drug regime: the 1961 Single Convention on Narcotic Drugs and the 1971 Convention on Psychotropic Substances. The two conventions institute a variety of controls; only one article in each convention is devoted to penal provisions (Articles 36 and 22, respectively). As the administrative measures drove the drug trade underground and created a criminal black market, the regime's focus gradually shifted to criminalization. Yet this late development of the regime should not obscure the fact that drug control, to this day, involves administrative measures and that historically such measures have been the linchpin of the drug regime.

This book has suggested that noncriminal measures are an integral part of the efforts against illicit trade and hence essential to their analysis. Furthermore, the *actors* most relevant to the analysis are not necessarily the criminals themselves. The targets of the regulatory efforts are often legitimate actors who operate within the legal, mainstream economy. Through participation in domestic and international political processes, these actors can voice their concerns about international regulation and shape it to fit their interests. In many cases, governments' resistance to international regulation can be traced to the influence of these actors, be they banks, arms manufacturers, or antiquities dealers. An analysis of the efforts against illicit trade must therefore examine the world of criminality *as well as the realm of legality* that are not antithetical, but inextricably linked.

## The Role of Weaker Countries

The literature on illicit trade has focused on drugs as a primary domain; human trafficking and money laundering have also received considerable scholarly attention.[15] This book has diversified this set of cases, offering an analysis of international cooperation against the illicit trade in small arms and in antiquities. Studying small arms and antiquities, however, represents more than an empirical contribution. It is theoretically significant in that it calls attention to the role of weaker countries in initiating and shaping the international efforts against illicit trade, and moves away from attributing these efforts solely to powerful countries.

Indeed, the existing literature has emphasized the key role of powerful countries in international crime control. Andreas and Nadelmann, for example, suggest that "international crime control efforts ultimately reflect the interests and agendas of those states best able to coerce and co-opt others" and that "the models, methods, and priorities of international crime control are substantially determined and exported by the most powerful states in the international system." Through global prohibition regimes, Andreas and Nadelmann argue, the United States and European countries have shaped moral views worldwide and have imposed their own norms on foreign governments. By contrast, "[l]ess powerful and especially less developed countries have typically played a more secondary and reactive role" in the evolution of these regimes.[16]

The attribution of the efforts against illicit trade to the initiative of powerful countries largely stems from the empirical focus of the literature on drugs, money laundering, and human trafficking. Powerful countries—in particular, the United States—have indeed been at the forefront of the international efforts in these three areas. Yet extrapolating from this set of cases exaggerates the role of powerful countries. It overlooks the fact that weaker countries may be the ones demanding the suppression of illicit trade, against the wishes of powerful countries. While in some cases powerful countries are the leaders of the international efforts and weaker countries are the laggards, these roles could be reversed.

Instead of presupposing that powerful countries play a leading role, this book has treated the distribution of power as a variable. In some of the cases studied, powerful countries promoted cooperation; in others, weaker countries took the lead. As the theoretical framework has explained, power relations do affect the robustness of the cooperative outcome. Through coercion, powerful countries can overcome the absence of shared interest; they can bring reluctant countries to commit to and comply with stringent international regulation. Nevertheless, international agreements spearheaded by weaker countries can have important consequences. As shown in Chapter 4, the 1970 UNESCO Convention—initiated by Mexico and Peru and supported by many developing countries—has had a profound impact on the antiquities market. Prior to 1970 this market had been free from ethical constraints. In the years since, governments and the public in rich countries have gradually come to expect responsible behavior on the part of dealers and museums. Most importantly, the United States, the largest market, has enacted regulation to prevent the import of plundered material. Trading in looted antiquities—a practice once seen as perfectly legitimate— is considered today to be unethical and illegal, the subject of public scandals and criminal prohibitions. Without resorting to coercion, the UNESCO Convention has triggered a normative transformation of the antiquities market, turning the tide against the illicit trade and the plunder that it fuels. In the case of small arms, the regulatory efforts led by the weak African countries have been less successful. And yet, the 2001 Program of Action was not without impact. The PoA has made the efforts against gun violence a matter of international concern and the subject of financial and technical assistance. With the adoption of the PoA, the once-free trade in small arms has come under globally agreed, albeit very limited, constraints. All in all, considering the resistance of powerful countries and the highly circumscribed influence of weaker countries, the latter have scored some notable achievements in their international initiatives against illicit trade.

The correction to the literature's emphasis on powerful countries should not be misinterpreted. I do not claim that powerful countries lack a dominant role in the efforts against illicit trade. As this book has demonstrated, powerful countries and their coercive influence played a crucial role in establishing cooperation against human trafficking, drugs, money laundering, and counterfeits. Rather, I argue that the part of weaker countries in the efforts against illicit trade is more central than previously acknowledged. Weaker countries have led the international efforts against the illicit trade in small arms and in antiquities; it was weaker countries' concerns that motivated the campaigns against conflict diamonds and the illicit movement of hazardous wastes. In forging cooperation against illicit trade, both powerful countries and weaker ones have important roles.

## Explaining Variations

This book has sought to explain four types of observed variations: variations in government preferences across countries, across trades, and over time, as well as variation in the robustness of international regulation across trades. How has the existing literature viewed these variations?

Of the four, the most readily observable is the cross-country variation in government preferences with respect to a given trade. Even a cursory look would reveal that the international regulatory efforts against illicit trade are often controversial. Negotiations can be acrimonious, and even after an agreement has been concluded, ratification and compliance may not follow. The literature has indeed recognized that illicit trade can be the source of contention and political conflict among governments; it has explained the variation in government preferences with respect to specific trades. For example, the extensive literature on drugs explains why the United States has led the international efforts for drug control and why drug-producing countries have been ambivalent or altogether hostile toward these efforts.[17] My goal, however, has been to move beyond a trade-specific analysis and to offer a general explanation for the cross-country variation in government preferences. Some of the influences on government preferences that I highlight, such as commercial interests and moral entrepreneurs, have been addressed in the existing literature. But this book has integrated them into a single analytical framework that links the various illicit trades and reveals their political similarities.

The three other variations that this book explains have received little attention in existing studies of illicit trade.

The literature has overlooked the second variation: the different preferences that a given government may have across illicit trades. This oversight—the result of attributing the efforts against illicit trade to the initiative of powerful countries—has obscured an important fact: governments favoring international regulation to suppress certain trades may oppose the regulatory efforts against other trades. While the U.S. government has been at the forefront of the efforts against human trafficking, drugs, and counterfeits, it has opposed the international regulation of small arms. The British government has been supportive of the efforts against money laundering, but resisted the international control of antiquities for decades. This book has called attention to this overlooked variation and shed light on its causes.

Variation in government preferences over time has been noted occasionally, especially with respect to drugs. For example, H. Richard Friman explains why Germany's resistance to international drug control before World War I turned into greater willingness to cooperate in the aftermath of the war.[18] The transformation of Britain's position—from sponsoring the opium trade to participating in the drug regime—has also been studied.[19] Overall, however, the literature has not offered a general explanation for why noncooperative countries might become more cooperative in the absence of coercion. The theoretical framework of this book allows us to systematically account for preference change over time, which was the focus of Chapter 4. Growing concerns about the secondary externalities of the antiquities trade—and, in the case of Britain, concerns about primary externalities as well—led the U.S. and British governments to reverse their longstanding support for free trade in antiquities and join the UNESCO Convention.

Finally, the literature has tended to overlook the variation in the robustness of international regulation. Framing these regulatory regimes as "global prohibitions" has created a sense of uniformity, masking important differences in institutional features. While in many cases these regimes are based on legally binding treaties, some rely on non-legally binding agreements. Certain regimes establish highly specific commitments, while others leave significant discretion to governments. In some cases, governments have delegated monitoring and enforcement powers to international organs; in others, they have not. Christine Jojarth's book *Crime, War, and Global Trafficking* (2009) is the first study to provide an in-depth analysis of these variations. Jojarth offers a functionalist account, in which the design of international institutions is shaped by the attributes of the policy problem: asset specificity (the loss countries would suffer if cooperation breaks down and the likelihood that such a breakdown might occur); behavioral uncertainty (the difficulty of detecting noncompliance); and environmental uncertainty (the difficulty of understanding the causes, consequences, or remedies for a problem). International power politics and domestic politics are largely absent from Jojarth's analysis. They are only discussed in the concluding chapter of her book.[20] The present study, by contrast, has explained the variation in institutional design by combining domestic politics with the international distribution of power. Powerful governments, motivated by domestic political considerations, can establish robust international regulation; weaker governments have to settle for diluted regulation.


## Implications for International Relations

This section ties the analysis of cooperation against illicit trade to the broader international relations literature and to ongoing IR debates.

# The Effects of International Institutions

The role of international institutions in facilitating cooperation is an important theme in the IR literature and the subject of a lively scholarly debate. Realists have traditionally questioned the independent effects of international institutions on state behavior. In the realist view, international organizations (IOs) and treaties are merely a reflection of state interests and power.[21] Yet the extensive literature on international institutions, which has developed since the early 1980s, has shown otherwise. This literature has demonstrated that international institutions may indeed have significant effects: institutions allow states to work together in circumstances that would make cooperation challenging, if not impossible, otherwise. This literature has identified *direct* mechanisms by which IOs and treaties facilitate cooperation, such as offering opportunities for reciprocity, enhancing transparency, magnifying the reputational consequences of noncooperative behavior, and resolving disputes.[22] At the same time, the literature has increasingly explored the *indirect* effects that international institutions may have through their influence on the domestic political arena.[23]

Much of the evidence in this book suggests that international institutions play a limited independent role in fostering cooperation against illicit trade. This has been the case with the U.S.-led campaigns against drugs, money laundering, and counterfeits, which were examined in Chapter 6. In all three campaigns, the United States has employed international bodies to advance its goal of suppressing illicit trade: respectively, the UN, the Financial Action Task Force, and the WTO. This is consistent with the realist view of international institutions as instruments in the hands of powerful countries. The UN, FATF, and WTO gave the American agenda multilateral cover and encouraged governments to conform to the standards advocated by the United States. Consider the role of the UN in international drug control. The UN has promoted and entrenched the American vision of strict drug regulation through publicity and educational initiatives and through the provision of information, advice, and technical assistance.[24] But ultimately it is the United States and its coercive powers that have been the engine of the drug regime. The UN has merely facilitated and legitimized the American efforts.

International organizations have also played a relatively modest role in the cases of small arms and antiquities. The Program of Action on Small Arms (2001) and the 1970 UNESCO Convention were negotiated under the auspices of IOs: respectively, the UN and UNESCO (itself part of the UN system). These IOs performed various supportive functions, such as providing a venue for the negotiations, conducting background research, and circulating relevant information. The UNESCO secretariat, in fact, played an important role in drafting the 1970 convention. Yet the resulting agreements were still weak in their form and substantive obligations. Most importantly, both the PoA and the UNESCO Convention failed to establish monitoring and enforcement mechanisms. In fact, in the case of small arms the institutional context had a *negative* effect: the consensus rule underlying the negotiations gave veto power to regulation opponents. This led to an agreement that reflected the lowest common denominator in 2001 and to a deadlock at the 2006 Review Conference.

The IOs' efforts to encourage implementation and compliance have also met with limited success. The UN has sought to coordinate field projects, workshops, and technical assistance to support the PoA's implementation. Yet there was little that the UN could do vis-à-vis governments that were reluctant to put the PoA into effect. UNESCO encountered similar difficulties. The organization asked member states to report on their implementation of the 1970 convention and on the difficulties they had encountered.[25] UNESCO also engaged in educational efforts to raise awareness of the illicit antiquities trade and provided information, training, and advice for protecting the cultural heritage.[26] Yet UNESCO was unable to persuade noncooperative governments to participate in the efforts against looting. Whereas Martha Finnemore showed how UNESCO promoted the establishment of science policy bureaucracies,[27] no similar direct effect of UNESCO was evident with respect to antiquities. The vast majority of market countries had refused for decades to ratify the UNESCO Convention. Even after ratification, significant policy changes did not always follow, as the case of Britain demonstrates.

Overall, this experience seems to support the realist view: international institutions can do little to constrain governments that do not wish to be constrained. If they judge an agreement to be contrary to their interests, governments—especially powerful ones—will refuse to commit or comply. International institutions may facilitate cooperation when a shared interest exists, but they cannot transform governments' preference to maintain the noncooperative status quo.

Yet we may reach a different conclusion by broadening our perspective beyond direct institutional effects on state authorities and official policy. As the case of antiquities shows, treaties may have important indirect effects that are not necessarily the result of changes in government behavior. Treaties may work through *sensitization*: they can bring issues into the limelight, raise public awareness, and change the normative environment in a way that influences relevant nonstate actors.

Indeed, the 1970 UNESCO Convention had a dramatic effect on the antiquities market that was not a direct manifestation or result of government action. As discussed in Chapter 4, the convention's impact on national policy was limited. The United States implemented merely two of the convention's provisions and established import controls on archaeological material from a limited number of countries. The British accession to the convention did not result in any significant government effort to control the movement of antiquities. Yet the convention sparked a fundamental change in the public perception of the antiquities trade. It brought international attention to the problem of looting and transformed the ethical environment in which the antiquities market operates, with profound implications for the conduct of the trade. Until the 1960s, the market was governed by the principle of laissez-faire. Few people in the West had misgivings about importing, selling, buying, and possessing looted material; in fact, looted objects were not considered stolen. There was also no recognition of the archaeological destruction that was a by-product of the demand for antiquities. If anything, antiquities were considered to be better off in American museums than "rotting away in tropical jungles."[28] The 1970 UNESCO Convention changed all that. It put antiquities on the international agenda as a *problem*, a problem for which art-market countries were in large part responsible. The convention also established that antiquities belonged to the countries where they were found and that those countries were entitled to retain antiquities as part of their cultural heritage. The result was a reversal of market countries' presumption that antiquities could and should move freely across borders.

The implications have been far-reaching. Since the early 1970s, museums in the United States have come under media scrutiny and have been embroiled in embarrassing scandals once their unscrupulous conduct was revealed. Awareness of the ethical concerns involved has made the American public more sympathetic to the claims of source countries and more critical of the art market and its practices. Courts have criminally convicted dealers who traded in looted antiquities. All these developments have cast a shadow over the antiquities trade, putting trade participants under pressure to conform to ethical standards. Anxious to maintain their reputation and avoid criminal sanctions, dealers and museums had to start paying attention to the provenance of antiquities and to verify their legitimacy: willful blindness to antiquities' illegal origin became more difficult to sustain. As a result, disclosure and dissemination of information have increased in this traditionally secretive market. While the illicit trade in antiquities has not yet been eliminated, the raising of the ethical bar has had important effects.

These effects were not the result of government *compliance* with the UNESCO Convention. They would not have occurred, however, without that convention and the light that it shone on looting and on the complicity of art markets. The UNESCO Convention demonstrates how international institutions can raise awareness and bring attention to problems and, in fact, problematize issues that were not seen as problematic before. Institutions sometimes transform the normative landscape and profoundly alter the conduct of non-state actors, even when the behavior of state authorities themselves sees limited change.

## Problematizing Shared Interest

This book's emphasis on absence of shared interest among governments departs from one of the prominent approaches to the study of international cooperation: neoliberal institutionalism. Institutionalists have traditionally assumed that "the possibility of cooperation is present in most modern international issues."[29] They have therefore downplayed the variation in government preferences, taking mutual interest in cooperation as given.[30] Institutionalist analysis has focused on situations of political market failure[31] in which cooperation is obstructed by problems such as informational constraints or incentives to defect. Even when distributional problems have been acknowledged, shared interest constituted the premise of the analysis.[32] The institutionalist literature has examined how international institutions allow governments to establish cooperation that promotes common interests and realizes joint gains.

Yet the international regulatory efforts against illicit trade are not based on shared interests and joint gains: certain governments consider them welfare-diminishing rather than welfare-enhancing. The principal challenge to these efforts is not uncertainty or incentives to cheat on an agreement, but the conflicting preferences of governments. When certain governments face a massive gun or drug problem while other governments support actors who supply these goods, there is little common ground. We risk overlooking this major obstacle—lack of shared interest—if we take the mutual-gains assumption as the premise of our analysis, as the institutionalist literature does. Assuming that cooperation benefits all actors misses the fact that preferences may diverge sharply and that certain governments actually favor a noncooperative outcome. The general theoretical point is that mutual gains and shared interest should be problematized, rather than taken for granted. Analysis of discord should not begin by asking why states failed to capture joint gains. Instead, the starting point should be: Were there any joint gains to be captured? Kenneth Oye made this point in 1985: "When you observe conflict, think Deadlock—the absence of mutual interest—before puzzling over why a mutual interest was not realized."[33] Yet, as Daniel Drezner observes, IR studies often implicitly assume that all participating actors can increase their utility through cooperation.[34] As this book has demonstrated, such an assumption should be avoided.

## The Evolution and Spread of Norms

Various parts of this book are consistent with the constructivist understanding of international norm dynamics and civil society activism. Margaret Keck and Kathryn Sikkink have put forth the boomerang model, in which

NGOs unable to influence their own governments seek international allies to bring pressure to bear on their governments from outside.[35] This dynamic was clearly manifested in the human trafficking case: Israeli NGOs, frustrated with the lack of government responsiveness, brought in the United States and thereby brought about policy change. Overall, this book has emphasized civil society's pressure on governments and its use of information and expertise to influence policy. These are recurring themes in the constructivist literature.[36] Yet the development of international norms against illicit trade conforms only partially to Martha Finnemore and Kathryn Sikkink's influential model of the evolution of norms.[37]

According to Finnemore and Sikkink, the norm life-cycle begins with norm entrepreneurs: individuals or NGOs that are motivated by altruism, empathy, and ideational commitment. These actors attempt to persuade a critical mass of states to embrace new norms. Of the three main cases examined in this book, only human trafficking is consistent with this mechanism of norm emergence. A coalition of evangelical Christians and feminists, motivated by religious sentiments and notions of dignity and equality, convinced the U.S. government to launch an international campaign against the trade in persons. Yet the international control of small arms and antiquities did not originate with nonstate norm entrepreneurs. Rather, the initiative came from self-interested governments. Through international regulation of small arms, African governments sought to curb gun violence, a devastating problem for their societies and a threat to governments themselves. Mexico and Peru initiated the international regulation of antiquities in order to retain archaeological objects of national importance.

The next step in Finnemore and Sikkink's model is a tipping point: the number of states adopting the new norm reaches a critical mass. A norm cascade follows: in the face of international social pressure, additional states subscribe to the norm, as they seek legitimacy, conformity, and esteem. Once again, the human trafficking case comes closest to the model. The norm against human trafficking cascaded and gained wide adherence through coercive social pressure—the intentional tarnishing of governments' reputation—reinforced by economic penalties. This norm cascade, however, was *not* the result of a tipping point. Rather, the United States alone gave a seal of approval to cooperative governments and a stamp of disapproval to noncooperative governments. The United States defined appropriate behavior—minimum standards for the elimination of human trafficking—and pressured governments to conform to these standards.

In the case of antiquities, there is only partial evidence of a legitimacy-driven cascade. The early 1990s should probably have marked a tipping point: approximately 80 countries had already joined the 1970 UNESCO Convention at that time, including the United States, the largest market-country. Nevertheless, other market countries persisted in their rejection of the convention. Britain's decision to accede in 2002 was in part motivated by international social pressures and the desire to conform to widely accepted standards, in line with Finnemore and Sikkink's model. Yet Britain's policy shift also resulted from domestic pressures and self-interest in the protection and return of British cultural objects. Consistent with Finnemore and Sikkink's model, Britain's accession triggered a mini-cascade and encouraged additional market countries to join the convention.

The small-arms norms have failed to cascade. While all member states of the UN have formally endorsed the Program of Action, this document has not generated significant policy changes in countries that favor weak international control of small arms, especially in Asia, the Middle East, and North Africa. Norms on the prevention of bodily harm to vulnerable or innocent populations tend to resonate cross-culturally;[38] norms on small arms that are aimed at stopping the killing and maiming of innocent people should therefore have enjoyed relative success. This, however, has not been the case.

Overall, this experience demonstrates the power and limitations of international social pressure. A large number of countries subscribing to a norm may not, by itself, produce sufficient social pressure to trump powerful noncooperative incentives. However, coercive social pressure by a highly influential actor may indeed influence governments, especially if accompanied by an economic threat. International social pressure reinforced by domestic political pressures and by self-interest may also succeed where social influence alone might fail.

## Trade-Policy Analysis

Agreements to suppress illicit trade are quite different from agreements on trade liberalization. Most obviously, the two types of agreements have opposite goals. Whereas the latter are aimed at lowering trade barriers and facilitating commerce, the former establish controls and restrictions, making trade less free. More fundamentally, the efforts against illicit trade pose a different cooperation problem than does trade liberalization. The lowering of barriers to trade may raise domestic and international controversies; but overall, the premise of trade liberalization is the mutual gains generated by market integration. Mutual gains allow trade-liberalization agreements to be self-enforcing through reciprocity. For that reason, scholars tend to suggest that these agreements enjoy a high degree of compliance.[39] By contrast, agreements to suppress illicit trade do not provide mutual gains and cannot be self-enforced. The main obstacle to cooperation against illicit trade is that certain governments identify only losses from cooperation, whereas trade liberalization is typically characterized by mixed motives: governments identify both gains and losses from lowering barriers to trade. A further distinction is the identity of the targeted actors: trade-liberalization agreements set rules for governments; agreements against illicit trade are aimed at influencing the conduct of governments as well as that of nongovernmental, private actors.

The analysis of illicit trade departs from the study of conventional trade in yet another respect. The literature on the political economy of trade largely focuses on *material* influences, in particular the economic interests of industries and of the public.[40] By contrast, this book's theoretical and empirical accounts have highlighted moral concerns about welfare abroad. Moral concerns have played a growing role in trade policymaking in recent years. Notable examples are the American and European use of preferential trade agreements to promote human rights and the controversy over developing countries' access to affordable AIDS medications. In light of these developments, scholars have begun to explore the relationship between trade and ideational concerns, especially human rights.[41] This book joins the emerging literature on the role of values and moral beliefs in trade politics. In an age when governments increasingly seek to reconcile trade and human rights, trade-policy research can no longer consider only material influences while overlooking ideational ones. The two dimensions—the material and the ideational—shape many of the contemporary debates over trade, and trade-policy analysis should be sensitive to both.

## Environmental Cooperation

Chapter 2 has noted important similarities between international cooperation against illicit trade and international environmental cooperation. Both types of cooperative endeavor seek to mitigate transboundary negative externalities. Both target the commercial actors that generate those externalities. Yet this book's approach to illicit trade—with the focus on domestically shaped government preferences—differs from some of the conventional approaches to environmental cooperation. Studies of international environmental politics often highlight collective-action problems that hinder the provision of public goods.[42] Less attention has been paid to the variation in government preferences on international environmental regulation, and especially the possibility that some governments are entirely opposed to such regulation. An important exception is Detlef Sprinz and Tapani Vaahtoranta's analysis of international environmental policy. In their model, support for international environmental regulation varies across countries as a function of their ecological vulnerability to pollution and the economic costs of pollution abatement. The combination of the two factors creates a fourfold variation in preferences: "pusher" countries favor stringent international regulation; "dragger" countries oppose regulation; and "bystanders" and "intermediates" fall in between.[43] This book's model of international regulation against illicit trade presents a similar fourfold typology of preferences, ranging from strong support for regulation to outright opposition. A key difference between the two models is the origin of preferences. This book has treated the domestic political arena as a critical part of the story: preferences on international regulation are shaped by domestic actors and domestic political considerations. By contrast, Sprinz and Vaahtoranta attribute preferences to country-level factors, without incorporating domestic politics in their model.

The neglect of domestic politics—especially the role of industries—in the study of governments' environmental preferences reflects a broader tendency: mainstream approaches to international environmental governance have generally understated the impact of business on policymaking.[44] As Peter Newell notes: "Despite passing acknowledgement, there is little in the regime literature on the role of business in international environmental politics."[45] A growing body of literature has sought to remedy this gap.[46] Yet business interests and other domestic influences are yet to be integrated into a systematic account of governments' environmental preferences. The model developed in this book could be a starting point. It integrates concerns about the negative externalities borne by the public with the influence of market actors and civil society—a combination typical of environmental politics.

## The Primacy of Governments and Their Regulatory Powers

As Peter Andreas notes, the international political economy literature has focused on the retreat of the regulatory state and the liberalization of the global economy. It has overlooked the reassertion of governments' regulatory powers in certain areas.[47] This book reinforces Andreas's observation by demonstrating that world trade has *not* been moving invariably in one direction: the general trend of growing trade openness has been accompanied by a countertrend of trade regulation. While world trade has overall become more liberalized in recent decades,[48] specific goods have increasingly come under international rules and restrictions. This book is also consistent with Drezner's revisionist argument, according to which "governments remain the primary actors in global economic governance."[49] Drezner's analysis goes against much of the literature on globalization that has downplayed the role of governments while highlighting other forces, such as capital flows and global civil society.[50] Like Drezner's study, this book has shown that governments retain the ultimate power and authority to set international regulatory standards. Domestic and transnational actors may have a say in shaping regulation, but governments are those who aggregate the various influences into a national preference, on the basis of which they negotiate in international forums. In writing rules against illicit trade, as in other areas of international economic regulation, governments are at the helm.

## Policy Implications

### *The Value of Nonglobal Cooperation*

Illicit trade involves a large number of countries, with perpetrators and victims scattered worldwide. Small arms are exported by some 30 countries, such as China, Pakistan, Israel, and the United States; the illicit arms trade most affects sub-Saharan Africa and Latin America. Developing countries, such as Guatemala, Mali, and Cambodia have seen their antiquities plundered and illegally exported; the principal beneficiaries of this trade have been the United States, Western Europe, and Japan. The drug market is also global in nature, as is the market for counterfeit goods. Governments that seek to suppress illicit trade thus typically pursue global initiatives. A set of global rules, mutually agreed upon by all countries, is more efficient than a large set of bilateral agreements between individual victims and perpetrators. Given that victims and perpetrators are often in different regions, a global agreement is also preferable to agreements of regional scope. But bringing together victims and perpetrators in a global endeavor has a downside: a large variation in government preferences could render the regulatory agreement weak, especially when the distribution of power favors regulation opponents. When this is the case, nonglobal cooperation between governments with homogenous preferences—intraregionally or interregionally—may be an alternative.

The case of small arms demonstrates this point. While the UN small-arms process has established a weak global regulatory framework, African governments have made progress in stemming gun violence through several regional and subregional agreements.[51] Assistance from donor countries to governments in Africa and elsewhere has facilitated various measures, such as the implementation of gun legislation and weapons destruction. These limited initiatives do not fully compensate for the weakness of global cooperation and the unwillingness of arms-exporting countries to establish proper controls, but they certainly help alleviate a severe problem. When global cooperation is thwarted by conflicting government preferences, smaller-scale collaboration among like-minded governments offers a second-best, yet viable option.

## Civil Society Advocacy

This book has examined several civil society campaigns against illicit trade: American and British archaeologists urged their respective governments to curb the trade in looted antiquities; a coalition of feminists and evangelical Christians initiated the American efforts against human trafficking worldwide. This experience suggests several lessons and insights for successful advocacy—insights that reinforce existing scholarly notions of civil society and its impact on world politics.[52] First and foremost, the provision of information is an essential tool for shaping the policy agenda and policy outcomes. To maximize the impact on policymakers, activists need to use information strategically:

- The information should be as detailed and specific as possible. Specificity draws attention, dramatizes the problem, and makes it difficult for policymakers to dismiss the issue. Detailed information is more likely to convince policymakers that the problem is grave and must be addressed. Clemency Coggins's 1969 article was groundbreaking in its highly detailed documentation of looting. This was among the reasons for the article's policy impact.
- The information should convey the nature and magnitude of the problem in clear, concrete, and emphatic terms. Means such as pictures and victim testimonies may help. It should not be assumed that the problem speaks for itself; the reasons for tackling it must be spelled out and explained. When the 1970 UNESCO Convention came before Congress, legislators were not aware of the widespread looting caused by the illicit trade in antiquities; it was archaeologists who informed them about the dire consequences of the trade. Victims' testimonies educated members of Congress about sex trafficking and helped convince them that the United States should act to eliminate this practice.
- The information should identify the culprits—the actors who contribute to and benefit from the problem—and dispel the notion that existing reality is natural or immutable. Identification of those responsible also creates a sense of indignation that can motivate action. Coggins's 1969 article revealed how American museums benefited from looting, and policymakers found it difficult to remain indifferent.
- The issue should be framed in a way that resonates with policymakers' beliefs, values, and sense of social responsibility. By labeling the campaign against human trafficking "abolitionist," the evangelical-feminist coalition evoked strong emotions in policymakers and enhanced their receptiveness to the coalition's goals.
- An effective campaign advances specific policy proposals and explains how they would address the problem effectively. Activists should convince policymakers that solving the problem is within reach, and that the solution is

in the policymakers' own hands. The consequences of inaction should be emphasized. American archaeologists employed this last tactic during the congressional debate on the UNESCO Convention. To put pressure on legislators, they argued that the stalled debate allowed looting to continue to thrive.

The provision of information is a powerful tool, but activists may also appeal to policymakers' electoral considerations and public-image concerns. The evangelical-feminist coalition successfully exploited these concerns to press policymakers for action against human trafficking. The coalition sought to demonstrate the broad public support for its cause, promised that public opinion would reward policymakers for acting to curb human trafficking, and threatened that inaction would arouse widespread anger. Both the promise and threat were credible, since the coalition encompassed groups from across the political spectrum, including the large evangelical constituency. Yet even the British archaeologists, electorally insignificant, took advantage of policymakers' responsiveness to the public climate. The growing public concern about the practices of the London art market made the government more responsive to the archaeologists' pleas. These episodes suggest that policymakers are more attentive if they believe that the advocacy group holds sway over public opinion or that its goals enjoy popular support.

Another lesson from the antiquities case is that public scandals provide a political opportunity and can help activists promote their cause. Scandals cause shock and anger that activists can build on to transform the public's and policymakers' perceptions and induce a policy change.[53]

## Domestic Consultation to Facilitate Cooperation

Consultative mechanisms may help to resolve domestic controversies over international cooperation. Both the U.S. government in 1969 and the British government in 2000 wished to join the international efforts against the illicit antiquities trade in the face of resistance from influential domestic actors. In both cases, the means of bringing those actors on board was an advisory panel representing all relevant stakeholders: the ASIL Panel in the United States and the Illicit Trade Advisory Panel in Britain. By convening these panels, the two governments sent a dual message: we intend to join the international efforts, but would like to do so while minimizing the adverse consequences to domestic constituencies. This message forced domestic actors to compromise. Pro-cooperation actors realized that their wish for decisive, enthusiastic government action would not be fulfilled. Actors opposed to cooperation accepted that they could not altogether prevent the government from joining the cooperative efforts. All actors saw it as being in their interest to mutually agree upon a course of action and recommend it to the government. The ASIL Panel and the Illicit Trade Advisory Panel can serve as useful models for governments that face domestic opposition over treaty ratification and implementation.

## Conclusion

This book has examined the international response to some of the most pressing policy challenges of the 21st century. How can we prevent rebels, criminals, and terrorists from obtaining guns and using them to wreak havoc? How can we eliminate the exploitation and abuse of human-trafficking victims? How can we preserve our cultural heritage that is under constant threat of plunder? International regulatory agreements are far from a fully satisfactory solution. International regulation shifts the burden of addressing these problems to governments that have little desire to do so. It asks them to compromise their own interests and those of domestic constituencies for the sake of helping foreign countries. Even international cooperation that builds on shared interest may be ineffective; cooperative endeavors that lack the cornerstone of common interest hardly constitute a panacea.

And yet, the Israeli experience with human trafficking demonstrates that coercion can induce cooperation and that indifference to illicit trade may be replaced, under pressure, with vigorous action. The antiquities case shows that intransigent governments—even the most powerful ones—can become more cooperative over time and reverse long-held practices that abetted illicit trade. Furthermore, the same case shows that campaigns against illicit trade can transform the normative environment. Prior to the 1970 UNESCO Convention, the trade in plundered objects and their possession and display had been uncontroversial—indeed, a respectable tradition. Today, dealers and museums involved with looted antiquities are deemed complicit in the theft and destruction of archaeology. All this does not mean, of course, that the eradication of illicit trade is within easy reach. Small arms, human trafficking, drugs, antiquities, and other illicit trades present enormously complex challenges that will continue to occupy the policy agenda in years to come. This book does suggest, however, that there is room for cautious optimism.

# NOTES

*Chapter 1*

1. Two works mark the beginning of the modern study of international cooperation: an edited volume on international regimes (Krasner 1983) and Robert Keohane's *After Hegemony* (Keohane 1984). Some notable contributions to the vast literature on international cooperation and institutions include: Dai 2007; Davis 2004; Drezner 2007; Fearon 1998; Goldstein et al. 2001; Hawkins et al. 2006; Koremenos, Lipson, and Snidal 2001; Krasner 1991; Martin 1992a; Milner 1997; Snidal 1985; Thompson 2009.

2. Nadelmann 1990.

3. See, for example, Berdal and Serrano 2002; Friman 2009a; Friman and Andreas 1999a; Kyle and Koslowski 2001; Naím 2005; van Schendel and Abraham 2005; Williams 1999.

4. Naím 2005, chap. 11; Williams 2001, 112–113.

5. See Andreas 2004, 642–643; Friman and Andreas 1999b, 5–6.

6. Most notably, the 1841 Treaty of London for the Suppression of the African Slave Trade, the 1862 Treaty between the United States and Great Britain for the Suppression of the Slave Trade, and the General Act of the Brussels Conference of 1890.

7. International Agreement for the Suppression of the White Slave Traffic, 1904; International Opium Convention, 1912.

8. Andreas 2002; Raustiala 1999, 117–121.

9. UNODC 2010a, 31–32.

10. See, for example, Koremenos 2005; Simmons 2010.

11. See, for example, Goldstein, Rivers, and Tomz 2007 and Rosendorff and Milner 2001 (trade); Morrow 2007 and Valentino, Huth, and Croco 2006 (the laws of war); Moravcsik 2000 and Simmons 2009 (human rights); Barrett 2003 and Mitchell 1994 (the environment).

12. Garcia 2006.

13. Simmons 2001.

14. Agreement on Trade-Related Aspects of Intellectual Property Rights.

15. Sell 2003.

16. Clapp 2001.

17. Nadelmann 1990.

18. Andreas and Nadelmann 2006, 20–21; Nadelmann 1990, 484–486.

19. Andreas and Nadelmann 2006, 22, 228–229; Nadelmann 1990, 486.

20. Andreas and Nadelmann 2006, 21; Nadelmann 1990, 485.

21. Jojarth 2009, 14.

22. Ibid., 60, 71, 279–285.

23. Ibid., 286.

24. Single Convention on Narcotic Drugs, 1961, Article 9(4).

25. Moravcsik 1997, 2008, and 2010.

26. Drezner 2007, 6, 39–40; Moravcsik 1997, 544.

27. Moravcsik 1997, 541–547.

28. United Nations Conference to Review Progress Made in the Implementation of the Program of Action to Prevent, Combat and Eradicate the Illicit Trade in Small Arms and Light Weapons in All Its Aspects, New York, June 26–July 7, 2006.

*Chapter 2*

1. Cukier and Sidel 2006, chap. 2; Small Arms Survey 2004, chap. 6; Small Arms Survey 2005, chap. 9; Small Arms Survey 2006, chap. 8.

2. UNDCP 1997.

3. le Billon 2001; Lujala, Gleditsch, and Gilmore 2005.

4. Brodie, Doole, and Renfew 2001; Brodie and Tubb 2002.

5. Cukier and Sidel 2006, 139–152.

6. Prott and O'Keefe 1988.

7. Raustiala 1999, 118–121; Andreas 2002, 41–42.

8. Cukier and Sidel 2006, chap. 6; Small Arms Survey 2006, chap. 6.

9. Mitchell and Keilbach 2001, 891–896. See also Mitchell 2010, 33–34.

10. Yandle 1983, 1984, and 1999.

11. DeSombre 2000, 39–47. See also Hafner-Burton 2009, 14–15, 25–26.

12. Simmons 2010, 286.

13. Naím 2005, 13.

14. Ibid., 6.

15. Small Arms Survey 2002, 128–129; Small Arms Survey 2008, chaps. 2 and 4.

16. Program of Action to Prevent, Combat and Eradicate the Illicit Trade in Small Arms and Light Weapons in All Its Aspects (UN Doc. A/CONF.192/15), Section II, Article 11.

17. Small Arms Survey 2008, 127–131.

18. The Forty Recommendations (as revised in 2003), Recommendations 5, 10, and 11. For the text, see Financial Action Task Force 2010.

19. The Forty Recommendations, Recommendation 23.

20. An example of independent participation is the representation of the diamond industry in the Kimberley Process by the World Diamond Council. Kantz 2007.

21. Moravcsik 1997, 516–520 and 2010.

22. Moravcsik 1997, 525–528.

23. Moravcsik 1997, 528–530.

24. On theory synthesis and analytic eclecticism see Andreas and Nadelmann 2006, 7–8; Moravcsik 2003; Sil and Katzenstein 2010.

25. Moravcsik 1997, 541–547.

26. See Grossman and Helpman 2001.

27. Moravcsik 1998, 23.

28. Ibid., 22.

29. For example, H. Richard Friman argues that "the Japanese have participated in bilateral and multilateral drug control efforts through a wide range of different ministries whose objectives often compete." Friman 1996, 68.

30. Andreas and Nadelmann 2006, 41; Musto 1999, 294–295.

31. Friman 2009b, 59–60; Mares 2006, 76.

32. David Lumsdaine's account of foreign aid emphasizes the public's interest in alleviating poverty overseas. Gary Bass links 19th century humanitarian intervention to the horrified reaction of publics in the West to atrocities abroad. Lumsdaine 1993; Bass 2008.

33. Grant and Taylor 2004, 390–391.

34. See Sell and Prakash 2004, 147–150 (arguing that NGOs have both instrumental goals and normative concerns).

35. See, for example, Kaufmann and Pape 1999.

36. See Price 1998, 621–623.

37. Grant and Taylor 2004, 390–393. Two publications by the NGO Global Witness played an important part in the campaign: *A Rough Trade: The Role of Companies and Governments in the Angolan Conflict* (1998) and *Conflict Diamonds: Possibilities for the Identification, Certification and Control of Diamonds* (2000).

38. Becker, Murphy, and Grossman 2006, 44.

39. See, for example, Wyler and Cook 2009, 23–24.

40. Reno 2009.

41. Mertha 2005, 155–156; Serrano 2009, 145.

42. Jojarth 2009, 149–150.

43. Helleiner 1999, 59, 74.

44. On the benefits of regulation for businesses see generally Stigler 1971.

45. DeSombre 2000, 34–36.

46. Drezner 2007, 43–45.

47. Gillies 2010, 113.

48. Haufler 2001, 26–27 and 2002, 170–171; Vogel 2008, 268.

49. Bernhagen 2008, 83; DeSombre 2000, 39, 44–45.

50. Barton et al. 2006, 30–31.

51. On lobbying, see Grossman and Helpman 2001.

52. Bernhagen 2008, 84–85.

53. This literature typically claims that consumers prefer free trade, which allows them to enjoy cheap imports and raises their real incomes. However, consumers do not shape trade policy through lobbying. The costs of protectionism are diffuse, and the severity of the collective action problem

facing consumers makes their lobbying efforts negligible compared to industries demanding protection. Oatley 2008, 82–83.

54. Inciardi 1999; McBride, Terry, and Inciardi 1999.

55. A notable example is the Drug Policy Alliance, an organization "promoting alternatives to the drug war that are grounded in science, compassion, health and human rights." http://www.drugpolicy.org (accessed May 11, 2011).

56. Martin 1992b, 25.

57. The international political conflict over antiquities is examined in Chapter 4, pp. 120–127.

58. Mitchell and Keilbach 2001, 902.

59. Simmons 2009, 116–117 and 2010, 275–276.

60. Simmons 2009, 123–125.

61. Dai 2007, chap. 4; Simmons 2009, 135–148.

62. Mitchell and Keilbach 2001, 896.

63. DeSombre 2000, 163–165; Martin 1992b, 56.

64. See, for example, Bewley-Taylor 2001, 203 (arguing that Colombia's economy suffered in 1997 after the country was declared by the United States to have made insufficient efforts against drug traffickers). See also Lebovic and Voeten 2006, 868 and 2009; Simmons 2000a.

65. Johnston 2001, 499–502.

66. Friman 2009b, 53–55.

67. Lebovic and Voeten 2009, 81–82; Simmons 2009, 122–123.

68. See Raustiala 1999, 111–112.

69. Thompson 2009, 27–31.

70. See Hafner-Burton 2008 (demonstrating the limited effectiveness of naming and shaming by NGOs as a means of exerting pressure on human rights violators).

71. Davis 2004, 156.

72. U.S. Department of State 2001.

73. Hafner-Burton 2005, 600–602.

74. Lake and Powell 1999, 14, 25.

Chapter 3

1. Annan 2000, 52.

2. Convention for the Control of the Trade in Arms and Ammunition, and Protocol. Signed at Saint-Germain-en-Laye, September 10, 1919.

3. Saint-Germain Convention, Article 1.

4. Stone 2000, 217–218.

5. Engelbrecht and Hanighen 1934, 268.

6. Stone 2000, 219–220.

7. The Saint-Germain Convention was not a League of Nations initiative, but the League took up the cause of promoting the convention. The League was also supposed to play a role in the convention's operation.

8. Stone 2000, 222–223.

9. Quoted in Stone 2000, 223–224.

10. Stone 2000, 229–230.

11. The Geneva Convention established five categories of arms: (1) arms for warfare (including, among others, rifles, cannons, and tanks); (2) arms for both military and other use; (3) vessels of war and their armament; (4) aircrafts; and (5) gunpowder and explosives.

12. Small Arms Survey 2007, 39.

13. Small Arms Survey 2004, 7.

14. UN Commodity Trade Statistics Database.

15. Small Arms Survey 2006, chap. 3 and 2009, chap. 1. The value of the small-arms trade is modest compared with the trade in major conventional weapons, which is estimated at $39–56 billion (2005 data). SIPRI 2007, 389.

16. Small Arms Survey 2005, 117 and 2006, 88.

17. The value of the global illicit drug market in 2003 was estimated at $94 billion at the wholesale level and $322 billion based on retail prices. UNODC 2005, 1:127.

18. Small Arms Survey 2005, 230.

19. Geneva Declaration Secretariat 2008, 15, 42.

20. Geneva Declaration Secretariat 2008, chap. 3.

21. Geneva Declaration Secretariat 2008, 75; Small Arms Survey 2004, 174–175, 200; UNODC 2011, 39.

22. Report of the Secretary-General to the Security Council on the subject of small arms (S/2008/258), April 17, 2008, 2–3.

23. Cukier and Sidel 2006, 28–31; Small Arms Survey 2006, chap. 8.

24. Small Arms Survey 2003, chap. 4.

25. Yankey-Wayne 2006, 83–84.

26. UN General Assembly Resolution 49/75 G, Assistance to States for curbing the illicit traffic in small arms and collecting them, December 15, 1994.

27. Boutros-Ghali 1995, para. 63.

28. UN General Assembly Resolution 50/70 B, December 12, 1995.

29. Report of the Panel of Governmental Experts on Small Arms, UN Doc. A/52/298, Annex, August 27, 1997, paras. 58–61.

30. Ibid., paras. 79–80.

31. UN General Assembly Resolution 52/38 J, December 9, 1997.

32. Report of the Group of Governmental Experts on Small Arms, UN Doc. A/54/258, August 19, 1999.

33. UN General Assembly Resolution 53/77 E, December 4, 1998.

34. Declaration of a Moratorium on Importation, Exportation and Manufacture of Light Weapons in West Africa, adopted by the Economic Community of West African States (ECOWAS).

35. Nairobi Declaration on the Problem of the Proliferation of Illicit Small Arms and Light Weapons in the Great Lakes Region and the Horn of Africa.

36. Declaration concerning Firearms, Ammunition and Other Related Materials in the Southern African Development Community; Protocol on the Control of Firearms, Ammunition and Other Related Materials in the Southern African Development Community (SADC) Region.

37. Bamako Declaration on an African Common Position on the Illicit Proliferation, Circulation and Trafficking of Small Arms and Light Weapons.

38. Inter-American Convention against the Illicit Manufacturing of and Trafficking in Firearms, Ammunition, Explosives, and Other Related Materials.

39. EU Program for Preventing and Combating Illicit Trafficking in Conventional Arms.

40. Legal Framework for a Common Approach to Weapons Control Measures (Nadi Framework).

41. Biting the Bullet 2006, 3; Krause 2002, 248; Rogers 2009, 117.

42. United Nations Conference on the Illicit Trade in Small Arms and Light Weapons in All Its Aspects, New York, July 9–20, 2006.

43. International Instrument to Enable States to Identify and Trace, in a Timely and Reliable Manner, Illicit Small Arms and Light Weapons.

44. Program of Action, Section II, para. 33.

45. Program of Action, Section I, para. 5.

46. Geneva Declaration Secretariat 2008, 2–5.

47. Crowley, Isbister, and Meek 2002.

48. World Bank 1995.

49. Shleifer 1998; Shleifer and Vishny 1998, chap. 9.

50. Pierre 1982, 3. Emphasis in the original.

51. Pierre 1982; Krause 1991.

52. Byman and Cliff 1999; Klieman 1992.

53. Bueno de Mesquita et al. 2003; Lai and Morey 2006, 388–389.

54. See, for example, Poe, Tate, and Keith 1999; Regan and Henderson 2002; Davenport and Armstrong 2004.

55. Lai and Morey 2006, 389–390.

56. Elkins, Guzman, and Simmons 2006; Simmons 2009, chap. 3.

57. Geneva Declaration Secretariat 2008, 67, 75; UNODC 2011, 39.

58. The Source is UNODC International Homicide Statistics, available at http://www.unodc.org/documents/data-and-analysis/IHS-rates-05012009.pdf (accessed January 22, 2012). For most countries, the UNODC's dataset provides two estimates: one based on criminal justice sources and another based on public health sources. When this is the case, I use an average of the two figures.

59. The source is United Nations Surveys of Crime Trends and Operations of Criminal Justice Systems; and Cukier and Sidel 2006.

60. The source is IMF World Economic Outlook Database 2011.

61. The source is OECD Statistics.

62. Small Arms Survey 2006 and the NISAT database of small-arms transfers were used to identify countries that export small arms worth at least $10 million annually (based on 2003 sales date). Data on the ownership of the small-arms industry are from Butterworth-Hayes 2004, Kiss 2004, Saferworld 2002, and Weidacher 2005.

63. The source is Polity IVd.

64. The source is La Porta et al. 1999.

65. The value of small-arms exports in 2003 is from *Small Arms Survey* 2006; the value of total exports in 2003 is from WTO Trade Statistics.

66. The number of international organizations in which a country was a member in 2000, Correlates of War data.

67. Small Arms Survey 2007, 47.

68. Erickson 2008.

69. Cooper 2000.

70. LaPierre 2006. On the NRA's involvement in the UN small-arms process, see Bob 2010; Rogers 2009, 182–184. NRA board members participated in the official American delegations to the UN small-arms conferences in 2001 and 2006.

71. The American preference for weak international regulation was not the result of industry opposition, as American arms manufacturers are not heavily dependent on exports. Furthermore, the United States already operates an advanced system of export controls; international controls would have imposed only limited costs on the industry. Erickson 2010.

72. On the American ambivalence toward arms control see Tannenwald 2001, 54–58.

73. Statement by Senegal during the General Debate of the First Committee, 55th Session of the UN General Assembly, October 4, 2000.

74. Statement by Colombia during the UN Conference on the Illicit Trade in Small Arms and Light Weapons in All Its Aspects, July 9, 2001.

75. Statement by Canada at the First Preparatory Committee for the UN Conference on the Illicit Trade in Small Arms and Light Weapons in All Its Aspects, February 28, 2000.

76. Statement by China at the First Preparatory Committee for the UN Conference on the Illicit Trade in Small Arms and Light Weapons in All Its Aspects, February 29, 2000; Statement by Pakistan at the First Preparatory Committee for the UN Conference on the Illicit Trade in Small Arms and Light Weapons in All Its Aspects, March 1, 2000.

77. Statement by Egypt during the UN Conference on the Illicit Trade in Small Arms and Light Weapons in All Its Aspects, July 10, 2001.

78. Statement by Belarus at the Second Preparatory Committee for the UN Conference on the Illicit Trade in Small Arms and Light Weapons in All Its Aspects, January 11, 2001.

79. Statement by Syria during the UN Conference on the Illicit Trade in Small Arms and Light Weapons in All Its Aspects, July 11, 2001.

80. Statement by the United States during the UN Conference on the Illicit Trade in Small Arms and Light Weapons in All Its Aspects, July 9, 2001.

81. For example, The Nairobi Protocol for the Prevention, Control and Reduction of Small Arms and Light Weapons in the Great Lakes Region and the Horn of Africa, signed 2004.

82. Program of Action, Section II, paras. 24–31.

83. Biting the Bullet 2006, 28; Kytömäki 2006.

84. UN General Assembly Resolution 61/89, Towards an Arms Trade Treaty: Establishing Common International Standards for the Import, Export and Transfer of Conventional Arms, December 6, 2006.

85. Program of Action, Section II, para. 2.

86. Cattaneo and Parker 2008.

87. Biennial meetings of states (BMS) were held in 2003, 2005, 2008, and 2010. The BMS are generally low-level meetings and do not serve as a forum for major negotiations.

88. Biting the Bullet 2006.

89. See note 43.

90. UN Doc. A/62/163, August 30, 2007.

91. Axelrod 1984, 181; Downs and Rocke 1987.

92. On the controversies that surrounded the establishment of the NPT, see Koremenos 2001, 305–308.

93. Marking arms at the time of import was a major point of contention during the negotiations of the International Tracing Instrument. The instrument ultimately included a strong recommendation to mark at import, but not an obligation.

94. Parker 2011, 15–20.

95. Krause 2002, 256–259; Laurance and Stohl 2002, 4; Rogers 2009, 184–188.

96. See Price 1998.

97. Bob 2010.

98. Engelbrecht and Hanighen 1934, 269. Emphasis in the original.

*Chapter 4*

1. Brodie and Doole 2001, 1.

2. Brodie 2002a, 1.

3. Elia 2009, 250; Prott 1995, 57. Also discarded and destroyed are mundane objects or fragmentary pieces that are not marketable, yet may carry archaeological value.

4. Tubb and Brodie 2001, 105.

5. Bauer 2008, 701–702.

6. Renfrew 2000, 19. Emphasis in the original.

7. Brodie, Doole, and Watson 2000, 10–11; Chippindale et al. 2001, 4–8; Gerstenblith 2001, 198–199; Gerstenblith 2007, 170–172; Gill and Chippindale 1993; Renfrew 2000, 19–20.

8. Alva 2001; Askerud and Clément 1997; Gado 2001; Gilgan 2001. Among nondeveloping countries, Italy and Greece are notable victims of looting. Elia 2001; Marthari 2001.

9. Brodie 2006a, 52–53; Chippindale and Gill 2000; Elia 2009, 240; Gerstenblith 2007, 178.

10. Tubb and Brodie 2001, 106.

11. Ibid., 110; Mackenzie 2005, 47–50.

12. Brodie 2002a, 2; Brodie, Doole, and Watson 2000, 29; Brodie and Renfrew 2005, 353.

13. Ede 1995, 211. See also Mackenzie 2005, 35.

14. Ede 1998, 129.

15. Ibid., 130; Elia 2009, 244–248 (rejecting the old collection and chance find arguments as myths); Gill and Chippindale 2006, 313–314 (arguing that "old collections" may be a front for looted objects); Mackenzie 2005, 52–55.

16. Elia 2009, 241. See also Bauer 2008, 698.

17. Renfrew 2000, 16.

18. Brodie 2006b, 10–11; Renfrew 2006, 246.

19. Brodie, Doole, and Watson 2000, 25.

20. Holowell 2006; Matsuda 1998.

21. It has been estimated, for example, that looters in the Petén region of Central America received \$200–\$500 each for objects that might ultimately sell for \$100,000. Brodie, Doole, and Watson 2000, 13. See also Alva 2001, 93; Borodkin 1995, 378.

22. For example, in the very poor village of Ghor es-Safi, Jordan, an entire community participated in robbing the remains of the ancient city of Zoar. Politis 2002, 257–259.

23. Borodkin 1995, 391–393; Gerstenblith 2001, 212–213.

24. For examples of antiquities legislation, see Prott and O'Keefe 1988.

25. Alva 2001, 95; Özgen 2001, 119; Prott 1995, 58.

26. Some transit markets are in geographically advantaged states, which traders and smugglers inevitably pass through because of their proximity to the source country or their regional-hub role (e.g., antiquities looted from Cambodia are brought to Hong Kong; loot from the Palestinian Territories goes through Israel). The second type of transit market is the art-market state that offers auctions, art fairs, and services such as valuation and restoration. Notable examples are Britain, Belgium, Germany, and Switzerland. Kersel 2006, 191–192; Prott and O'Keefe 1989, 532–535.

27. Kersel 2006, 189–193.

28. The UNESCO Convention addresses the illicit trade in cultural property. Article 1 defines "cultural property" in very broad terms that include a range of objects beyond antiquities, yet antiquities have been at the heart of the convention.

29. Jote 1994, 193.

30. O'Keefe 2000, 9–10, 14.

31. Abramson and Huttler 1973, 933–934; Askerud and Clément 1997, 9; Jote 1994, 196.

32. UNESCO Doc. 11 C/DR/186, December 1, 1960.

33. Records of the General Conference of UNESCO, Eleventh Session, Paris, 1960, Resolution 4.412(d).

34. UNESCO/CUA/115, April 14, 1962, 10.

35. UNESCO/CUA/115, 3. Another indication was the reluctance of many countries to ratify the Protocol to the Convention for the Protection of Cultural Property in the Event of Armed Conflict, 1954.

36. UNESCO Doc. 12 C/PRG/10, July 27, 1962, Annex II, 1.

37. Records of the General Conference of UNESCO, Twelfth Session, Paris, 1962, Resolution 4.413; UNESCO/CUA/123, July 15, 1963, 6.

38. UNESCO/CUA/123, Annex, 14.

39. UNESCO/CUA/123 Add. I, March 21, 1964, Annex I, 17.

40. Ibid., 22.

41. Ibid., 15–16.

42. Ibid., 23–24.

43. UNESCO Doc. 15 C/15, August 22, 1968, Annex, 11.

44. The text of the preliminary draft convention is in UNESCO Doc. SHC/MD/3,August 8, 1969, Annex. The text was drafted by a principal expert and four consultants from various parts of the world.

45. UNESCO Doc. SHC/MD/5, February 27, 1970, Annex I, 3.

46. Ibid., 12.

47. Ibid., 16.

48. UNESCO Doc. SHC/MD/5 Add. 1, April 10, 1970, 7.

49. UNESCO Doc. SHC/MD/5 Add. 2, April 22, 1970, 3.

50. UNESCO Doc. SHC/MD/5, Annex I, 21.

51. Ibid.

52. Ibid., 21–23.

53. UNESCO Doc. 20 C/84, September 15, 1978, 11, 34–35, 42; UNESCO Doc. 22 C/93, August 30, 1983, 3–4.

54. UNESCO Doc. 20 C/84, 12, 35.

55. UNESCO Doc. 22 C/93, 3.

56. UNESCO Doc. 20 C/84, 42.

57. Ibid., 44–45.

58. UNESCO Doc. 22 C/93, 3–4.

59. Prott and O'Keefe 1983, 60.

60. Ibid., 123.

61. Ibid., 123–129.

62. UK House of Commons 2000, III:339–340.

63. UNIDROIT 1996, 68.

64. UNIDROIT 1996, 77.

65. Spiegler and Kaye 2001, 128.

66. Author's interview with lawyer James Fitzpatrick, Washington, D.C., May 2008. Fitzpatrick has represented antiquities dealers since the mid-1970s.

67. Spiegler and Kaye 2001, 128.

68. Ibid.; Prott 1997, 13.

69. Meyer 1973, 12–14.

70. Coggins 1969, 94.

71. Bator 1983, 4.

72. Author's interview with Clemency Coggins, Boston, June 2008. At the time of writing, Coggins is a professor of archaeology and art history at Boston University.

73. Bator 1983, 2.

74. Ibid., 2–4. At the insistence of *Art Journal,* Coggins's original article did not identify the museums by name, but referred to them as "American museums." Coggins named the museums in a list published in 1970. See that list in Meyer 1973, 213–218.

75. Bator 1983, 4.

76. Coggins, interview.

77. Coggins 1970; Coggins 1972.

78. Coggins 1970, 10–14; Coggins 1972, 264.

79. Bator 1983, 4–5 footnote 12; Meyer 1973, 86–100.

80. Elisabetta Povoledo, "Ancient Vase Comes Home to a Hero's Welcome," *New York Times*, January 19, 2008.

81. Bator 1983, 4 fn 11; Meyer 1973, 102–106.

82. Bator 1983, 5 fn 13; Meyer 1973, 144–145.

83. See, for example, a series of *New York Times* articles by journalist Robert Reinhold on the theft of Mayan archaeology: "Looters Impede Scholars Studying Maya Mystery," *New York Times*, March 26, 1973; "Traffic in Looted Maya Art is Diverse and Profitable," *New York Times*, March 27, 1973; "Elusive Maya Glyphs Yielding to Modern Technique," *New York Times*, March 28, 1973.

84. Meyer 1973, xi.

85. Ibid., 123–124.

86. U.S. Senate 1970, III; U.S. Senate 1971, I.

87. Author's interview with Mark Feldman, Washington, D.C., May 2008; U.S. Senate 1971, 2, 5. Mexico assisted with the return of stolen cars to the United States pursuant to the 1936 U.S.-Mexico Convention for the Recovery and Return of Stolen or Embezzled Motor Vehicles, Trailers, Airplanes or Component Parts of Any of Them.

88. Author's correspondence with Mark Feldman, December 2008.

89. Feldman, interview.

90. Treaty of Cooperation between the United States of America and the United Mexican States Providing for the Recovery and Return of Stolen Archaeological, Historical and Cultural Properties, 1970.

91. U.S. Senate 1971, 3–4.

92. Feldman, interview. The treaty authorized the U.S. Attorney General, upon Mexican request, to institute a civil action in a federal court to recover and return pre-Columbian and colonial objects of outstanding importance as well as significant historical documents.

93. Bator 1983, 6 fn 16.

94. Feldman, interview.

95. Feldman and Bettauer 1970, 2.

96. Bator 1983, 95–97. The Secretariat Draft is in UNESCO Doc. SHC/MD/5, Annex III. This was a revised version of the preliminary draft convention discussed earlier.

97. Feldman and Bettauer 1970, 3, 41–42.

98. Another principle that guided the U.S. delegation was nonretroactivity. This was of particular importance to American museums concerned about a possible threat to their existing collections. The third goal was to bring source countries to strengthen their own protection of cultural heritage and to liberalize antiquities export policy (for example, through exchanges with museums). Feldman, interview; DuBoff et al. 1976, 113–115; U.S. Senate 1978, 17–18.

99. Bator 1983, 97–99.

100. Feldman and Bettauer 1970, 4–6.

101. Bator 1983, 68.

102. Feldman, interview.

103. U.S. Senate 1972a, V, XI–XIII. See also U.S. Senate 1972b, 11. Mark Feldman confirms that while U.S. relations with the hemisphere were indeed a concern, the main issue was the extent of archaeological depredation and the desire to respond to what was seen as a real problem abroad. Feldman, interview.

104. DuBoff et al. 1976, 112, 115; U.S. House 1979, 6; U.S. Senate 1978, 19.

105. U.S. Senate 1972a, XII.

106. U.S. Senate 1972a, VI. The State Department report included Article 7(a) among the convention's important provisions, but made clear that "this provision would apply primarily to institutions controlled by the Federal Government." Ibid. See also U.S. Senate 1972b, 11–12.

107. Bator 1983, 94–95.

108. Bator 1983, 101–102.

109. O'Keefe 2000, 41 (referring to Article 2 of the 1970 UNESCO Convention).

110. See the reservation and understandings in U.S. Senate 1972b, 9.

111. Bator 1983, 6 fn 16, 96; *Congressional Record* 1970, 20366 (June 18); Feldman and Bettauer 1970, 2–3; U.S. Senate 1972a, XII.

112. U.S. Senate 1978, 17.

113. DuBoff et al. 1976, 111; U.S. House 1977a, 42.

114. Resolution adopted by the Council of the Archaeological Institute of America at its meeting of December 30, 1970. Reprinted in DuBoff 1975, 569.

115. The Society for American Archaeology and the American Anthropological Association joined the AIA in actively supporting the UNESCO Convention.

116. U.S. House 1976, 53–54, 65; U.S. Senate 1978, 60–61, 68–69.

117. U.S. House 1977a, 132.

118. U.S. House 1979, 31, 34.

119. U.S. House 1977a, 87, 97; U.S. House 1979, 31.

120. U.S. House 1977a, 111; U.S. House 1979, 32.

121. U.S. Senate 1978, 61.

122. Ibid., 61, 72, 75.

123. Ibid., 61, 68–69.

124. U.S. House 1979, 30.

125. Letter from Clemency Coggins to Senator Abraham Ribicoff, February 27, 1978 (Clemency Coggins's files).

126. Ibid.

127. Letter from Clemency Coggins to Senator Ribicoff, November 27, 1978 (Clemency Coggins's files).

128. Author's interview with Clemency Coggins, Boston, May 2008.

129. July 1982 Public Action Alert by the Archaeological Institute of America (Clemency Coggins's files).

130. Letter from Clemency Coggins to Robert E. Lighthizer, Chief Counsel, Senate Finance Committee, July 31, 1982 (Clemency Coggins's files).

131. U.S. House 1976, 18.

132. U.S. House 1977a, 31, 42.

133. U.S. House 1976, 18, 21; U.S. House 1977a, 31–32.

134. U.S. House 1976, 22; U.S. House 1977a, 33.

135. DuBoff et al. 1976, 111; U.S. Senate 1978, 55.

136. U.S. House 1976, 20; U.S. House 1977a, 31, 34, 44.

137. U.S. House 1977a, 41, 44–45, 114; U.S. Senate 1978, 50–51.

138. U.S. Senate 1978, 50.

139. Author's interview with James Fitzpatrick, Washington D.C., May 2008.

140. Fitzpatrick, interview.

141. The dealers also proposed to involve Congress in the imposition of import restrictions, by establishing import controls through congressional legislation on a case-by-case basis; by submitting agreements with source countries to Senate ratification; or by allowing either the House or the Senate to veto import restrictions before they go into effect. U.S. House 1976, 22–23; U.S. House 1977a, 36.

142. Fitzpatrick, interview.

143. U.S. House 1977a, 38; U.S. House 1979, 40, 43.

144. U.S. House 1977a, 32, 37–38.

145. *United States v. McClain*, 545 F.2d 988 (5th Cir. 1977); 593 F.2d 658 (5th Cir. 1979).

146. Gerstenblith 2006, 69; Yasaitis 2005, 98–99.

147. U.S. House 1979, 44–45.

148. Fitzpatrick, interview.

149. U.S. House 1977a, 31, 39; U.S. Senate 1978, 50–51.

150. U.S. House 1977a, 39–40.

151. Fitzpatrick, interview.

152. Fitzpatrick, interview.

153. Fitzpatrick, interview.

154. U.S. House 1977a, 123–124, 137–138.

155. American Association of Museums, Code of Ethics for Museums.

156. Meyer 1973, 74–75. The University of Pennsylvania Museum 1970 declaration is reprinted in Meyer 1973, 254–255. This policy applied only to purchases, but not to gifts from collectors. The museum adopted a more stringent acquisition policy in 1978.

157. Report of the Committee on the Acquisition of Works of Art and Antiquities, adopted as official Harvard University policy on November 29, 1971. Reprinted in Meyer 1973, 255–259.

158. Among those museums were the Field Museum of Natural History in Chicago, the Brooklyn Museum, the University of California Museum in Berkeley, the Arizona State Museum, and the Smithsonian Institution. Hamilton 1975, 357. See also Bator 1983, 81 fn 144.

159. 1971 Harvard report, note 157.

160. Hamilton 1975, 361.

161. Meyer 1973, 76.

162. Joint Professional Policy on Museum Acquisitions, 1973, reprinted in DuBoff 1975, 563–564 and U.S. Senate 1978, 181–182; U.S. House 1979, 67–68.

163. U.S. House 1977a, 25; U.S. Senate 1978, 53, 179–181.

164. U.S. House 1976, 64–65.

165. U.S. House 1979, 65–66.

166. U.S. House 1976, 50–51.

167. U.S. House 1977a, 7, 19–20. The Metropolitan also shared the dealers' criticism of the *McClain* decision and asked that the implementing legislation overturn it. U.S. House 1977a, 4–5.

168. U.S. House 1979, 68–69.

169. U.S. House 1977a, 93–94 (Bowers Museum, Santa Ana, CA), 100 (Everson Museum of Art, Syracuse, N.Y.), 131 (Mint Museum of Art, Charlotte, N.C.).

170. Congressman Mikva sponsored the House version of the implementing legislation.

171. U.S. Senate 1978, 21.

172. U.S. House 1977b, 4, 19.

173. U.S. Senate 1978, 33–34, 45–46.

174. U.S. Senate 1978, 36–37, 71–72, 145–146.

175. USIA was an agency working to further the dialogue between American citizens and institutions and their foreign counterparts and to promote acceptance of U.S. policies by foreign publics. The delegation of authority under the CPIA to the USIA is in Executive Order 12555 of March 10, 1986.

176. Convention on Cultural Property Implementation Act, Sec. 303(a) (1)(C)(i) and 303(c)(1).

177. Pearlstein 2005, 19–21; U.S. Senate 1985, 14–15.

178. Coggins 1998, 58; Hingston 1999, 135–143.

179. Agreements have been signed with the following countries: Bolivia, Cambodia, Canada (agreement expired), China, Colombia, Cyprus, El Salvador, Greece, Guatemala, Honduras, Italy, Mali, Nicaragua, and Peru. Several of the agreements were preceded by emergency restrictions.

180. 333 F.3d 393 (2nd Cir. 2003).

181. Gerstenblith 2006, 70–74.

182. Pearlstein 2005, 22.

183. Author's interview with lawyer William Pearlstein who represents antiquities dealers and collectors, New York, May 2008; Fitzpatrick, interview; Fitzpatrick 1998.

184. Pearlstein, interview.

185. Specifically, the dealers argue that the 1997 bilateral agreement with Canada was meant to placate Canadian anger over the Helms-Burton Act. They also maintain that in 2007 the State Department expanded the agreement with Cyprus to include coins, contrary to CPAC's expert opinion, in light of Cyprus's help in the War on Terror. Fitzpatrick, interview; Fitzpatrick 1998, 76–77.

186. Ewing 1999, 180–181; Pearlstein 2005, 24–27.

187. Fitzpatrick, interview; Pearlstein, interview.

188. Elisabetta Povoledo, "Getty Agrees to Return 40 Antiquities to Italy," *New York Times*, August 2, 2007; Waxman 2008, chaps. 13–14.

189. See Ramos and Duganne 2000.

190. The cultural heritage community includes organizations such as the Lawyers' Committee for Cultural Heritage Preservation and SAFE—a coalition of scholars, professionals, educators, and students dedicated to the protection of cultural heritage worldwide.

191. Author's telephone interview with Patty Gerstenblith, May 2008; author's telephone interview with Nancy Wilkie, April 2008. Patty Gerstenblith is a professor of law and founding president of the Lawyers' Committee for Cultural Heritage Preservation. Nancy Wilkie is a professor of archaeology and former president of the Archaeological Institute of America.

192. Brodie 2006b, 10; Cuno 2008, 9.

193. Cuno 2008, 140. See also Waxman 2008, 196.

194. Coggins 1970, 13. Alan Shestack points out that art museum directors serve at the pleasure of the board of trustees. The board may fire a director who fails to expand and improve the museum's collections. Shestack 1999, 98. Competition among museums has also fueled aggressive acquisitions. Meyer 1973, 64–65.

195. Author's telephone interview with James Cuno, director of the Art Institute of Chicago, May 2008; Cuno 2008, 12–14, 153–155, and chap. 5. Practically speaking, Cuno calls for long-term loans of antiquities and the reinstatement of partage: an arrangement practiced in the late 19th and early 20th centuries for the sharing of archaeological finds between the foreign excavating team and local authorities.

196. Author's telephone interview with Anita Difanis, AAMD director of government affairs, May 2008. The arguments made by the museum community echo those of John Henry Merryman, a leading scholar of art law. See, for example Merryman 1986 and 2005.

197. AAMD, *Survey Shows Museum Antiquities Purchases are Less than 10% of Global Trade*, February 7, 2006; Cuno 2008, 4–5; Cuno, interview; Difanis, interview. On the return of antiquities from American art museums to Italy and Greece, see Gill and Chippindale 2006 and 2007.

198. Brodie 2006b, 14–17; Elia 2009.

199. Brodie 2002b, 188–190, 194–198.

200. The antiquities market constitutes only a small part of the total British art market. ITAP 2000, Annex A, paras. 7–8. Yet, controls on antiquities were seen as a potential threat to the entire art market.

201. Boylan 1995, 94–95.

202. See Article 5(b) of the 1970 UNESCO Convention. The British government also interpreted the convention as requiring governmental supervision of archaeological excavations as well as regulation of the conduct of curators, collectors, and dealers. UK House of Commons 2000, II:227.

203. Office of Arts and Libraries, "1970 UNESCO Convention concerning the Illicit Import, Export and Transfer of Ownership of Cultural Property," n.d.

204. For example, it was thought that implementation of the UNESCO Convention would require altering the civil law to limit the circumstances that allowed giving good title to illegally exported objects.

205. The government feared that the convention's requirements concerning exports would heavily burden the dealers; so would the requirement in Article 10(a) that dealers keep registers of their stock, including the origin and supplier of each item.

206. Quoted in UK House of Commons 2000, I:xx–xxi.

207. Hansard HL vol. 578 col. WA33 (February 17, 1997).

208. Hansard HC vol. 344 col. 222W (February 9, 2000).

209. Author's interview with Norman Palmer, professor of law, barrister, and chairman of the Illicit Trade Advisory Panel, London, June 2007.

210. ITAP 2000, para. 97.

211. Hansard HL vol. 578 col. 553 (February 18, 1997).

212. UK House of Commons 2000, II:11–12.

213. Addyman 2001.

214. Palmer, interview; ITAP 2000, Annex A, paras. 23–32.

215. Palmer, interview.

216. Author's interview with archaeologist Neil Brodie, research director at the Illicit Antiquities Research Center, University of Cambridge, Cambridge, UK, June 2007; Brodie, Doole, and Watson 2000, 53; Alan Riding, "14 Roman Treasures, on View and Debated," *New York Times*, October 25, 2006.

217. Brodie, Doole, and Watson 2000, 26–27; Watson 1997.

218. Brodie, interview.

219. UK House of Commons 2000, II:28–29, 33.

220. Author's interview with Colin Renfrew, professor of archaeology at the University of Cambridge and a member of the House of Lords, Cambridge, UK, June 2007. For example, Renfrew asked "[w]hether the reputation of London as an international art market of probity may be damaged by evidence of the public sale of looted antiquities smuggled from their country of origin, and whether [the government] will take steps to monitor the scale of this illicit trade in the United Kingdom." Hansard HL vol. 578 col. 553 (February 18, 1997).

221. Brodie, interview; Brodie, Doole, and Watson 2000, 9; Chippindale and Gill 2001.

222. Website of the Illicit Antiquities Research Center, http://www.mcdonald.cam.ac.uk/projects/iarc/info/us.htm (accessed May 25, 2011). The Center closed in 2007.

223. Brodie, Doole, and Watson 2000, 42.

224. Ibid., 43.

225. Author's interview with Maurice Davies, deputy director of the Museums Association, London, June 2007.

226. Davies, interview; UK House of Commons 2000, II:10–23.

227. Randy Kennedy and Hugh Eakin, "Met Chief, Unbowed, Defends Museum's Role," *New York Times*, February 28, 2006; Deborah Solomon,

"Stolen Art?," *New York Times*, February 19, 2006. See also Waxman 2008, chap. 8.

228. Author's interview with Robert Anderson, former director of the British Museum, Cambridge, UK, June 2007. According to the 1998 Policy Statement on the Acquisition of Antiquities by the Trustees of the British Museum, the museum refuses to acquire objects that have been illegally excavated and/or illegally exported from their countries of origin.

229. Anderson, interview.

230. Davies, interview.

231. Ede 1995, 213 and 1998, 130; UK House of Commons 2000, II:57–59.

232. Author's interview with Anthony Browne, chairman of the British Art Market Federation, London, June 2007.

233. Author's interview with James Ede, antiquities dealer and chairman of the Antiquities Dealers Association, London, June 2007.

234. UK House of Commons 2000, II:78.

235. Palmer, interview.

236. Author's telephone interview with Anthony Browne, chairman of the British Art Market Federation, December 2008; Ede, interview; author's interview with David Gaimster, general secretary of the Society of Antiquaries and former senior policy advisor for cultural property at the Department for Culture, Media, and Sport, London, June 2007.

237. Browne, interviews.

238. Regulation 3911/92 changed the export licensing system for cultural goods in Britain. For antiquities imported from an EU country, the Regulation conditions an export license upon documentary proof of the legality of the previous export from the EU country of origin.

239. Cook 1995, 189; Morrison 1995, 208–209.

240. Wickham-Jones 2000.

241. Gaimster, interview.

242. Renfrew, interview.

243. Palmer, interview.

244. Eggers and Hainmueller 2009.

245. Heffernan 2003; Wickham-Jones 2000, 12.

246. ITAP 2000, para. 1.

247. Ibid., paras. 8–10.

248. Ibid., paras. 46–53.

249. See UK House of Commons 2000, II:80–81.

250. Palmer, interview; ITAP 2000, paras. 54–61.

251. Another obstacle was the convention's requirement that dealers maintain registers of cultural property in their stock. The Panel was satisfied that "the current requirements for dealers to register for VAT and to keep records of their transactions meet this obligation." ITAP 2000, paras. 56–59.

252. Palmer, interview.

253. Gaimster, interview.

254. Palmer, interview.

255. ITAP 2000, paras. 61–62. ITAP's endorsement of the UNESCO Convention and rejection of the UNIDROIT Convention were the reverse of the recommendations issued by the House of Commons' Culture, Media, and Sport Committee. That committee recommended that Britain accede to the UNIDROIT Convention, rather than to the UNESCO Convention. UK House of Commons 2000, I:xxix.

256. ITAP 2000, paras. 66–76.

257. Ibid., paras. 77–83.

258. Ibid., paras. 84–95.

259. Author's interview with Roger Bland, head of the Department of Portable Antiquities and Treasure at the British Museum and secretary of ITAP, London, July 2007.

260. Palmer, interview.

261. Minister for the Arts Tessa Blackstone, quoted in Department for Culture, Media, and Sport press release, August 1, 2002.

262. ITAP 2001, paras. 23–28.

263. Mackenzie and Green 2008.

264. See UK Department for Culture, Media, and Sport and Home Office 2004, paras. 17–18.

265. Browne, interview (December 2008).

266. ITAP 2001, para. 39.

267. See Mackenzie 2011, 139–141.


*Chapter 5*

1. The number of human trafficking victims worldwide is the subject of much controversy, and estimates vary widely. According to the U.S. government, approximately 800,000 people are trafficked across borders annually, yet the Government Accountability Office has questioned this number. U.S. Department of State 2008a, 7; U.S. Government Accountability Office 2006, 10–21. See also Feingold 2010.

2. Scully 2001.

3. Ibid., 77.

4. Doezema 2000, 25–26; Nadelmann 1990, 513–514.

5. Doezema 2000, 27; Scully 2001, 84; Walkowitz 1980.

6. Bruch 2004, 8.

7. International Agreement for the Suppression of the White Slave Traffic, Article 1.

8. Article 23(c) of the Covenant of the League of Nations entrusted the League "with the general supervision over the execution of agreements with regard to the traffic in women and children."

9. Demleitner 1994, 169–172.

10. Quoted in Scully 2001, 88.

11. Nadelmann 1990, 516.

12. Demleitner 1994, 174–175.

13. Friman and Reich 2007, 6–7.

14. Article 6 of the convention asks States Parties to "take all appropriate measures, including legislation, to suppress all forms of traffic in women and exploitation of prostitution of women."

15. U.S. Department of State 2002a, 1.

16. U.S. Department of State 2008a, 1.

17. Hertzke 2004, 160–164.

18. Hertzke 2004, chap. 6.

19. Author's interview with Michael Horowitz, McLean, VA, May 2008.

20. Michael Specter, "Traffickers' New Cargo: Naive Slavic Women," *New York Times*, January 11, 1998.

21. Horowitz, interview.

22. Author's interview with a member of a faith-based organization, Washington, D.C., May 2008.

23. Dempsey 2010, 1744.

24. Author's interview with Norma Ramos, co-executive director of the Coalition Against Trafficking in Women, New York, May 2008; Dempsey 2010.

25. Hughes 2001.

26. Chuang 2010; Soderlund 2005.

27. Berman 2006; Weitzer 2007.

28. Chuang 2006.

29. Hertzke 2004, 318–321.

30. Horowitz, interview.

31. Horowitz, interview.

32. Member of a faith-based organization, interview.

33. Author's interview with John Miller, former director of the State Department's Office to Monitor and Combat Trafficking in Persons, Washington, D.C., May 2008.

34. Horowitz, interview.

35. U.S. Senate 2000a, 3.

36. Ibid., 26–28.

37. Ibid., 88–90. The victims were brought before Congress by Laura Lederer, who at the time directed the Protection Project for human-trafficking research at Harvard University.

38. See Wellstone 2001, 190–192.

39. U.S. Senate 2000a, 35.

40. Ibid., 42.

41. Letter from Christian and Jewish leaders to Speaker of the House Dennis Hastert, Representative Richard Gephardt, and Senators Trent Lott and Tom Daschle, June 16, 1999 (Michael Horowitz's files).

42. Stolz 2005, 420–422.

43. U.S. House 1999, 78–81; U.S. Senate 2000a, 12–13.

44. DeStefano 2007, 18–29.

45. U.S. House 1999, 8, 11.

46. U.S. Senate 2000a, 11.

47. Horowitz, interview.

48. U.S. House 1999, 12–13, 85; U.S. Senate 2000a, 8–9, 15–16.

49. U.S. House 1999, 13.

50. U.S. House 1999, 11–12, 67–68, 85–86.

51. U.S. Senate 2000a, 7.

52. Author's telephone interview with Laura Lederer, former executive director of the Senior Policy Operating Group on Trafficking in Persons, June 2010.

53. Ditmore and Wijers 2003; Gallagher 2001, 984–985; Raymond 2002, 493–497.

54. Hertzke 2004, 203–204.

55. Stetson 2004, 261.

56. Horowitz, interview.

57. Letter from Christian and Jewish leaders to Speaker of the House et al.; Letter from William Bennett to Speaker of the House Dennis Hastert, November 1, 1999; Letter from Commissioner John Busby, The Salvation Army, to senior members of the House of Representatives, October 27, 1999; Letter from Richard Cizik, National Association of Evangelicals, to Representative Benjamin Gilman, chairman of the House International Relations Committee, October 29, 1999 (Michael Horowitz's files).

58. Letter from Jessica Neuwirth and nine others to President Clinton, January 3, 2000 (Michael Horowitz's files). See also Philip Shenon, "Feminist Coalition Protests U.S. Stance on Sex Trafficking Treaty," *New York Times*, January 13, 2000.

59. William Bennett and Charles Colson, "The Clintons Shrug at Sex Trafficking," *Wall Street Journal*, January 10, 2000.

60. Letter from Barbara Ledeen, Independent Women's Forum, to Representative Henry Hyde, March 16, 2000; Letter from Rabbi David Saperstein, Religious Action Center of Reform Judaism, to Representative Zoe Lofgren, March 31, 2000; Letter from Pamela Shifman and Monique Widyono, Equality Now, to the U.S. House of Representatives, March 16, 2000; Letter from the Southern Baptist Convention to the House Judiciary Committee, March 14, 2000 (Michael Horowitz's files).

61. See Articles 3(a) and 3(b) of the UN Protocol. Chuang 2010, 1676–1677.

62. Trafficking Victims Protection Act, Secs. 108, 110. In addition to withholding aid, the United States may seek to deny noncompliant governments any loan or other funds provided by multilateral development banks and the International Monetary Fund.

63. Michael Horowitz, Memo to the Files, March 12, 2002; Letter from religious and feminist leaders to President Bush, June 28, 2002 (Michael Horowitz's files).

64. E-mail from Michael Horowitz to Elliott Abrams, senior director for democracy, human rights, and international operations at the National Security Council, December 12, 2001 (Michael Horowitz's files). Emphasis in the original.

65. E-mail from Michael Horowitz to Elliott Abrams, January 17, 2002 (Michael Horowitz's files).

66. Letter from religious and feminist leaders to President Bush, June 28, 2002 (Michael Horowitz's files).

67. Skinner 2008, 111–112.

68. In 2002 a Fox News affiliate in Ohio aired an investigative report featuring U.S. service members in South Korea patronizing bars and other establishments that offered prostitution services. This prompted several members of Congress to express concerns that American soldiers were knowingly obtaining the services of trafficked persons and perhaps even protecting brothels. There were also reports that employees of DynCorp, a U.S. government contractor in Bosnia, had engaged in sex trafficking. The inspector general of the Department of Defense investigated these allegations and issued two reports on DoD's response to human trafficking in South Korea and in Bosnia and Kosovo. See U.S. Department of Defense 2003a and 2003b.

69. White House Press Release, February 25, 2003. See also the State Department's 2004 document "The Link Between Prostitution and Sex Trafficking" (U.S. Department of State 2004) and the position expressed in U.S. Department of State 2008a, 24: "The United States Government opposes prostitution and any related activities, including pimping, pandering, or maintaining brothels as contributing to the phenomenon of trafficking in persons, and maintains that these activities should not be regulated as a legitimate form of work for any human being. Those who patronize the commercial sex industry form a demand which traffickers seek to satisfy."

70. See the text in http://www.un.org/webcast/ga/58/statements/usaeng030923.htm (accessed August 15, 2011).

71. Hertzke 2004, 334.

72. Letter from John Miller, director of the TIP Office, to Senator Sam Brownback, October 2003 (Michael Horowitz's files).

73. U.S. Government Accountability Office 2006, 26.

74. Ibid., 29–31.

75. Ibid., 33.

76. Weitzer 2007, 458, 461.

77. Gershuni 2004, 137; Levenkron and Dahan 2003, 19; Parliamentary Inquiry Committee on Trafficking in Women 2005. Israeli NGOs claimed that the actual number of victims was significantly higher than the official estimates.

78. Gershuni 2004, 135–136; Gruenpeter Gold and Ben Ami 2004, 8; Levenkron and Dahan 2003, 10–13.

79. Levenkron and Dahan 2003, 19–23.

80. Ibid., 24–32.

81. Gershuni 2005, 1–2; author's interview with Rahel Gershuni, government coordinator of the battle against trafficking in persons, Jerusalem, June 2007. See also Amir and Amir 2004, 145–146.

82. State-Attorney Directive 2.2 regarding Investigation and Prosecution of Soliciting Prostitution, Rendering Prostitution Services, and Managing Massage Parlors, January 1994.

83. Gershuni 2005, 2; Levenkron and Dahan 2003, 38, 42–43.

84. Gershuni 2004, 139.

85. Levenkron and Dahan 2003, 33–34.

86. Ben-Israel and Levenkron 2005, 17.

87. Simmons and Lloyd 2010.

88. Author's interview with Nomi Levenkron, legal advisor, Hotline for Migrant Workers, Tel Aviv, June 2007.

89. Gershuni, interview; Levenkron, interview.

90. Report of the Interministerial Task Force for Addressing and Monitoring the Phenomenon of Trafficking in Women for Prostitution, Jerusalem, November 20, 2002 (in Hebrew).

91. Gershuni, interview.

92. Amnesty International 2000.

93. Gershuni 2005, 3.

94. Criminal Hearing Request 7542/00, *Chanukov v. The State of Israel* (October 27, 2000).

95. Author's interview with MK Zehava Galon, chair of the Knesset Subcommittee for the Battle against Trafficking in Women, Jerusalem, June 2007. The Knesset Subcommittee for the Battle against Trafficking in Women is a permanent committee that replaced the Parliamentary Inquiry Committee on Trafficking in Women.

96. Galon, interview; Gershuni 2007a, 11; Levenkron, interview.

97. Gershuni 2007b.

98. U.S. Department of State 2006, 44.

99. U.S. Department of State 2001, 88.

100. Dan Ben-Eliezer, Ministry of Foreign Affairs, Protocol no. 14 of the meeting of the Parliamentary Inquiry Committee on Trafficking in Women, July 18, 2001 (in Hebrew).

101. Levenkron, interview.

102. Protocol no. 25 of the meeting of the Parliamentary Inquiry Committee on Trafficking in Women, March 4, 2002 (in Hebrew).

103. See, for example, MK Yuri Stern, Protocol no. 25 of the Parliamentary Inquiry Committee.

104. Gershuni, interview; Levenkron, interview; Levenkron and Dahan 2003, 40; MK Zehava Galon, Protocol no. 25 of the Parliamentary Inquiry Committee.

105. Gruenpeter Gold and Ben Ami 2004, 9; Levenkron and Dahan 2003, 41.

106. In January 2002 State-Attorney Directive 2.2 was revised. The new directive called for special attention to enforcement against sex trafficking, including both deterrence and punishment.

107. Gershuni 2004, 140–146.

108. Protocol no. 14 of the Parliamentary Inquiry Committee.

109. Galon, interview; Gershuni, interview; author's interview with Ady Schonmann, Office of the Legal Adviser, Ministry of Foreign Affairs, Jerusalem, June 2007.

110. MK Colette Avital, Protocol no. 14 of the Parliamentary Inquiry Committee.

111. Meir Sheetrit, minister of justice, Protocol no. 25 of the Parliamentary Inquiry Committee.

112. MK Colette Avital, Protocol no. 14 of the Parliamentary Inquiry Committee.

113. Johnston 2001, 501–506.

114. Gerhuni, interview; Galon, interview; Schonmann, interview.

115. Johnston 2001, 501.

116. Yoni Lerman, Hotline for Migrant Workers, Protocol no. 25 of the Parliamentary Inquiry Committee.

117. Gershuni, interview.

118. Schonmann, interview.

119. Galon, interview.

120. Nathan 2009a, 2–3; Protocol no. 22 of the meeting of the Knesset Subcommittee for the Battle against Trafficking in Women, February 15, 2011 (in Hebrew).

121. Protocol no. 14 of the meeting of the Parliamentary Inquiry Committee on Trafficking in Women.

122. Johnston 2001, 502.

123. U.S. Department of State 2008a, 18–19.

124. Israeli authorities use the term "foreign workers" (*ovdim zarim*) rather than "migrant workers" so as not to imply that the workers might become permanent residents or citizens of Israel.

125. State Comptroller of Israel 2005, 377. This figure includes both workers with valid residence permits and workers without valid residence permits.

126. Worker's Hotline 2002, 6. See also State Comptroller of Israel 2003, 654–655.

127. Bartram 1998; State Comptroller of Israel 1996, 477–480; Worker's Hotline 2002, 6.

128. State Comptroller of Israel 1996, 479–480; State Comptroller of Israel 2003, 655.

129. Worker's Hotline 2002, 7.

130. Rozen et al. 2003, 7–8; State Comptroller of Israel 2003, 649, 655–656; Worker's Hotline 2002, 8–9.

131. Until 2006, charging of any recruitment fees was prohibited. In 2006 the law was changed to allow a maximal recruitment fee of approximately $1,000.

132. Rozen et al. 2003, 13.

133. Worker's Hotline 2002, 12.

134. HCJ (High Court of Justice) 4542/02 *Kav LaOved (Worker's Hotline) et al. v. The Government of Israel et al.*, [2006] (1) Israel Law Reports 260, 288.

135. Rozen et al. 2003, 14–15.

136. Rozen et al. 2003, 12; Worker's Hotline 2002, 14.

137. Rozen et al. 2003, 9–11; author's interview with Yuval Livnat, legal advisor, Worker's Hotline, Tel Aviv, June 2007.

138. UNODC 2010b; U.S. Department of State 2008a, 19–20.

139. State Comptroller of Israel 1996, 480–481; State Comptroller of Israel 2003, 656–657.

140. State Comptroller of Israel 2003, 657.

141. Illegal workers were those who entered Israel on a tourist visa and worked without a permit; workers with a permit who continued to work past the expiration of their permit; workers who worked for an employer other than the one specified in their permit; and workers who entered Israel illegally without any visa.

142. State Comptroller of Israel 2003, 658–661.

143. Rozen et al. 2003, 35–42, 52–53, 57–58; State Comptroller of Israel 2005, 381–382.

144. Rozen et al. 2003, 24–26; State Comptroller of Israel 1999, 282–283; State Comptroller of Israel 2005, 379–380, 389–392.

145. Author's interview with MK Ran Cohen, chair of the Knesset Committee on Foreign Workers, Tel Aviv, June 2007; author's interview with Rony Yedidia, formerly at the Consular Division, Israel's Ministry of Foreign Affairs, Cambridge, MA, May 2007.

146. Rozen et al. 2003, 25; State Comptroller of Israel 2005, 390–391.

147. Gershuni, interview; Rozen et al. 2003, 29.

148. Gershuni, interview.

149. Cohen, interview; Livnat, interview.

150. HCJ 4542/02, 283.

151. HCJ 4542/02, 311.

152. Cohen, interview.

153. U.S. Department of State 2005, 128.

154. This category of countries that require special scrutiny was not part of the original Trafficking Act of 2000, but was added in the Trafficking Victims Protection Reauthorization Act of 2003.

155. U.S. Department of State 2006, 145–146.

156. Livnat, interview.

157. Prohibition of Trafficking in Persons (Legislative Amendments) Law, 5766–2006.

158. MK Galon proposed an anti-trafficking law in 2003. The law enacted in 2006 consolidated Galon's bill and a government bill.

159. Author's interview with Commander Dorit Ben-Meir, investigations and intelligence officer at the Emigration Administration, Ramla, June 2007.

160. Gershuni, interview

161. Cohen, interview.

162. Livnat, interview.

163. Nathan 2009a, 2–3, 7–8; Nathan 2009b, 16–20; U.S. Department of State 2008a, 146; U.S. Department of State 2010, 185.

164. Berman 2007; Nathan 2007 and 2009c, 7–8.

165. Nathan 2011.

166. For example, workers were often unable to tell when their passport was taken and by whom. Author's interview with Commander Ziva Agami-Cohen, former head of the Crime Unit at the Emigration Administration, Lod, June 2007.

167. Agami-Cohen, interview

168. Cohen, interview; Livant, interview.

169. Schonmann, interview.

170. Mertus and Bertone 2007.

171. Mertus and Bertone 2007, 47.

172. Richards 2004, 156–157.


### Chapter 6

1. U.S. Department of State 2003, II-10.

2. The first international agreement on human trafficking was signed in 1904, slightly prior to the 1909 emergence of international drug control. Yet unlike drug control, the efforts against human trafficking have not been continuous: the contemporary American campaign against human trafficking does not build on the historical endeavors in this area.

3. Cartwright 1999; Office of National Drug Control Policy 2004; UNDCP 1997.

4. Office of National Drug Control Policy 2004.

5. Mokdad et al. 2004, 1242.

6. UNODC 2009a, 13.

7. UNODC 2008, 173–177. According to official Chinese estimates, opium addiction affected 23.3 percent of the male adult population in 1906. UNODC 2009a, 25.

8. McAllister 2000, 24–25; UNODC 2009a, 32, 46; Walker 1991, 14–15.

9. The missionaries also considered opium as an obstacle to their efforts to spread Christianity due to the drug's corruptive influence and the damage to churches' reputation from Westerners' involvement in providing the drug. McAllister 2000, 21; Reins 1991, 109–110; Taylor 1969, 27–31; Walker 1991, 26–27.

10. Taylor 1969, 217, 328.

11. Bewley-Taylor 2001, 18–19; McAllister 2000, 27, 30–31; Musto 1999, 30–31, 39; Taylor 1969, 29, 329. The U.S. government was anxious to improve Sino-American relations that had reached a low point with a 1905 embargo against American goods organized by Chinese merchants. Chinese anger was the result of restrictions on Chinese migration to the United States and mistreatment of Chinese immigrants.

12. Bewley-Taylor 2001, 19; Bruun, Pan, and Rexed 1975, 10; Musto 1992, 33; Musto 1999, 25–28; Taylor 1969, 31–48, 328; UNODC 2009a, 31.

13. Taylor 1969, 58–59, 83, 152–154; UNODC 2009a, 41–42.

14. Bewley-Taylor 2001, 17; McAllister 2000, 16–19, 30; Musto 1992, 31–32; Musto 1999, 3–7, 43–44, 294–295; Spillane and McAllister 2003, S5–S6. Anti-drug campaigns in early 20th century Europe were similarly fueled by the association of drugs with "dangerous" groups inside and outside the state, such as Germans, Communists, or bohemian artists. This construction of threat allowed governments to establish a sense of national unity, limit the impact and spread of "foreign" ideas, and regulate social behavior. Buxton 2006, 46–47.

15. Musto 1999, 8–10, 33–34, 46–48.

16. Bewley-Taylor 2001, 21, 23, 25–27; McAllister 2000, 35, 39; Musto 1992, 33–35; Musto 1999, 33–35, 45; Taylor 1969, 59, 114–116, 130–131.

17. Bewley-Taylor 2001, 48; McAllister 2000, 58; Taylor 1969, 67, 83, 131, 145, 153, 159, 163–164, 226, 302.

18. McAllister 2000, 31. See Perl 2006, 2 ("The primary goal of U.S. international narcotics policy is to reduce the supply of illicit narcotics flowing into the United States."); U.S. Department of State 2008b, I:16–17.

19. Bewley-Taylor 2001, 6, 36–37; Buxton 2006, 32; Jojarth 2009, 102–103; McAllister 2000, 235, 249–250; Walker 1992, 275.

20. Bayer and Ghodse 1999; McAllister 2000, 112; UNODC 2009a, 8, 82.

21. Taylor 1969, 67, 163–164.

22. Trocki 1999, 73–74. Opium production and sale provided as much as 1/3 of government revenue in British India at certain points in the 19th century. Opium farms in French Indochina contributed approximately 30 percent of colonial revenues (1861–1882), and in the Netherlands East Indies (today's Indonesia) such farms provided 35 percent of total tax revenue (1816–1925). UNODC 2009a, 21.

23. Taylor 1969, 52, 68.

24. McAllister 2000, 21–25; Reins 1999, 110–111, 114; UNODC 2009a, 29–32, 46; Walker 1991, 14–15.

25. Buxton 2006, 27–28; McAllister 2000, 22; Taylor 1969, 64–73, 80.

26. McAllister 2000, 81; Taylor 1969, 193, 217.

27. Bruun, Pan, and Rexed 1975, 13; McAllister 2000, 29, 32, 66, 160; Taylor 1969, 77, 99; UNODC 2009a, 52.

28. McAllister 2000, 114–115, 235, 248–249; Taylor 1969, 180, 198, 217.

29. Taylor 1969, 308.

30. McAllister 2000, 67, 119, 167, 183; Taylor 1969, 52, 110, 301.

31. Jojarth 2009, 103–106.

32. U.S. Department of State 2003, II-9: "Destroying a lucrative crop, even an illegal one, carries enormous political, economic and social ramifications for the producing country. It inevitably means attacking the livelihood of a large—and often the poorest—sector of the population. Democratic governments that take away vital income without any quid pro quo seldom survive for long." See also Perl 2006, 9.

33. Buxton 2006, 129–130; UNODC 2009a, 67.

34. Hinojosa 2007, 85–86; Mares 2006, 116, 118; U.S. Government Accountability Office 2008.

35. Bruun, Pan, and Rexed 1975, 223–224; Friman 1996, 26–32.

36. Friman 1996, chap. 2; McAllister 2000, 32–33; Taylor 1969, 94, 102, 113.

37. Bruun, Pan, and Rexed 1975, 155; McAllister 2000, 79.

38. Friman 1996, 24–25; McAllister 2000, 60–61, 66, 71–72, 97–99; Taylor 1969, 248.

39. Bruun, Pan, and Rexed 1975, 153–156, 159; McAllister 2000, 194–195, 205, 223, 226–234, 240, 243–244, 250.

40. Bruun, Pan, and Rexed 1975, 158–159; McAllister 2000, 97, 100, 112–113, 229.

41. McAllister 2000, 90–91, 98, 106; Taylor 1969, 133, 236–237, 242–243.

42. Friman 1996, 11; McAllister 2000, 32–34; Taylor 1969, 92, 101–102, 106–107, 113.

43. Mares 1992, 337; Musto 1992, 40.

44. Bruun, Pan, and Rexed 1975, 153, 256, 265; McAllister 2000, 110, 127, 194–195, 231–232, 240, 244.

45. McAllister 2000, 43, 95.

46. Bewley-Taylor 2001, 22; McAllister 2000, 29–30; Taylor 1969, 76–77.

47. Bayer and Ghodse 1999; McAllister 2000, 32–35; Taylor 1969, 87–88, 93–96, 102–120; UNODC 2008, 191.

48. UNODC 2009a, 52–53.

49. McAllister 2000, 67, 71–72, 76–77; Taylor 1969, 184, 197–202.

50. Bewley-Taylor 2001, 29, 33; Taylor 1969, 214, 217, 253; Wright 1934, 475.

51. McAllister 1992, 148.

52. See Chapter 3, p. 86.

53. Bruun, Pan, and Rexed 1975, 117–118; McAllister 1992, 148–151, 157–158; McAllister 2000, 206–207.

54. Permanent Central Opium Board and Drug Supervisory Body.

55. See Articles 9, 12–14, 19–20, 29–31, 34, 36 of the Single Convention on Narcotic Drugs. Bewley-Taylor 2001, 143–144; McAllister 1992, 152–153; McAllister 2000, 208–209; UNODC 2009a, 60–62.

56. Bayer and Ghodse 1999; Bruun, Pan, and Rexed 1975, 253–259; McAllister 2000, 201–202, 226–230.

57. Bruun, Pan, and Rexed 1975, 260–261, 265; McAllister 1992, 153–161; McAllister 2000, 206, 209, 226–234, 240–241.

58. McAllister 2000, 243–246, 250; UNODC 2009a, 66–80; U.S. Department of State 2008b, 15.

59. Taylor 1969, 92–96, 141–144; UNODC 2009a, 51.

60. McAllister 2000, 123; Taylor 1969, 200–202, 210, 215, 296–297; UNODC 2009a, 57.

61. Convention for Limiting the Manufacture and Regulating the Distribution of Narcotic Drugs.

62. Taylor 1969, 248–250, 253, 259–261; UNODC 2009a, 55–56.

63. McAllister 2000, 107–108, 113; Taylor 1969, 244.

64. Bewley-Taylor 2001, 30, 39–41; Friman 1996, chap. 3; McAllister 2000, 100, 111–113, 117, 120, 132–133.

65. Bewley-Taylor 2001, 44–45; Friman 1996, 63–69; McAllister 2000, 151–153, 160–161.

66. Bewley-Taylor 2001, 59–61, 65–66, 71–72; McAllister 2000, 165–171.

67. Bewley-Taylor 2001, 84–89, 137, 143, 159–160; Bruun, Pan, and Rexed 1975, 18; McAllister 2000, 235–236.

68. UNODC 2009b, 1–2. Emphasis in the original.

69. International Narcotics Control Board 2010, 31. The Board is also authorized to recommend that parties to the drug conventions stop importing drugs from or exporting drugs to noncompliant countries. This authority has rarely been invoked. Jojarth 2009, 123–124.

70. Bewley-Taylor 2001, 171–173, 186.

71. Bewley-Taylor 2001, 199–201; Craig 1980; McAllister 2000, 145; Walker 1989, 119–133; Walker 1992, 270, 273.

72. Bewley-Taylor 2001, 186–188; Friesendorf 2007, 79–83; Walker 1994, 26–28.

73. National Security Decision Directive 221, April 8, 1986; Bewley-Taylor 2001, 188; Friesendorf 2007, 83–84, 88; Walker 1992, 275; Walker 1994, 29–30.

74. Bewley-Taylor 2001, 188–193.

75. Storrs 2003.

76. Ayling 2005, 378, 381; Bewley-Taylor 2001, 203; Perl 2006, 9.

77. See, for example, Hinojosa 2007, 40–43, 57–61.

78. Friman 2010, 88–91.

79. Ayling 2005; Bewley-Taylor 2001, 202–206; Buxton 2006, 140; Storrs 2001, 6.

80. U.S. Senate 2000b, 2 (Senator Chuck Grassley).

81. McWilliams 1992, 24–26.

82. Bruun, Pan, and Rexed 1975, 13, 136; McAllister 2000, 50–52; Taylor 1969, 151, 215, 218, 223, 268–269; UNODC 2009a, 52–53, 55. The United States was, however, involved with the League of Nations' drug organs. The United States participated in the work of the Opium Advisory Committee in an unofficial or consultative capacity and considered the Permanent Central Opium Board to be independent from the League.

83. McAllister 2000, 87, 111.

84. Bewley-Taylor 2001, 115; McAllister 2000, 163, 166, 169, 183.

85. Bewley-Taylor 2001, 123–129; Friman 2009b, 59; Rubin 2004, 5.

86. Bewley-Taylor 2001, 197–198, 204; Storrs 2003, 2–3.

87. See Friman 2009b.

88. Bruun, Pan, and Rexed 1975, 161.

89. Bewley-Taylor 2001, 36, 116; McAllister 2000, 32, 52–53, 64, 101, 247.

90. Jojarth 2009, 139.

91. Jojarth 2009, 140–141; Reuter and Truman 2004, 25.

92. Reuter and Truman 2004, 40–42, 175.

93. Gilmore 2004, 22–23, 31; Reuter and Truman 2004, 140–141.

94. UNODC 2009b, 235–249.

95. Moghadam 2009, 49–50.

96. Gilmore 2004, 93.

97. Gilmore 2004, 35–43.

98. The Forty Recommendations, Recommendations 5, 10, 11, and 13.

99. Reuter and Truman 2004, 98–101. See also Jojarth 2009, 149–150; Simmons 2000b, 248.

100. Jojarth 2009, 151.

101. Bartlett 2002, 7–9; Harvey 2004, 336, 341; Reuter and Truman 2004, 130–131.

102. Reuter and Truman 2004, 46–47.

103. According to a rough estimate, the U.S. federal government spent approximately $1.5 billion on the AML regime in fiscal year 2003; for the entire public sector, including state and local spending, the total may have been $3 billion. Reuter and Truman 2004, 95–98.

104. Pieth and Aiolfi 2003, 7.

105. Pieth and Aiolfi 2003, 8–9, 20.

106. Jojarth 2009, 150–151; Simmons 2000b, 247–248; U.S. Department of State 2002b, XII-11, XII-167.

107. Bartlett 2002.

108. Wechsler 2001, 46.

109. Helleiner 1999, 74 and 2002, 184. Cf. Oatley and Nabors 1998.

110. Simmons 2000b, 248.

111. Section 4702 of the Anti-Drug Abuse Act of 1988.

112. Jojarth 2009, 142–143; Simmons 2000b, 249.

113. Of the 36 members, two are international organizations: the European Commission and the Gulf Cooperation Council. The FATF has a small secretariat that is located in, but is independent of, the OCED headquarters in Paris. Upon its establishment in 1989 the FATF was given a five-year extendable mandate. In 2004 the FATF's mandate was renewed for an eight-year period.

114. Jojarth 2009, 166. See, for example, Recommendations 1, 4, and 10.

115. Financial Action Task Force 2010, 2.

116. Simmons 2000b, 262.

117. Ibid.

118. Financial Action Task Force 2009, 12–15. The mutual-evaluation process is a key component of the FATF's work and a critical tool for ensuring compliance with the 40 Recommendations; yet the Recommendations themselves do not establish the process and its procedure. The third round of evaluations that began in January 2005 was guided by the FATF reference documents: *Methodology for Assessing Compliance with the FATF 40 Recommendations and the FATF 9 Special Recommendations* (2004) and *AML/CFT Evaluations and Assessments: Handbook for Countries and Assessors* (2004).

119. Financial Action Task Force 2007a, 3.

120. Financial Action Task Force 2000a, 6.

121. Financial Action Task Force 2000b, 12; Financial Action Task Force 2001, 18.

122. Wechsler 2001, 52.

123. Financial Action Task Force 2007b, 3–4.

124. Brillo 2010; Drezner 2007, 143–145.

125. Jojarth 2009, 168.

126. Financial Action Task Force 2009, 17.

127. Financial Action Task Force 2009, 6.

128. The eight FSRBs are the Asia/Pacific Group on Money Laundering, the Caribbean Financial Action Task Force, the Council of Europe Committee of Experts on the Evaluation of Anti-Money Laundering Measures and the Financing of Terrorism, the Financial Action Task Force on Money Laundering in South America, the Middle East and North Africa Financial Action Task Force, the Eurasian Group on Combating Money Laundering and Financing of Terrorism, the Eastern and Southern Africa Anti-Money Laundering Group, and the Intergovernmental Action Group against Money Laundering in West Africa.

129. Naím 2005, 109–110. See also OECD 2008, 68.

130. Dimitrov 2009, 15–16; Maskus 2000, 44–49; OCED 2008, 137–153.

131. Matthews 2002, 12–13; Sell and Prakash 2004, 154.

132. Sell 2003, 50–51, 80–81, 86; Sell and Prakash 2004, 157–158.

133. Matthews 2002, 18–21; Sell 2003, 46–49, 78–87, 99–100, 103.

134. Although counterfeits do not originate exclusively from developing countries, the scale of counterfeiting in developing countries tends to be higher. OECD 2008.

135. Deere 2009, 10; Dimitrov 2009.

136. Dimitrov 2009, 64–65; Maskus, Dougherty, and Mertha 2005, 302–306; OECD 2008, 154; Ryan 1998, 80.

137. Matthews 2002, 108–111; Maskus, Dougherty, and Mertha 2005, 298–302, 311–313; OECD 2008, 140.

138. Maskus, Dougherty, and Mertha 2005, 303, 305.

139. Drahos 2002, 768–769; Matthews 2002, 8–13; Sell 1998, 107–130.

140. Deere 2009, 48–49; Matthews 2002, 15–16, 25–27; Sell 1998, 133–135; Sell 2003, 85–86, 91–94.

141. Sell 2003, 85.

142. Deere 2009, 52–53, 55; Matthews 2002, 15–16; Ryan 1998, 72–79; Sell 2003, 90, 108.

143. Quoted in Sell 2003, 88. See also Matthews 2002, 21.

144. Sell 2003, 48, 82, 89–91.

145. Matthews 2002, 20–24; Sell 2003, 1–2, 96, 101–106.

146. Matthews 2002, 17, 24, 30; Sell 2003, 107–108.

147. Deere 2009, 55; Drahos 2002, 774–776; Matthews 2002, 31–33, 44; Ryan 1998, 93, 112; Sell 2003, 108–111.

148. Matthews 2002, 45; Ryan 1998, 12–13, 92–93, 112; Sell 2003, 110.

149. Deere 2009, 156–159, 179; Sell 2003, 122–138; U.S. Trade Representative 2009, 8–10.

150. Deere 2009, 48–50, 115, 159–160; Matthews 2002, 25–27; Mertha 2005, 39–41, 56–57; Ryan 1998, 80; Sell 2003, 92–93, 98–99, 123–125, 138–139; U.S. Trade Representative 2006.

151. Deere 2009, 114–120, 129, 151–154, 161.

152. Deere 2009, 161–162, 164–166; U.S. Trade Representative 2006.

153. Mertha 2005, 10–11, 43–52, 101–102, 126–129, 150–156, 212–217.

154. U.S. Trade Representative 2010, 19.

155. Sell 2003, 106–107.

156. Mertha 2005, 19, 185; OECD 2008, 87–89, 312; Phillips 2005, 99–100.

157. Sell 2003, 139–153; Das 2003.

### Chapter 7

1. Friman 2009b, 50–51.

2. Naím 2005, 219.

3. Ibid., 219–228.

4. Ibid., 2005, 218.

5. Ibid., 2005, 231–232.

6. Ibid., 220. Emphasis in the original.

7. Friman 2009b, 51.

8. Abraham and van Schendel 2005.

9. Andreas and Nadelmann 2006, 228–229; Nadelmann 1990, 486.

10. See Friman 2009b, 52–53 for a critique.

11. Andreas and Nadelmann 2006, 18; Nadelmann 1990, 481.

12. Program of Action, Section II, Articles 11, 14, and 17.

13. Program of Action, Section II, Article 3.

14. Bruun, Pan, and Rexed 1975, 225–226.

15. For example, Aronowitz 2009; Edwards and Gill 2003; Friman 1996; Liddick 2004; Mares 2006; Walker 1989, Williams 1999; Williams 2001; and Zhang 2007.

16. Andreas and Nadelmann 2006, 9–10, 20.

17. Bewley-Taylor 2001; McAllister 2000; Taylor 1969.

18. Friman 1996, 20–26.

19. Andreas and Nadelmann 2006, 38–39; Brown 1973.

20. Jojarth 2009, 279–285.

21. Mearsheimer 1995; Morgenthau 1985, chap. 18.

22. For example, Abbott and Snidal 1998; Keohane 1984; Simmons 2000a. See Simmons and Martin 2002 for an overview.

23. For example, Grieco et al. 2011; Mansfield, Milner, and Rosendorff 2002; Simmons 2009.

24. Donnelly 1992.

25. See UNESCO Doc. 20 C/84, September 15, 1978; UNESCO Doc. 22 C/93, August 30, 1983; UNESCO Doc. 24 C/24, August 20, 1987.

26. For example, Askerud and Clément 1997; The Fight against the Illicit Trafficking of Cultural Objects: The 1970 Convention: Past and Future (UNESCO information kit, 2011, CLT/2011/CONF.207/6).

27. Finnemore 1996, chap. 2.

28. U.S. House 1977a, 131.

29. Koremenos, Lipson, and Snidal 2001, 765.

30. Keohane 1984, 6.

31. Ibid., 85.

32. The Rational Design Project, for example, has emphasized the following obstacles to cooperation: distributional problems, enforcement problems, number of actors and asymmetries among them, and uncertainty. Koremenos, Lipson, and Snidal 2001, 773–779.

33. Oye 1985, 7.

34. Drezner 2007, 53–54.

35. Keck and Sikkink 1998.

36. For example, Carpenter 2007; Price 1998; Ron, Ramos, and Rodgers 2005.

37. Finnemore and Sikkink 1998.

38. Keck and Sikkink 1998, 27, 204.

39. See Simmons 2010, 283–286.

40. See, for example, Grossman and Helpman 1994; Kono 2006; Mansfield, Milner, and Rosendorff 2002.

41. For example, Aaronson and Zimmerman 2008; Hafner-Burton 2009.

42. For example, Barrett 2003; Young 1989. For an overview, see Neumayer 2001.

43. Sprinz and Vaahtoranta 1994.

44. Bernhagen 2008, 79.

45. Newell 2005, 23.

46. For example, DeSombre 2000; Levy and Newell 2005.

47. Andreas 2004, 645–647.

48. See, for example, Milner and Kubota 2005.

49. Drezner 2007, 33–34.

50. Ibid., 13–22.

51. For example, Protocol on the Control of Firearms, Ammunition, and Other Related Materials in the Southern African Development Community (SADC) Region, signed in 2001 and in force since 2004.

52. See Keck and Sikkink 1998, 18–20.

53. See Mitchell 2003, 440–441; Sell and Prakash 2004, 152 (arguing that a crisis or an exogenous shock may create political opportunities and facilitate a policy change).

# REFERENCES

Aaronson, Susan Ariel, and Jamie M. Zimmerman. 2008. *Trade Imbalance: The Struggle to Weigh Human Rights Concerns in Trade Policymaking*. Cambridge and New York: Cambridge University Press.

Abbott, Kenneth W., and Duncan Snidal. 1998. Why States Act through Formal International Organizations. *Journal of Conflict Resolution* 42(1): 3–32.

Abraham, Itty, and Willem van Schendel. 2005. Introduction: The Making of Illicitness. In *Illicit Flows and Criminal Things: States, Borders, and the Other Side of Globalization*, edited by Willem van Schendel and Itty Abraham, 1–37. Bloomington: Indiana University Press.

Abramson, Ronald D., and Stephen B. Huttler. 1973. The Legal Response to the Illicit Movement of Cultural Property. *Law & Policy in International Business* 5: 932–970.

Addyman, Peter. 2001. Antiquities without Archaeology in the United Kingdom. In *Trade in Illicit Antiquities: The Destruction of the World's Archaeological Heritage*, edited by Neil Brodie, Jennifer Doole, and Colin Renfrew, 141–144. Cambridge: McDonald Institute for Archaeological Research.

Alva, Walter. 2001. The Destruction, Looting and Traffic of the Archaeological Heritage of Peru. In *Trade in Illicit Antiquities: The Destruction of the World's Archaeological Heritage*, edited by Neil Brodie, Jennifer Doole, and Colin Renfrew, 89–96. Cambridge: McDonald Institute for Archaeological Research.

Amir, Delila, and Menachem Amir. 2004. The Politics of Prostitution and Trafficking of Women in Israel. In *The Politics of Prostitution: Women's Movements, Democratic States and the Globalisation of Sex Commerce*, edited by Joyce Outshoorn, 144–164. Cambridge and New York: Cambridge University Press.

Amnesty International. 2000. *Israel: Human Rights Abuses of Women Trafficked from Countries of the Former Soviet Union into Israel's Sex Industry*. May 18. AI index: MDE 15/17/00.

Andreas, Peter. 2002. Transnational Crime and Economic Globalization. In *Transnational Organized Crime and International Security: Business as Usual?*, edited by Mats Berdal and Mónica Serrano, 37–52. Boulder, Colo.: Lynne Rienner.

Andreas, Peter. 2004. Illicit International Political Economy: The Clandestine Side of Globalization. *Review of International Political Economy* 11(3): 641–652.

Andreas, Peter, and Ethan Nadelmann. 2006. *Policing the Globe: Criminalization and Crime Control in International Relations.* New York: Oxford University Press.

Annan, Kofi A. 2000. *"We the Peoples": The Role of the United Nations in the 21st Century.* New York: United Nations.

Aronowitz, Alexis A. 2009. *Human Trafficking, Human Misery: The Global Trade in Human Beings.* Westport, Conn.: Praeger.

Askerud, Pernille, and Etienne Clément. 1997. *Preventing the Illicit Traffic in Cultural Property: A Resource Handbook for the Implementation of the 1970 UNESCO Convention.* Paris: UNESCO.

Axelrod, Robert. 1984. *The Evolution of Cooperation.* New York: Basic Books.

Ayling, Julie. 2005. Conscription in the War on Drugs: Recent Reforms to the U.S. Drug Certification Process. *International Journal of Drug Policy* 16(6): 376–383.

Barrett, Scott. 2003. *Environment and Statecraft: The Strategy of Environmental Treaty-Making.* Oxford and New York: Oxford University Press.

Bartlett, Brent L. 2002. The Negative Effects of Money Laundering on Economic Development. Study for the Asian Development Bank, regional technical assistance project no. 5967, Countering Money Laundering in the Asian and Pacific Region.

Barton, John H., Judith L. Goldstein, Timothy E. Josling, and Richard H. Steinberg. 2006. *The Evolution of the Trade Regime.* Princeton, N.J.: Princeton University Press.

Bartram, David V. 1998. Foreign Workers in Israel: History and Theory. *International Migration Review* 32(2): 303–325.

Bass, Gary J. 2008. *Freedom's Battle: The Origins of Humanitarian Intervention.* New York: Alfred A. Knopf.

Bator, Paul M. 1983. *The International Trade in Art.* Chicago: University of Chicago Press. Midway Reprint, 1988 (page references are to the reprint edition).

Bauer, Alexander A. 2008. New Ways of Thinking about Cultural Property: A Critical Appraisal of the Antiquities Trade Debates. *Fordham International Law Journal* 31: 690–724.

Bayer, I., and H. Ghodse. 1999. Evolution of International Drug Control, 1945–1995. *Bulletin on Narcotics* 51 (1 and 2). United Nations International Drug Control Program. Vienna.

Becker, Gary S., Kevin M. Murphy, and Michael Grossman. 2006. The Market for Illegal Goods: The Case of Drugs. *Journal of Political Economy* 114(1): 38–60.

Ben-Israel, Hanny, and Nomi Levenkron. 2005. *The Missing Factor: Clients of Trafficked Women in Israel's Sex Industry.* Hotline for Migrant Workers and the Hebrew University in Jerusalem.

Berdal, Mats, and Mónica Serrano. 2002. *Transnational Organized Crime and International Security: Business as Usual?* Boulder, Colo.: Lynne Rienner.

Berman, Jacqueline. 2006. The Left, the Right, and the Prostitute: The Making of U.S. Antitrafficking in Persons Policy. *Tulane Journal of International and Comparative Law* 14: 269–293.

Berman, Jonathan. 2007. *Freedom Inc.: Binding Migrant Workers to Manpower Corporations in Israel.* Worker's Hotline and Hotline for Migrant Workers. April.

Bernhagen, Patrick. 2008. Business and International Environmental Agreements: Domestic Sources of Participation and Compliance by Advanced Industrialized Democracies. *Global Environmental Politics* 8(1): 78–110.

Bewley-Taylor, David, R. 2001. *The United States and International Drug Control, 1909–1997.* London and New York: Continuum.

Biting the Bullet. 2006. *Reviewing Action on Small Arms 2006: Assessing the First Five Years of the UN Programme of Action.* International Alert, Saferworld, and the University of Bradford, in cooperation with IANSA.

Bob, Clifford. 2010. Packing Heat: Pro-gun Groups and the Governance of Small Arms. In *Who Governs the Globe?*, edited by Deborah D. Avant, Martha Finnemore, and Susan K. Sell, 183–201. New York: Cambridge University Press.

Borodkin, Lisa J. 1995. The Economics of Antiquities Looting and a Proposed Legal Alternative. *Columbia Law Review* 95: 377–417.

Boutros-Ghali, Boutros. 1995. *Supplement to an Agenda for Peace: Position Paper of the Secretary-General on the Occasion of the Fiftieth Anniversary of the United Nations.* A/50/60—S/1995/1. January 3.

Boylan, Patrick J. 1995. Illicit Trafficking in Antiquities and Museum Ethics. In *Antiquities: Trade or Betrayed: Legal, Ethical, and Conservation Issues*, edited by Kathryn Walker Tubb, 94–104. London: Archetype Publications.

Brillo, Bing Baltazar C. 2010. The Politics of the Anti-Money Laundering Act of the Philippines: An Assessment of the Republic Act 9160 and 9194. *Asian Social Science* 6(8): 109–125.

Brodie, Neil. 2002a. Introduction. In *Illicit Antiquities: The Theft of Culture and the Extinction of Archaeology*, edited by Neil Brodie and Kathryn Walker Tubb, 1–22. London and New York: Routledge.

Brodie, Neil. 2002b. Britannia Waives the Rules? The Licensing of Archaeological Material for Export from the UK. In *Illicit Antiquities: The Theft of Culture and the Extinction of Archaeology*, edited by Neil Brodie and Kathryn Walker Tubb, 185–204. London and New York: Routledge.

Brodie, Neil. 2006a. An Archaeologist's View of the Trade in Unprovenanced Antiquities. In *Art and Cultural Heritage: Law, Policy and Practice*, edited by Barbara T. Hoffman, 52–63. Cambridge and New York: Cambridge University Press.

Brodie, Neil. 2006b. Introduction. In *Archaeology, Cultural Heritage, and the Antiquities Trade*, edited by Neil Brodie, Morag M. Kersel, Christina Luke, and Kathryn Walker Tubb, 1–24. Gainesville, Fla.: University Press of Florida.

Brodie, Neil, and Jennifer Doole. 2001. Illicit Antiquities. In *Trade in Illicit Antiquities: The Destruction of the World's Archaeological Heritage*, edited by Neil Brodie, Jennifer Doole, and Colin Renfrew, 1–6. Cambridge: McDonald Institute for Archaeological Research.

Brodie, Neil, Jennifer Doole, and Colin Renfrew, eds. 2001. *Trade in Illicit Antiquities: The Destruction of the World's Archaeological Heritage*. Cambridge: McDonald Institute for Archaeological Research.

Brodie, Neil, Jenny Doole, and Peter Watson. 2000. *Stealing History: The Illicit Trade in Cultural Material*. Cambridge: McDonald Institute for Archaeological Research.

Brodie, Neil, and Colin Renfrew. 2005. Looting and the World's Archaeological Heritage: The Inadequate Response. *Annual Review of Anthropology* 34: 343–361.

Brodie, Neil, and Kathryn Walker Tubb, eds. 2002. *Illicit Antiquities: The Theft of Culture and the Extinction of Archaeology*. London and New York: Routledge.

Brown, J.B. 1973. Politics of the Poppy: The Society for the Suppression of the Opium Trade, 1874–1916. *Journal of Contemporary History* 8(3): 97–111.

Bruch, Elizabeth M. 2004. Models Wanted: The Search for an Effective Response to Human Trafficking. *Stanford Journal of International Law* 40: 1–45.

Bruun, Kettil, Lynn Pan, and Ingemar Rexed. 1975. *The Gentlemen's Club: International Control of Drugs and Alcohol*. Chicago: University of Chicago Press.

Bueno de Mesquita, Bruce, Alastair Smith, Randolph M. Siverson, and James D. Morrow. 2003. *The Logic of Political Survival*. Cambridge, Mass.: MIT Press.

Butterworth-Hayes, Philip, ed. 2004. *Jane's World Defence Industry*. Coulsdon, UK: Jane's Information Group.

Buxton, Julia. 2006. *The Political Economy of Narcotics: Production, Consumption and Global Markets*. London and New York: Zed Books.

Byman, Daniel L., and Roger Cliff. 1999. *China's Arms Sales: Motivations and Implications*. Santa Monica, Calif.: Rand.

Carpenter, R. Charli. 2007. Setting the Advocacy Agenda: Theorizing Issue Emergence and Nonemergence in Transnational Advocacy Networks. *International Studies Quarterly* 51(1): 99–120.

Cartwright, William S. 1999. Costs of Drug Abuse to Society. *Journal of Mental Health Policy and Economics* 2(3): 133–134.

Cattaneo, Silvia, and Sarah Parker. 2008. *Implementing the United Nations Programme of Action on Small Arms and Light Weapons: Analysis of the National Reports Submitted by States from 2002 to 2008*. UNIDIR. Geneva.

Chippindale, Christopher, and David W. J. Gill. 2000. Material Consequences of Contemporary Classical Collecting. *American Journal of Archaeology* 104(3): 463–511.

Chippindale, Christopher, and David W. J. Gill. 2001. On-Line Auctions: A New Venue for the Antiquities Market. *Culture Without Context* 9: 4–13.

Chippindale, Christopher, David Gill, Emily Salter, and Christian Hamilton. 2001. Collecting the Classical World: First Steps in a Quantitative History. *International Journal of Cultural Property* 10(1): 1–31.

Chuang, Janie. 2006. The United States as Global Sheriff: Using Unilateral Sanctions to Combat Human Trafficking. *Michigan Journal of International Law* 27: 437–494.

Chuang, Janie A. 2010. Rescuing Trafficking from Ideological Capture: Prostitution Reform and Anti-Trafficking Law and Policy. *University of Pennsylvania Law Review* 158: 1655–1728.

Clapp, Jennifer. 2001. *Toxic Exports: The Transfer of Hazardous Wastes from Rich to Poor Countries*. Ithaca, N.Y.: Cornell University Press.

Coggins, Clemency. 1969. Illicit Traffic of Pre-Columbian Antiquities. *Art Journal* 29(1): 94–98, 114.

Coggins, Clemency. 1970. The Maya Scandal: How Thieves Strip Sites of Past Cultures. *Smithsonian* 1(7): 8–17.

Coggins, Clemency. 1972. Archaeology and the Art Market. *Science* 175(4019): 263–266.

Coggins, Clemency Chase. 1998. United States Cultural Property Legislation: Observations of a Combatant. *International Journal of Cultural Property* 7(1): 52–68.

Cook, Brian F. 1995. The Trade in Antiquities: A Curator's View. In *Antiquities: Trade or Betrayed: Legal, Ethical and Conservation Issues*, edited by Kathryn Walker Tubb, 181–192. London: Archetype Publications.

Cooper, Neil. 2000. The Pariah Agenda and New Labour's Ethical Arms Sales Policy. In *New Labour's Foreign Policy: A New Moral Crusade?*, edited by Richard Little and Mark Wickham-Jones, 147–167. Manchester and New York: Manchester University Press.

Craig, Richard B. 1980. Operation Intercept: The International Politics of Pressure. *The Review of Politics* 42(4): 556–580.

Crowley, Michael, Roy Isbister, and Sarah Meek. 2002. *Building Comprehensive Controls on Small Arms Manufacturing, Transfer and End-Use*. Biting the Bullet, Briefing 13. BASIC (British American Security Information Council), International Alert, and Saferworld.

Cukier, Wendy, and Victor W. Sidel. 2006. *The Global Gun Epidemic: From Saturday Night Specials to AK-47s*. Westport, Conn.: Praeger Security International.

Cuno, James. 2008. *Who Owns Antiquity? Museums and the Battle Over Our Ancient Heritage*. Princeton, N.J.: Princeton University Press.

Dai, Xinyuan. 2007. *International Institutions and National Policies*. Cambridge and New York: Cambridge University Press.

Das, Keshab. 2003. The Domestic Politics of TRIPs: Pharmaceutical Interests, Public Health, and NGO Influence in India. Globalization and Poverty research program.

Davenport, Christian, and David A. Armstrong II. 2004. Democracy and the Violation of Human Rights: A Statistical Analysis from 1976 to 1996. *American Journal of Political Science* 48(3): 538–554.

Davis, Christina L. 2004. International Institutions and Issue Linkage: Building Support for Agricultural Trade Liberalization. *American Political Science Review* 98(1): 153–169.

Deere, Carolyn. 2009. *The Implementation Game: The TRIPS Agreement and the Global Politics of Intellectual Property Reform in Developing Countries.* Oxford and New York: Oxford University Press.

Demleitner, Nora V. 1994. Forced Prostitution: Naming an International Offense. *Fordham International Law Journal* 18: 163–197.

Dempsey, Michelle Madden. 2010. Sex Trafficking and Criminalization: In Defense of Feminist Abolitionism. *University of Pennsylvania Law Review* 158: 1729–1778.

DeSombre, Elizabeth R. 2000. *Domestic Sources of International Environmental Policy: Industry, Environmentalists, and U.S. Power.* Cambridge, Mass.: MIT Press.

DeStefano, Anthony M. 2007. *The War on Human Trafficking: U.S. Policy Assessed.* New Brunswick, N.J.: Rutgers University Press.

Dimitrov, Martin K. 2009. *Piracy and the State: The Politics of Intellectual Property Rights in China.* New York: Cambridge University Press.

Ditmore, Melissa, and Marjan Wijers. 2003. The Negotiations on the UN Protocol on Trafficking in Persons. *Nemesis* 4: 79–88.

Doezema, Jo. 2000. Loose Women or Lost Women? The Re-emergence of the Myth of White Slavery in Contemporary Discourses of Trafficking in Women. *Gender Issues* 18(1): 23–50.

Donnelly, Jack. 1992. The United Nations and the Global Drug Control Regime. In *Drug Policy in the Americas*, edited by Peter H. Smith, 282–304. Boulder, Colo.: Westview.

Downs, George W., and David M. Rocke. 1987. Tacit Bargaining and Arms Control. *World Politics* 37(3): 297–325.

Drahos, Peter. 2002. Developing Countries and International Intellectual Property Standard-Setting. *Journal of World Intellectual Property* 5(5): 765–789.

Drezner, Daniel W. 2007. *All Politics is Global: Explaining International Regulatory Regimes.* Princeton, N.J.: Princeton University Press.

DuBoff, Leonard D., ed. 1975. *Art Law: Domestic and International.* South Hackensack, N.J.: Fred B. Rothman & Co.

DuBoff, Leonard D., James A.R. Nafziger, André Emmerich, Mark B. Feldman, James McAlee, and Paul M. Bator. 1976. Proceedings of the Panel on the U.S. Enabling Legislation of the UNESCO Convention on the Means of Prohibiting and Preventing the Illicit Import, Export and Transfer of Ownership of Cultural Property. *Syracuse Journal of International Law and Commerce* 4: 97–139.

Ede, James. 1995. The Antiquities Trade: Towards a More Balanced View. In *Antiquities: Trade or Betrayed: Legal, Ethical and Conservation Issues*, edited by Kathryn Walker Tubb, 211–214. London: Archetype Publications.

Ede, James. 1998. Ethics, the Antiquities Trade, and Archaeology. *International Journal of Cultural Property* 7(1): 128–131.

Edwards, Adam, and Peter Gill, eds. 2003. *Transnational Organised Crime: Perspectives on Global Security.* London and New York: Routledge.

Eggers, Andrew C., and Jens Hainmueller. 2009. MPs for Sale? Returns to Office in Postwar British Politics. *American Political Science Review* 103(4): 513–533.

Elia, Ricardo J. 2001. Analysis of the Looting, Selling, and Collecting of Apulian Red-Figure Vases: A Quantitative Approach. In *Trade in Illicit Antiquities: The Destruction of the World's Archaeological Heritage*, edited by Neil Brodie, Jennifer Doole, and Colin Renfrew, 145–153. Cambridge: McDonald Institute for Archaeological Research.

Elia, Ricardo J. 2009. Mythology of the Antiquities Market. In *Cultural Heritage Issues: The Legacy of Conquest, Colonization, and Commerce*, edited by James A.R. Nafziger and Ann M. Nicgorski, 239–255. Leiden: Martinus Nijhoff.

Elkins, Zachary, Andrew T. Guzman, and Beth A. Simmons. 2006. Competing for Capital: The Diffusion of Bilateral Investment Treaties, 1960–2000. *International Organization* 60(4): 811–846.

Engelbrecht H.C., and F.C. Hanighen. 1934. *Merchants of Death: A Study of the International Armament Industry.* New York: Dodd, Mead & Company.

Erickson, Jennifer L. 2008. When Do the Takers Become the Makers? The Promotion of "Responsible Arms Trade" Norms. Cornell University. Unpublished manuscript.

Erickson, Jennifer L. 2010. Social Incentives for Policy Commitment: International Reputation and "Responsible" Arms Export Controls. Paper presented at the annual convention of the International Studies Association, New Orleans, February.

Ewing, Douglas C. 1999. What is "Stolen"? The McClain Case Revisited. In *The Ethics of Collecting Cultural Property: Whose Culture? Whose Property?*, 2nd ed., edited by Phyllis Mauch Messenger, 177–183. Albuquerque: University of New Mexico Press.

Fearon, James D. 1998. Bargaining, Enforcement, and International Cooperation. *International Organization* 52(2): 269–305.

Feingold, David A. 2010. Trafficking in Numbers: The Social Construction of Human Trafficking Data. In *Sex, Drugs, and Body Counts: The Politics of Numbers in Global Crime and Conflict*, edited by Peter Andreas and Kelly M. Greenhill, 46–74. Ithaca, N.Y.: Cornell University Press.

Feldman, Mark B., and Ronald J. Bettauer. 1970. *Report of the United States Delegation to the Special Committee of Governmental Experts to Examine the Draft Convention on the Means of Prohibiting and Preventing the Illicit Import, Export and Transfer of Ownership of Cultural Property.* Submitted to the Secretary of State. July 27.

Financial Action Task Force. 2000a. *Report on Non-Cooperative Countries and Territories.* Paris. February 14.

Financial Action Task Force. 2000b. *Review to Identify Non-Cooperative Countries or Territories: Increasing the Worldwide Effectiveness of Anti-Money Laundering Measures.* Paris. June 22.

Financial Action Task Force. 2001. *Review to Identify Non-Cooperative Countries or Territories: Increasing the Worldwide Effectiveness of Anti-Money Laundering Measures*. Paris. June 22.

Financial Action Task Force. 2007a. *Summary of the Third Mutual Evaluation Report: Anti-Money Laundering and Combating the Financing of Terrorism—Greece*. Paris. June 29.

Financial Action Task Force. 2007b. *Annual Review of Non-Cooperative Countries and Territories 2006–2007: Eighth NCCT Review*. Paris. October 12.

Financial Action Task Force. 2009. *Financial Action Task Force Annual Report 2008–2009*. Paris. July.

Financial Action Task Force. 2010. *FATF 40 Recommendations, October 2003*. Paris.

Finnemore, Martha. 1996. *National Interests in International Society*. Ithaca, N.Y.: Cornell University Press.

Finnemore, Martha, and Kathryn Sikkink. 1998. International Norm Dynamics and Political Change. *International Organization* 52(4): 887–917.

Fitzpatrick, James F. 1998. Stealth UNIDROIT: Is USIA the Villain? *NYU Journal of International Law and Politics* 31: 47–77.

Friesendorf, Cornelius. 2007. *US Foreign Policy and the War on Drugs: Displacing the Cocaine and Heroin Industry*. London and New York: Routledge.

Friman, H. Richard. 1996. *NarcoDiplomacy: Exporting the U.S. War on Drugs*. Ithaca, N.Y.: Cornell University Press.

Friman, H. Richard, ed. 2009a. *Crime and the Global Political Economy*. Boulder, Colo.: Lynne Rienner.

Friman, H. Richard. 2009b. Externalizing the Costs of Prohibition. In *Crime and the Global Political Economy*, edited by H. Richard Friman, 49–65. Boulder, Colo.: Lynne Rienner.

Friman, H. Richard. 2010. Numbers and Certification: Assessing Foreign Compliance in Combating Narcotics and Human Trafficking. In *Sex, Drugs, and Body Counts: The Politics of Numbers in Global Crime and Conflict*, edited by Peter Andreas and Kelly M. Greenhill, 75–109. Ithaca, N.Y.: Cornell University Press.

Friman, H. Richard, and Peter Andreas, eds. 1999a. *The Illicit Global Economy and State Power*. Lanham, Md.: Rowman & Littlefield.

Friman, H. Richard, and Peter Andreas. 1999b. Introduction: International Relations and the Illicit Global Economy. In *The Illicit Global Economy and State Power*, edited by H. Richard Friman and Peter Andreas, 1–23. Lanham, Md.: Rowman & Littlefield.

Friman, H. Richard, and Simon Reich. 2007. Human Trafficking and the Balkans. In *Human Trafficking, Human Security, and the Balkans*, edited by H. Richard Friman and Simon Reich, 1–19. Pittsburgh, Pa.: University of Pittsburgh Press.

Gado, Boubé. 2001. The Republic of Niger. In *Trade in Illicit Antiquities: The Destruction of the World's Archaeological Heritage*, edited by Neil Brodie, Jennifer Doole, and Colin Renfrew, 57–72. Cambridge: McDonald Institute for Archaeological Research.

Gallagher, Anne. 2001. Human Rights and the New UN Protocols on Trafficking and Migrant Smuggling: A Preliminary Analysis. *Human Rights Quarterly* 23(4): 975–1004.

Garcia, Denise. 2006. *Small Arms and Security: New Emerging International Norms*. London and New York: Routledge.

Geneva Declaration Secretariat. 2008. *Global Burden of Armed Violence*. Geneva.

Gershuni, Rahel. 2005. The Response of the Israeli Government to Trafficking in Persons: A Study in Shifting Institutional Attitudes. Presented at the College of Management Law School, Rishon LeZion, Israel. December 22.

Gershuni, Rahel. 2007a. Trafficking in Persons in Israel. Israel's Ministry of Justice. March.

Gershuni, Rahel. 2007b. Israel's National Coordinator of the Battle against Trafficking in Persons. Israel's Ministry of Justice. March.

Gershuni, Rochelle. 2004. Trafficking in Persons for the Purpose of Prostitution: The Israeli Experience. *Mediterranean Quarterly* 15(4): 133–146.

Gerstenblith, Patty. 2001. The Public Interest in the Restitution of Cultural Objects. *Connecticut Journal of International Law* 16: 197–246.

Gerstenblith, Patty. 2006. Recent Developments in the Legal Protection of Cultural Heritage. In *Archaeology, Cultural Heritage, and the Antiquities Trade*, edited by Neil Brodie, Morag M. Kersel, Christina Luke, and Kathryn Walker Tubb, 68–92. Gainesville, Fla.: University Press of Florida.

Gerstenblith, Patty. 2007. Controlling the International Market in Antiquities: Reducing the Harm, Preserving the Past. *Chicago Journal of International Law* 8: 169–195.

Gilgan, Elizabeth. 2001. Looting and the Market for Maya Objects: A Belizean Perspective. In *Trade in Illicit Antiquities: The Destruction of the World's Archaeological Heritage*, edited by Neil Brodie, Jennifer Doole, and Colin Renfrew, 73–87. Cambridge: McDonald Institute for Archaeological Research.

Gill, David W.J., and Christopher Chippindale. 1993. Material and Intellectual Consequences of Esteem for Cycladic Figures. *American Journal of Archaeology* 97(4): 601–659.

Gill, David, and Christopher Chippindale. 2006. From Boston to Rome: Reflections on Returning Antiquities. *International Journal of Cultural Property* 13(3): 311–331.

Gill, David, and Christopher Chippindale. 2007. From Malibu to Rome: Further Developments on the Return of Antiquities. *International Journal of Cultural Property* 14(2): 205–240.

Gillies, Alexandra. 2010. Reputational Concerns and the Emergence of Oil Sector Transparency as an International Norm. *International Studies Quarterly* 54(1): 103–126.

Gilmore, William C. 2004. *Dirty Money: The Evolution of International Measures to Counter Money Laundering and the Financing of Terrorism*. 3rd ed. Strasbourg: Council of Europe Publishing.

Goldstein, Judith L., Miles Kahler, Robert O. Keohane, and Anne-Marie Slaughter, eds. 2001. *Legalization and World Politics*. Cambridge, Mass.: MIT Press.

Goldstein, Judith L., Douglas Rivers, and Michael Tomz. 2007. Institutions in International Relations: Understanding the Effects of the GATT and the WTO on World Trade. *International Organization* 61(1): 37–67.

Grant, J. Andrew, and Ian Taylor. 2004. Global Governance and Conflict Diamonds: The Kimberley Process and the Quest for Clean Gems. *The Round Table* 93(375): 385–401.

Grieco, Joseph M., Christopher Gelpi, Jason Reifler, and Peter D. Feaver. 2011. Let's Get a Second Opinion: International Institutions and American Public Support for War. *International Studies Quarterly* 55(2): 563–583.

Grossman, Gene M., and Elhanan Helpman. 1994. Protection for Sale. *American Economic Review* 84(4): 833–850.

Grossman, Gene M., and Elhanan Helpman. 2001. *Special Interest Politics*. Cambridge, Mass.: MIT Press.

Gruenpeter Gold, Leah, and Nissan Ben Ami. 2004. *National NGOs Report to the Annual UN Commission on Human Rights: Evaluation of National Authorities Activities and Actual Facts on the Trafficking in Persons for the Purpose of Prostitution in Israel*. Awareness Center. Tel Aviv. April.

Hafner-Burton, Emilie M. 2005. Trading Human Rights: How Preferential Trade Agreements Influence Government Repression. *International Organization* 59(3): 593–629.

Hafner-Burton, Emilie M. 2008. Sticks and Stones: Naming and Shaming the Human Rights Enforcement Problem. *International Organization* 62(4): 689–716.

Hafner-Burton, Emilie M. 2009. *Forced to be Good: Why Trade Agreements Boost Human Rights*. Ithaca, N.Y.: Cornell University Press.

Hamilton, Wardlaw. 1975. Museum Acquisitions: The Case for Self-Regulation. In *Art Law: Domestic and International*, edited by Leonard D. DuBoff, 347–362. South Hackensack, N.J.: Fred B. Rothman & Co.

Harvey, Jackie. 2004. Compliance and Reporting Issues Arising for Financial Institutions from Money Laundering Regulations: A Preliminary Cost Benefit Study. *Journal of Money Laundering Control* 7(4): 333–346.

Haufler, Virginia. 2001. *A Public Role for the Private Sector: Industry Self-Regulation in a Global Economy*. Washington, D.C.: Carnegie Endowment for International Peace.

Haufler, Virginia. 2002. Industry Regulation and Self-Regulation: The Case of Labour Standards. In *Enhancing Global Governance: Towards A New Diplomacy?*, edited by Andrew F. Cooper, John English, and Ramesh Thakur, 162–186. Tokyo and New York: United Nations University Press.

Hawkins, Darren G., David A. Lake, Daniel L. Nielson, and Michael J. Tierney, eds. 2006. *Delegation and Agency in International Organizations*. Cambridge and New York: Cambridge University Press.

Heffernan, Richard. 2003. New Labour and Thatcherism. In *The New Labour Reader*, edited by Andrew Chadwick and Richard Heffernan, 49–58. Cambridge: Polity Press.

Helleiner, Eric. 1999. State Power and the Regulation of Illicit Activity in Global Finance. In *The Illicit Global Economy and State Power*, edited by H. Richard Friman and Peter Andreas, 53–90. Lanham, Md.: Rowman & Littlefield.

Helleiner, Eric. 2002. The Politics of Global Financial Regulation: Lessons from the Fight Against Money Laundering. In *International Capital Markets: Systems in Transition*, edited by John Eatwell and Lance Taylor, 177–204. Oxford and New York: Oxford University Press.

Hertzke, Allen D. 2004. *Freeing God's Children: The Unlikely Alliance for Global Human Rights*. Lanham, Md.: Rowman & Littlefield.

Hingston, Ann Guthrie. 1999. U.S. Implementation of the UNESCO Cultural Property Convention. In *The Ethics of Collecting Cultural Property: Whose Culture? Whose Property?*, 2nd ed., edited by Phyllis Mauch Messenger, 129–147. Albuquerque: University of New Mexico Press.

Hinojosa, Victor J. 2007. *Domestic Politics and International Narcotics Control: U.S. Relations with Mexico and Colombia, 1989–2000*. New York: Routledge.

Holowell, Julie. 2006. Moral Arguments on Subsistence Digging. In *The Ethics of Archaeology: Philosophical Perspectives on Archaeological Practice*, edited by Chris Scarre and Geoffrey Scarre, 69–93. Cambridge and New York: Cambridge University Press.

Hughes, Donna M. 2001. The "Natasha" Trade: Transnational Sex Trafficking. *National Institute of Justice Journal* 246: 8–15.

Inciardi, James A. 1999. American Drug Policy: The Continuing Debate. In *The Drug Legalization Debate*, 2nd ed., edited by James A. Inciardi, 1–8. Thousand Oaks, Calif.: Sage.

International Narcotics Control Board. 2010. *Report of the International Narcotics Control Board for 2009*. E/INCB/2009/1. New York: United Nations.

ITAP (Illicit Trade Advisory Panel). 2000. *Report of the Ministerial Advisory Panel on Illicit Trade*. Department for Culture, Media, and Sport. London. December. Available at http://webarchive.nationalarchives.gov.uk/+/http://www.culture.gov.uk/reference_library/publications/4693.aspx (accessed July 27, 2011).

ITAP. 2001. Progress Report of the Ministerial Advisory Panel on the Illicit Trade in Cultural Objects. Available at http://www.culture.gov.uk/images/publications/ITAPProgressReport2001.pdf (accessed July 27, 2011).

Johnston, Alastair Iain. 2001. Treating International Institutions as Social Environments. *International Studies Quarterly* 45(4): 487–515.

Jojarth, Christine. 2009. *Crime, War, and Global Trafficking: Designing International Cooperation*. Cambridge and New York: Cambridge University Press.

Jote, Kifle. 1994. *International Legal Protection of Cultural Heritage*. Stockholm: Juristförlaget.

Kantz, Carola. 2007. The Power of Socialization: Engaging the Diamond Industry in the Kimberley Process. *Business and Politics* 9(3): Article 2.

Kaufmann, Chaim D., and Robert A. Pape. 1999. Explaining Costly International Moral Action: Britain's Sixty-year Campaign Against the Atlantic Slave Trade. *International Organization* 53(4): 631–668.

Keck, Margaret E., and Kathryn Sikkink. 1998. *Activists beyond Borders: Advocacy Networks in International Politics*. Ithaca, N.Y.: Cornell University Press.

Keohane, Robert O. 1984. *After Hegemony: Cooperation and Discord in the World Political Economy*. Princeton, N.J.: Princeton University Press.

Kersel, Morag M. 2006. From the Ground to the Buyer: A Market Analysis of the Trade in Illegal Antiquities. In *Archaeology, Cultural Heritage, and the Antiquities Trade*, edited by Neil Brodie, Morag M. Kersel, Christina Luke, and Kathryn Walker Tubb, 188–205. Gainesville, Fla.: University Press of Florida.

Kiss, Yudit. 2004. *Small Arms and Light Weapons Production in Eastern, Central, and Southeast Europe*. Small Arms Survey, Occasional Paper 13. October.

Klieman, Aharon. 1992. *Double-Edged Sword: Israel Defense Exports as an Instrument of Foreign Policy* (in Hebrew). Tel Aviv: Am Oved.

Kono, Daniel Y. 2006. Optimal Obfuscation: Democracy and Trade Policy Transparency. *American Political Science Review* 100(3): 369–384.

Koremenos, Barbara. 2001. Loosening the Ties that Bind: A Learning Model of Agreement Flexibility. *International Organization* 55(2): 289–325.

Koremenos, Barbara. 2005. Contracting around International Uncertainty. *American Political Science Review* 99(4): 549–565.

Koremenos, Barbara, Chares Lipson, and Duncan Snidal. 2001. The Rational Design of International Institutions. *International Organization* 55(4): 761–799.

Krasner, Stephen D., ed. 1983. *International Regimes*. Ithaca, N.Y.: Cornell University Press.

Krasner, Stephen D. 1991. Global Communications and National Power: Life on the Pareto Frontier. *World Politics* 43(3): 336–366.

Krause, Keith. 1991. Military Statecraft: Power and Influence in Soviet and American Arms Transfer Relationships. *International Studies Quarterly* 35(3): 313–336.

Krause, Keith. 2002. Multilateral Diplomacy, Norm Building, and UN Conferences: The Case of Small Arms and Light Weapons. *Global Governance* 8(2): 247–263.

Kyle, David, and Rey Koslowski, eds. 2001. *Global Human Smuggling: Comparative Perspectives*. Baltimore: Johns Hopkins University Press.

Kytömäki, Elli. 2006. Regional Approaches to Small Arms Control: Vital to Implementing the UN Programme of Action. *Disarmament Forum* 2006(1): 55–64.

Lai, Brian, and Daniel S. Morey. 2006. Impact of Regime Type on the Influence of U.S. Foreign Aid. *Foreign Policy Analysis* 2(4): 385–404.

Lake, David A., and Robert Powell. 1999. International Relations: A Strategic-Choice Approach. In *Strategic Choice and International Relations*, edited by David A. Lake and Robert Powell, 3–38. Princeton, N.J.: Princeton University Press.

LaPierre, Wayne. 2006. *The Global War on Your Guns: Inside the U.N. Plan to Destroy the Bill of Rights*. Nashville: Nelson Current.

La Porta, Rafael, Florencio Lopez-de-Silanes, Andrei Shleifer, and Robert Vishny. 1999. The Quality of Government. *Journal of Law, Economics, and Organization* 15(1): 222–279.

Laurance, Edward, and Rachel Stohl. 2002. *Making Global Public Policy: The Case of Small Arms and Light Weapons.* Small Arms Survey, Occasional Paper 7. December.

le Billon, Philippe. 2001. Angola's Political Economy of War: The Role of Oil and Diamonds, 1975–2000. *African Affairs* 100(398): 55–80.

Lebovic, James H., and Erik Voeten. 2006. The Politics of Shame: The Condemnation of Country Human Rights Practices in the UNCHR. *International Studies Quarterly* 50(4): 861–888.

Lebovic, James H., and Erik Voeten. 2009. The Cost of Shame: International Organizations and Foreign Aid in the Punishing of Human Rights Violators. *Journal of Peace Research* 46(1): 79–97.

Levenkorn, Nomi, and Yossi Dahan. 2003. *Women as Commodities: Trafficking in Women in Israel 2003.* Hotline for Migrant Workers, Isha L'Isha—Haifa Feminist Center, and Adva Center.

Levy, David L., and Peter J. Newell, eds. 2005. *The Business of Global Environmental Governance.* Cambridge, Mass.: MIT Press.

Liddick, Donald R. Jr. 2004. *The Global Underworld: Transnational Crime and the United States.* Westport, Conn.: Praeger.

Lujala, Päivi, Nils Petter Gleditsch, and Elisabeth Gilmore. 2005. A Diamond Curse? Civil War and a Lootable Resource. *Journal of Conflict Resolution* 49(4): 538–562.

Lumsdaine, David Halloran. 1993. *Moral Vision in International Politics: The Foreign Aid Regime, 1949–1989.* Princeton, N.J.: Princeton University Press.

Mackenzie, S. R. M. 2005. *Going, Going, Gone: Regulating the Market in Illicit Antiquities.* Leicester, UK: Institute of Art and Law.

Mackenzie, Simon. 2011. Illicit Deals in Cultural Objects as Crimes of the Powerful. *Crime, Law and Social Change* 56(2): 133–153.

Mackenzie, Simon, and Penny Green. 2008. Performative Regulation: A Case Study in How Powerful People Avoid Criminal Labels. *British Journal of Criminology* 48(2): 138–153.

Mansfield, Edward D., Helen V. Milner, and B. Peter Rosendorff. 2002. Why Democracies Cooperate More: Electoral Control and International Trade Agreements. *International Organization* 56(3): 477–513.

Mares, David R. 1992. The Logic of Inter-American Cooperation on Drugs. In *Drug Policy in the Americas,* edited by Peter H. Smith, 329–342. Boulder, Colo.: Westview.

Mares, David R. 2006. *Drug Wars and Coffeehouses: The Political Economy of the International Drug Trade.* Washington, D.C.: CQ Press.

Marthari, Marisa. 2001. Altering Information from the Past: Illegal Excavations in Greece and the Case of the Early Bronze Age Cyclades. In *Trade in Illicit Antiquities: The Destruction of the World's Archaeological Heritage,* edited by Neil Brodie, Jennifer Doole, and Colin Renfrew, 161–172. Cambridge: McDonald Institute for Archaeological Research.

Martin, Lisa L. 1992a. Interests, Power, and Multilateralism. *International Organization* 46(4): 765–792.

Martin, Lisa L. 1992b. *Coercive Cooperation: Explaining Multilateral Economic Sanctions*. Princeton, N.J.: Princeton University Press.

Maskus, Keith E. 2000. *Intellectual Property Rights in the Global Economy*. Washington, D.C.: Institute for International Economics.

Maskus, Keith E., Sean M. Dougherty, and Andrew Mertha. 2005. Intellectual Property Rights and Economic Development in China. In *Intellectual Property and Development: Lessons from Recent Economic Research*, edited by Carsten Fink and Keith E. Maskus, 295–331. Washington, D.C. and New York: World Bank and Oxford University Press.

Matsuda, David. 1998. The Ethics of Archaeology, Subsistence Digging, and Artifact Looting in Latin America: Point, Muted Counterpoint. *International Journal of Cultural Property* 7(1): 87–97.

Matthews, Duncan. 2002. *Globalising Intellectual Property Rights: The TRIPs Agreement*. London and New York: Routledge.

McAllister, William B. 1992. Conflict of Interest in the International Drug Control System. In *Drug Control Policy: Essays in Historical and Comparative Perspective*, edited by William O. Walker III, 143–166. University Park, Pa.: Pennsylvania State University Press.

McAllister, William B. 2000. *Drug Diplomacy in the Twentieth Century: An International History*. London and New York: Routledge.

McBride, Duane C., Yvonne M. Terry, and James A. Inciardi. 1999. Alternative Perspectives on the Drug Policy Debate. In *The Drug Legalization Debate*, 2nd ed., edited by James A. Inciardi, 9–54. Thousand Oaks, Calif.: Sage.

McWilliams, John C. 1992. Through the Past Darkly: The Politics and Policies of America's Drug War. In *Drug Control Policy: Essays in Historical and Comparative Perspective*, edited by William O. Walker III, 5–41. University Park, Pa.: Pennsylvania State University Press.

Mearsheimer, John J. 1995. The False Promise of International Institutions. *International Security* 19(3): 5–49.

Merryman, John Henry. 1986. Two Ways of Thinking About Cultural Property. *American Journal of International Law* 80: 831–853.

Merryman, John Henry. 2005. Cultural Property Internationalism. *International Journal of Cultural Property* 12(1): 11–39.

Mertha, Andrew C. 2005. *The Politics of Piracy: Intellectual Property in Contemporary China*. Ithaca, N.Y.: Cornell University Press.

Mertus, Julie, and Andrea Bertone. 2007. Combating Trafficking: International Efforts and Their Ramifications. In *Human Trafficking, Human Security, and the Balkans*, edited by H. Richard Friman and Simon Reich, 40–60. Pittsburgh, Pa.: University of Pittsburgh Press.

Meyer, Karl E. 1973. *The Plundered Past*. New York: Atheneum.

Milner, Helen V. 1997. *Interests, Institutions, and Information: Domestic Politics and International Relations*. Princeton, N.J.: Princeton University Press.

Milner, Helen V., and Keiko Kubota. 2005. Why the Move to Free Trade? Democracy and Trade Policy in the Developing Countries. *International Organization* 59(1): 107–143.

Mitchell, Ronald B. 1994. Regime Design Matters: International Oil Pollution and Treaty Compliance. *International Organization* 48(3): 425–458.

Mitchell, Ronald B. 2003. International Environmental Agreements: A Survey of Their Features, Formation, and Effects. *Annual Review of Environment and Resources* 28: 429–461.

Mitchell, Ronald B. 2010. *International Politics and the Environment*. London: Sage.

Mitchell, Ronald B., and Patricia M. Keilbach. 2001. Situation Structure and Institutional Design: Reciprocity, Coercion, and Exchange. *International Organization* 55(4): 891–917.

Moghadam, Assaf. 2009. Motives for Martyrdom: Al-Qaida, Salafi Jihad, and the Spread of Suicide Attacks. *International Security* 33(3): 46–78.

Mokdad, Ali H., James S. Marks, Donna F. Stroup, and Julie L. Gerberding. 2004. Actual Causes of Death in the United States, 2000. *JAMA* 291(10): 1238–1245.

Moravcsik, Andrew. 1997. Taking Preferences Seriously: A Liberal Theory of International Politics. *International Organization* 51(4): 513–553.

Moravcsik, Andrew. 1998. *The Choice for Europe: Social Purpose and State Power from Messina to Maastricht*. Ithaca, N.Y.: Cornell University Press.

Moravcsik, Andrew. 2000. The Origins of Human Rights Regimes: Democratic Delegation in Postwar Europe. *International Organization* 54(2): 217–252.

Moravcsik, Andrew. 2003. Theory Synthesis in International Relations: Real Not Metaphysical. *International Studies Review* 5(1): 131–136.

Moravcsik, Andrew. 2008. The New Liberalism. In *The Oxford Handbook of International Relations*, edited by Christian Reus-Smit and Duncan Snidal, 234–254. Oxford and New York: Oxford University Press.

Moravcsik, Andrew. 2010. Liberal Theories of International Relations: A Primer. Princeton University. Unpublished manuscript.

Morgenthau, Hans J. 1985. *Politics among Nations: The Struggle for Power and Peace*. 6th ed. New York: McGraw-Hill.

Morrison, Carolyn. R. 1995. United Kingdom Export Policies in Relation to Antiquities. In *Antiquities: Trade or Betrayed: Legal, Ethical and Conservation Issues*, edited by Kathryn Walker Tubb, 205–210. London: Archetype Publications.

Morrow, James D. 2007. When Do States Follow the Laws of War? *American Political Science Review* 101(3): 559–572.

Musto, David F. 1992. Patterns in U.S. Drug Abuse and Response. In *Drug Policy in the Americas*, edited by Peter H. Smith, 29–44. Boulder, Colo.: Westview.

Musto, David F. 1999. *The American Disease: Origins of Narcotic Control*. 3rd ed. New York: Oxford University Press.

Nadelmann, Ethan A. 1990. Global Prohibition Regimes: The Evolution of Norms in International Society. *International Organization* 44(4): 479–526.

Naím, Moisés. 2005. *Illicit: How Smugglers, Traffickers, and Copycats are Hijacking the Global Economy*. New York: Doubleday.

Nathan, Gilad. 2007. *Problems in Employing Foreign Workers in Construction through Corporations* (in Hebrew). Knesset Research and Information Center. Jerusalem. August 6.

Nathan, Gilad. 2009a. *Police Treatment of Victims of Human Trafficking for the Purposes of Labor and Prostitution* (in Hebrew). Knesset Research and Information Center. Jerusalem. November 10.

Nathan, Gilad. 2009b. *Migrant Workers and Human Trafficking Victims: Government Policy and Immigration-Authority Activity* (in Hebrew). Knesset Research and Information Center. Jerusalem. October 20.

Nathan, Gilad. 2009c. *Foreign Workers in Israel: Central Issues and Update* (in Hebrew). Knesset Research and Information Center. Jerusalem. February 2.

Nathan, Gilad. 2011. *Addressing the Illegal Charging of Recruitment Fees from Foreign Workers* (in Hebrew). Knesset Research and Information Center. Jerusalem. January 25.

Neumayer, Eric. 2001. How Regime Theory and the Economic Theory of International Environmental Cooperation Can Learn from Each Other. *Global Environmental Politics* 1(1): 122–147.

Newell, Peter J. 2005. Business and International Environmental Governance: The State of the Art. In *The Business of Global Environmental Governance*, edited by David L. Levy and Peter J. Newell, 21–45. Cambridge, Mass.: MIT Press.

Oatley, Thomas. 2008. *International Political Economy: Interests and Institutions in the Global Economy*. 3rd ed. New York: Pearson/Longman.

Oatley, Thomas, and Robert Nabors. 1998. Redistributive Cooperation: Market Failure, Wealth Transfers, and the Basle Accord. *International Organization* 52(1): 35–54.

OECD. 2008. *The Economic Impact of Counterfeiting and Piracy*. Paris: OECD Publishing.

Office of National Drug Control Policy. 2004. *The Economic Costs of Drug Abuse in the United States, 1992–2002*. Washington, D.C. December.

O'Keefe, Patrick J. 2000. *Commentary on the UNESCO 1970 Convention on Illicit Traffic*. Leicester, UK: Institute of Art and Law.

Oye, Kenneth A. 1985. Explaining Cooperation under Anarchy: Hypotheses and Strategies. *World Politics* 38(1): 1–24.

Özgen, Engin. 2001. Some Remarks on the Destruction of Turkey's Archaeological Heritage. In *Trade in Illicit Antiquities: The Destruction of the World's Archaeological Heritage*, edited by Neil Brodie, Jennifer Doole, and Colin Renfrew, 119–120. Cambridge: McDonald Institute for Archaeological Research.

Parker, Sarah. 2011. *Improving the Effectiveness of the Programme of Action on Small Arms: Implementation Challenges and Opportunities*. UNIDIR. Geneva.

Parliamentary Inquiry Committee on Trafficking in Women. 2005. *Final Report of the Parliamentary Inquiry Committee on Trafficking in Women* (in Hebrew). Jerusalem. March.

Pearlstein, William G. 2005. Cultural Property, Congress, the Courts, and Customs: The Decline and Fall of the Antiquities Market? In *Who Owns the*

Past? *Cultural Policy, Cultural Property, and the Law*, edited by Kate Fitz Gibbon, 9–31. Piscataway, N.J.: Rutgers University Press.

Perl, Raphael. 2006. *Drug Control: International Policy and Approaches.* Congressional Research Service. February 2.

Pierre, Andrew. 1982. *The Global Politics of Arms Sales.* Princeton, N.J.: Princeton University Press.

Pieth, Mark, and Gemma Aiolfi. 2003. *Anti-Money Laundering: Levelling the Playing Field.* Basel Institute on Governance. Basel.

Phillips, Tim. 2005. *Knockoff: The Deadly Trade in Counterfeit Goods.* London and Sterling, Va.: Kogan Page.

Poe, Steven C., C. Neal Tate, and Linda Camp Keith. 1999. Repression of the Human Right to Personal Integrity Revisited: A Global Cross-National Study Covering the Years 1976–1993. *International Studies Quarterly* 43(2): 291–313.

Politis, Konstantinos D. 2002. Dealing with the Dealers and Tomb Robbers: The Realities of the Archaeology of the Ghor es-Safi in Jordan. In *Illicit Antiquities: The Theft of Culture and the Extinction of Archaeology*, edited by Neil Brodie and Kathryn Walker Tubb, 257–267. London and New York: Routledge.

Price, Richard. 1998. Reversing the Gun Sights: Transnational Civil Society Targets Land Mines. *International Organization* 52(3): 613–644.

Prott, Lyndel V. 1995. National and International Laws on the Protection of the Cultural Heritage. In *Antiquities: Trade or Betrayed: Legal, Ethical and Conservation Issues*, edited by Kathryn Walker Tubb, 57–72. London: Archetype Publications.

Prott, Lyndel V. 1997. *Commentary on the UNIDROIT Convention.* Leicester, UK: Institute of Art and Law.

Prott, Lyndel V., and P.J. O'Keefe. 1983. *National Legal Control of Illicit Traffic in Cultural Property.* CLT-83/WS/16. UNESCO. Paris. May 11.

Prott, Lyndel V., and Patrick J. O'Keefe. 1988. *Handbook of National Regulations concerning the Export of Cultural Property.* Paris: UNESCO.

Prott, Lyndel, and P.J. O'Keefe. 1989. *Law and the Cultural Heritage.* Vol. 3, *Movement.* London and Edinburgh: Butterworths.

Ramos, Maria, and David Duganne. 2000. *Exploring Public Perceptions and Attitudes about Archaeology.* Society for American Archaeology. February.

Raustiala, Kal. 1999. Law, Liberalization & International Narcotics Trafficking. *New York University Journal of International Law and Politics* 32: 89–145.

Raymond, Janice G. 2002. The New UN Trafficking Protocol. *Women's Studies International Forum* 25(5): 491–502.

Regan, Patrick M., and Errol A. Hendeson. 2002. Democracy, Threats and Political Repression in Developing Countries: Are Democracies Internally Less Violent? *Third World Quarterly* 23(1): 119–136.

Reins, Thomas D. 1991. Reform, Nationalism and Internationalism: The Opium Suppression Movement in China and the Anglo-American Influence, 1900–1908. *Modern Asian Studies* 25(1): 101–142.

Renfrew, Colin. 2000. *Loot, Legitimacy and Ownership: The Ethical Crisis in Archaeology*. London: Duckworth.

Renfrew, Colin. 2006. Museum Acquisitions: Responsibilities for the Illicit Traffic in Antiquities. In *Archaeology, Cultural Heritage, and the Antiquities Trade*, edited by Neil Brodie, Morag M. Kersel, Christina Luke, and Kathryn Walker Tubb, 245–257. Gainesville, Fla.: University Press of Florida.

Reno, William. 2009. Illicit Commerce in Peripheral States. In *Crime and the Global Political Economy*, edited by H. Richard Friman, 67–84. Boulder, Colo.: Lynne Rienner.

Reuter, Peter, and Edwin M. Truman. 2004. *Chasing Dirty Money: The Fight Against Money Laundering*. Washington, D.C.: Institute for International Economics.

Richards, Kathy. 2004. The Trafficking of Migrant Workers: What are the Links Between Labour Trafficking and Corruption? *International Migration* 42(5): 147–168.

Rogers, Damien. 2009. *Postinternationalism and Small Arms Control: Theory, Politics, Security*. Farnham, UK: Ashgate.

Ron, James, Howard Ramos, and Kathleen Rodgers. 2005. Transnational Information Politics: NGO Human Rights Reporting, 1986–2000. *International Studies Quarterly* 49(3): 557–588.

Rosendorff, B. Peter, and Helen V. Milner. 2001. The Optimal Design of International Trade Institutions: Uncertainty and Escape. *International Organization* 55(4): 829–857.

Rozen, Sigal, Ella Keren, Nomi Levenkron, Shevy Korzen, and Ronen Steinberg. 2003. *"For You Were Strangers": Modern Slavery and Trafficking in Human Beings in Israel*. Hotline for Migrant Workers. Tel Aviv. February.

Rubin, Barnett R. 2004. *Road to Ruin: Afghanistan's Booming Opium Industry*. Center for American Progress and Center on International Cooperation. October 7.

Ryan, Michael P. 1998. *Knowledge Diplomacy: Global Competition and the Politics of Intellectual Property*. Washington, D.C.: Brookings Institution Press.

Saferworld. 2002. *Arms Production, Exports and Decision-Making in Central and Eastern Europe*. London. June.

Scully, Eileen. 2001. Pre-Cold War Traffic in Sexual Labor and Its Foes: Some Contemporary Lessons. In *Global Human Smuggling: Comparative Perspectives*, edited by David Kyle and Rey Koslowski, 74–106. Baltimore: Johns Hopkins University Press.

Sell, Susan K. 1998. *Power and Ideas: North-South Politics of Intellectual Property and Antitrust*. Albany: State University of New York Press.

Sell, Susan K. 2003. *Private Power, Public Law: The Globalization of Intellectual Property Rights*. Cambridge: Cambridge University Press.

Sell, Susan K., and Aseem Prakash. 2004. Using Ideas Strategically: The Contest Between Business and NGO Networks in Intellectual Property Rights. *International Studies Quarterly* 48(1): 143–175.

Serrano, Mónica. 2009. Drug Trafficking and the State in Mexico. In *Crime and the Global Political Economy*, edited by H. Richard Friman, 139–157. Boulder, Colo.: Lynne Rienner.

Shestack, Alan. 1999. The Museum and Cultural Property: The Transformation of Institutional Ethics. In *The Ethics of Collecting Cultural Property: Whose Culture? Whose Property?*, 2nd ed., edited by Phyllis Mauch Messenger, 93–101. Albuquerque: University of New Mexico Press.

Shleifer, Andrei. 1998. State versus Private Ownership. *Journal of Economic Perspectives* 12(4): 133–150.

Shleifer, Andrei, and Robert W. Vishny. 1998. *The Grabbing Hand: Government Pathologies and Their Cures*. Cambridge, Mass.: Harvard University Press.

Sil, Rudra, and Peter J. Katzenstein. 2010. Analytic Eclecticism in the Study of World Politics: Reconfiguring Problems and Mechanisms across Research Traditions. *Perspectives on Politics* 8(2): 411–431.

Simmons, Beth A. 2000a. International Law and State Behavior: Commitment and Compliance in International Monetary Affairs. *American Political Science Review* 94(4): 819–835.

Simmons, Beth A. 2000b. International Efforts against Money Laundering. In *Commitment and Compliance: The Role of Non-Binding Norms in the International Legal System*, edited by Dinah Shelton, 244–263. Oxford and New York: Oxford University Press.

Simmons, Beth A. 2001. The International Politics of Harmonization: The Case of Capital Market Regulation. *International Organization* 55(3): 589–620.

Simmons, Beth A. 2009. *Mobilizing for Human Rights: International Law in Domestic Politics*. New York: Cambridge University Press.

Simmons, Beth A. 2010. Treaty Compliance and Violation. *Annual Review of Political Science* 13: 273–296.

Simmons, Beth A., and Paulette Lloyd. 2010. Subjective Frames and Rational Choice: Transnational Crime and the Case of Human Trafficking. Available at SSRN: http://ssrn.com/abstract=1653473.

Simmons, Beth A., and Lisa L. Martin. 2002. International Organizations and Institutions. In *Handbook of International Relations*, edited by Walter Carlsnaes, Thomas Risse, and Beth A. Simmons, 192–211. Thousand Oaks, Calif.: Sage.

SIPRI. 2007. *SIPRI Yearbook 2007: Armaments, Disarmament and International Security*. Oxford: Oxford University Press.

Skinner, E. Benjamin. 2008. *A Crime So Monstrous: Face-to-Face with Modern-Day Slavery*. New York: Free Press.

Small Arms Survey. 2002. *Small Arms Survey 2002: Counting the Human Cost*. Oxford and New York: Oxford University Press.

Small Arms Survey. 2003. *Small Arms Survey 2003: Development Denied*. Oxford and New York: Oxford University Press.

Small Arms Survey. 2004. *Small Arms Survey 2004: Rights at Risk*. Oxford and New York: Oxford University Press.

Small Arms Survey. 2005. *Small Arms Survey 2005: Weapons at War.* Oxford and New York: Oxford University Press.

Small Arms Survey. 2006. *Small Arms Survey 2006: Unfinished Business.* Oxford and New York: Oxford University Press.

Small Arms Survey. 2007. *Small Arms Survey 2007: Guns and the City.* Cambridge and New York: Cambridge University Press.

Small Arms Survey. 2008. *Small Arms Survey 2008: Risk and Resilience.* Cambridge and New York: Cambridge University Press.

Small Arms Survey. 2009. *Small Arms Survey 2009: Shadows of War.* Cambridge and New York: Cambridge University Press.

Snidal, Duncan. 1985. Coordination versus Prisoners' Dilemma: Implications for International Cooperation and Regimes. *American Political Science Review* 79(4): 923–942.

Soderlund, Gretchen. 2005. Running from the Rescuers: New U.S. Crusades Against Sex Trafficking and the Rhetoric of Abolition. *NWSA Journal* 17(3): 64–87.

Spiegler, Howard N., and Lawrence M. Kaye. 2001. American Litigation to Recover Cultural Property: Obstacles, Options, and a Proposal. In *Trade in Illicit Antiquities: The Destruction of the World's Archaeological Heritage,* edited by Neil Brodie, Jennifer Doole, and Colin Renfrew, 121–132. Cambridge: McDonald Institute for Archaeological Research.

Spillane, Joseph, and William B. McAllister. 2003. Keeping the Lid On: A Century of Drug Regulation and Control. *Drug and Alcohol Dependence* 70(3): S5–S12.

Sprinz, Detlef, and Tapani Vaahtoranta. 1994. The Interest-Based Explanation of International Environmental Policy. *International Organization* 48(1): 77–105.

State Comptroller of Israel. 1996. *Annual Report 46 for the Year 1995* (in Hebrew). Jerusalem.

State Comptroller of Israel. 1999. *Annual Report 49 for the Year 1998* (in Hebrew). Jerusalem.

State Comptroller of Israel. 2003. *Annual Report 53B for the Year 2002* (in Hebrew). Jerusalem.

State Comptroller of Israel. 2005. *Annual Report 55B for the Year 2004* (in Hebrew). Jerusalem.

Stetson, Dorothy McBride. 2004. The Invisible Issue: Prostitution and Trafficking of Women and Girls in the United States. In *The Politics of Prostitution: Women's Movements, Democratic States and the Globalisation of Sex Commerce,* edited by Joyce Outshoorn, 245–264. Cambridge and New York: Cambridge University Press.

Stigler, George J. 1971. The Theory of Economic Regulation. *Bell Journal of Economics and Management Science* 2(1): 3–21.

Stolz, Barbara. 2005. Educating Policymakers and Setting the Criminal Justice Policymaking Agenda: Interest Groups and the "Victims of Trafficking and Violence Act of 2000." *Criminal Justice* 5(4): 407–430.

Stone, David R. 2000. Imperialism and Sovereignty: The League of Nations' Drive to Control the Global Arms Trade. *Journal of Contemporary History* 35(2): 213–230.

Storrs, K. Larry. 2001. *Drug Certification Requirements and Proposed Congressional Modifications in 2001.* Congressional Research Service. November 6.

Storrs, K. Larry. 2003. *Drug Certification/Designation Procedures for Illicit Narcotics Producing and Transit Countries.* Congressional Research Service. September 22.

Tannenwald, Nina. 2001. U.S. Arms Control Policy in a Time Warp. *Ethics & International Affairs* 15(1): 51–70.

Taylor, Arnold H. 1969. *American Diplomacy and the Narcotics Traffic, 1900–1939: A Study in International Humanitarian Reform.* Durham, N.C.: Duke University Press.

Thompson, Alexander. 2009. *Channels of Power: The UN Security Council and U.S. Statecraft in Iraq.* Ithaca, N.Y.: Cornell University Press.

Tomz, Michael, Jason Wittenberg, and Gary King. 2003. *CLARIFY: Software for Interpreting and Presenting Statistical Results.* Version 2.1. Stanford University, University of Wisconsin, and Harvard University. January 5. Available at http://gking.harvard.edu/.

Trocki, Carl A. 1999. *Opium, Empire, and the Global Political Economy: A Study of the Asian Opium Trade, 1750–1950.* London and New York: Routledge.

Tubb, Kathryn Walker, and Neil Brodie. 2001. From Museum to Mantelpiece: The Antiquities Trade in the United Kingdom. In *Destruction and Conservation of Cultural Property,* edited by Robert Layton, Peter G. Stone, and Julian Thomas, 102–116. London and New York: Routledge.

UK Department for Culture, Media and Sport and Home Office. 2004. *Government Response to "Cultural objects: developments since 2000" (HC 59), Report of the Culture, Media and Sport Select Committee, Session 2003–2004.* February.

UK House of Commons. 2000. Culture, Media and Sport Committee. Seventh Report. *Cultural Property: Return and Illicit Trade.* London: The Stationery Office.

UNDCP (United Nations International Drug Control Program). 1997. *Economic and Social Consequences of Drug Abuse and Illicit Trafficking.* SOC/NAR/771. UNDCP Technical Series no. 6. Vienna.

UNIDROIT. 1996. *Diplomatic Conference for the Adoption of the Draft UNIDROIT Convention on the International Return of Stolen or Illegally Exported Cultural Objects, Rome, 7 to 24 June 1995: Acts and Proceedings.* Rome: UNIDROIT.

UNODC (United Nations Office on Drugs and Crime). 2005. *World Drug Report 2005.* Vienna: UNODC.

UNODC. 2008. *World Drug Report 2008.* Vienna: UNODC.

UNODC. 2009a. *A Century of International Drug Control.* Vienna: UNODC.

UNODC. 2009b. *World Drug Report 2009.* Vienna: UNODC.

UNODC. 2010a. *The Globalization of Crime: A Transnational Organized Crime Threat Assessment.* Vienna: UNODC.

UNODC. 2010b. *Human Trafficking Indicators.* Vienna. October 11.

UNODC. 2011. *2011 Global Study on Homicide: Trends, Contexts, Data.* Vienna: UNODC.

U.S. Department of Defense. Office of the Inspector General. 2003a. *Assessment of DoD Efforts to Combat Trafficking in Persons: Phase I—United States Forces Korea.* Case H03L88433128. July 10.

U.S. Department of Defense. Office of the Inspector General. 2003b. *Assessment of DoD Efforts to Combat Trafficking in Persons: Phase II—Bosnia-Herzegovina and Kosovo.* Case H03L88433128. December 8.

U.S. Department of State. 2001. *Victims of Trafficking and Violence Protection Act of 2000: Trafficking in Persons Report.* Washington, D.C. July.

U.S. Department of State. 2002a. *Victims of Trafficking and Violence Protection Act 2000: Trafficking in Persons Report.* Washington, D.C. June.

U.S. Department of State. Bureau for International Narcotics and Law Enforcement Affairs. 2002b. *International Narcotics Control Strategy Report.* Washington, D.C. March.

U.S. Department of State. Bureau for International Narcotics and Law Enforcement Affairs. 2003. *International Narcotics Control Strategy Report.* Washington, D.C. March.

U.S. Department of State. 2004. *The Link Between Prostitution and Sex Trafficking.* Washington, D.C. November 24.

U.S. Department of State. 2005. *Trafficking in Persons Report.* Washington, D.C. June.

U.S. Department of State. 2006. *Trafficking in Persons Report.* Washington, D.C. June.

U.S. Department of State. 2008a. *Trafficking in Persons Report.* Washington, D.C. June.

U.S. Department of State. Bureau for International Narcotics and Law Enforcement Affairs. 2008b. *International Narcotics Control Strategy Report.* March.

U.S. Department of State. 2010. *Trafficking in Persons Report.* Washington, D.C. June.

U.S. Government Accountability Office. 2006. *Human Trafficking: Better Data, Strategy, and Reporting Needed to Enhance U.S. Antitrafficking Efforts Abroad.* GAO–06–825. Washington, D.C. July.

U.S. Government Accountability Office. 2008. *Plan Colombia: Drug Reduction Goals Were Not Fully Met, but Security Has Improved; U.S. Agencies Need More Detailed Plans for Reducing Assistance.* GAO–09–71. Washington, D.C. October.

U.S. House. 1976. Committee on Ways and Means. Subcommittee on Trade. *Written Comments on H.R. 14171.* 94th Cong., 2nd sess. August 3.

U.S. House. 1977a. Committee on Ways and Means. Subcommittee on Trade. *UNESCO Convention on Cultural Property: Hearings on H.R. 5643.* 95th Cong., 1st sess. April 26. Serial 95–28.

U.S. House. 1977b. Committee on Ways and Means. *Implementation of Convention on Cultural Property.* 95th Cong., 1st sess. September 21. Report 95–615.

U.S. House. 1979. Committee on Ways and Means. Subcommittee on Trade. *Cultural Property Treaty Legislation: Hearing on H.R. 3403.* 96th Cong., 1st sess. September 27. Serial 96–52.

U.S. House. 1999. Committee on International Relations. Subcommittee on International Operations and Human Rights. *Trafficking of Women and Children in the International Sex Trade: Hearing.* 106th Cong., 1st sess. September 14. Serial 106–66.

U.S. Senate. 1970. *Treaty with Mexico Providing for the Recovery and Return of Stolen Archaeological, Historical and Cultural Properties: Message from the President of the United States.* 91st Cong., 2nd sess. September 23.

U.S. Senate. 1971. Committee on Foreign Relations. *Recovery and Return of Stolen Archaeological, Historical and Cultural Properties.* 92nd Cong., 1st sess. February 9. Executive Report 92–1.

U.S. Senate 1972a. *Convention on Ownership of Cultural Property: Message from the President of the United States.* 92nd Cong., 2nd sess. February 2.

U.S. Senate. 1972b. Committee on Foreign Relations. *Convention on Ownership of Cultural Property.* 92nd Cong., 2nd sess. August 8. Executive Report 92–29.

U.S. Senate. 1978. Committee on Finance. Subcommittee on International Trade. *Convention on Cultural Property Implementation Act: Hearing on H.R. 5643 and S. 2261.* 95th Cong., 2nd sess. February 8.

U.S. Senate. 1985. Committee of the Judiciary. Subcommittee on Criminal Law. *Relating to Stolen Archaeological Property: Hearing on S. 605.* 99th Cong., 1st sess. May 22. Serial J–99–27.

U.S. Senate. 2000a. Committee on Foreign Relations. Subcommittee on Near Eastern and South Asian Affairs. *International Trafficking in Women and Children: Hearings.* 106th Cong., 2nd sess. February 22 and April 4.

U.S. Senate. 2000b. *A Review of the President's Annual Certification Process: Hearing before the Senate Caucus on International Narcotics Control.* 106th Cong., 2nd sess. March 21.

U.S. Trade Representative. 2006. *2006 Special 301 Report.* Washington, D.C. April 28.

U.S. Trade Representative. 2009. *2009 Special 301 Report.* Washington, D.C. April 30.

U.S. Trade Representative. 2010. *2010 Special 301 Report.* Washington, D.C. April 30.

Valentino, Benjamin, Paul Huth, and Sara Croco. 2006. Covenants without the Sword: International Law and the Protection of Civilians in Times of War. *World Politics* 58(3): 339–377.

van Schendel, Willem, and Itty Abraham, eds. 2005. *Illicit Flows and Criminal Things: States, Borders, and the Other Side of Globalization.* Bloomington: Indiana University Press.

Vogel, David. 2008. Private Global Business Regulation. *Annual Review of Political Science* 11: 261–282.

Walker, William O. III. 1989. *Drug Control in the Americas.* Albuquerque: University of New Mexico Press.

Walker, William O. III. 1991. *Opium and Foreign Policy: The Anglo-American Search for Order in Asia, 1912–1954*. Chapel Hill: University of North Carolina Press.

Walker, William O. III. 1992. International Collaboration in Historical Perspective. In *Drug Policy in the Americas*, edited by Peter H. Smith, 265–281. Boulder, Colo.: Westview.

Walker, William O. III. 1994. U.S. Narcotics Foreign Policy in the Twentieth Century: An Analytical Overview. In *Drugs and Foreign Policy: A Critical Review*, edited by Raphael F. Perl, 7–39. Boulder, Colo.: Westview.

Walkowitz, Judith R. 1980. The Politics of Prostitution. *Signs* 6(1): 123–135.

Watson, Peter. 1997. *Sotheby's: Inside Story*. London: Bloomsbury.

Waxman, Sharon. 2008. *Loot: The Battle over the Stolen Treasures of the Ancient World*. New York: Times Books.

Wechsler, William F. 2001. Follow the Money. *Foreign Affairs* 80(4): 40–57.

Weidacher, Reinhilde. 2005. *Behind a Veil of Secrecy: Military Small Arms and Light Weapons Production in Western Europe*. Small Arms Survey, Occasional Paper 16.

Weitzer, Ronald. 2007. The Social Construction of Sex Trafficking: Ideology and Institutionalization of a Moral Crusade. *Politics & Society* 35(3): 447–475.

Wellstone, Paul. 2001. *The Conscience of a Liberal: Reclaiming the Compassionate Agenda*. New York: Random House.

Wickham-Jones, Mark. 2000. Labour's Trajectory in Foreign Affairs: The Moral Crusade of a Pivotal Power? In *New Labour's Foreign Policy: A New Moral Crusade?*, edited by Richard Little and Mark Wickham-Jones, 3–32. Manchester and New York: Manchester University Press.

Williams, Phil, ed. 1999. *Illegal Immigration and Commercial Sex: The New Slave Trade*. London and Portland, Ore.: Frank Cass.

Williams, Phil. 2001. Crime, Illicit Markets, and Money Laundering. In *Managing Global Issues: Lessons Learned*, edited by P.J. Simmons and Chantal de Jonge Oudraat, 106–150. Washington, D.C.: Carnegie Endowment for International Peace.

Worker's Hotline. 2002. *Kav LaOved Annual Report 2002*. Tel Aviv.

World Bank. 1995. *Bureaucrats in Business: The Economics and Politics of Government Ownership*. New York: Oxford University Press.

Wright, Quincy. 1934. The Narcotics Convention of 1931. *American Journal of International Law* 28: 475–486.

Wyler, Liana Sun, and Nicolas Cook. 2009. *Illegal Drug Trade in Africa: Trends and U.S. Policy*. Congressional Research Service. September 30.

Yandle, Bruce. 1983. Bootleggers and Baptists: The Education of a Regulatory Economist. *Regulation* 7(3): 12–16.

Yandle, Bruce. 1984. Intertwined Interests, Rent Seeking and Regulation. *Social Science Quarterly* 65(4): 1002–1012.

Yandle, Bruce. 1999. Bootleggers and Baptists in Retrospect. *Regulation* 22(3): 5–7.

Yankey-Wayne, Valerie. 2006. The Human Dimension of the United Nations Programme of Action on Small Arms: The Key Role of Africa. *Disarmament Forum* 2006(1): 83–93.

Yasaitis, Kelly Elizabeth. 2005. National Ownership Laws as Cultural Property Protection Policy: The Emerging Trend in *United States v. Schultz*. *International Journal of Cultural Property* 12(1): 95–113.

Young, Oran R. 1989. The Politics of International Regime Formation: Managing Natural Resources and the Environment. *International Organization* 43(3): 349–375.

Zhang, Sheldon X. 2007. *Smuggling and Trafficking in Human Beings: All Roads Lead to America.* Westport, Conn.: Praeger.

# INDEX

Renfrew, Colin 159–160, 165–166,
     314
reputation 17, 27, 38, 40–41, 43, 51,
     54, 68, 84, 86, 145, 152, 154,
     157, 163, 165, 170–171, 204–
     209, 246, 253–255, 260–261,
     264, 270, 288, 290
Review Conference on Small Arms
     10, 15, 67, 73, 92–93, 96,
     99–100, 274, 287
Ribicoff, Abraham 139, 149
Royal Academy of Arts 158–159
Russia 62, 92, 102–112, 183, 195,
     198, 260

Salvation Army 181
sanctions 17, 20, 50–51, 54, 108,
     110, 185–193, 205, 207, 209,
     247, 266–267, 269–270
Saperstein, David 182
scandals 16–17, 85–86, 130–133,
     146, 152, 156, 158–160, 163,
     165–166, 170–172, 201,
     254–255, 274, 283, 288, 296
*Schultz* decision 151–152
secondary externalities 11–12, 17,
     19, 21, 32, 36–38, 44–46, 56,
     68, 83, 86, 98, 124, 128, 130,
     135, 152, 155, 158, 165, 171,
     179, 194, 227–228, 251, 275,
     285
Section 301 of the U.S. Trade Act
     266–269
Self-enforcement 49
Senate 134–135, 137, 147–149, 152,
     165, 183, 185, 246
     Finance Committee 140, 144
     Foreign Relations Committee 132,
     135, 183
Senegal 90
Sevso Treasure 158
sex trafficking 17, 19, 37–38, 51,

58, 175–189, 195–209, 212,
     216–223, 273, 280, 295
sex work 57, 181–182, 188, 190–
     191, 194
Shanghai Opium Commission 227,
     231, 235
shared interest 4, 9, 11, 18, 21,
     47–52, 54, 56–57, 95, 99, 120,
     127, 193, 209, 235, 248, 266,
     271, 274, 276–278, 283, 287,
     289, 297
Sheetrit, Meir 203
Sikkink, Kathryn 289–291
Simmons, Beth 49
Single Convention on Narcotic
     Drugs 8, 226, 237–240, 244,
     281
slave trade 5, 180, 185
small arms 3, 5, 7, 10, 18–19,
     22–26, 59–112, 238, 248–249,
     274–276, 279–284, 286–287,
     290–291, 294
Smith, Chris 183
Somalia 47–48, 81, 83
Sotheby's 159, 161
South Africa 80, 103–112
South Korea 54, 80, 191, 267–268
Southern African Development
     Community 65
Southern Baptist Convention 182
Soviet Union 6, 178, 195, 198, 238
Spain 83
Specter, Michael 180
Sprinz, Detlef 292–293
Sri Lanka 80, 89
State Department 16, 19, 54,
     131–136, 141–142, 147, 150,
     152, 154, 156–157, 172, 176,
     179, 187, 189–193, 202–208,
     217–218, 241, 262
state-owned enterprises 70–71,
     75–78, 80–81, 86–88, 90, 92,
     101, 279